A CRITICAL EDITION OF
YEATS'S *A VISION* (1925)

A CRITICAL EDITION OF YEATS'S *A VISION* (1925)

Edited by
George Mills Harper
and Walter Kelly Hood

MACMILLAN
PRESS

First edition 1978
Reprinted 1987

Published by
THE MACMILLAN PRESS LTD
Houndmills, Basingstoke, Hampshire RG21 2XS
and London
Companies and representatives
throughout the world

Printed in Great Britain by
Antony Rowe Ltd
Chippenham

British Library Cataloguing in Publication Data
Yeats, William Butler
A critical edition of Yeats's *A Vision* (1925)
1. Occult sciences
I. Title II. Harper, George Mills   III. Hood, Walter Kelly
133   BF1411
ISBN 0-333-21299-1

Contents

Preface

'Privately printed for subscribers only' and signed by the author, *A Vision* was first issued by T. Werner Laurie on 15 January 1926 (though dated 1925) in an edition of 600 copies, with brown-paper woodcuts and parchment half-binding. Because this never-reissued volume is greatly different from its 1937 revision, students and scholars who seek to understand the development of Yeats's mind and art during a most important period (1917–25) have long been faced with a serious lacuna.

The present edition reproduces Yeats's original work by a process of photo-lithography; the only differences between Yeats's original text and the present one, therefore, consist of the use of less expensive paper and binding, of the introduction of lineation, of the substitution of ordinary for brown paper for the woodcuts (facing the title page and pages xv and 8), and of the use of black rather than red ink for the upper cone and its annotations in the diagram of the historical cones (p. 177). Otherwise, no changes of any kind have been made in Yeats's text, which retains its original pagination. As recent scholarship has shown, many of Yeats's prose texts were 'improved' without note after his death; while the present format entails endnotes rather than more convenient footnotes, it also allows absolutely accurate reproduction of the original—and only —text of Yeats's 1925 *Vision*.

The scholarly apparatus of this edition consists of an Editorial Introduction tracing the development of the book (particularly, Yeats's indebtedness to Mrs Yeats's mediumship and to his background in psychical research), of endnotes, of a Bibliography of works cited by page, of an Index to the Editorial Introduction and to Yeats's text and the Notes (and including approximate birth-and-death dates for all historical personages). Although Harper was primarily responsible for the Editorial Introduction and Hood for the Notes, this was a communal effort in which the editors were joined by their wives (one read and ordered Yeats's Automatic Script; the other compiled the Index); Harper was responsible for contributing most of the information about Yeats's unpublished manuscripts, both in Editorial Introduction and in Notes.

In the Notes, the aim was to gloss Yeats's freely allusive prose, to identify the numerous persons and places in his references, to point to literary 'sources' where they were known, to record significant variants in Yeats's manuscripts or galley and page proofs, and occasionally to elucidate the ideas (or content). Complete annotation, even of what the editors fancifully supposed they indubitably knew, would have greatly increased the size of the book and made its cost prohibitive to the audience for whom it was intended. Without oversimplifying what is surely the most abstruse work of one of the most complex minds of his time, the editors have attempted to suggest the immense reading and thought which *A Vision* manifests and to provide, in Editorial Introduction and Notes, a partial guide for those who wish to understand the development of Yeats's 'System'.

A few formal matters which are not discussed elsewhere or which require the reader's initial comprehension require explanation. Unless otherwise indicated, quotations from Yeats's poems and plays are from the two standard 'variorum' editions, mentioned in the List of Abbreviations. In the numerous quotations from Yeats's unpublished papers, the use of *sic* was eschewed as superfluous except in a few unusually confusing instances. After Yeats's text and before the Index appear a List of Abbreviations and a Bibliography; the former contains short references to all editions of Yeats's works herein cited and to some frequently used terms, while the latter includes all works (by authors other than Yeats) cited by page. In the Bibliography, the asterisk is used to mark those editions of works which (according to present evidence) Yeats probably knew; the method has unavoidably excluded many annotations.

Acknowledgments

This volume would not have been possible without the approval and assistance of Miss Anne Yeats, Senator Michael B. Yeats, and A. P. Watt Ltd. The editors are indebted to many of their students, colleagues, and friends who have so willingly assisted them in their search for sources and meaning. The editors are also indebted, directly or indirectly, to hundreds of editors, authors, and publishers of books which they have consulted—in particular, to Macmillan, whose many publications by and about Yeats (including such commentaries as those of Jeffares) have been indispensable to this work.

Finally, the editors are indebted to the following institutions and foundations for financial assistance without which the research for this edition would have been much more difficult. In particular, Harper is indebted to research support from Florida State University and to the National Endowment for the Humanities (1976–7) for a Fellowship for Independent Study and Research; Hood, to research support from Tennessee Technological University and to the National Endowment for the Humanities for a Summer Stipend (1976).

Editorial Introduction

A Vision is a strange and often disordered attempt to use the methods of empirical science to explain 'The Way of the Soul between the Sun and the Moon'.[1] 'Man becomes free from the four *Faculties*', Yeats wrote, 'through those activities where everything is said or done for the sake of something else, where all is evidence, argument, language, symbol, number, morality, mechanism, merchandise'.[2] Although he liked to quote Plato's admonition that none should enter the doors of the Academy who were 'ignorant of Geometry',[3] Yeats was not concerned with proving that the cones of his 'Principal Symbol' 'govern all the movements of the planets'; for he thought, 'as did Swedenborg in his mystical writings, that the forms of geometry can have but a symbolic relation to spaceless reality, *Mundus Intelligibilis*' (*VB* 69–70). The symbolic forms of psychic geometry projected in *VA* were not in fact based primarily on Plato or Swedenborg or others of the classical writers Yeats liked to cite but rather on the experiments and thinking of his many friends and fellow students, first in the Hermetic Order of the Golden Dawn and more significantly in the Society for Psychical Research.[4] He was an active member of the GD from 1890 to 1922 and an Associate Member of the SPR from 1913 to 1928. It is no chance that the first version of his visionary conception of human experience was conceived when he was writing 'Swedenborg, Mediums and the Desolate Places' and 'Preliminary Examination of the Script of E[lizabeth] R[adcliffe]',[5] and that the 'revised form' of the second version was written (though not finished) by Sept 1928.[6] The impact of the SPR is clear in the opening lines of a revised draft of 'Dramatis Personae': 'This book would be different if it had not come from those who claim to have died many times and in all they say assume their own existence. In this it resembles nothing of philosophy from the time of Descartes but much that is ancient.'[7] 'I begin with the Daimon', Yeats continued, 'and of the Daimon I know little but comfort myself with this saying of Marcion's "Neither can we think say or know anything of the Gospels".' Nevertheless, he concluded in a draft dated Oct 1929, '[I] write with confidence what my instructors have said, or what I have deduced from their diagrams.' His instructors did indeed convey a strange conglomeration of ideas and suggestions: 'What is . . . new in this book', the fictional Owen Aherne wrote in a rejected passage, 'is not any ingenious description of abstract forms and movement but that it interprets by their means all thought, all history and the difference between man and man.' It is not surprising surely that such an ambitious book should sometimes baffle and confuse. If, as we assume, Aherne was speaking for Yeats, *A Vision* (both versions) may well be the most important work in the canon to the understanding of his art and thought if not his life. By examining briefly the inception of *VA* and the circumstances and people surrounding Yeats while it was being written and by annotating the unidentified allusions and references to art and literature in the book, we hope this edition will illuminate one of the strangest spiritual auto-biographies of the our time.

Like most profound works of art, *VA* cannot readily be traced to a single stimulant or moment of conception. Yeats himself frequently suggested that it was a development of *Per Amica Silentia Lunae,* implying thereby that the curious student should examine its sources. Anyone who studies the activities of Yeats in the months immediately preceding the composition of *PASL* will be aware that it originated in spiritualistic experiments, including many seances and numerous books and articles he read on the subject.[8] The most important of these psychic experiences were the experiments in automatic writing which Yeats observed, conducted, and analyzed. Although the experiments of Lady Edith Lyttelton were not the most extensive or most important of these, Yeats said that one of them was the stimulus of the System outlined and explained in *VA.* In the CF which Yeats used to 'codify' the extensive experiments in automatic writing which he and his wife conducted immediately following their marriage on 20 Oct 1917, he recorded the origin of his book as follows:

> System said to develop from a script showed me in 1913 or 14. An image in that script used. (This refers to script of Mrs. Lyttelton, & a scrap of paper by Horton concerning chariot with black & white horses). This told in almost earliest script of 1917.

Since there was in Yeats's mind a direct relationship between Lady Lyttelton's script and William Thomas Horton's 'scrap of paper' and since these prophetic writings were greatly important to Yeats for the remainder of his life, we are fortunate, not only that both have been preserved, but also that the sequence of images and events which culminated in the composition of *VA* can be traced in detail. Long after the occurrence of the events described, Lady Lyttelton wrote of the powerful impression made by Yeats which led her to record the script he referred to in the CF. Finding 'support and sympathy in his friendship', she began 'experimenting in the puzzled and bewildered way' with automatic writing after the death of her husband on 5 Jy 1913.[9] As she recalled in 1940, 'Much of it fitted into what are called cross-correspondences, that is, referred to the writings of other automatists of which I knew absolutely nothing—and seemed to me to be drawn from some common source'. She believed that the 'strange sentences' which came from her pencil had a 'further source' than her 'unaided imagination'. Not knowing how to account for or explain her experiments, she wrote to Yeats, 'a trained and experienced occultist', in Nov 1913, telling him of her 'perplexities' and reminding him of a promise to show her a paper he had been writing on 'the subject of contact with another world of being' (i.e., the essay on Miss Radcliffe). In Apr 1914 Yeats visited Lady Lyttelton and showed her his paper and 'some automatic script whether his own or some-one else's I am not now sure'. After his visit and probably as a direct result of it, she produced several automatic scripts focused on Yeats. In the first of these, dated 24 Apr 1914, the Control[10] informed her that 'Yeats . . . can help he has great gifts. Ask him about Zoroaster, perhaps he will understand—& the planets in His care.'[11] On 9 May she was told that 'Yeats is a prince with an evil counsellor'. On 15 June she recorded a bewildering but most important message:

Zoroaster & the planets. If this is not understood tell him to think of the double harness—of Phaeton, the adverse principle
The hard rings on the surf
Despair is the child of folly
If the invidious suggestion is not quelled there may be trouble.

Further references to Yeats were made in scripts of 22, 24, 26, 27, and 29 June. Between the excerpts of 22 and 24 June, Lady Lyttelton wrote a note to Yeats: 'I copy what followed a day or two later for tho' I do not know that it has anything to do with you it mentions planets & somehow may connect with Phaeton'. The excerpt for 27

June concludes with what may have been a veiled warning that surely appealed to Yeats: 'In the midst of death we are in life—the inversion is what I *mean*.'

'With some trepidation', as she recalled in 1940, Lady Lyttelton sent these excerpts to Yeats on 12 Jy 1914, concluding her brief note apologetically: 'To me it is all quite incomprehensible.' Prompt, as usual, Yeats replied on 18 Jy: 'I will not write fully about your automatic writing as I have not had time to look up the Miltonic allusion and that to Phaeton.'[12] Concerning the allusions to *Thus Spake Zarathustra*, which Yeats had 'read with great excitement some years ago', he concluded that 'they [the Controls] are harping on some duality, but what duality I do not know, nor do I know of an evil counsellor'. Puzzled over the symbolic significance of her script, Yeats observed:

> The worst of this cross correspondence work is that it seems to start the controller dreaming, and following associations of the mind, echoes of echoes. I wonder if they mean that my evil counsellor is a spirit and that he has come from reading Zarathustra—but no that is not it. . . . I cannot make it out.

Two days later, however, partial illumination came by means of cross correspondence through a prophetic message from Yeats's long-time friend William Thomas Horton. On 20 Jy 1914 he attended one of Yeats's Monday Evenings at 18 Woburn Buildings. The conversation focused on spiritualism, including most likely the automatic writing of Lady Lyttelton's script. Sometime that evening the skeptical Horton gave Yeats the 'scrap of paper' referred to in the CF. Dated 20 Jy and written on two small sheets, this prophetic warning seemed to corroborate Yeats's theory of cross correspondence:

> The fight is still raging round you while *you* are busy trying to increase the speed & usefulness of your chariot by means of a dark horse you have paired with the winged white one which for so long has served you faithfully & well.
> Unless you give the dark horse wings & subordinate it to the white winged horse the latter will break away & leave you to the dark horse who will lead your chariot into the enemies camp where you will be made a prisoner. Conquor & subordinate the

dark horse to the white one or cut the dark horse away, from your chariot, & send it adrift.[13]

Yeats was 'struck'. Although he was busy preparing to go to Ireland (probably on Saturday, 25 Jy), he wrote again to Lady Lyttelton before he left. Describing Horton as 'a curious being, a mystic and artist', Yeats enclosed the warning note and explained his reason for sending it:

> It is as you will see very nearly what your controls say. Notice their allusion to the horses of Phaeton and to the sign, the sun (Leo).[14] I do not understand it in the least except that both you and he speak of a dual influence and bad. I know of none on this earth. Horton may think it means spiritism which he dislikes but I did not ask him. "The inversion" in your script is a technical mystic term for the evil power.

Horton's criticism was indeed directed at spiritism. On Saturday, 25 Jy, not having had any response to his prophetic note, he wrote a strongly censorious letter to his 'dear old friend': 'I pray God you will take to heart the warning I gave you. It makes me absolutely sick to see & hear you so devoted to Spiritualism & its investigation. . . . To see you on the floor among those papers searching for an automatic script, where one man finds a misquotation among them, while round you sit your guests, shocked me for it stood out as a terrible symbol.'[15]

Lady Lyttelton wrote to Yeats on 28 Jy enclosing two further extracts about Yeats from scripts of the day before, but he did not respond, and she presumed that she 'was not on the track or he did not want to go into the matter'. Nevertheless, Yeats told her 'long after . . . that the warning had been real and justifiable, though he did not understand it at the time'. In fact, the meaning of her warning was probably not clear to him until he was moved to record its cross correspondence with Horton's in the CF.

Although Horton's much stronger mythical warning was also disregarded, it remained in the storehouse of Yeats's subconscious mind to be recalled 'in almost earliest script of 1917'. Although he recorded that his wife had surprised him 'by attempting automatic writing' 'on the afternoon of October 24th 1917, four days after marriage' (VB 8), he did not preserve these early experiments until 5 Nov. On that day, in the second of two sessions, the Control offered

the following information in answer to unrecorded questions by
Yeats:

> yes but with gradual growth
> yes—one white one black both winged
> both winged both necessary to you
> one you have the other found
> the one you have by seeking is—
> you find by seeking it in the one you have[16]

These tantalizingly ambiguous responses contain the images Yeats
had in mind when he wrote the note in the CF. Horton's prophetic
warning is central to *VA* and may have lodged in Yeats's subconscious for the remainder of his life. During a Sleep of 11 Jan 1921,
for example, the Control informed Yeats that 'all communications
such as ours were begun by the transference of an image later from
another mind. The image is selected by the Daimon from telepathic
impacts & one is chosen, not necessarily a recent one.' 'For
instance', Yeats commented, 'the script about black & white horses
may have been from Horton who wrote it to me years before.' If the
spirit of Horton (d. 19 Feb 1919) was, as Yeats believed, 'conscious of
the transmission' of 'that image', it was surely pleased; but it may
have been shocked at the implications of the System which Yeats
had erected on such a frail foundation. Aware of that possibility,
Yeats had consulted Thomas (the Control), who assured him that
the dead Horton 'believes now much that he denied before, he says
you are right, he says he is so happy that he weeps . . .' (AS, 24 May
1919).

   How the image in Lady Lyttelton's script and Horton's 'scrap of
paper' was developed into the System is a puzzle which will
perhaps never be fully resolved, but some conjectural observations
may be made. In the AS for 5 Nov 1917 the Control informed Yeats
that both white and black horses are 'necessary to you'. In effect, if
we explicate the answers to the unrecorded questions Yeats probably asked, the Control had told him that man comes into the world
with one (white), but must find the other (black) 'by seeking it in the
one you have'. Yeats, his mind stored with astrological symbolism,
associated the white and black horses with the sun and moon,
which form the basic antitheses of *VA*. On the very first page of
preserved Script the Control speaks to Yeats of an 'enmity' which is
now stopped: 'that which was inimical was an evil spiritual influ-

ence that is now at an end.' Despite the ambiguity and the vacuum caused by the absence of Yeats's questions, one point is clear from the beginning of the AS: '☉ in ☽ [is] sanity of feeling' and '☽ in ☉ [is] Inner to outer more or less' (5 Nov 1917). The dark unruly horse of the moon is equated symbolically to the inner, subjective, and 'antithetical self'; the white horse of the sun to the outer, objective, and daily or 'primary self'. The Control's (and Yeats's) opposition to Horton's spiritual psychology is strongly stated: both horses are winged and both are necessary. According to the Control, 'The enmity of the two creates the third—the Evil Persona', which 'comes from the clash & discord of the two natures, while the artistic self comes from the harmonizing of the two, or rather of the effort of the one to harmonize with the other'.

These rather careful distinctions were made in an eight-page typescript dated 8 Nov, which is the first of Yeats's efforts to 'codify' the AS during or near the time of its production. As the first session in which the questions asked of the Control and the hour are recorded, this Script is important. The two questions suggest themes that run throughout *VA* and link it clearly to *PASL*:

1. What is the relation between the Anima Mundi & the Antithetical Self?
2. What quality in the Anima Mundi compels the relationship?

The Control chose to answer the second question first because he considered it the 'most important', and we may assume that Yeats did also:

It is the purely instinctive & cosmic quality in man which seeks completion in its opposite which is sought by the subconscious self in anima mundi to use your own term while it is the conscious mind that makes the E[vil] P[ersona] in consciously seeking its opposite & then emulating it.

Thus, in the first few days of the AS, Yeats, his wife, and the Control established the psychological polarities, suggested by Lady Lyttelton's script and Horton's note, from which the System developed.

In the months ahead Yeats and his Instructors (including George, in one sense) conducted what is surely the most extensive and varied series of psychical researches ever recorded by an important creative mind. Although a great number of English and continental people, including many friends of Yeats, were conducting various forms of spiritualistic research, most of them were observing and recording seances; and none, to my knowledge, ever attempted the kind of spiritual quest described in *VA*. Day after day for months on end, often in a state of emotional and intellectual exhiliration, the three co-equal experimenters sought to explain the human personality, the course of Western civilization, and the evolution of the soul after death. Unlike many of his friends in the SPR, Yeats was aware that these philosophic goals could be achieved only through myth, and he believed that the myth would ultimately be most meaningful and enduring in the poems and plays which the System made possible. Several were written while the AS was being recorded, as we have pointed out in the notes to this volume.

Because it will not be possible to examine here the scope and variety of the AS and Sleeps, I have prepared a Table which will suggest the enormous expenditure of time and creative effort, though not the diversity and intellectual complexity which they represent.

A brief explanation may be useful. With some few exceptions, I have taken the dates and places directly from the notebooks which Yeats systematically identified and preserved. The number of pages perhaps approximates but certainly is not the total: a considerable number of questions without answers or vice versa have been preserved, and Yeats himself occasionally noted losses in the CF. It is possible that much more than I estimate is lost or misplaced.[17] By my count thirty-six notebooks of AS and three of Sleeps are preserved. But Yeats, who was usually careful with facts, stated that he had compiled a considerably greater number: 'Exposition in sleep came to an end in 1920, and I began an exhaustive study of some fifty copy-books of automatic script, and of a much smaller number of books recording what had come in sleep' (*VB* 17–18). But Yeats is talking in round numbers, and he is surely incorrect in the date: three notebooks record many Sleeps in 1920 and 1921, several in 1922, and a few as late as Nov 1923.

During this period, Yeats and George experimented with several variations recorded as Sleeps. The first mention was made in an undated entry (between 21 and 28 Mar 1920): 'New Method. George speaks while asleep'. On 18 Feb 1921 Yeats 'decided with consent of "Carmichael" [the Control] to stop all sleep for the present. "Interpreter" is not well enough'. Nothing except a brief account of some psychic experiences in Wells and Glastonbury is recorded

AUTOMATIC SCRIPT

Date	Place	No. of sessions	No. of questions	Pages preserved
24 Oct–4 Nov 1917	Ashdown Forest ——	——	——	——
5–12 Nov 1917	Ashdown Forest	13	33	93
20 Nov–7 Dec 1917	London	21	723	284
21–25 Dec 1917	Ashdown Forest	4	136	77
31 Dec 1917–1 Jan 1918	London or Oxford	2	81	26
2 Jan–5 Mar 1918	Oxford	55	1778	591
11 Mar 1918	Dublin	1	——	2
14–27 Mar 1918	Glendalough	9	225	91
30 Mar–2 Apr 1918	Glenmalure	5	143	37
7 Apr–2 May 1918	Coole	11	173	69
9 May–9 Sept 1918	Ballinamantane	54	1004	431
14–17 Sept 1918	Rosses Point	3	77	22
18 Sept 1918	Sligo	1	24	7
21–23 Sept 1918	Ballylee	3	47	18
24 Sept–11 Dec 1918	Dublin	33	595	212
16–22 Dec 1918	Enniskerry	7	150	61
24 Dec 1918–8 Jan 1919	Dublin	9	131	80
9–17 Jan 1919	Lucan	7	112	61
19 Jan–16 Feb 1919	Dublin	15	134	77
20–29 Mar 1919	Dundrum	9	258	84
31 Mar 1919	Dublin	1	18	5
1 Apr–6 May 1919	Dundrum	28	605	190
21–25 May 1919	London	3	67	16
28–29 May 1919	Oxford	2	33	10
31 May–8 June 1919	London	4	68	28
16–30 June 1919	Ballylee	12	226	108
2–3 Jy 1919	Kilkenny	2	——	8
14–24 Jy 1919	Ballylee	6	90	43
25 Jy 1919	Galway	1	18	5
26 Jy–1 Aug 1919	Oughterard	7	128	53
2–15 Aug 1919	Ballylee	14	279	92
20 Aug 1919	Renvyle	1	——	3
22 Aug–23 Sept 1919	Ballylee	28	524	208
12–27 Oct 1919	Oxford	17	226	99
30 Oct 1919	London	1	——	1
4 Nov 1919–4 Jan 1920	Oxford	42	398	232
7 Jan 1920	London	1	11	6
27 Jan–1 Feb 1920	New York City	2	9	4
1 Mar 1920	Chicago, Illinois	1	8	5
21 Mar 1920	Portland, Oregon	1	16	9

Date	Place	No. of sessions	No. of questions	Pages preserved
24 Mar 1920	Train, on way to San Francisco	1	——	7
28–29 Mar 1920	Pasadena, Calif.	2	25	11
29 Apr 1920	Train, Cleveland to New York City	1	1	1
16–17 May 1920	New York City	2	——	6
20 June 1920	London	1	——	1
15–24 Sept 1920	Oxford	4	26	8
25–26 Jan 1921	Stone Cottage	2	19	7
4 June 1921	Shillingford	1	——	2
Undated: 'Examination of my horoscope. . .'	?	1	40	10
Undated, random script	?	?	13	126
TOTALS		450	8672	3627

SLEEPS AND MEDITATIONS

Dates recorded	Place	No. of sessions	Pages preserved
28 Mar–28 Apr 1920	Pasadena, New York City, Chicago, 'on train'	20	22
10–14 May 1920	Travelling	2	3
15 May–12 June 1920	New York City	8	16
28 May 1920	Montreal	1	107 (28 May 1920–
30 May 1920	SS *Megantu*	2	9 Feb 1921
19 June–12 Aug 1920	Holland Place, London	16 & 6 'notes to sleeps'	inclusive)
13 Aug 1920–11 Jan 1921	Oxford	41 & 7 'notes'	
11 Jan–9 Feb 1921	Oxford	'various'	
19 Jan 1921	Wells	2	98 (19 Jan 1921–
18 Feb 1921	Oxford	2	18 Sept 1922
6–10 Apr 1921	Shillingford	4	inclusive)
12 Apr 1921	Dorchester	1	
19–25 Apr 1921	Shillingford	4	
4–27 Sept 1921	Thame	7	

Dates recorded	Place	No. of sessions	Pages preserved
7 Oct 1921–15 Jan 1922	Oxford	11	
2 May 1922	Ballylee	11	
16–26 June 1922	Ballylee	5	17
4–6 Jy 1923	Ballylee or Dublin	3	7
14 Jy–27 Nov 1923	Dublin	10	
21 Mar 1924	Dublin	1	[included in 17pp. above]
TOTALS		164	270

from that date till 6 Apr, when 'All communication by external means—sleeps—whistles—voices—renounced, as too exacting for George. Philosophy is now coming in a new way. I am getting it in sleep & when half awake, & George has correspondential dreams or visions.' They continued to use this method of communication until the summer of 1922. At the top of a page headed 'Notes June 23' Yeats wrote, 'Sleeps are now [being?] typed & put in a different book.' But only a few such typed records are preserved. Moreover, three pages later, under the same date, Yeats noted: ' "Philosophic sleeps" have ceased to avoid consequent frustration, but two nights ago George began talking in her sleep. She seemed a different self with more knowledge & confidence.' On 18 Sept 1922, to keep the record straight, Yeats made a significant entry:

In I think July we decided to give up "sleeps" "automatic writing" & all such means & to discovering mediumship, & to get our further thought by "positive means". Dionertes consented but said that when we came to write out account of life after death we could call Elder & resume sleeps etc for a time.

The remaining pages in this notebook do not record further Sleeps.

A year later, however, beginning on 4 Jy 1923 and ending on 27 Nov, Yeats recorded a series of eleven Sleeps (or 'Talks' about them). Dionertes had apparently fulfilled his promise that 'help would be given' for the 'account of life after death'. An entry for 26 Oct makes clear that Yeats was in fact working on what was to become 'The Gates of Pluto' and that he had chosen the title for his book:

> About three weeks ago had a sleep which had a statement about covens now incorporated in chapter on covens in ''A Vision''. The part however about the smaller wheel which corresponds to the romantic, musical movement etc. is my own.[18]

Yeats's comment about his own contribution illustrates what well may be an irresolvable problem for the critic who attempts to distinguish between the thought of Yeats and his Communicators or between Yeats and George. Fairly involved in the relatively obvious simple question-and-answer method of the first AS, the problem becomes increasingly complex as Yeats and George moved through the Script, to George's Sleeps, to Yeats's Sleeps, to more 'positive means'. Even Yeats was not always sure whether 'interpretation [was] from Dionertes or from me, he confirming' (14 Jy 1923).

Because Yeats considered it important to be precise about dates and related facts, we may be sure that his recorded quest for visionary truth by means of the AS and Sleeps covered a period of more than seven years (from 24 Oct 1917 to 27 Nov 1923).

My count of the number of sessions is less exact than that of the total number of pages, chiefly because two or more Sleeps are often discussed in one entry and all are usually recorded from one to several days after the experience. Although a great number of brief intervals (e.g., 'wait ten minutes') are carefully noted in the AS, I have counted as separate sessions only those in which the questions begin with a new set of numbers. I am less certain about the precise total of Yeats's questions. When the number of questions asked do not coincide with those answered, I have accepted the larger total, but have not attempted to estimate by unnumbered answers the unrecorded questions (there are hundreds, frequently at the opening and closing of sessions). Nor can I be wholly accurate about the identity of the Controls, Guides, etc., who usually announce themselves by both names and signs but occasionally only by signs, which are not always distinctive. Although there were many of these Communicators (Yeats's final generic term), they changed far less often than he implied (*VB* 9), and only three (Thomas, Ameritus, and Dionertes) presided with great regularity. According to Yeats, 'Guides are called by such names as leaf, Rose etc while Spirits who have been men are given such names as Thomas, Dionertes etc' (23 May 1920). Also present but not answering questions were individual Daimons, including his daughter Anne's after her birth on 24 Feb 1919. With very few exceptions the dates and places and usually the exact times of beginning (but not ending) are carefully noted at the head of each session of AS and many Sleeps.

In the beginning (5–12 Nov 1917) there was apparently little clear direction to questions or answers. After their return from Ashdown Forest to London on 13 Nov, however, Yeats probably talked about his 'incredible experience' (*VB* 8) to numerous friends and acquaintances, from many of whom he no doubt solicited advice. Following an interval of seven days without AS, he renewed his quest with far greater vigor and precision. Although he may have had some master plan in mind, he followed no very logical sequence, and he adjusted and expanded as he went. There are many suggestions, especially in the first year or so (even as early as 21 Feb 1918), that only a few more months would be needed to complete the AS, and Yeats was regularly urged by the Control and the Medium to reread and codify.

Initially, he recalls, his codification took the form of 'a small concordance in a large manuscript book' and then 'a much larger, arranged like a card index' (*VB* 18). Since very few dates are recorded in this CF, I cannot accurately determine when it was compiled, but numerous undated quotations from and references to the AS and succeeding Sleeps make it possible to establish dates before which many of the notes cannot have been made. With some few exceptions, chiefly concerning Yeats's immediate family and Iseult and Maud Gonne, the CF excludes the purely personal and other peripheral (sometimes humourous) matter in the AS and Sleeps.

But much of the excluded material is not extraneous, strictly speaking. From one perspective *VA* was stimulated by and based on the mystery of Yeats's relations with three women: his wife and Iseult and Maud Gonne. The AS was begun four days after his marriage, much of the early Script is concerned with Iseult's knots or complexes, and great numbers of questions (but fewer answers) are devoted directly or indirectly to Maud. Several times throughout the AS, Yeats suggests that her refusals to accept him in 1896 and for the last time some twenty years later were responsible for the power of his poetry: 'How am I to describe in writing of system her influence during those 20 years?' he asked on 4 May 1919. Six years later he admitted that he had not resolved the problem: '. . . I have not even dealt with the whole of my subject, perhaps not even with what is most important, writing nothing about the Beatific Vision, little of sexual love' (*VA* xii). Perhaps he realized, as he codified in the CF, that sexual love and its transformation, the Beatific Vision, were too personal to be treated in a book founded on 'a regular scientific method discovered by experiment' (AS, 10 Jan 1919). As a result, the great question of the mystery of sexual love is avoided or treated obliquely in the CF; and the names of the several women who had changed the course of his life, though placed in their proper Phases in the AS, were omitted from *VA*: his wife, Florence Farr Emery, Mrs Patrick Campbell, Olivia Shakespear, Iseult and Maud Gonne, and Lady Gregory.

Although there is not space here to consider the CF in detail, even a brief description will perhaps suggest its importance to an understanding of Yeats's methods and thought as he prepared to write his book. Arranged alphabetically and consisting of some 750 three by five cards (chiefly postal), it was compiled over a considerable period of time, a few cards having been added after the publication of *VA*. Of greatest general interest perhaps are the headings under which Yeats chose to codify the AS and order his thought. As the CF now stands, the first card, perhaps intentionally out of place alphabetically, is headed 'Anima Mundi, Genius etc' and dated 8 Nov 1917. Concerning itself with the first two recorded questions in the AS (see p. xvii above) and using for the first time Yeats's terms for the psychological and cosmological polarities of Antithetical Self and Daily or Primary Self, this card and indeed the date itself may have assumed symbolic significance in his mind. The next two cards—about 'After Life State'—were probably written much later: Card 3, discussing red and black gyres (*VA* 178), first mentioned on 19 June 1920, is written on a personal card with the printed address 42 Fitzwilliam Square, Dublin, to which the Yeatses moved in Aug 1928. Other cards under the letter *A*, frequently out of order, are filed under such headings as 'Automatism', 'Astrology', 'Anne' (and 'Anne Hyde'), 'Anne, Michael etc', 'Abstraction', and 'Automatic Faculty'. The cards about the Yeats children, Anne and Michael (usually referred to in the AS and Sleeps as the third and fourth Daimons), are remarkable. Yeats quotes from an AS for 20 Mar 1919 (the first Script after Anne's birth) in which he had been told that Anne was a spiritual descendant of a seventeenth-century woman named Anne Hyde, and warned that 'the son and daughter needed by them [the Controls] as symbols are the only children we must have . . .; more would destroy system'. Also related is a curious entry under *B* which refers to Michael: 'Black Eagle=Heir= 4th Daimon'. Although there are numerous references to the Black Eagle in the AS and Sleeps, nothing was made of this symbol in *VA*.

The ten other cards under *B* are concerned with 'Beatific Vision', 'Birth', 'Body', 'Before Life', 'Beauty' and 'Berenices Hair'. As might be expected, most of these are related to entries under other letters. For example, one card under *C* is headed 'CM, IM, BV' (i.e., Critical Moment, Initiatory Moment, and Beatific Vision). Extremely important in the AS, these three psychological states receive little attention in the book, perhaps because they usually refer to crises in the lives of Yeats, George, Maud, Iseult, and other intimate associates (often intentionally unnamed). There are almost 100 cards under *C* with such headings as 'Cones or Wheels', 'Cardinal Points', 'Cycles', 'Colour', 'Covens Memory', 'CB, Spirit, PB' (i.e., Celestial Body, Spirit, and Passionate Body), 'CB, Mask', 'Christ, Judas, etc', 'Conditional Memory', 'Contraries', 'Contact', and 'Crossings', with various modifications and additions which often refer to other cards.

Although this unsystematic process occasionally led Yeats to link seemingly illogical subjects, it provided a convenient cross-reference enabling him to turn readily to related ideas under other headings. For example, he could refer to cards about Anne and Michael under *A* and *B* by the heading '3 & 4 Daimon': '3D=13 cycle, 4D=combined cycles of two unlikes (self & George for instance)'. Although the headings fall into some 125 topics, there are two or three times that many, including variations. For example, Christ is the subject of at least three separate headings: 'Christ', 'Christ, Holy Ghost, etc', and 'Christ, Judas, etc'. But Christ is also the subject of one card headed 'Initiate' ('the Perfect Man') and of several under the heading of 'Masters'. Following no apparent logic, the headings are chosen primarily as reminders of ideas and experiences recorded in the great storehouse of the AS and Sleeps or Yeats's thoughts about them. As he struggled to absorb his 'incredible experience' and bring order out of chaos, he filed cards under such suggestive and diverse headings as 'Diagrams', 'Definitions', 'Expiation', 'Fragrances', 'Freewill', 'Fate & Destiny', 'Frustration', 'Guides', 'Good & Evil', 'Harmonization & Discord', 'Images', 'Invocation', 'Ideal Lover & Overshadower', 'Joy', 'Karma', 'Knots', 'Luck', 'Love', 'Lightning Flash', 'Light & Dark', 'Memories Astral Light', 'Moral Despair', 'Mediumship', 'Metre & Rhythm', 'Myth', 'Opposites', 'Planets', 'Planes', 'Quarters', 'Records', 'Return', 'Setting Forth', 'Symbols', 'Sex', 'Shock', 'Stages of the Work', 'Sin & Excess', 'Style', 'Teacher & Victim', 'Tables', 'Transference', 'Ugliness', 'Victimage', and numerous extensions and modifications.

Also, of course, there are many cards filed under headings directly related to sections in *VA* such as 'Faculties', 'Masks', 'Historical Cone', 'Hunchback', 'Lists', 'Principles', 'Phases', and 'Shiftings'.

Careful not to take credit himself for ideas transmitted by the Control and recorded by George, Yeats consistently enclosed phrases and passages in quotation marks and resorted to numerous devices such as 'I am told that . . .', 'I find on separate sheet . . .', 'As given by control', 'Drawn by me but corrected, probably by control', and 'Copied from Script with corrections'. Also, by occasional (but far too few) references to dates of the AS, he reminded himself of the source of his ideas and quotations: e.g., 'Long important Script July 29, 1919' and 'Horary for April 21, 1919. 9 P M to show mediums Daimon'. Although Yeats's 'codification' of the AS appears to be his attempt to extract material which might be appropriate to *VA*, the CF records considerable information which he very wisely rejected for the book: the most suggestive if not the most significant of this material is contained in the numerous cards concerning Initiatory Moments, Critical Moments, Lightning Flashes, and related concepts. Since the biographical information suggested or recorded in these data (including several dates frequently repeated in both AS and CF) obviously refers to emotional crises, Yeats is deliberately obscure about the events to which he and George alluded. It may be that he refrained because 'she does not want me to write system for publication—not as exposition—but only to record & to show to a few people' (13 Sept 1922), or perhaps he decided, in the words of one Control, that we should 'be content in mystery not always explained' (20 Mar 1918).

Whatever the reason, Yeats had decided by 18 Sept 1922 'to get our further thought by "positive means" '. Although chronological order is less clear from this point, there are occasional dates and clues in letters, notebooks, and rejected manuscripts (or typescripts) which cast considerable light on the sometimes vacillating but more positive methods by which Yeats sought to order the exposition of the amazing revelations. He had already outlined his thought about 'The Twenty-Eight Embodiments' (*VA* 38-117) in the CF (some 115 cards are devoted to the Phases), and had begun organizing other sections of his book in an early notebook, most of which is in George's hand and must have been compiled while the AS was being written. Precise as usual, George writes at one point that the information she has recorded was 'Corrected by Thomas on Sunday in April 1918'; and Yeats observes near the end of the notebook that 'one spirit gives name as Thomas of Dorlowicz'. Since he was the first important Control to appear, these entries suggest that this notebook was compiled while the AS was being written. Also suggesting an early date is a very elementary version of 'The Table of the Four Faculties' (*VA* 30–3). Occupying only a half-page, the chart omits Phases 1, 8, 15, and 22 and lists the remaining twenty-four under designations for the Four Faculties: Ego, Mask, Genius, and Personality of Fate (only Mask was retained in *VA*).

Many of the headings in this notebook illustrate the kind of codifying the Yeatses had achieved at this stage: 'Zodiacal Signs', 'Wisdom of Two', 'Ugliness & Beauty', 'Sex', 'Spirit after Death', 'Phases', 'Seven Planes', 'Passionate Body', 'Primary and Anti', 'Cuchulain Plays', 'Mask', 'Ann Hyde', 'Inititate', 'Guides', 'Genius', 'Funnel', 'Ego', 'Dreaming Back', etc. One list is headed 'Symbol'; others explain the symbolic properties of 'Colours', 'Plants', and 'Beasts' (including insects and birds). Many of these and other headings also appear in the CF, which was perhaps being compiled at the same time but finally included many more details and recorded materials covering a longer period of time.

Another notebook, which revises and recasts much of the information in the early one, can be dated more accurately. Identified as the 'Property of W B Yeats, 4 Broad St, Oxford, England', it was probably compiled after he moved to that address (before 12 Oct 1919). It contains a reference to 'nativity of second child' (born 22 Aug 1921), entries spanning a period from 1 Nov 1922 to 27 Nov 1923, and a notation dated Jan 1925. It also contains several of the lists (not always in final form) which ultimately became part of the book (Four Automatonisms, Four Conditions of Mask, etc.) as well as several which were not used (Seven Planes, Colours, etc.). A fairly detailed diagram of a double cone relates years to Phases from Christ's birth to 2000. On 1 Nov 1922 Yeats noted 'Dates corrected since', presumably to what they were in the final form (*VA* 178). A greatly expanded chart of the Four Faculties is now close in language and format to the Table in *VA*. But there is one significant difference: the characteristics of the Phases are listed in six columns: Ego, Good Mask, Evil Mask, Evil Genius, Creative Genius, Personality of Fate (Mask is not divided for Phases 1 through 8). Obviously displeased with such a hexadic conception of the nature of man, Yeats found a means of compressing the six headings into the Four Faculties. His cosmic vision was essentially and consistently tetradic, based upon such occult sources as the Cabala, Neoplatonism, Boehme, and

Blake.[19] Besides 'The Table of Four Faculties', Yeats discovered ten other tetradic lists of characteristics in the human psyche (*VA* 33–6), and numerous other important tetradic divisions are listed in this notebook: especially, Head, Heart, Loins, and Fall as they are related to four zodiacal signs and four cardinal points, Four Daimons, and Four Memories ('declared to be frustration'). It is surely significant that Yeats is puzzled that two of his tables 'are divided into ten divisions'. 'They were given me in this form', he explained, 'and I have not sufficient confidence in my knowledge to turn them into the more convenient twelve-fold divisions' (*VA* 34n). Three pages concerned with 'After Death State' are marked through and labeled 'Partly muddled. Dreaming Back & Return etc'. One entry defines 'Three forms of Dream Image' ('Ideal thought when lived becomes image'). Several pages are devoted to the discussion (including 'Summing up') of Initiatory and Critical Moments in his and George's lives. Finally, and perhaps most importantly, this notebook contains eleven closely related entries (chiefly Sleeps from 4 Jy to 27 Nov 1923) concerned primarily with material which became part of *VA*, Book IV.

Since Yeats speaks (in an entry for 26 Oct) about material 'now incorporated in chapter on covens in "A Vision" ', it is clear that he was already composing, but just when he began or the precise order in which sections of the book were written is not clear. Again, however, there are occasional clues in the AS, the Sleeps, and the CF; and some evidence may be found in rejected manuscripts and typescripts. Yeats planned to make the order of composition clear by dating the sections as he accumulated information. Although he dated the completion of five sections (*VA* xiii, xxiii, 117, 215, and 252), the dates are useful primarily to establish the fact that Books I and II (undated) were finished well before the remainder. But the manuscripts and typescripts provide illuminating information not only about the chronology of composition but also about the development of Yeats's thought. He began writing *VA* as a dialogue between Michael Robartes and Owen (first John) Aherne (sometimes Ahearne or A Herne). As Yeats pointed out in a note to 'The Phases of the Moon', he took their names from three stories he had written years before (see *VP* 821). Yeats preserved two bodies of materials representing early attempts to write his book in this dialogue form: 132 pages of manuscript and 31 legal-sized pages of typescript. The disordered and often repetitive manuscripts (falling roughly into four different versions or fragments of the narrative) are revised, organized, and expanded in the typescript, one page of which records that it is a 'second dictation'. Containing chiefly the framework story which became the Introduction to *VA* and a considerable discussion of Phases 1 to 21, the typescript breaks off abruptly with an observation by Aherne (three times signed John or J.): 'I notice that you place not only Napoleon but Milton at Twenty-one.' Intending publication apparently, Yeats revised this typescript with some care and added several notes and insertions. It contains little material which ultimately became part of *VA* after Book I, and was abandoned, presumably because Yeats found the structural device and perhaps the fiction itself too restrictive for his purpose.

Although neither the manuscript versions nor the typescript can be dated with certainty, a letter to Lady Gregory suggests that Yeats began writing in London immediately after the honeymoon at Ashdown Forest (20 Oct to 12 Nov 1917). He wrote from Oxford on 4 Jan 1918 about the 'very profound, very exciting mystical philosophy . . . coming in strange ways to George and myself', then added: 'I am writing it all out in a series of dialogues about a supposed medieval book, the *Speculum Angelorum et Hominum* by Giraldus, and a sect of Arabs called the Judwalis (diagrammatists). Ross has helped me with the Arabic' (*L* 643–4). This letter verifies the plan that had already been decided upon and recorded in the AS. On 1 Jan, when Yeats asked for information about 'the second circle', the Control said: 'That must go into another dialogue. You cannot use it with this one and as far as psychology of the individual is concerned it is not necessary.' Clearly the pattern of investigations had assumed some definite directions to be developed in a series of dialogue essays, the first of which was to explore the 'psychology of the individual'.

Since one manuscript draft, probably the earliest, leaves blanks on three separate pages for the title of Giraldus's book and on one page for his name, Yeats almost certainly began writing before he and George left London to return to Ashdown Forest for the Christmas holidays (see *L* 634). During the week from 13 to 20 Nov when no Script was recorded, Yeats had surely talked with friends who had more experience then he in spiritualistic experiments, including members of the SPR. Also, at this time (certainly before 20 Dec) he had consulted Sir Edward Denison Ross, Director of the School of Oriental Studies in London University, about Arabian names and a title for his fictional Arabic Book. He and George returned to their investigations on 20 Nov with renewed confidence and a sense of direction lacking in the earlier Script. From that date through 7 Dec they conducted twenty-one sessions on thirteen separate days and recorded the results in 284 pages representing 723 questions and answers (some of both are lost). At the end of that amazing metaphysical exploration Yeats may have been prompted to write the first tentative pages of what was to culminate some eight years later in the most difficult and exciting of his books.

But a question in the AS for 21 Nov suggests that Yeats was already composing: 'For example in my essay Keats, Mrs Campbell etc was anti gaining victory?' The Control replied, 'No, Campbell anti losing; Keats yes, Gregory yes, Landor yes.' In the intense and extended sessions of the next few days Yeats asked and received answers to many of the questions upon which *VA* was based: Blake's 'terms Head, Heart, Loins', good and evil, ugliness and beauty, conscious and subconscious, the 28 stages, etc. Intermingled with these are many clearly related personal questions which were omitted from or veiled in the book: for example, a 'Freudian analysis' of Iseult's knots, the reason Yeats and George were 'chosen for each other', and the 'identity papers' (of Maud Gonne most likely). There are also suggestions in terminology and questions that Yeats had a partial plan in mind: he speaks of 'purpose of vision' and asks about symbolic values. In two long and very important sessions on 30 Nov, the Control comes 'to clear up your essay'. He offers material for 'your myth', and Yeats summarizes 'our myth this stage' and asks if the System is 'a new creation' or an old one known to 'initiates in many lands'. Although the answer to this question is lost, Yeats obviously expected to learn that he, the Medium, and the Controls were reviving and explaining a system that had been stored for long ages in the Anima Mundi, On 6 Dec Yeats was told to 'get the machinery of individual finished before going on'. The following day he 'described what I thought happened in my essay on Anima Mundi' and was told that 'Anima Mundi is too vague, it comprises the soul of innocence in the natural world & does not apply to after death states'. By 7 Dec apparently Yeats had conceived the outline of his System and had begun organizing it in the form of a dialogue.

At the opening of one manuscript version—perhaps the first—Aherne inquires about Yeats's essay on Anima Mundi: 'Have you read "Per Amica Silentia Lunae," which Macmillan & Co have just published for Mr Yeats?' 'Yes', Robartes replies, 'and it has shocked me & puzzled me, shocked especially in the second of the two essays by its dogmatic certainty.' A few pages later Robartes speaks of having 'read Rosa Alchemica when it came out in Savoy',[20] and both he and Aherne complain of the treatment they received in Yeats's story. Blank spaces are left for the title and author of the mythical book which is said to have been published in 1599.

In another unfinished manuscript version, perhaps the second in chronological order, a space originally blank now names the book as *Speculum Angelorum et Hominis* of Giraldus printed in 1594. His tribe is called Bacleones [?], 'an Arab sect well known at Fez in the time of Leo Africanus'. Since 'Bacleones' was changed to 'Judwalis' and 'Hominis' to 'Hominum' in the letter to Lady Gregory on 4 Jan, I assume that this manuscript was written prior to that date.[21] Two of the early versions refer to 'an ancient Arab MS called "The Camels Back" '[22] which contains the doctrines of the *Speculum*. The most extensive of the four manuscripts speaks of 'a student of "The Way of the Soul" '[23] who had set up in Damascus as a doctor. Among the other pieces of evidence suggesting a quite early date for these manuscripts, two are expecially important: (1) one contains a considerably revised page of 'The Phases of the Moon' (ll. 95–106); (2) another contains a sentence in a speech by Robartes which became the opening song for *The Only Jealousy of Emer*. Finished on 14 Jan 1918 (*L* 645), this play receives far more attention than any other of Yeats's creative works in the AS and Sleeps.

By the time the Yeatses returned to Ashdown Forest about 20 Dec, he had apparently written at least a few pages and had come to some definite conclusions about the early parts of the book to be. On 22 Dec the Control instructed Yeats to 'finish all codifying' and 'clear up as you go'. Yeats responded: 'I make statement of psychology of whole scheme as I see it & ask assent.' Reminded of 'your pledge of secrecy', Yeats must have planned the essay in the R-A TS within the next few days. There was no more AS until 29 Dec and then a veritable creative outburst after the move to Oxford, a day or so later. Sometime during the extremely productive month of January (see Table, p. xix above), he may have reorganized some 130 manuscript pages (often repetitious) into the thirty-one pages (plus notes) of the TS. Incorporating much of the material in the manuscripts, it covers with less detail and less order the outlines of the narrative of the Introduction (*VA* xv–xxiii) and the exposition of 'The Twenty-Eight Embodiments' (*VA* 38–117).

There is some evidence that Yeats planned an essay or series of essays on the model of *PASL*, which is mentioned in all four of the manuscript fragments. In one version Aherne says that 'it was published today'; in another Robartes speaks of not being 'able to rest . . . since I have seen that essay', the very title of which 'suggests that he has had it all at second hand'. The TS opens with a discussion of the book. 'Why that title "Through the friendly silence of the Moon" ', Robartes asks; 'why "silence" and why "moon"?' And he speaks of the doctrine of the soul 'as crudely stated in Per Amica'.

Such comments might, of course, be merely a part of the literary hoax by which Yeats was to maintain his 'pledge of secrecy'. But there is evidence that he intended to publish the TS as dialogue essays reminiscent of Oscar Wilde's. After line 5 of page 18 Yeats drew a line across the page and wrote 'Second conversation'. The 'second dictation' of a rejected sentence from page 10 suggests that he conceived his book as a series of such conversations: 'You will not understand me fully', Robartes said, 'until you have studied for yourself the diagrams which I will give you [and even then before I can describe detail accurately I shall have spent—if you find patience to listen—some days in exposition].'[24] Since Yeats made many revisions (including additions) in the TS, we may be sure that he intended to publish it—whether in periodicals, in a small book like *PASL*, or in a big book as yet not fully planned.

Essentially these two 'Conversations' represent Yeats's condensation and reflection upon the philosophical (but not the extensive personal) matter treated in the AS from 5 Nov 1917 to 30 Jan 1918. On that date Yeats was informed that 'There are three stages. One is passed, the second begins, the third depends on you.' The following day, in two amazing sessions (24 pages, 121 questions), attention was shifted to a new issue, primarily the 'separation of the spirit at death'.

Although Robartes spoke of 'diagrams which I will give you', the TS has none. The First Conversation (pp. 1–18) contains a rather rambling and somewhat unorganized account of the narrative in the Introduction and portions of the exposition in 'The Great Wheel' (without the table and lists in *VA* 30–7). The Second Conversation (pp. 18–31) is concerned almost exclusively with 'The Twenty-Eight Embodiments', though as a narrative rather than the mechanically organized section in *VA* 38–117. Because Robartes is forced to do most of the talking in this essay, the dialogue is less appealing than that of the First Conversation. The restrictions imposed by the form may have influenced Yeats to abandon it without completing the Second Conversation, which breaks off with a rhetorical question about the reason for placing Napoleon and Milton at P 21.

Since Napoleon was ultimately moved to P 20 and Milton was rejected, these two Examples illustrate Yeats's uncertainty and also cast some light on the date of the R-A TS. Yeats began the search for appropriate Examples on 21 Dec 1917, in the first session of the AS after the return to Ashdown Forest, and some of the names proposed continued to be problems until finally placed or rejected: Tennyson and Keats at P 12, Wordsworth and Rossetti at 14, Dante at 17, Goëthe at 18, Browning at 19, F.W.H. Myers at 23. Yeats asked for but did not receive Examples for Phases 1 through 8. On 22 Dec he requested the Phases of George Herbert and George Russell (the lost answer was probably 25), and he learned that Thomas, the Control, belonged to 18. When Yeats moved to Oxford (probably on 30 Dec), the first task was to find Examples for the Phases. On 1 Jan 1918, he was informed that Nietzsche belonged at 12 and Zarathustra at 18. On 2 Jan Yeats asked the Control to 'place events of Christs history on diagram of lunar phases' (see n. to p. 244, 12–15), and he received the Phases of several people: Lady Gregory (24), Maud Gonne and Helen of Troy (16) (there is 'no flawless woman'), Synge (23) and Landor (17); Yeats also learned that there is 'no human being at either' 1 or 15. The Control insisted that Yeats 'go on with lists' the following day, and other names were added: Shakespeare and Chaucer (20), Milton and Horace (21), Homer and Botticelli (17), Virgil (12), Motesquieu, Dürer, and Plutarch (18), Herodotus (3), Michelangelo and Balzac (23), Socrates and Pascal (27), Savonarola (20), Schopenhauer and Carlyle (11), Verlaine (13), Dostoievski (22) and his Idiot (8), Calvin and Luther (25), Flaubert (21), Tolstoy and Whitman (6), the Cubists (9), Lassalle (10). On 4 Jan the Control asked to be given 'all lists', and Yeats named fifteen people and received Phases for all but one: Defoe (4), Meredith and Cervantes (20), Jane Austen (the Control did 'not want to'), Velasquez (19), Burne-Jones (17), Watts and Titian (18), Richelieu and Napoleon (21), Cromwell (19), Mazarin (24), Parnell (10), and O'Connell (23). Yeats requested 'a man for 9' but received no answer.

On the following day he asked for and received many of the descriptive phrases for Good and Bad (i.e., True and False) Masks (see *VA* 30–3), all of which were 'subject to revision'. Following the discussion of these characteristics, Yeats asked the Control to 'take up affinities of souls', and he received a triadic list of related Phases, beginning with his own: 17, 12, 24; 18, 13, 25, etc. He also learned that Olivia Shakespear's Phase was 20 but could not get Florence Farr's because the Medium had seen her only twice.

Throughout most of Jan, Yeats and his assistants continued to work with Phases and related matters, and he was perhaps prepared to compose the two Conversations in the R-A TS. During this month George drew up a careful list (ultimately filed with the AS of 2 June) of names they had placed. Although the list of names for Phases 1 through 9 is lost, what remains is instructive. Several names have been marked through and shifted to other Phases. Among these are Keats and Tennyson, now moved to 14. Since both are discussed as representatives of this Phase on 24 Jan, the list was surely drawn up before that date. And the R-A TS, which discusses names not on the list and also cites Keats as the 'perfect type' for 14, was surely later. Yeats places himself at 17 and George at 18, but omitted both in *VA*, perhaps because their inclusion would have seemed too personal.

The opening sentence of the Second Conversation probably refers to this list: 'I notice on one of the interpolated pages', Aherne remarks, 'a long list in your hand writing of European poets, philosophers and men of action classified under the different phases.' 'In fact', Robartes replies, speaking for Yeats, 'I have had to re-study the whole system in relation to the interests of the first thirty years of my life. Here and there I have even added the name of some man who has come to interest me in the last few months.' Among the new artists, many of whom 'belong to phases between 8 & 11', Robartes 'placed the Cubists at nine', Augustus John at 10 or 11, Ezra Pound (Aherne's 'enemy') at 12, and Charles Conder at 14. Helen of Troy has also been shifted to 14, the Phase of Iseult Gonne and Robert Gregory.

By this time apparently extensive vistas were opening up, and Yeats decided that his original plan for 'a series of dialogues' was inadequate. On 6 Feb the Control spoke of matters not to be decided until 'the third stage', which 'may be very long' off and would require further preparation. On 21 Feb he suggested that 'Perhaps another 3 months' would be needed, but he was less certain a week later: 'I am not going to give you much for another month; you must meditate far more, meditate on some spiritual image.' There was no further Script until 4 Mar, when a convocation of six Controls and

Guides gathered to counsel and direct. Speaking for the first time of 'the book', they informed Yeats that they were

> not pleased because you talk too freely of spirits & of initiation. . . . You may speak of the actual system but you may not tell of any personal thought, image, or information we give nor of the forms & processes we give for your own contemplation nor of such demand & restrictions as we make nor of the life we demand that you should live. Only speak of those actual machineries of the philosophy that may be in the book.

After some unrecorded question by Yeats, they warned him further not to imply that the System was coming 'through your own initiation or psychic power'. He might 'imply *invention*' or 'dreams but not *guidance of spirits in your life*. That is always wrong because you speak to unbelievers'. Because 'the only value is in the whole', they 'do not *wish* the spirit source revealed'. Clearly, they wanted Yeats to avoid sensationalizing his experience by conversations with incredulous friends and students who gathered at his Monday Evenings in Oxford. The Controls advised Yeats that he might 'say a good deal is of supernormal & the rest invention & deduction', but they warned him very sternly that he must 'never mention *any* personal message; these . . . are the most important of all our communicaions'. This warning may not be the only reason for the exclusion of personal materials from *VA*, but Yeats surely thought it reason enough. As a result, a large percentage of the great mass of AS and Sleeps was no longer considered suitable for the book. Since the names of numerous close friends were still in the lists and he continued to ask questions about his art and his intimate personal affairs, especially with women, the experiments obviously served two functions: one therapeutic and private, the other creative and public. The Controls concluded their advice with an assurance that a trip to Ireland, the first since marriage, was 'quite safe'. And the voyage home was symbolically related to what he had been learning: 'All life is a return to its beginnings—there is no new thought or feeling.'

The following day, probably Yeats's last in Oxford for many months, the Control reiterated that he was 'not going to begin writing on the system till you are again settled'—that is, in Ireland. When Yeats asked an oblique question about the possible reincarnation of the dead child of Anne Hyde through him and George (see p. xxiv above), he was informed that he would not be able to decide until 'the third stage' was reached and that he 'ought to tabulate the system as far as you have gone to make your mind fertile and critical'. In response to some unrecorded question the Control said that he would 'deal with that in the period of describing mediumship & vision', which may have been the subject planned for the third stage.

The symbolic crossing to Ireland made, the Yeatses stopped in Dublin, and he communicated briefly (on 11 Mar) with Anne Hyde (who did 'not want medium to know'). In Glendalough by 14 Mar, they renewed their visionary quest with a series of sessions devoted primarily to Dreaming Back and the relationship of the Passionate Body to the Celestial Body.

There are surprizingly few clues to assist us in dating the sections of the expanded book Yeats now had in mind. Because he needed much more information, however, we may be relatively sure that he did not return to composition for some time, perhaps several months. And even while he wrote, his plan continued to change and expand, as he suggested in a rejected typescript: 'P.S. I have dated the various sections of this book because my knowledge grew as I wrote, and there are slight changes of emphasis, and blank spaces that need explanation.' Despite that note he dated only three of the Books: I ('Finished at Thoor, Ballylee, 1922, in a time of Civil War'), III ('Finished at Capri, February, 1925'), and IV ('Finished at Syracuse, January, 1925'). Besides two of the poems, he also dated the Dedication (February, 1925) and Introduction (May, 1925). As completion dates, however, they tell us very little about the actual time or chronological order of composition and may even be misleading. For example, the four dates in 1925 may suggest that he composed everything except Book I in a burst of energy that winter and spring.

But we know that he worked at *VA* over a long period of time, and in fact much more than Book I may have been drafted by the end of 1922. The manuscript of the 'Introduction by Owen Aherne' is dated 'Dec 1922', and there is some evidence that *VA* through Book II was finished by that date. A much-revised typescript includes Aherne's 'Introductory Chapter', Parts I and II (covering *VA*, Book I), and the beginning of Part III. This typescript ends abruptly with four hand-written etceteras, suggesting perhaps that the remainder was written or in progress. But Yeats almost surely did not have this typescript in mind when he noted in *VA* that Book I was 'Finished at Thoor, Ballylee, 1922'. He was in Ballylee as late as 18 Sept (the date of the last notebook entry); on 9 Oct he had been in Dublin 'for a couple of weeks' when he wrote to Olivia Shakespear that he was 'busy writing out the system—getting a "Book A" written that can be typed and shown to interested persons and talked over' (*L* 690). He refers to the typescript (131 pages) of three Parts, the first two of which were intended as divisions of 'Book A', as it was entitled and then crossed out at the top of page 3 (it was also labeled 'preliminary'). By 1 Dec Werner Laurie was ready to accept the book at once, but Yeats was 'insisting on his reading a hundred pages or so first' (*L* 694). (Parts I and II reach 125 pages by Yeats's numbering.) His plan is clear in a letter to Olivia on 18 Dec: 'If Laurie does not repent, a year from now should see the first half published. It will need another volume to finish it' (*L* 695). Presumably, Book B (originally Part III) was to be the other volume needed for completion of his plan. Although the typescript has only five pages of Part III, we can be relatively sure that it was to have contained the remainder of *VA* as Yeats then conceived it. Apparently, Yeats still had in mind two small books of two parts each on the order and indeed an extension of *PASL*.

But if he was still working on the typescript of Book A on 18 Dec, what version was finished at Ballylee, which he left at the end of Sept? He may, of course, refer to a manuscript from which the typescript was made, or he may refer to a different manuscript labelled, in large letters on page 6, 'Version B'. Although it opens as a dialogue between Robartes and Aherne, the form is soon abandoned. This manuscript of 114 pages (plus some notes and other matter) by Yeats's count contains much of the material in the typescript of Book A, but the organization, except the discussion of the Phases, is significantly different. Divided into eight sections (one has three sub-sections) marked by small Roman numerals, Version B is obviously thought of as an organic unit.

The first seven sections are designed to lead into VIII, which is a detailed exposition of twenty-three of the twenty-eight embodiments. Phases 1, 14, and 15 are omitted entirely, perhaps because they required additional care or thought; Phases 27 and 28 are barely outlined, perhaps because of the rush to leave Ballylee 'in a time of Civil War'.[25]

Having completed his experiments (with the exception of a few Sleeps in 1923) and a draft of Version B, Yeats must have begun rewriting as soon as he was settled at 82 Merrion Square in Dublin. First, apparently, he carefully revised the manuscript. As he prepared Book A, based upon this revision, he expanded and reordered: the first seven sections were replaced by eleven, and section VIII became Part II. A section of the manuscript entitled 'Why Kusta ben Luki was banished from court & under what circumstances he returned' was revised and cut to become an unnumbered introductory section called 'The Dance of the Four Royal Persons', and two important new sections were added: 'The Four Perfections and the Four Automatonisms' and 'The Daimon, the Sexes, Unity of Being, Natural and Supernatural Unity'. He also made a note on a blank page facing the exposition about P 16 that he intended to 'Put unity of being in Chapter by itself'. The other major organizational change was to combine two untitled sections (III and IV) into one called 'The Geometrical Foundation', which was to be the opening of Part III (originally Book B). The episode about Flaubert (see *VA* 128) was symbolically significant in Yeats's cosmic vision. Perhaps the most rewritten part of *VA*, it was introduced at one stage of composition by a passage from Plato's *Republic*, Book X, which was also important to Yeats's mythopoeic chart of the soul's journey through life. According to Plato's myth, when 'all the souls had chosen their lives', Lachesis 'dispatched with each of them the Destiny he had selected to guard his life & satisfy his choice'. The Destiny then 'led the soul to Clotho in such a way as to pass beneath her hand & the whirling motion of the distaff & thus ratified the fate which each had chosen'.[26] Why Yeats rejected this passage as epigraph is not clear: it may be that he thought Plato had emphasized Chance rather than Choice in the soul's odyssey.

Although the typescript of Book A is much revised, the copy which went to Werner Laurie was most likely clean. Since there are few typing errors or blanks, we may be sure that Yeats dictated to the typist, revising as he rewrote. At this time he reached a fundamental structural decision to drop the dialogue form. It was therefore necessary to rewrite section 1 of Version B, and the first form of 'Aherne's Introduction' was the result. The manuscript was probably finished in Dec 1922, the date at the end. He left blanks for the word *Hominorum* in the title of Giraldus's book and for the Arabic title of the 'learned book' once possessed by the Judwalis. Although the basic narrative of the 'Introduction' remained unchanged through the publication of *VA*, Yeats revised and expanded it for Laurie, who must have received Book A and the five opening pages of Book B in early 1923. On 13 Mar, in an unpublished letter to Laurie, Yeats wrote, 'I promised you a hundred pages'. Perhaps the typescript was already or soon to be completed.

How much more, if any, of Book B had been written at this time I cannot determine, but the revision of 'Aherne's Introduction' suggests that Yeats had the basic divisions of *VA* in mind. Speaking of Robartes' 'diagrams and notes', Yeats wrote: 'This bundle . . . described the *mathematical law* of history, that bundle the adventure of the soul after death, that other the interaction between the living and the dead and so on.'[27]

Unfortunately, we have few dates to assist us in establishing the composition of 'Dove or Swan' (*VA*, Book III), originally entitled simply 'History'. But there is evidence that Yeats wrote the manuscript (61 pages plus a few notes on unnumbered pages) soon after completing the typescript of 100 plus pages for Laurie. One notebook of Sleeps, the last entry of which is dated 9 Feb 1921, contains six miscellaneous pages with notes concerning dates, Phases, diagrams, and references to historical figures. Since two of the notes (on Oxford stationery) quote from *The Education of Henry Adams* and relate his observations to dates and Phases in Yeats's historical outline, it seems likely that Yeats made the notes while he was reading *The Education* in preparation for the essay on 'History'. Writing to AE on 14 Mar 1921, Yeats said: 'I have read all Adams and find an exact agreement even to dates with my own "law of history" ' (*L* 666). Yeats's discussion of the period 'A.D. 1220 to 1300' is clearly indebted to Adams, and an additional reference to Constantine in a revision of a typescript based on the manuscript comes directly from the notes on Oxford stationery. That is, while revising the first draft he had again consulted his notes or Adams's books. As he wrote in the typescript, 'Mont St Michel rises before me, symbolical of all.'

Yeats originally intended his discussion of History to fall into two parts (but not numbered as such). The first was to be a brief consideration of the 2000 years B.C., the second a much more extended consideration of the Christian era. The discussion of each of these cycles was also to be divided. The pre-Christian cycle was to have two sections: '2000 B.C. to 500 B.C.' and 'B.C. 500 to A.D. 1'.[28] There is some evidence in both manuscript and typescript that Yeats wrote and abandoned a longer essay about the pre-Christian era, perhaps because it was 'a time of which I am ignorant and of which even the latest research has discovered little'. The first page of the manu-

script, which begins with the section on 'B.C. 500 to A.D. 1',
is numbered both 1 and 19. Since parallel sets of numbers are
continued throughout, it seems clear that Yeats had cut the first
eighteen pages and renumbered the whole. This assumption is
corroborated by the fact that two typescripts, one a revision
of the other, begin with the same dates and are numbered from
1.

   Yeats originally planned to break his discussion of the 2000 years
of the Christian cycle into small units approximating the divisions in
'The Historical Cones' (*VA* 178). Each period of 1000 years was to be
broken into twelve chronological units to which the twenty-eight
Phases were assigned. As a result, there were in effect two complete
cycles of 1000 years in the greater cycle of 2000 years. Discovering
the inflexibility of his plan, he admitted apologetically in the typescript that 'it is of course impossible to do more than select a more or
less arbitrary general date for a change that varies from country to
country (cf. *VA* 187). Nevertheless, he made numerous changes in
both manuscript and typescript before rejecting the scheme for the
simpler one ultimately adopted (see *VA* 185 and 196). There is
evidence in the revised typescript that he planned descriptive topical headings in addition to dates and Phases. For example, a section
which was first headed 'A.D. to A.D. 100' was expanded and
revised to read:

The First Fountain

The climax of secular order, & the incarnation. First Fountain
Phases 2. 3. 4
A.D. 1 to A.D. 120.

The first two lines were marked through, and nothing more was
made of The Four Fountains, which may have been conceived as a
kind of tetradic parallel in the history of civilization to The Four
Faculties in the history of the soul.

   Despite the tone of sophisticated insouciance in the essay on
History, Yeats was frequently hesistant, perhaps a bit uncom-
fortable, at taking all knowledge for his province. In both manuscript
and typescript there are many half-apologetic tags and excuses such
as 'I think' or 'wonder if' or 'see in this change'. And finally, in a
rejected passage, he defended himself appropriately by taking
refuge in the supranatural: 'Hitherto I have described the past or but
the near future, but now I must plunge beyond the reach of the

senses.' Although he revised both extensively, he was obviously still uneasy, and he read history voraciously and perceptively between the revision of the typescript and the final version 'Finished at Capri, February, 1925'. 'Dove or Swan' is a remarkable essay, with which Yeats continued to be pleased, repeating it 'without change' in *VB* (but see n. to p. 210, 26).

Although Yeats surely expected 'The Gates of Pluto' to be the summation or crowning achievement of *VA*, he was finally disappointed with it. In a rejected manuscript (c. 1929) Yeats admitted that 'a long section called the "Gates of Pluto" now fills me with shame. It contains a series of unrelated statements & inaccurate deductions from the symbols & were little but hurried notes recorded for our future guidance' (see n. to p. 217 and cf. *VB* 19 and 23). Since the system of *VA* came 'from certain dead men who in all they say assume their own existence',[29] Yeats obviously intended almost from the beginning that one or more of his essays should be concerned with the difficult psychological and philosophical questions explored in Book IV. On 30 Jan 1918, the Control informed him that there were to be three stages in their explorations: 'One is passed, the second begins, the third depends on you'. When Yeats asked for a definition of the second stage, he learned that 'it is of two parts—firstly of man & the spirits, secondly of the spirits & God'. He began at once, devoting many sessions and hundreds of questions to the subject in the next two weeks. (He was informed on 6 Feb that 'it may be very long before you can arrive at' the third stage.) Although Yeats frequently received ambiguous answers, he knew precisely what he needed to learn, as his opening questions on 31 Jan demonstrate: 'Describe separation of the spirit at death'; 'What is the state of spirit immediately after separation from body'. And he learned before the day's arduous work (two sessions, 121 questions) was over that the first four of the soul's seven planes of existence were directly related or parallel to the four elements: (1) Physical (earth), (2) Passionate (water), (3) Spirits of the Dead (air), (4) Celestial Body (fire). He had of course learned long before from a GD study manual, 'Liber Hodos Chamelionis', that 'the sphere of Sensation which surroundeth the whole Physical body of a Man is called the "Magical Mirror of the Universe" '. In two important sessions on 1 Feb Yeats pursued the subject vigorously. George drew the first tentative diagrams of what was to become 'The Separation of the Four Principles', and she made a list of sub-topics which perhaps represents a tentative outline of Book IV: '(1) The newly dead, (2)

Funnel life dreaming back, (3) Funnel life shifting, (4) Life between, (5) Spirits at I, (6) Spirits at XV, (7) Guides.'

Although Yeats noted that Book IV was 'Finished at Syracuse, January, 1925' (*VA* 252), he no doubt worked on it long before, and an early draft, much different from the final, may have been written in 1923. Eleven Sleeps and Meditations covering the period from 4 Jy to 27 Nov are primarily concerned with the subject matter of 'The Gates of Pluto' and may be the direct result of the Control's consent (on 18 Sept 1922) 'that when we came to write out account of life after death we could . . . resume sleeps etc for a time'. In the account of a Sleep dated 26 Oct 1923 Yeats refers to a 'chapter on covens in "A Vision" ': he claims as his own (rather than the Control's) 'the part . . . about the smaller wheel which corresponds to the romantic musical movement, etc' (see n. 18 above). Still entitled simply 'Book Four', it was to have two main divisions: (1) 'Death, the Soul, and the Life after Death': (2) 'The Soul between Death and Birth'. At this stage Yeats must have intended to 'count the life before death and the life after as two halves of a single Wheel and measure it upon that' (*VA* 161). For some unexplainable reason that structural plan was not satisfactory, and Yeats ultimately transferred much of the material from 'Death, the Soul, and the Life after Death' to *VA*, Book II, where in fact it often seems illogically placed. The first section of the typescript of 'Book Four', entitled 'Michael Robartes and the Judwali Doctor' (see parenthetical paragraphs in *VA* 245–7), contains a reference which may assist in dating its composition. The Arab boy in the narrative dreamed 'that men placed him between the forks of a tree, and that a woman, while musicians beat drums and blew horns, shot him dead with an arrow'. This 'old ceremony connected with tree worship' was, according to Owen Aherne, similar to a 'dream or vision . . . Mr Yeats had once'. Aherne refers to an article by Yeats about 'dreams and visions' of 'the cabbalistic tree of life' and 'a naked woman . . . shooting an arrow at a star'.[30] Since the explanatory notes were based upon information provided by a 'learned man' from Oxford in an unpublished letter dated 5 Apr 1923, the reference in the typescript was obviously written after—probably soon after—that date. The record of a Sleep dated 9 Jy also refers to 'my archer vision' which, Yeats wrote, 'would be idea from spiritual memory'.

There is evidence in letters to and from Dulac that Yeats was trying to complete *VA* at this time. On 24 Jy Dulac wrote that he had 'done a sketch in pencil of the portrait of Gyraldus by an unknown artist of the early sixteenth century', and he asked Yeats for 'a few particulars' about Giraldus.[31] Dulac mailed the sketch on 30 Sept: 'It is a little "early" in style', he wrote, 'but I think it is better suited to a book of that kind than the "Dürer" manner.' And he asked Yeats 'about the other diagrams': 'tell me when you want them and what they are in detail.'[32] Yeats replied on 14 Oct: 'The portrait of Giraldus is admirable. I enclose the sketch for the diagram. . . . The book will be finished in I hope another month—it contains only a little of my system but the rest can follow' (*L* 699–700).

Since Dionertes returned as late as 27 Nov to communicate important information about Phantasmagoria, Shiftings, Dreaming Back, 'Japanese story of two lovers' (cf. *VA* 225), as well as Yeats's own 'inference' four times noted parenthetically, we may assume that he was still at work on Part II of Book Four, 'The Soul between Death and Birth', which was to become 'The Gates of Pluto'.

Fortunately, he preserved an almost complete but extensively revised typescript which contains, though not in a finished state, much of the material in twelve of the sixteen sections of *VA*, Book IV. A manuscript of section XI is close to the final version and was probably written later. Sections I, XV, and XVI had not yet been written. Section XV, 'Mythologies', was added in GP; the other two were perhaps written when Yeats decided to abandon the original two-part structure and redundant titles: I 'Death, the Soul, and the Life after Death'; II 'The Soul between Death and Birth'. He may have been conscious of the similarity between these titles and those of books written by two famous investigators of psychic phenomena named in the typescript: J. H. Hyslop's *Life after Death* and Camille Flammarion's trilogy *Before Death, At the Moment of Death*, and *After Death*. Upon deciding to use only the material in Part II for Book IV, Yeats chose a new title from a passage in Cornelius Agrippa's *De Occulta Philosophia*, which he had quoted with approval in 'Swedenborg, Mediums and the Desolate Places' (*VBWI* 332). And he probably wrote 'Stray Thoughts' (section I) to accommodate his choice.

The decision to restructure Book IV (and II as a result) may have been the prime reason that he could not finish *VA* in 'another month' as he had optimistically predicted on 14 Oct 1923 (*L* 699). Three and a half months later he wrote resignedly to Dulac: 'I am still very far from finished, so there is no hurry about your design. I work for days and then find I have muddled something, and have to do it all again, especially whenever I have to break new ground' (*L* 703).[33]

On 26 May 1924 he was 'codifying fragments of the philosophy' which still absorbed him two months later (*L* 705, 707).

Also, as a result of the decision to restructure, Yeats may have decided to dedicate his book 'To Vestigia' (Moina Mathers), an 'old fellow student' in the GD. Sometime after MacGregor Mathers' death in 1918, Moina returned to London and met Yeats again for the first time in many years. 'When the first draft of this dedication was written', according to Yeats, 'I had not seen you for more than thirty years, nor knew where you were nor what you were doing' (*VA* ix). In fact, the time cannot have been more than twenty-five years: Yeats visited the Matherses in Paris in Apr 1898 (*L* 298), and he had seen Moina again before Jan 1924 when she wrote of 'your conversation' and expressed 'the pleasure I had had in meeting you again'.[34] If, then, Yeats had not seen Moina for many years when 'the first draft of this dedication was written' (*VA* ix), it would have predated the meeting she refers to. Almost certainly, however, this draft was written in the summer of 1924, and it may have been partially responsible for the delay in completion of *VA*. Moina wrote to Yeats on 5 Jan 1924 of the 'violent' shock she had received over 'your caricature portrait of S.R.M.D.' in *The Trembling of the Veil* (1922).[35] 'With this awful book of yours between us I can never meet you again or be connected with you in any way save you make such reparation as may lie in your power'.[36] Yeats replied on 8 Jan with 'suggestions' which she considered 'quite the best that could be made under the circumstances' (12 Jan).[37] When Yeats offered still further concessions in a letter of 28 Jan, she thanked him warmly and suggested that 'a certain re-construction of "SR's" character in your book would be the solution'.[38] Although Yeats changed the sketch little in subsequent printings, he obviously wanted to make the reparation she sought, and he may have decided that 'it was plain that I must dedicate my book to you' (*VA* ix).

Yeats preserved two distinctly different versions of the Dedication and an Epilogue also addressed 'To Vestigia'. There is almost certain evidence in the opening of the rejected 'first draft' that it was written in the summer of 1924.

A couple of summers ago I walked some four miles from an old tower some twice a week to where an old friend [lived]. When conversation began to flag as it will with old friends who know each others thoughts [she] would take up the "Consuelo" of George Sand [or] its sequel & read out a Chapter. As she read you came into my memory, as you were when I saw you *nearly* thirty years ago. [my italics]

The old tower was Ballylee, where he had lived 'a couple of summers ago' (i.e., in 1922). While there, he reported to Olivia Shakespear, on 27 Jy 1922, that 'an old friend' had indeed been reading to him: 'Did you ever read George Sand's *Consuelo* and its sequel? Lady Gregory has read them out to me—a chapter at a time—during the summer' (*L* 687).[39] Almost certainly, then, the 'first draft' of the Dedication was written in the summer of 1924 after Yeats had seen Moina again. Since he was usually careful with dates and facts, he surely had some symbolic date and span of time in mind: the first draft reads 'nearly thirty years ago', the second was changed to 'for thirty [years]', and the third (dated 'February, 1925') was further altered to 'more than thirty years', the exact phrase with which the rejected Epilogue begins. What Yeats had in mind is perhaps suggested in the opening sentence of the second draft: 'Thirty years ago a number of young men & women, you & I among the number, were accustomed to meet in London & in Paris, to discuss mystical philosophy.' A rejected passage in the Epilogue is illuminating: 'Yet it may be that [you] will dislike [my] book, for I do not know what you have thought these thirty years[,] they were all so long ago[,] those meetings of fellow students'. Since Yeats was remembering experiences after Moina moved to Paris in 1892, he was apparently being intentionally vague when he widened the span still further in the final version to 'nearly forty years ago' (*VA* ix). And indeed the Dedication was most likely an afterthought, Yeats's effort to appease the anger aroused by an indiscreet 'caricature portrait'.

Whatever the reason for Yeats's studied ambiguity it is important to note that the rejected Epilogue and all versions of the Dedication are addressed to Yeats's 'old fellow students' in the GD and that they maintain an air of secrecy demanded of an Adept in the Order. As might be expected, the AS contains many overtones of and numerous references to the GD and several of its members, for Yeats was seriously involved in its problems during the writing of the AS and Sleeps.[40] 'All those strange students who were my friends', one draft reads, 'are dead or estranged.' The most important of the estranged was Moina Mathers, whom Yeats was clearly trying to mollify without betraying her identity to the reading public: 'I call you the name that we all knew you by & that none but we have ever known.' The most important of the dead was W. T.

Horton, who, if living, would have been asked 'to accept the dedication' (*VA* x). Several others are referred to without being named in
the first draft: Audrey Locke, Horton's Platonic friend, and the only
one who had not been a member of the GD; Allan Bennett, the
Burmese monk; Florence Farr, who spent the last years of her life
teaching in Ceylon; MacGregor Mathers, who died a bitter man;
Dorothea Hunter, a clairvoyant friend of the 1890s; Maud Gonne,
who had sought escape in 'violent revolutionary hatred'; and 'the
learned brassfounder in the North of England' (not mentioned in
the first draft), who may have been Thomas Henry Pattinson.[41] 'I
have written this book', Yeats explained in the first draft, 'for a
handful of fellow students, who are dead or estranged; & when I am
alarmed at the thought of publishing so singular a book I encourage
myself with the certainty that they would have considered it important.' 'They would have understood', he continued, 'that perhaps
the little chapters signed John Aherne are all that he or I can say for
some years yet as to how it all came.' Yeats perhaps rejected this
draft of the Dedication because it was too personal (Maud, Mac-
Gregor, and Dorothea were omitted from the final version) or
because it would suggest that his book was addressed to a coterie
and was therefore too esoteric.[42]

Although considerable revision of his book remained to be made,
Yeats felt a great relief that he had almost completed 'these few
pages [which] have taken me many months of exhausting labour'.
'Three times this morning', he wrote in one manuscript, 'I had given
up in despair lest I not remember that this task has been laid upon
me by those who cannot speak being dead & who if I fail may never
find another interpreter.' 'Lacking me', he added, 'Kusta ben Luka
himself once so learned & so elequent could now . . . but twitter like
a swallow'; 'like him I offer no metaphysical system but a science,
like other sciences proved by its predictions.'[43]

Yeats was not wholly satisfied with his nearly completed book,
but he was 'impatient to be done with it, to feel that I cannot touch it
again for some years to come that I may begin before it [is] too late,
the works of art that it seems to me to have made possible'. He was
conscious that he had perhaps 'not even dealt . . . with the most
important part, for I have said little of sexual love nothing of the
souls reality'.[44] He had been warned by the Controls and the
Medium that it was too personal; he had failed to treat the soul's
reality because he felt inadequate for the task. He was emotionally
spent as he finished the first draft of the Dedication 'To Vestigia':

Something that has troubled my life for years has *been folded up & smoothed out & laid away;*[45] & yet I declare that I have not invented one detail of this system, that alone has made it possible that I may end my life without wholly lacking an emotion or emphasis on my [purity?].

Whatever the inadequacy of his book, however, Yeats was certain that the creation of it had rid his mind of abstraction: he had 'been purified by desire'. On 23 Apr 1925 he recorded his relief and partial frustration in a notebook devoted chiefly to after-thoughts about his exhausting spiritual quest: 'Yesterday I finished "A Vision", I can write letters again & idle'.[46]

But the restless seeker could not remain idle. Although he thought briefly that the 'Knots' 'had been taken out' and his mind 'set in order', he was already thinking of re-making the chart he had plotted for 'the way of the soul'. 'Doubtless', he said in the revised Dedication, 'I must complete what I have begun'. In fact, he did begin almost immediately to revise and restructure the book which had consumed seven and one-half years of his life. But 'defects of my own' made it impossible to finish 'The Soul in Judgment', biographically the most important of the books in the revised version (see *VB* 23). But he was convinced that the end of life is not the end of existence: the visionary voyage would go on. Yeats had learned from Thomas in that 'almost earliest script' of 5 Nov 1917 that 'you find by seeking'. And Thomas himself may have learned from William Blake that 'the spriritual cone has no BC or AD'[47] for the

Human Forms identified, living, going forth & returning wearied
Into the Planetary lives of Years, Months, Days & Hours.[48]

Yeats too was certain, long before he reordered the 'incredible experience' codified in *VA*, that 'Going and returning are the typical eternal motions, they characterize the visionary forms of eternal life'.[49]

Notes

1 *A Vision* (London: T. Werner Laurie, 1925), p. xix. Hereafter cited as *VA* (as distinct from *VB*, 1937) and followed by page numbers when appropriate. For other abbreviations used throughout this essay and the notes at the end of the book see 'List of Abbreviations'.

2 From a rejected typescript (5 May 1928) entitled 'Dramatis Personae', originally planned as Book I of *VB*. Since the great mass of manuscript and typescript materials (several thousand pages in all) of the various stages of development of *VA* and *VB* are not yet ordered and described (though now available for examination in the Yeats Archives at the State University of New York at Stony Brook), my citations from them may on occasion seem vague, ambiguous, or even tantalizingly imprecise. But I will describe, as fully as space permits, the nature and scope of the materials, especially those relating to *VA*; and I will cite dates, circumstances, and places when they seem relevant. Fortunately, many such details are carefully recorded—especially in the Automatic Script (hereafter cited as AS), Sleeps, and Card File (hereafter cited as CF).

3 Typescript of 'Dramatis Personae'.

4 Hereafter cited as GD and SPR.

5 In *VBWI* 311–36 and Harper, *YO* 130–71.

6 See letter from Wyndham Lewis, in which he asks 'when it is likely to appear in its revised form', *LWBY* 484.

7 An earlier draft reads: '. . . since Descartes taught the living to assume theirs'.

8 See, for example, the note in 'Swedenborg, Mediums and the Desolate Places' in which Yeats names ten writers whose 'well-known books' on spiritualistic research he had read. He had also 'made considerable use' of four journals. 'I have myself', he concluded, 'been a somewhat active investigator' (*VBWI* 324).

9 I am indebted to the National Library of Ireland for permission to quote from Lady Lyttelton's unpublished 'Reminiscences of Yeats' (part of MS. 5919) written in 1940 at the request of Joseph Hone.

10 I have used the term *Control* to identify the personality of the spirit which makes use of the Medium to deliver direct or relayed messages to sitters. Yeats distinguished between the various Controls and Guides (see p. xxii above), but sometimes referred to them as Communicators or Instructors; he usually referred to his wife, George, as the Medium or Interpreter.

11 I am quoting chiefly from copies of excerpts made by Lady Lyttelton now in the library of Senator Michael B. Yeats. She preserved the originals and copied from them when she wrote her 'Reminiscences', which includes somewhat different excerpts.

12 I am indebted to Senator Michael B. Yeats for permission to quote from this and the following letter from Yeats transcribed in Lady Lyttelton's 'Reminiscences'.

13 I have been unable to locate Horton's executor. I am indebted to Senator Michael B. Yeats for the opportunity to examine this and other unpublished materials referred to or cited herein.

14 Yeats was no doubt aware that both Horton and Lady Lyttelton were recalling the myth of the black and white horses from Plato's *Phaedrus* (secs. 255–6). Lady Lyttelton copied Horton's note and returned it.

15 *LWBY* 296–7.

16 The AS contains little capitalization and punctuation, which I have supplied only when it seems necessary for clarity.

17 Mrs Yeats is said to have told someone that she had destroyed part of the AS. Because she was so careful to preserve almost every scrap of Yeats's work, I remain skeptical.

18 In a 'Chapter' of an early typescript entitled 'Gyres of Nations, Epochs, and of Movements of Creative Thought', Yeats argued that 'from Nietzsche onward, the romantic movement must find some complement in the development of music, for its growing excitement, for its rage, for its embittered distinction'.

19 In one of the early manuscripts in the form of a dialogue, Michael Robartes speaks for Yeats: 'Blake conceived of man as fourfold, while in the Mind, & as threefold now that he is fallen, & I find that I must follow him.'

20 First published in *The Savoy*, No. 2 (Apr 1896), 56–70.

21 Since, however, a third manuscript and the R-A TS both read 'Hominis', it is possible that Wade's transcription of the letter to Lady Gregory is incorrect.

22 See p. xvi, 33. 'The Camel's Back' is referred to in 'Appendix by Michael Robartes', which Yeats apparently prepared for *VA* after he abandoned the dialogue form. See Harper, *YO* 210–15.

23 Yeats borrowed the title of W. T. Horton's *The Way of the Soul*. On 23 Oct 1912 he wrote to ask Yeats 'what you think of it' (unpub. letter). Sometime after June 1922, when he received a dedicatory copy of Cecil French's *Between Sun and Moon* (*LWBY* 424), Yeats must have changed his fictitious title to 'The Way of the Soul Between the Sun and the Moon' (see n. to p. xix, 11–12).

24 The passage in brackets is crossed through.

25 In one of the notebooks of Sleeps two pages before an entry dated 18 Sept [1922] Yeats recorded: 'I write amid a civil war – no trains, no letters, no papers, no news. For many days we have not known what is happening beyond the horizon. Are they fighting in Limerick? It is not known.' On 4

Oct the Yeatses had 'been in Dublin for about 10 days' (unpub. ltr. to W. F. Stead).

26 Yeats was quoting from *The Republic of Plato*, ed J. L. Davies and D. J. Vaughan, new ed. London: Macmillan, 1885, p. 369. A gift copy still in Yeats's library, it is inscribed 'W. B. Yeats from Lionel Johnson. 1893'.

27 Cf. *VA* xx.

28 I have regularized punctuation and word order in the chronological headings.

29 See n. 2 above.

30 'A Biographical Fragment', *The Criterion*, I, No. 4 (Jy 1923), 315–21.

31 *LWBY* 439.

32 Ibid, 439–40.

33 But he had taken time off to write 'my Essay on Stockholm' and to answer many letters of congratulation over the award of the Nobel Prize (see *L* 703).

34 *LWBY* 448.

35 See pp. 210–13 for the sketch she objected to. 'S Rioghail Mo Dhream' was one of Mathers' mottoes in the GD.

36 *LWBY* 447–8.

37 Ibid. Yeats's replies to these letters have not been discovered.

38 Ibid, 451.

39 George Sand's 'stirring book . . . Consuelo' is also cited in the 'chapter on covens' (in the rejected Part I of Book IV) which Yeats referred to in the record of a Sleep dated 26 Oct 1923 (see n. 18 above).

40 See *YGD* 121–56.

41 Ibid, 197.

42 Also, George had urged him to restrict the circulation to a select group.

43 From an early manuscript draft of *VA*, Book I.

44 From a manuscript draft of the Dedication. Cf. *VA* xii.

45 The italicized passage was revised to read: 'been taken out & set in order'.

46 MS 13576, p. 275, National Library of Ireland. There is also a microfilm in the Yeats Archives at the State University of New York at Stony Brook.

47 AS, 9 Feb 1919.

48 *Jerusalem*, Plate 99, ll. 2–3.

49 *WWB*, I, 401.

A VISION

Portrait of Giraldus
from the Speculum Angelorum et Homenorum

A VISION

AN EXPLANATION OF LIFE
FOUNDED UPON THE WRITINGS
OF GIRALDUS AND UPON CER-
TAIN DOCTRINES ATTRIBUTED
TO KUSTA BEN LUKA

By
WILLIAM
BUTLER
YEATS

LONDON
PRIVATELY PRINTED FOR SUBSCRIBERS ONLY BY
T. WERNER LAURIE, LTD.
1925

I thank Messrs Macmillan & Co., the publishers of my book " Later Poems," for permission to reprint from that work " The Phases of the Moon."

W. B. Y.

Printed in Great Britain by
The Dunedin Press, Limited, Edinburgh.

A VISION

This edition consists of six hundred copies numbered and signed.

This is No. 513

This edition consists of six hundred copies numbered and signed.

This is No. 513

CONTENTS

DEDICATION

TO VESTIGIA

IT is a constant thought of mine that what we write is often a commendation of, or expostulation with the friends of our youth, and that even if we survive all our friends we continue to prolong or to amend conversations that took place before our five-and-twentieth year. 5 Perhaps this book has been written because a number of young men and women, you and I among the number, met nearly forty years ago in London and in Paris to discuss mystical philosophy. You with your beauty and your learning and your mysterious gifts were held by 10 all in affection, and though, when the first draft of this dedication was written, I had not seen you for more than thirty years, nor knew where you were nor what you were doing, and though much had happened since we copied the Jewish Schemahamphorasch with its seventy- 15 two Names of God in Hebrew characters, it was plain that I must dedicate my book to you. All other students who were once friends or friends' friends were dead or estranged. Florence Farr coming to her fiftieth year, dreading old age and fading 20 beauty, had made a decision we all dreamt of at one time or another, and accepted a position as English

ix

teacher in a native school in Ceylon that she might study oriental thought, and had died there. Another had become a Buddhist monk, and some ten years ago a traveller of my acquaintance found him in a Burmese monastery. A third lived through that strange adventure, perhaps the strangest of all adventures—Platonic love. When he was a child his nurse said to him—" An Angel bent over your bed last night," and in his seventeenth year he awoke to see the phantom of a beautiful woman at his bedside. Presently he gave himself up to all kinds of amorous adventures, until at last, in I think his fiftieth year but when he had still all his physical vigour, he thought " I do not need women but God." Then he and a very good, charming, young fellow-student fell in love with one another and though he could only keep down his passion with the most bitter struggle, they lived together platonically, and this they did, not from prejudice, for I think they had none, but from a clear sense of something to be attained by what seemed a most needless trampling of the grapes of life. She died, and he survived her but a little time during which he saw her in apparition and attained through her certain of the traditional experiences of the saint. He was my close friend, and had he lived I would have asked him to accept the dedication of a book I could not expect him to approve, for in his later life he cared for little but what seemed to him a very simple piety. We all, so far as I can remember, differed from ordinary students of philosophy or religion through our belief that truth cannot be discovered but may be revealed, and that if a man do not lose faith, and if he go through certain preparations, revelation will find him at the fitting moment. I remember a learned brassfounder in the North of England who visited us occasionally, and was convinced that there was a certain moment in every year which, once known, brought with it " The Summum

Bonum, the Stone of the Wise." But others, for it was
clear that there must be a vehicle or symbol of communication, were of opinion that some messenger would make
himself known, in a railway train let us say, or might
be found after search in some distant land. I look   5
back to it as a time when we were full of a phantasy
that has been handed down for generations, and is now
an interpretation, now an enlargement of the folk-lore
of the villages. That phantasy did not explain the world
to our intellects which were after all very modern, but 10
it recalled certain forgotten methods of meditation and
chiefly how so to suspend the will that the mind became
automatic, a possible vehicle for spiritual beings. It
carried us to what we had learned to call *Hodos
Chameliontos.*   15

II

SOME were looking for spiritual happiness or for some
form of unknown power, but I had a practical object.
I wished for a system of thought that would leave my
imagination free to create as it chose and yet make all
that it created, or could create, part of the one history, 20
and that the soul's. The Greeks certainly had such a
system, and Dante—though Boccaccio thought him a
bitter partisan and therefore a modern abstract man—
and I think no man since. Then when I had ceased all
active search, yet had not ceased from desire, the   25
documents upon which this book is founded were put
into my hands, and I had what I needed, though it may
be too late. What I have found indeed is nothing new,
for I will show presently that Swedenborg and Blake
and many before them knew that all things had their   30
gyres; but Swedenborg and Blake preferred to explain
them figuratively, and so I am the first to substitute for

Biblical or mythological figures, historical movements and actual men and women.

III

I HAVE moments of exaltation like that in which I wrote " All Souls' Night," but I have other moments when remembering my ignorance of philosophy I doubt if I can make another share my excitement. As I most fear to disappoint those that come to this book through some interest in my poetry and in that alone, I warn them from that part of the book called " The Great Wheel " and from the whole of Book II, and beg them to dip here and there in the verse and into my comments upon life and history. Upon the other hand my old fellow students may confine themselves to what is most technical and explanatory; thought is nothing without action, but if they will master what is most abstract there and make it the foundation of their visions, the curtain may ring up on a new drama.

I could I daresay make the book richer, perhaps immeasurably so, if I were to keep it by me for another year, and I have not even dealt with the whole of my subject, perhaps not even with what is most important, writing nothing about the Beatific Vision, little of sexual love; but I am longing to put it out of reach that I may write the poetry it seems to have made possible. I can now, if I have the energy, find the simplicity I have sought in vain. I need no longer write poems like " The Phases of the Moon " nor " Ego Dominus Tuus," nor spend barren years, as I have done some three or four times, striving with abstractions that substituted themselves for the play that I had planned.

IV

DOUBTLESS I must someday complete what I have begun, but for the moment my imagination dwells upon a copy of Powys Mather's " Arabian Nights " that awaits my return home. I would forget the wisdom of the East and remember its grossness and its romance. Yet when I wander upon the cliffs where Augustus and Tiberius wandered, I know that the new intensity that seems to have come into all visible and tangible things is not a reaction from that wisdom but its very self. Yesterday when I saw the dry and leafless vineyards at the very edge of the motionless sea, or lifting their brown stems from almost inaccessible patches of earth high up on the cliff-side, or met at the turn of the path the orange and lemon trees in full fruit, or the crimson cactus flower, or felt the warm sunlight falling between blue and blue, I murmured, as I have countless times, " I have been part of it always and there is maybe no escape, forgetting and returning life after life like an insect in the roots of the grass." But murmured it without terror, in exultation almost.

W. B. Y.

CAPRI, *February*, 1925.

The Great Wheel

INTRODUCTION

By OWEN AHERNE

IN the spring of 1917 I met in the National Gallery a man whom I had known in the late Eighties and early Nineties, and had never thought to see again. Michael Robartes and I had been intimate friends and fellow-students for a time, and later, after matters of theological difference arose between us, I lost sight of him, but heard a vague rumour that he was wandering or settled somewhere in the Near East. At first I was not certain if this were indeed he, and passed him in hesitation several times, but his athletic body, and his skin that had seemed, even when I first met him, sundried and sundarkened, his hawk-like profile, could belong to no other man. I wish the thirty years had changed me as little, for I saw no change in that erect body except that the hair that had been some kind of red, was grey, and in places, fading into white. I had known him as an uncompromising Pre-Raphaelite, and there he stood before the story of Griselda pictured in a number of episodes, the sort of thing he had admired thirty years ago. Even when I had made him understand who I was I drew him from the picture with difficulty, because his indignation that the authorities of the gallery had not thought it was worth saving from the German bombs had heightened his admiration for all pictures of

5

10

15

20

that type and his need for its expression. "The old painters," he said, "painted women with whom they would if they could have spent the night or a life, battles they would if they could have fought in, and all manner

5 of desirable houses and places, but now all is changed, and God knows why anybody paints anything. But why should we complain, things move by mathematical necessity, all changes can be dated by gyre and cone, and pricked beforehand upon the Calendar." I

10 brought him to a seat in the middle of the room, and I had begun to speak of the changed world we met in when he said : "Where is Yeats? I want his address. I am lost in this town and I don't know where to find anybody or anything." I felt a slight chill, for

15 we had both quarrelled with Mr Yeats on what I considered good grounds. Mr Yeats had given the name of Michael Robartes and that of Owen Aherne to fictitious characters, and made those characters live through events that were a travesty of real events. "Remem-

20 ber," I said, "that he not only described your death but represented it as taking place amid associations which must, I should have thought, have been highly disagreeable to an honourable man." "I was fool enough to mind once," he said, "but I soon found that he had

25 done me a service. His story started a rumour of my death that became more and more circumstantial as it grew. One by one my correspondents ceased to write. My name had become known to a large number of fellow-students, and but for that rumour I could not have lived

30 in peace even in the desert. If I had left no address I could never have got it out of my head that there was a vast heap of their letters lying somewhere, or even crossing the desert upon camel back." I did not know where Mr Yeats lived, but said that we could find out

35 from Mr Watkins the book-seller in Cecil's Court : and having so found out, he said we must call upon Mr Yeats,

and we started, keeping as much as possible from the
main streets that we might have silence for our talk.
" What have you to say to Yeats ? " I said, and instead
of answering he began to describe his own life since our
last meeting. " You will remember the village riot 5
which Yeats exaggerated in ' Rosa Alchemica.' A couple
of old friends died of their injuries, and that, and certain
evil results of another kind, turned me for a long time
from my favourite studies. I had all through my early
life periods of pleasure, or at least of excitement, that 10
alternated with periods of asceticism. I went from Paris
to Rome, and from Rome to Vienna, in pursuit of a
ballet dancer, and in Vienna we quarrelled. I tried to
forget my sorrow in wine, but in a few weeks I had tired
of that, and then, with some faint stirring of the old 15
interest I went to Cracow, partly because of its fame
as a centre of printing, but more I think because Dr.
Dee and his friend Edward Kelly had in Cracow practised
alchemy and scrying. There I took up with a fiery
handsome girl of the poorer classes, and hired a couple 20
of rooms in an old tumble-down house. One night I
was thrown out of bed and when I lit my tallow candle
found that the bed, which had fallen at one end, had
been propped up by a joint stool and an old book bound
in calf. In the morning I found that the book was called 25
' Speculum Angelorum et Hominorum,' had been written
by Giraldus and printed at Cracow in 1594, a good
many years before the celebrated Cracow publications,
and was of a very much earlier style both as to woodcut
and type. It was very dilapidated and all the middle 30
pages had been torn out; but at the end of the book
were a number of curious allegorical pictures; a woman
with a stone in one hand and an arrow in the other; a
man whipping his shadow; a man being torn in two by
an eagle and some kind of wild beast; and so on to the 35
number of eight and twenty; a portrait of Giraldus and

b

a unicorn; and many diagrams where gyres and circles grew out of one another like strange vegetables; and there was a large diagram at the beginning where lunar phases and zodiacal signs were mixed with various
5 unintelligible symbols—an apple, an acorn, a cup. My beggar maid had found it, she told me, on the top shelf in a wall cupboard where it had been left by the last tenant, an unfrocked priest who had joined a troup of gypsies and disappeared, and she had torn
10 out the middle pages to light our fire. What little remained of the text was in Latin, and I was piecing the passages together and getting a little light on two or three of the diagrams when a quarrel with my beggar maid plunged me into wine and gloom once more. Then
15 turning violently from all sensual pleasure I decided to say my prayers at the Holy Sepulchre, and from there I went to Damascus that I might learn Arabic for I had decided to continue my prayers at Mecca, and hoped to get there in disguise. I had gone the greater portion of
20 the way when I saw certain markings upon the sands which corresponded almost exactly to a diagram in the ' Speculum.' Nobody could explain them or say who made them, but when I discovered that an unknown tribe of Arabs had camped near by a couple of nights
25 before and that they had moved in a northerly direction, I took the first opportunity of plunging into the desert in pursuit. I went from tribe to tribe for several months, learnt nothing and found myself at last in a remote town where, thanks to a small medicine chest which I always
30 carry, I became first doctor, and then a kind of steward to an Arab chief or petty king. I constantly spoke about those markings upon the sand but learnt nothing till our town or village was visited by a tribe of Judwalis. There are several tribes of this strange sect, who are
35 known among the Arabs for the violent contrasts of character amongst them, for their licentiousness and

their sanctity. Fanatical in matters of doctrine, they seem tolerant of human frailty beyond any believing people I have met. One of them, an old man well known for his piety, asked me to prescribe for some complaint of his. When he came into my house, the book lay open upon a table, the frontispiece spread out : he turned towards it because it was European, and everything European filled him with curiosity, and then, pointing to the lunar phases and the mythological emblems, declared that he saw the doctrines of his tribe. The Judwali had once possessed a learned book called " The Way of the Soul between the Sun and the Moon " and attributed to a certain Kusta ben Luka, Christian Philosopher at the Court of Harun Al-Raschid, and though this, and a smaller book describing the personal life of the philosopher, had been lost or destroyed in desert fighting some generations before his time, its doctrines were remembered, for they had always consti- tuted the beliefs of the Judwalis who look upon Kusta ben Luka as their founder. As my attempt to under- stand the diagrams of Giraldus, in the absence of other intellectual interests, had come to fill all my thoughts, I persuaded him to accept me into his tribe and for some years wandered with the Judwalis, though not always with the same tribe. I found that though their Sacred Book had been lost they had a vast doctrine which was constantly explained to their growing boys and girls by the aid of diagrams drawn by old religious men upon the sands, and that these diagrams were in many cases identical with those in the " Speculum Angelorum et Hominorum." I am convinced, however, that this doctrine did not originate with Kusta ben Luka, for certain terms and forms of expression suggest some remote Syriac origin. I once told an old Judwali of my conviction upon this point but he merely said that Kusta ben Luka had doubtless been taught by the desert djinns who lived to a great age and remembered ancient languages."

We had come by this to the little Bloomsbury court where Mr Yeats had his lodging; but when I told him 5 so, he said, " No, it will be better to write and make an appointment. He is almost certain to be out." The evening had begun to darken and I pointed to a gleam of light through a slit in the curtain of the room on the second floor, but he said " No, no, I will write," and 10 then " I have great gifts in my hands and I stand between two enemies; Yeats that I quarrelled with and have not forgiven; you that quarrelled with me and have not forgiven me." He began to walk away and I followed, and presently we fell into talk about indifferent 15 things. I dined with him at the hotel and after dinner he brought out diagrams and notes, and began explaining their general drift. The sheets of paper which were often soiled and torn were rolled up in a bit of old camel skin and tied in bundles with bits of cord and bits of 20 an old shoe-lace. This bundle, he explained, described the mathematical law of history, that bundle the adventure of the soul after death, that other the interaction between the living and the dead and so on. He saw that I was interested and asked if I would arrange 25 them for publication. Such things fascinate me and I consented and from then on for months we were travelling companions, and he explained notes and diagrams in words almost as obscure. Certainly no man had ever less gift of expression. He came with me to France and 30 later on to Ireland because of his wish to see once more places that he had known. In Dublin we stayed for a time in my Dominick Street house, described so extravagantly in " The Tables of the Law," which keeps its eighteenth century state, though slum children play upon 35 its steps and the windows of the next house are patched with brown paper. On a walking tour in Connaught we

passed Thoor Ballylee where Mr Yeats had settled for the
summer, and words were spoken between us slightly
resembling those in " The Phases of the Moon," and I
noticed that as his friendship with me grew closer, his
animosity against Mr Yeats revived.   5

Suddenly, however, our friendship was shattered by a
violent scene like those of our youth. We had returned
to London and I had there written eighty or ninety
pages of exposition. He complained in exaggerated
language that I interpreted the system as a form of   10
Christianity, that only those aspects of character that
were an expression of Christianity interested me—
primary character to use the terms of the philosophy—
and that I was neither informed nor interested when I
came to the opposite type. I contended that there could   15
be nothing incompatible between his system and
Christianity. St. Clement of Alexandria had taught the
re-birth of the Soul and had remained a saint, and in
our own time the Capuchin Archbishop Passivalli has
taught it and keeps his mitre. Through lack of it, I said,   20
the mediæval Church got into a labyrinth of absurdity
about Limbo and unbaptised children, but a certain number of modern Catholics have come to think that God may
very well command a soul that has left its work unfinished
to leave Purgatory and return to the world. Nothing,   25
however, would persuade him, and he declared that he
would give all his material to Mr Yeats and let him do
what he liked with it. Now it was my turn to get angry,
for I had spent much toil upon his often confused and
rambling notes. " You will give them to a man," I   30
said, " who has thought more of the love of woman
than of the love of God." " Yes," he replied, " I want
a lyric poet, and if he cares for nothing but expression,
so much the better, my desert geometry will take care
of the truth." I replied—I think it better to set my   35
words down without disguise—"Mr Yeats has intellectual

belief but he is entirely without moral faith, without
that sense, which should come to a man with terror and
joy, of a Divine Presence, and though he may seek, ánd
may have always sought it, I am certain that he will not

5 find it in this life." This increased Robartes' anger, for I
had almost repeated words of his own, and he accused
Christianity of destroying Greco-Roman art and science,
because it thought nothing mattered but faith.   I denied
this but said that even barbarism had not been too great a

10 price to pay for pity and a conscience, and I reminded
him that the system itself made the realisation of God
one half of life. He then used ungenerous words, revived
a quarrel of thirty years before, said that I was always
the same, that I was but a free man for a moment, and

15 even asked if I had consulted my confessor.* He called
next day with some kind of an apology but said I must
come to see Mr Yeats and that he had made an appointment for us both. At Mr Yeats's Bloomsbury lodging
he talked of his travels and his discovery, and as during

20 the night I had thought the matter over and thought
myself well out of a troublesome and thankless work, I
helped his exposition. He had brought the Giraldus
diagrams, and they seemed to interest Mr Yeats at first
sight as much as they had Robartes himself. Mr Yeats

25 consented to write the exposition on the condition that
I wrote the introduction and any notes I pleased, and
would have persuaded me to accept a portion of the
profits but this I refused as later on I may publish my
own commentary.

30 Two days later Robartes returned to Mesopotamia,
for the armistice had made some spot, where he planned
to spend his declining years, habitable once more, and
from that day to this I have heard neither of him nor
from him. This silence that has closed round him has

---

* I think Mr Aherne has remembered his own part in this
conversation more accurately than that of his opponent.—W. B. Y.

made it natural to write, as I know he wished that I should, as if his conversation and his foibles were already a part of history. In all probability he will never read what Mr Yeats or I have written, and he has lived so long out of Europe that he has no friends to find offence in a too candid record.

Mr Yeats's completed manuscript now lies before me. The system itself has grown clearer for his concrete expression of it, but I notice that if I made too little of the *antithetical* phases he has done no better by the *primary*. I think too that Mr Yeats himself must feel that the abstract foundation needs some such exploration as I myself had attempted. The twelve rotations associated with the lunar and solar months of the Great Year first arose, as Mr Yeats understands, from the meeting and separation of certain spheres. I consider that the form should be called elliptoid, and that rotation as we know it is not the movement that corresponds most closely to reality. At any rate I can remember Robartes saying in one of his paradoxical figurative moods that he pictured reality as a number of great eggs laid by the Phœnix and that these eggs turn inside out perpetually without breaking the shell.

O. A.

London, *May*, 1925.

BOOK I

WHAT THE CALIPH PARTLY LEARNED

A VISION

I. THE WHEEL AND THE PHASES OF THE MOON

An old man cocked his ear upon a bridge;
He and his friend, their faces to the South,
Had trod the uneven road. Their boots were soiled,
Their Connemara cloth worn out of shape;
They had kept a steady pace as though their beds,   5
Despite a dwindling and late risen moon,
Were distant still. An old man cocked his ear.

AHERNE

What made that sound?

ROBARTES

       A rat or water-hen
Splashed, or an otter slid into the stream.
We are on the bridge; that shadow is the tower,   10
And the light proves that he is reading still.
He has found, after the manner of his kind,
Mere images; chosen this place to live in
Because, it may be, of the candle light
From the far tower where Milton's platonist   15
Sat late, or Shelley's visionary prince :
The lonely light that Samuel Palmer engraved,

An image of mysterious wisdom won by toil;
And now he seeks in book or manuscript
What he shall never find.

AHERNE

Why should not you
Who know it all ring at his door, and speak
5   Just truth enough to show that his whole life
Will scarcely find for him a broken crust
Of all those truths that are your daily bread;
And when you have spoken take the roads again?

ROBARTES

He wrote of me in that extravagant style
10   He had learned from Pater, and to round his tale
Said I was dead; and dead I choose to be.

AHERNE

Sing me the changes of the moon once more;
True song, though speech : " mine author sung it me."

ROBARTES

Twenty-and-eight the phases of the moon,
15   The full and the moon's dark and all the crescents,
Twenty-and-eight, and yet but six-and-twenty
The cradles that a man must needs be rocked in :
For there's no human life at the full or the dark.
From the first crescent to the half, the dream
20   But summons to adventure and the man
Is always happy like a bird or a beast;
But while the moon is rounding towards the full
He follows whatever whim's most difficult
Among whims not impossible, and though scarred,
25   As with the cat-o'-nine-tales of the mind,
His body moulded from within his body
Grows comelier. Eleven pass, and then

Athena takes Achilles by the hair,
Hector is in the dust, Nietzsche is born,
Because the hero's crescent is the twelfth.
And yet, twice born, twice buried, grow he must,
Before the full moon, helpless as a worm.   5
The thirteenth moon but sets the soul at war
In its own being, and when that war's begun
There is no muscle in the arm; and after
Under the frenzy of the fourteenth moon
The soul begins to tremble into stillness,   10
To die into the labyrinth of itself!

AHERNE

Sing out the song; sing to the end, and sing
The strange reward of all that discipline.

ROBARTES

All thought becomes an image and the soul
Becomes a body : that body and that soul   15
Too perfect at the full to lie in a cradle,
Too lonely for the traffic of the world :
Body and soul cast out and cast away
Beyond the visible world.

AHERNE

                    All dreams of the soul
End in a beautiful man's or woman's body.   20

ROBARTES

Have you not always known it?

AHERNE

                    The song will have it
That those that we have loved got their long fingers
From death, and wounds, or on Sinai's top,
Or from some bloody whip in their own hands.

They ran from cradle to cradle till at last
Their beauty dropped out of the loneliness
Of body and soul.

ROBARTES

The lover's heart knows that.

AHERNE

It must be that the terror in their eyes
5 Is memory or foreknowledge of the hour
When all is fed with light and heaven is bare.

ROBARTES

When the moon's full those creatures of the full
Are met on the waste hills by country men
Who shudder and hurry by : body and soul
10 Estranged amid the strangeness of themselves,
Caught up in contemplation, the mind's eye
Fixed upon images that once were thought,
For separate, perfect, and immovable
Images can break the solitude
15 Of lovely, satisfied, indifferent eyes.

And thereupon with aged, high-pitched voice
Aherne laughed, thinking of the man within,
His sleepless candle and laborious pen.

ROBARTES

And after that the crumbling of the moon :
20 The soul remembering its loneliness
Shudders in many cradles; all is changed,
It would be the world's servant, and as it serves,
Choosing whatever task's most difficult
Among tasks not impossible, it takes
25 Upon the body and upon the soul
The coarseness of the drudge.

AHERNE

Before the full
It sought itself and afterwards the world.

ROBARTES

Because you are forgotten, half out of life,
And never wrote a book, your thought is clear.
Reformer, merchant, statesman, learned man,
Dutiful husband, honest wife by turn,   5
Cradle upon cradle, and all in flight and all
Deformed because there is no deformity
But saves us from a dream.

AHERNE

And what of those
That the last servile crescent has set free?

ROBARTES

Because all dark, like those that are all light,   10
They are cast beyond the verge, and in a cloud,
Crying to one another like the bats;
And having no desire they cannot tell
What's good or bad, or what it is to triumph
At the perfection of one's own obedience;   15
And yet they speak what's blown into the mind;
Deformed beyond deformity, unformed,
Insipid as the dough before it is baked,
They change their bodies at a word.

AHERNE

And then?

ROBARTES

When all the dough has been so kneaded up   20
That it can take what form cook Nature fancy
The first thin crescent is wheeled round once more.

AHERNE

But the escape; the song's not finished yet.

ROBARTES

Hunchback and Saint and Fool are the last crescents.
The burning bow that once could shoot an arrow
Out of the up and down, the wagon wheel
5   Of beauty's cruelty and wisdom's chatter—
Out of that raving tide—is drawn betwixt
Deformity of body and of mind.

AHERNE

Were not our beds far off I'd ring the bell,
Stand under the rough roof-timbers of the hall
10   Beside the castle door, where all is stark
Austerity, a place set out for wisdom
That he will never find; I'd play a part;
He would never know me after all these years
But take me for some drunken country man;
15   I'd stand and mutter there until he caught
" Hunchback and Saint and Fool," and that they came
Under the three last crescents of the moon,
And then I'd stagger out. He'd crack his wits
Day after day, yet never find the meaning.

20   *And then he laughed to think that what seemed hard*
Should be so simple—a bat rose from the hazels
And circled round him with its squeaky cry,
The light in the tower window was put out.

2. THE DANCE OF THE FOUR ROYAL PERSONS

By Owen Aherne

MICHAEL ROBARTES gives the following account of
the diagram called " The Great Wheel " in Giraldus.
A Caliph who reigned after the death of Harun Al-Raschid
discovered one of his companions climbing the wall
that encircled the garden of his favourite slave, and   5
because he had believed this companion entirely devoted
to his interests, gave himself up to astonishment. After
much consideration he offered a large sum of money to
any man who could explain human nature so completely
that he should never be astonished again. Kusta ben   10
Luka, now a very old man, went to the palace with his
book of geometrical figures, but the Caliph, after he had
explained them for an hour, banished him from the
palace, and declared that all unintelligible visitors were
to be put to death. A few days later four black but   15
splendidly dressed persons stood at the city gate and
announced that they had come from a most distant
country to explain human nature, but that the Caliph
must meet them on the edge of the desert. He came
attended by his Vizir, and asked their country. " We   20
are," said the eldest of the four, " the King, the Queen,
the Prince and the Princess of the Country of Wisdom.
It has reached our ears that a certain man has pretended
that wisdom is difficult, but it is our intention to reveal
all in a dance." After they had danced for several   25

minutes the Caliph said : " Their dance is dull, and they
dance without accompaniment, and I consider that nobody has ever been more unintelligible." The Vizir gave
the order for their execution, and while waiting the
5   tightening of the bow-strings, each dancer said to the
executioner : " In the Name of Allah, smooth out the
mark of my footfall on the sand." And the executioner
replied, " If the Caliph permit." When the Caliph
heard what the dancers had said, he thought, " There
10 is certainly some great secret in the marks of their feet."
He went at once to the dancing place, and, having stood
for a long time looking at the marks, he said : " Send
us Kusta ben Luka, and tell him that he shall not die."
Kusta ben Luka was sent for, and from sunrise to sunset
15 of the day after, and for many days, he explained the
markings of the sand. At last the Caliph said : " I now
understand human nature; I can never be surprised
again : I will put the amount of the reward into a tomb
for the four dancers." Kusta ben Luka answered : " No,
20 Sire, for the reward belongs to me." " How can that
be ? " said the other, " for you have but explained the
marks upon the sand, and those marks were not made
by your feet." " They were made by the feet of my
pupils," said ben Luka. " When you banished me from
25 the Palace they gathered in my house to console me,
and the wisest amongst them said, ' He that dies is the
chief person in the story,' and he and three others offered
to dance what I chose." " The reward is yours," said
the Caliph, " and henceforth let the figure marked by
30 their feet be called the Dance of the Four Royal Persons,
for it is right that your pupils be rewarded for dying."

According to the Robartes MSS. the Dance of the Four
Royal Persons is one of the names for the first figure
drawn by the Judwali elders for the instruction of youth
35 and is identical with the " Great Wheel " of Giraldus.

I am inclined to see in the story of its origin a later

embodiment of a story that it was the first diagram drawn upon the sand by the wife of Kusta ben Luka, and that its connection with the lunar phases, the movements and the nature of the *Four Faculties* and their general application to the facts of human life, were fully explained before its geometrical composition was touched upon. The Judwali doctor of Bagdad, who is mentioned elsewhere in this book, said that the whole philosophy was so expounded in a series of fragments which only displayed their meaning, like one of those child's pictures which are made up out of separate cubes, when all were put together. The object of this was, it seems, to prevent the intellect from forming its own conclusions, and so thwarting the Djinn who could only speak to curiosity and passivity. I cannot, however, let this pass without saying that I doubt the authenticity of this story, which Mr Yeats has expanded into the poem " Desert Geometry or The Gift of Harun Al-Raschid," at least in its present form, and that an almost similar adventure is attributed in one of the Robartes documents to a Mahometan grammarian of a much later date. I will, however, discuss all these matters at length in my own book upon the philosophy and its sources.

O. A.

May, 1925.

PART I

3. THE GREAT WHEEL

I

ANTITHETICAL AND PRIMARY

THE diagram of the Great Wheel shows a series of
numbers and symbols which represent the Lunar phases;
and all possible human types can be classified under one
or other of these twenty-eight phases. Their number is
5   that of the Arabic Mansions of the Moon but they are used
merely as a method of classification and for simplicity
of classification their symbols are composed in an entirely
arbitrary way. As the lunar circle narrows to a crescent
and as the crescent narrows to a still narrower crescent,
10   the Moon approaches the Sun, falls as it were under his
influence; and for this reason the Sun and Moon in
diagram 1 are considered to be imposed one upon another.
They may be coloured gold and silver respectively.
The first phase is therefore full Sun as it were, and the
15   15th Phase full Moon, while Phases 8 and 22 are half
Sun and half Moon. In Book II is described the
geometrical foundation of this symbolism and of the
other characters of the wheel. When one uses the
phases, in popular exposition or for certain symbolic
20   purposes, one considers full Sun as merely the night
when there is no moon, and in representing any phase
visibly one makes the part which is not lunar dark. The

12

Sun is objective man and the Moon subjective man, or more properly the Sun is *primary* man and the Moon *antithetical* man—terms that will be explained later. Objective and Subjective are not used in their metaphysical but in their colloquial sense. Murray's diction- 5

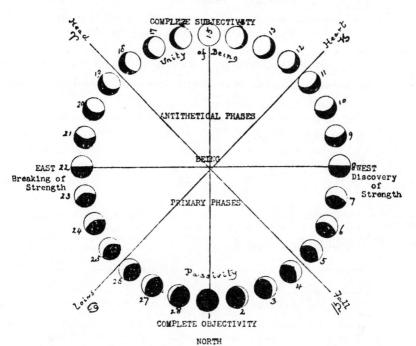

ary describes the colloquial use of the word " objective " thus. All that " is presented to consciousness as opposed to consciousness of self, that is the object of perception or thought, the non-ego." And again, objective when used in describing works of art means " dealing with or 10 laying stress upon that which is external to the mind, treating of outward things and events rather than inward thought ", " treating a subject so as to exhibit the

actual facts, not coloured by the opinions or feelings of
the writer." The volume of Murray's dictionary containing letter S is not yet published, but as " subjective "
is the contrary to " objective " it needs no further
5 definition. Under the Sun's light we see things as they
are, and go about our day's work, while under that of
the Moon, we see things dimly, mysteriously, all is sleep
and dream. All men are characterised upon a first
analysis by the proportion in which these two characters
10 or *Tinctures*, the objective or *primary*, the subjective or
antithetical, are combined. Man is said to have a series
of embodiments (any one of which may be repeated) that
correspond to the twenty-eight fundamental types. The
First and *Fifteenth*, being wholly objective and sub-
15 jective respectively, are not human embodiments, as
human life is impossible without the strife between the
Tinctures.

II

THE FOUR FACULTIES

INCARNATE man has *Four Faculties* which constitute
the *Tinctures*—the *Will*, the *Creative Mind*, the *Body of*
20 *Fate*, and the *Mask*. The *Will* and *Mask* are predominately Lunar or *antithetical*, the *Creative Mind* and
the *Body of Fate* predominately Solar or *primary*. When
thought of in isolation, they take upon themselves the
nature now of one phase, now of another. By *Will** is
25 understood feeling that has not become desire because

---

* I have changed the " creative genius " of the Documents
into *Creative Mind* to avoid confusion between " genius " and
Daimon; and " Ego " into *Will* for " Ego " suggests the total
man who is all *Four Faculties*. *Will* or self-will was the only word
I could find not for man but Man's root. If Blake had not
given " selfhood " a special meaning it might have served my
turn.
September, 1925.

there is no object to desire; a bias by which the soul is classified and its phase fixed but which as yet is without result in action; an energy as yet uninfluenced by thought, action, or emotion; the first matter of a certain personality—choice. If a man's *Will* is at say Phase 17 we say that he is a man of Phase 17, and so on. By *Mask* is understood the image of what we wish to become, or of that to which we give our reverence. Under certain circumstances it is called the *Image*. By *Creative Mind* is meant intellect, as intellect was understood before the close of the seventeenth century—all the mind that is consciously constructive. By *Body of Fate* is understood the physical and mental environment, the changing human body, the stream of Phenomena as this affects a particular individual, all that is forced upon us from without, Time as it affects sensation. The *Will* when represented in the diagram is always opposite the *Mask*, the *Creative Mind* always opposite the *Body of Fate*.

The *Will* looks into a painted picture. The *Creative Mind* looks into a photograph, but both look into something which is the opposite of themselves. The picture is that which is chosen, while the photograph is heterogeneous. The photograph is fated, because by fate is understood that which comes from without, whereas the *Mask* is predestined, *Destiny* being that which comes to us from within. We best express the heterogeneousness of the photograph if we call it a photograph of a crowded street, which the *Creative Mind*—when not under the influence of the *Mask*—contemplates coldly; while the picture contains but few objects and the contemplating *Will* is impassioned and solitary.

All *Four Faculties* influence each other and the object of the diagram of the Wheel is to show when and in what proportions. When the *Will* predominates, and there is strong desire, the *Mask* or *Image* is sensuous, but when *Creative Mind* predominates it is abstract. When the *Mask* predominates it is idealised, when *Body of Fate* predominates it is concrete, and so on. An object is sensuous if I relate it to myself, " *my* fire, *my* chair," etc., but it is concrete if I say " *a* chair, *a* fire," and abstract if I but speak of it as the representative of a class—" *the* chair, *the* fire," etc.

III

The Place of the Four Faculties on the Wheel

A MAN whose *Will* is at Phase 17 will have his *Creative Mind* at Phase 13 and his *Mask* at Pnase 3 and his *Body of Fate* at Phase 27; while a man whose *Will* is at Phase 3 would have all these positions exactly reversed. When *Will* is at Phase 15, *Creative Mind* is there also. On the other hand, when *Will* is at Phase 22, *Will* and *Body of Fate* are superimposed, while *Creative Mind* and *Mask* are superimposed at Phase 8. The points on diagram 1 marked *Head, Heart, Loins* and *Fall* mark where the four faculties are at equal distances from one another and that in part is why they are also represented by cardinal signs. They have also another significance which will be explained later.

Will and *Mask* are opposite in *Tincture, Creative Mind* and *Body of Fate* are opposite in *Tincture*. The one has the *primary* in the exact strength of the *antithetical* in the other, and vice versa. The *primary* and *antithetical* define the inclination of the *Will*, and through the *Will* affect the other three; this may be called the difference in quality. A *Will* at Phase 18 would have the exact amount of *antithetical* inclination that a *Will* at Phase 4 would have of *primary*. On the other hand, a *Will* at Phase 18 and *Creative Mind* at Phase 12 are exactly the same in the proportions of their *Tinctures*, have exactly the same quality of *Tincture* but move in opposite directions—one is going from Phase 1 to Phase 28 and the other from Phase 28 to Phase 1. It is therefore necessary to consider both direction and quality.

The relations between *Will* and *Mask*, *Creative Mind* and *Body of Fate* are called *oppositions,* and upon some occasions *contrasts,* while those between *Will* and *Creative Mind*, *Mask* and *Body of Fate* are called—for reasons which will appear later—*discords.*

Between Phase 12 and Phase 13, and between Phase 4 and Phase 5 in diagram 1 occurs what is called " the *opening* of the *tinctures,*" and between Phase 18 and Phase 19, and between Phase 4 and Phase 5 what is called " the *closing.*" This means that between Phase 12 and Phase 13 each Tincture divides into two, and closes up again between Phase 18 and Phase 19. Between Phase 26 and Phase 27 the Tinctures become one *Tincture*, and between Phase 4 and Phase 5 become two again. The *antithetical* before Phase 15 becomes the *primary* after Phase 15, and vice versa—that is to say, the thoughts and emotions that are in nature *antithetical* before Phase 15 are in nature *primary* after Phase 15; the man who before Phase 15 is harsh in his judgment of himself will turn that harshness to others after Phase 15.

The geometrical reasons both for this interchange and for the closing and opening of the *Tinctures* are discussed in Book II.

IV

DRAMA OF THE FACULTIES AND OF THE TINCTURES, ETC.

ONE can describe *antithetical* man by comparing him to the *Commedia del Arte* or improvised drama of Italy. The stage manager having chosen his actor, the *Will*, chooses for this actor, that he may display him the better,

B

a scenario, *Body of Fate*, which offers to his *Creative Mind* the greatest possible difficulty that it can face without despair, and in which he must play a rôle and wear a *Mask* as unlike as possible to his natural character (or *Will*) and leaves him to improvise, through *Creative Mind*, the dialogue and the details of the plot. He must discover a being which only exists with extreme effort, when his muscles are as it were all taut and all his energies active, and for that reason the *Mask* is described as " A form created by passion to unite us to ourselves." Much of what follows will be a definition or description of this deeper being, which may become the unity described by Dante in the Convito.

For *Primary* Man one must go to the Decline of the *Commedia del Arte* for an example. The *Will* is weak and cannot create a rôle, and so, if it transform itself, does so after an accepted pattern, some traditional clown or pantaloon. It has perhaps no object but to move the crowd, and if it " gags " it is that there may be plenty of topical allusions. In the *primary* phases Man must cease to desire *Mask* and *Image* by ceasing from self-expression, and substitute a motive of service for that of self-expression. Instead of the created *Mask* he has an imitative *Mask*; and when he recognises this, his *Mask* may become an image of mankind. The author of " The Imitation of Christ " was certainly a man of a late *primary* phase. It is said that the *antithetical Mask* is free, and the *primary Mask* enforced; and the free *Mask* is personality, a union of qualities, while the enforced mask is character, a union of quantities, and of their limitations—that is to say, of those limitations which give strength precisely because they are enforced. Personality, no matter how habitual, is a constantly renewed choice, and varies from an individual charm, in the more *antithetical* phases, to a hard objective dramatisation, which differs from character mainly because it is a dramatisation, in phases where the *antithetical Tincture* holds its predominance with difficulty.

Antithetical men are, like Landor, violent in themselves because they hate all that impedes their personality, but are in their intellect (*Creative Mind*) gentle, but *primary* men whose hatreds are impersonal are violent in their intellect but gentle in themselves as doubtless Robespierre was gentle.

The *Mask* before Phase 15 is described as " a revelation " because through it the being obtains knowledge of itself, sees itself in personality; while after Phase 15 it is a " concealment," for the being grows incoherent, vague and broken, as its intellect (*Creative Mind*) is more and more concerned with objects that have no relation to its unity but a relation to the unity of Society or of material things, known through the *Body of Fate*, and adopts a personality which it more and more casts outward, more and more dramatises. It is now a dissolving violent phantom which would grip itself and hold itself together. The being of *Antithetical Man* is described as full of rage before Phase 12, against all in the world that hinders its expression, but after Phase 12 the rage is a knife turned against itself. After Phase 15, but before Phase 19, the being is full of phantasy, a continual escape from, and yet acknowledgment of all that allures in the world, a continual playing with all that must engulf it. The *primary* is that which serves, the *antithetical* is that which creates.

At Phase 8 is the " Discovery of Strength," an embodiment in sensuality, for the imitation that held it to the norm of the race has ceased and the personality with its own norm has not begun. *Primary* and *antithetical* are equal and fight for mastery; and when this fight is ended through the conviction of weakness

and the preparation for rage, the *Mask* becomes once more voluntary. At Phase 22 is the " Breaking of Strength," for here the being makes its last attempt to impose its personality upon the world, before the *Mask* becomes
5 enforced once more and Character is once more born.

To these two phases, perhaps to all phases, the being may return up to four times before it can pass on. It is claimed, however, that four times is the utmost possible. By being is understood that which divides
10 into *Four Faculties*, by individual the *Will* analysed in relation to itself, by personality the *Will* analysed in relation to the *Mask*. It is because of the antithesis between *Will* and *Mask* that subjective natures are called *antithetical*, while those in whom individuality and
15 *Creative Mind* predominate, and who are content with things as they find them, are called *primary*. Personality is strongest near Phase 15, individuality near Phase 22 and Phase 8.

V

RULE FOR DISCOVERING TRUE AND FALSE MASKS

WHEN the Will is in antithetical phases the True Mask
20 *is the effect of Creative Mind of opposite phase upon that phase; and the False Mask is the effect of Body of Fate of opposite phase upon that phase.*

The True *Mask* of Phase 17 for instance is " Simplification by intensity " and is derived from Phase 3 modified
25 by the *Creative Mind* of that phase, which is described as " Simplicity " and is from Phase 27 which is that of the Saint.

The False *Mask* of Phase 17 is " Dispersal " and is derived from Phase 3, modified by the *Body of Fate*
30 which is from Phase 13 and is described as " Interest."

It will be found that this word describes with great accuracy the kind of " Dispersal " which weakens men of Phase 17 when they try to live in the *Primary Tincture.*

When the *Will* is in *primary* phases the True *Mask* is the effect of *Body of Fate* of opposite phase upon that phase; and the False *Mask* is the effect of *Creative Mind* of opposite phase upon that phase.

The True *Mask* of Phase 3, is " Innocence " and it is derived from Phase 17 modified by its *Body of Fate* which is described as " Loss " and derived from Phase 27, which is that of the Saint.

The False *Mask* of Phase 3 is " Folly " and is derived from Phase 17 modified by *Creative Mind* of that phase which is described as " Creative imagination through *antithetical* emotion." The *primary* Phase 3 when it attempts to live *antithetically* gives itself up to inconsequence because it cannot be creative in the *Mask.* On the other hand, when it lives according to the *Primary,* and is true to phase, it takes from its opposite phase delight in passing things, sees " a world in a grain of sand, Heaven in a wild flower " and becomes a child playing, knows nothing of consequence and purpose. " Loss " effects Phase 17 itself as an enforced withdrawal of *primary* desire for the *Body of Fate* is inimical to *antithetical* natures.

Only long familiarity with the system can make the whole table of *Masks, Creative Minds,* etc.—see sec. xii —intelligible; it should be studied by the help of these two following rules :—

In an antithetical phase the being seeks by the help of the Creative Mind to deliver the Mask from Body of Fate.

In a primary phase the being seeks by the help of the Body of Fate to deliver the Creative Mind from the Mask.

VI

Rule for finding the True and False Creative Mind

WHEN the Will is in antithetical phases the True Creative Mind is derived from the Creative Mind Phase modified by the Creative Mind of that phase; while the False Creative Mind is derived from the Creative Mind
5 *Phase, modified by the Body of Fate of that Phase.*

For instance the True *Creative Mind* of Phase 17 " Creative Imagination through *antithetical* Emotion " is derived from Phase 13 as that Phase is modified by its *Creative Mind* which is described as " Sincere
10 expression of Self."

The False *Creative Mind* of Phase 17 " Artificial self-realisation " is derived from Phase 13 as that phase is modified by its *Body of Fate* " Enforced Love."

Phase 17 has the same proportion of *Tinctures* as
15 Phase 13 but a different direction, is growing more *Primary* and so has intellectually what Phase 13 has emotionally, and is turning outward what Phase 13 turned inward.

Phase 13 stirred to creation by " Sincere expression
20 of self " stirs Phase 17 to creation of images; on the other hand Phase 13 stirred by " Enforced love "—which had to Phase 13 itself been an influence forcing the being to seek what to it was an impossible *primary* activity and so to a morbid self-absorption—becomes in
25 Phase 17 an " artificial dramatisation of the Self."

When the Will is in Primary Phases the True Creative Mind is derived from Creative Mind phase, modified by the Body of Fate of that phase; while the False Creative Mind is derived from the Creative Mind Phase modified
30 *by the False Creative Mind of that Phase.*

For instance the True *Creative Mind* of Phase 27 is

described as " Spiritual Receptivity " and is derived from Phase 3 as that phase is modified by its *Body of Fate* derived from Phase 13, and described as " Interest." While its false *Creative Mind* is described as " Pride " and is derived from Phase 3, modified by the False *Creative Mind* of that Phase which is derived from Phase 27 and described as " Abstraction." As will be seen later the phase of the Saint, Phase 27, has " Abstraction " for its great sin and escapes from this sin by " Humility."

Again two mirrors face one another. Phase 3 and Phase 27 are alike in *Tincture* but different in direction. The meaning of the interchange between " Pride " and " Abstraction " will grow clear from the exposition of the phase.

VII

RULE FOR FINDING BODY OF FATE

THE *Body of Fate* of any particular phase is the effect of the whole nature of its *Body of Fate* phase upon that particular phase. As, however, the *Body of Fate* is always *primary* it is in sympathy with the *primary* phase while it opposes the *antithetical* phase; in this it is the reverse of the *Mask* which is sympathetic to an *antithetical* phase but opposes a *primary*.

VIII

SUBDIVISIONS OF THE WHEEL

EXCLUDING the four phases of crisis (*Phases 8, 22, 15, 1,*) each quarter consists of six phases, or of two sets of three. In every case the first phase of each set can be described as a manifestation of power, the second of a code or arrangement of powers, and the third of a belief, the belief being an appreciation of, or submission to some quality which becomes power in the next phase. The reason of this is that each set of three is itself a wheel, and has the same character as the Great Wheel. The Phases 1 to 8 are associated with elemental earth, being phases of germination and sprouting; those between Phase 8 and Phase 15 with elemental *water*, because there the image-making power is at its height; those between Phase 15 and Phase 22 with elemental *air*, because through *air*, or space, things are divided from one another, and here intellect is at its height; those between Phase 22 and Phase 1 with elemental fire because here all things are made simple. The *Will* is strongest in First Quarter, *Mask* in second, *Creative Mind* in third, and the *Body of Fate* in fourth.

There are other divisions and attributions to be considered later.

IX

Discords, Oppositions and Contrasts.

THE being becomes conscious of itself as a separate being, because of certain facts of *opposition* and *discord*, the emotional *opposition* of *Will* and *Mask*, the intellectual *opposition* of *Creative Mind* and *Body of Fate*, discords between *Will* and *Creative Mind*, *Creative Mind* and *Mask*, *Mask* and *Body of Fate*, *Body of Fate* and *Will*. A *discord* is always the enforced understanding of the unlikeness of *Will* and *Mask* or of *Creative Mind* and *Body of Fate*. There is an enforced attraction between *opposites*, for the *Will* has a natural desire for the *Mask* and the *Creative Mind* a natural perception of the *Body of Fate*; in one the dog bays the Moon, in the other the eagle stares on the Sun by natural right. When, however, the *Creative Mind* deceives the *Will*, by offering it some *primary* image of the *Mask*, or when the *Will* offers to the *Creative Mind* an emotion that should 5 be turned towards the *Mask* alone, the *opposition* emerges again in its simplicity because of the jarring of the emotion, the grinding out of the *Image*. On the other hand it may be the *Mask* that slips on to the *Body of Fate* till we confuse what we would be with what 10 we must be. As the *discords* through the circling of the *Four Faculties* approach *opposition*, when as at Phase 15 (say) the *Creative Mind* comes to be opposite the *Mask*, they share the qualities of *Opposition*. As the *Faculties* approach to one another, on the other hand, *Discord* 15 gradually becomes identity, and one or other, according to whether it takes place at Phase 1 or Phase 15, is weakened and finally absorbed, *Creative Mind* in *Will* at Phase 15, *Will* in *Creative Mind* at Phase 1 and so on. While if it be at Phase 8 or Phase 22 first one predomin- 20 ates and then the other and there is instability.

Without this continual *discord* through *deception* there would be no conscience, no activity; and it will be seen later that *deception* is used as a technical term and may be substituted for " desire." Life is an 25 endeavour, made vain by the Four Sails of its Mill, to come to a double contemplation, that of the chosen *Image*, that of the Fated *Image*.

There are also *harmonies* but these which are geometrically connected with the centre of the figure 30 can be best considered in relation to another part of the System.

X

The Four Perfections and the Four Automatonisms

THE *Four Perfections* can only be understood when their phases come to be considered; it will be obvious for instance that self-sacrifice must be the typical virtue of phases where instinct or race is predominant, and
5 especially in those three phases that come before reflection. *Automatonism* in *antithetical phases* arises from the *Mask* and *Creative Mind*, when separated from the *Body of Fate* and *Will*, through refusal of, or rest from conflict; and in *primary phases* from the *Body of*
10 *Fate* and *Will*, when weary of the struggle for complete *primary* existence or when they refuse that struggle. It does not necessarily mean that the man is not true to phase or, as it is said, out of phase; the most powerful natures are precisely those who most often need
15 *automatonism* as a rest. It is perhaps an element in our enjoyment of art and literature, being awakened in our minds by rhythm and by pattern. He is, however, out of phase, if he refuse for anything but need of rest the conflict with the *Body of Fate* which is the source
20 of *antithetical* energy and so falls under *imitative* or *creative automatonism*, or if in *primary* phases he refuse conflict with the *Mask* and so falls under *obedient* or *instinctive automatonism*.

XI

The Daimon, the Sexes, Unity of Being, Natural and Supernatural Unity.

THE *Will* and the *Creative Mind* are in the light, but the
25 *Body of Fate* working through accident, in dark, while

Mask, or *Image*, is a form selected instinctively for those emotional associations which come out of the dark, and this form is itself set before us by accident, or swims up from the dark portion of the mind. But there is another mind, or another part of our mind in this darkness, that is yet to its own perceptions in the light; and we in our turn are dark to that mind. These two minds (one always light* and one always dark, when considered by one mind alone), make up man and *Daimon*, the *Will* of the man being the *Mask* of the *Daimon*, the *Creàtive Mind* of the man being the *Body of Fate* of the *Daimon* and so on. The Wheel is in this way reversed, as St. Peter at his crucifixion reversed by the position of his body the position of the crucified Christ : " Demon est Deus Inversus." Man's *Daimon* has therefore her energy and bias, in man's *Mask*, and her constructive power in man's fate, and man and *Daimon* face each other in a perpetual conflict or embrace. This relation (the *Daimon* being of the opposite sex to that of man) may create a passion like that of sexual love. The relation of man and woman, in so far as it is passionate, reproduces the relation of man and *Daimon*, and becomes an element where man and *Daimon* sport, pursue one another, and do one another good or evil. This does not mean, however, that the men and women of opposite phases love one another, for a man generally chooses a woman whose *Mask* falls between his *Mask* and his *Body of Fate*, or just outside one or other; but that every man is, in the right of his sex, a wheel, or group of *Four Faculties*, and that every woman is, in the right of her sex, a wheel which reverses the masculine wheel. In so far as man and woman are swayed by their sex they interact

* Light and dark are not used in this section as in the description of the phases, but as it were cross that light and dark at right angles. See diagrams in Sec. XVII, Book II.

September, 1925.

as man and *Daimon* interact, though at other moments
their phases may be side by side. The *Daimon* carries
on her conflict, or friendship with a man, not only through
the events of life, but in the mind itself, for she is in
5   possession of the entire dark of the mind. The things
we dream, or that come suddenly into our heads, are
therefore her *Creative Mind* (our *Creative Mind* is her
Body of Fate) through which her energy, or bias, finds
expression; one can therefore, if one will, think of man
10   as *Will* and *Creative Mind* alone, perpetually face to face
with another being who is also but *Will* and *Creative
Mind*, though these appear to man as the object of desire,
or beauty, and as fate in all its forms. If man seeks to
live wholly in the light, the *Daimon* will seek to quench
15   that light in what is to man wholly darkness, and there
is conflict and *Mask* and *Body of Fate* become evil; when
however in *antithetical* man the *Daimonic* mind is
permitted to flow through the events of his life (the
Daimonic Creative Mind) and so to animate his *Creative
20   Mind*, without putting out its light, there is Unity of
Being. A man becomes passionate and this passion
makes the *Daimonic* thought luminous with its peculiar
light—this is the object of the *Daimon*—and she so
creates a very personal form of heroism or of poetry.
25   The *Daimon* herself is now passionless and has a form
of thought, which has no need of premise and deduction,
nor of any language, for it apprehends the truth by a
faculty which is analogous to sight, and hearing, and
taste, and touch, and smell, though without organs. He
30   who attains Unity of Being is some man, who, while
struggling with his fate and his destiny until every
energy of his being has been roused, is content that he
should so struggle with no final conquest. For him fate
and freedom are not to be distinguished; he is no longer
35   bitter, he may even love tragedy like those " who love
the gods and withstand them "; such men are able to

bring all that happens, as well as all that they desire,
into an emotional or intellectual synthesis and so to
possess not the Vision of Good only but that of Evil.
They are described as coming after death into dark and
into light, whereas *primary* men, who do not receive
revelation by conflict, are in dark or in light. In the
Convito Dante speaks of his exile, and the gregariousness
it thrust upon him, as a great misfortune for such as he;
and yet as poet he must have accepted, not only that
exile, but his grief for the death of Beatrice as that
which made him *Daimonic*, not a writer of poetry alone
like Guido Cavalcanti. Intellectual creation accompanies
or follows in *antithetical* man, the struggle of the being to
overthrow its fate and this is symbolised by placing the
Creative Mind in the phase opposite to that of the *Body
of Fate*. Unity of Being becomes possible at Phase 12,
and ceases to be possible at Phase 18, but is rare before
Phase 13 and after Phase 17, and is most common at
Phase 17. When man is in his most *antithetical* phases
the *Daimon* is most *primary*; man pursues, loves, or
hates, or both loves and hates—a form of passion, an
antithetical image is imposed upon the *Daimonic* thought
—but in man's most *primary* phases the *Daimon* is at her
most *antithetical*. Man is now pursued with hatred, or
with love; must receive an alien terror or joy; and it
is to this final acceptance of the *Image* that we apply
the phrases " Unity with God," " Unity with Nature."
Unity with God is possible after Phase 26, though almost
impossible before Phase 27 which is called " The Saint,"
while Unity with Nature may take place after Phase 1,
and in its turn becomes impossible after Phase 4. But
for the possibility of this union man in his *primary*
phases would sink into a mechanical objectivity, become
wholly automatic. At Phase 26, however, he can escape
from that which he apprehends through the organs of
sense, by submission to that which he can apprehend

by the mind's eye and ear, its palate and its touch. When he is content to be pursued, to be ignored, to be hated even by that he so apprehends, he becomes the object not of hatred but of love, for the *Daimonic* mind,
5 being now *antithetical*, has passed from thought to passion. *Antithetical* man pursuing, or hungry, with a passion like that of the beasts, may be exalted with a passion first discovered and expressed by finer minds than his; and the *Daimon* so pursuing, so hungry, is also
10 so exalted, and we have therefore the right to describe our union with it, as union with Nature, or with God. When Phase 1 has been passed, the union is with nature.

According to the Solar symbolism, which is explained in Book II, two are not in light and two in dark, but
15 all four in light as contrasted to *Four Principles* that are solar and entirely dark.

XII

Table of the Four Faculties

EACH *Faculty* is placed after the number of the phase where it is formed, not after the phase which it affects.

	WILL.	MASK.	CREATIVE MIND.	BODY OF FATE.
1.	No	description except	entire plasticity.	
2.	Beginning of Energy.	*True.* Illusion. *False.* Delusion.	*True.* Physical activity. *False.* Cunning.	Enforced love of the world.
3.	Beginning of Ambition.	*True.* Simplification through intensity. *False.* Dispersal.	*True.* Super-sensitive receptivity. *False.* Pride.	Enforced love of another.

WILL.	MASK.	CREATIVE MIND.	BODY OF FATE.
4. Desire for Primary objects.	*True.* Intensity through emotions. *False.* Curiosity.	*True.* Abstract supersensitive thought. *False.* Fascination of sin.	Enforced intellectual action.
5. Separation from innocence.	*True.* Conviction. *False.* Domination.	*True.* Rhetoric. *False.* Spiritual arrogance.	Enforced belief.
6. Artificial Individuality.	*True.* Fatalism. *False.* Superstition.	*True.* Constructive emotion. *False.* Authority.	Enforced emotion.
7. Assertion of Individuality.	*True.* Self-analysis. *False.* Self-adaptation.	*True.* Creation through pity. *False.* Self-driven desire.	Enforced sensuality.
8. War between individuality and race.	*True.* Self-immolation. *False.* Self-assurance.	*True.* Amalgamation. *False.* Despair.	The beginning of true strength.
9. Belief takes place of individuality.	*True.* Wisdom. *False.* Self-pity.	*True.* Intellectual domination. *False.* Distortion.	Adventure that excites individuality.
10. The image-breaker.	*True.* Self-reliance. *False.* Isolation.	*True.* Dramatization of Mask. *False.* Self-desecration.	Humanity.
11. The consumer. The pyre-builder.	*True.* Consciousness of self. *False.* Self-consciousness.	*True.* Emotional intellect. *False.* The Unfaithful.	Natural law.
12. The Forerunner.	*True.* Self-realization. *False.* Self-abandonment.	*True.* Emotional philosophy. *False.* Enforced law.	Search.

WILL.	MASK.	CREATIVE MIND.	BODY OF FATE.
13. The sensuous man.	*True.* Renunciation. *False.* Emulation.	*True.* Creative imagination through antithetical emotion. *False.* Enforced self-realization.	Interest.
14. The obsessed man.	*True.* Oblivion. *False.* Malignity.	*True.* Vehemence. *False.* Opinionated will.	None except monotony
15.	No description except	entire beauty.	
16. The positive man.	*True.* Player on Pan's Pipes. *False.* Fury.	*True.* Emotional will. *False.* Terror.	Fool is his own Body of Fate.
17. The Daimonic man.	*True.* Innocence. *False.* Folly.	*True.* Subjective Truth. *False.* Morbidity.	None except impersonal action.
18. The emotional man.	*True.* Passion. *False.* Will.	*True.* Subjective philosophy. *False.* War between two forms of expression.	Hunchback is his own Body of Fate.
19. The assertive man.	*True.* Excess. *False.* Limitation.	*True.* Moral iconoclasm. *False.* Self-assertion.	Persecution.
20. The concrete man.	*True.* Justice. *False.* Tyranny.	*True.* Domination through emotional constriction. *False.* Reformation.	Objective action.
21. The acquisitive man.	*True.* Altruism. *False.* Efficiency.	*True.* Self-dramatization. *False.* Anarchy.	Success.

WILL.	MASK.	CREATIVE MIND.	BODY OF FATE.
22. Balance between ambition and contemplation.	*True.* Courage. *False.* Fear.	*True.* Versatility. *False.* Impotence.	Temptation versus strength.
23. The Receptive Man.	*True.* Facility. *False.* Obscurity.	*True.* Heroic sentiment. *False.* Dogmatic sentimentality.	Enforced triumph of achievement.
24. The end of ambition.	*True.* Organization. *False.* Inertia.	*True.* Ideality. *False.* Derision.	Enforced success in action.
25. The conditional man.	*True.* Rejection. *False.* Moral reformation.	*True.* Social intellect. *False.* Limitation.	Enforced failure of action.
26. The Multiple Man also called The Hunchback.	*True.* Self-exaggeration. *False.* Self-abandonment.	*True.* First perception of character. *False.* Mutilation.	Enforced Disillusion.
27. The Saint.	*True.* Self-expression. *False.* Self-absorption.	*True.* Simplicity. *False.* Abstraction.	Enforced Cost.
28. The Fool.	*True.* Serenity. *False.* Self-distrust.	*True.* Hope. *False.* Moroseness.	Enforced illusion.

XIII

CHARACTERS OF CERTAIN PHASES

FOUR PERFECTIONS

At P. 2, P. 3, P. 4 ...   Self-sacrifice
At P. 13   ...   ...   Self-knowledge
At P. 16, P. 17, P. 18   Unity of Being
At P. 27   ...   ...   Sanctity

c

Four Types of Wisdom

At P. 4 ... ... Wisdom of Desire
At P. 12 ... ... Wisdom of Intellect
At P. 18 ... ... Wisdom of Heart
At P. 26 ... ... Wisdom of Knowledge

Four Contests

5 At P. 1 ... ... Moral
At P. 8 ... ... Emotional
At P. 15 ... ... Physical
At P. 22 ... ... Spiritual or supersensual

Rage, Phantasy, etc.

From P. 8 to P. 12 Rage
10 From P. 12 to P. 15 Spiritual or supersensual Rage
From P. 15 to P. 19 Phantasy
From P. 19 to P. 22 Power

XIV

* General Character of Creative Mind affecting Certain Phases

(1) Affecting 28, 1, 2, from 2, 1, 28. Controlled.
(2) „ 8, 4, 5, 6 from 27, 26, 25, 24. Trans-
15 formatory.
(3) „ 7, 8, 9 from 23, 22, 21. Mathematical.
(4) „ 10, 11, 12 from 20, 19, 18. Intellectually passionate.
(5) „ 13 from 17. Stillness.

* This and the following Table are divided into ten divisions because they were given me in this form, and I have not sufficient confidence in my knowledge to turn them into the more convenient twelve-fold divisions. The relation of the Great Wheel and the Year is explained in Book II, and the makers of these tables may have had the old tenfold year in their minds.—W. B. Y.

(6) Affecting 14, 15 16 from 16, 15, 14. Emotional.

(7)   ,,   17, 18, 19, 20 from 18, 12, 11, 10.
              Emotionally passionate.

(8)   ,,   21, 22, 28 from 9, 8, 7. Rational.

(9)   ,,   24 from 6. Obedient.   5

(10)   ,,   25, 26, 27 from 8, 4, 5. Serenity.

XV

GENERAL CHARACTER OF BODY OF FATE

(1) Affecting 28, 1, 2 from 16, 15, 14. Joy.

(2)   ,,   8, 4, 5, 6, from 18, 12, 11, 10. Breathing.

(8)   ,,   7, 8, 9 from 9, 8, 7. Tumult.

(4)   ,,   10, 11, 12 from 6, 5, 4. Tension.   10

(5)   ,,   18 from 8. Disease.

(6)   ,,   14, 15, 16 from 2, 1, 28. The world.

(7)   ,,   17, 18, 19, 20 from 27, 26, 25, 24.
              Sorrow.

(8)   ,,   21, 22, 28 from 28, 22, 21. Ambition.   15

(9)   ,,   24 from 20. Success.

(10)   ,,   25, 26, 27 from 19, 18, 17. Absorption.

XVI

TABLE OF THE QUARTERS

THE FOUR CONTESTS OF THE ANTITHETICAL WITHIN ITSELF

First quarter. With body. ⎫
Second   ,,   With heart. ⎬ In the first quarter body
Third   ,,   With mind. ⎬ should win, in second 20
Fourth ,,   With soul. ⎭ heart, etc.

Four Automatonisms

First quarter.		Instinctive.
Second	,,	Imitative.
Third	,,	Creative.
Fourth	,,	Obedient.

Four Conditions of the Will

5
First quarter.		Instinctive.
Second	,,	Emotional.
Third	,,	Intellectual.
Fourth	,,	Moral.

Four Conditions of the Mask

First quarter.		Intensity (affecting Third Quarter)
10 Second	,,	Tolerance (affecting Fourth Quarter).
Third	,,	Convention or systematization (affecting First Quarter).
Fourth	,,	Self-analysis (affecting Second Quarter).

Defects of False Creative Mind which bring the False Mask

First quarter.		Sentimentality.
15 Second	,,	Brutality (desire for root facts of life).
Third	,,	Hatred.
Fourth	,,	Insensitiveness.

Note.—In *primary* Phases these defects separate *Mask* from *Body of Fate*, in *antithetical*, *Creative Mind* from 20 *Body of Fate*.

Elemental Attributions

Earth	...	First quarter	...
Water	...	Second quarter	...
Air	...	Third quarter	...
Fire	...	Fourth quarter	...

XVII

UNCLASSIFIED ATTRIBUTES

Mask worn — moral and emotional.
Mask carried —emotional.

ABSTRACTION

Strong at 6, 7, 8.
Strongest at 22, 23, 24, 25.
Begins at 19, less at 20, increase again at 21.

THREE ENERGIES

Images from self give emotion.
Images from world give passion.
Images from the supersensual give will.

4. THE TWENTY-EIGHT EMBODIMENTS

I

PHASE ONE AND THE INTERCHANGE OF THE TINCTURES

AS will be seen, when late phases are described, every achievement of a being, after Phase 22, is an elimination of the individual intellect and a discovery of the moral life. When the individual intellect lingers on, it is
5 arrogance, self-assertion, a sterile abstraction, for the being is forced by the growing *primary Tincture* to accept first the service of, and later on absorption in, the *primary* whole, a sensual or supersensual objectivity.

When the old *antithetical* becomes the new *primary*,
10 moral feeling is changed into an organisation of experience which must in its turn seek a unity, the whole of experience. When the old *primary* becomes the new *antithetical*, the old realisation of an objective moral law is changed into a subconscious turbulent instinct. The
15 world of rigid custom and law is broken up by " the uncontrollable mystery upon the bestial floor."

Phase 1 not being human can better be described after Phase 28.

II

Phase Two

Will—Beginning of Energy.

Mask (from *P. 16*). *True*—Player on Pan's Pipes. *False*—Fury.

Creative Mind (from *P. 28*). *True*—Hope. *False*—Moroseness. 5

Body of Fate (from *P. 14*)—"None except monotony."

When the man lives out of phase and desires the *Mask*, and so permits it to dominate the *Creative Mind*, he copies the emotional explosion of Phase 16 in so far as difference of phase permits. He gives himself to a violent 10 animal assertion and can only destroy, strike right and left as in the rage of a child, seek satisfaction of bodily need full of ignorance and gloom.

> " But when they find the frowning Babe,
> Terror strikes through the region wide : 15
> They cry ' The babe ! the babe is born ! '
> And flee away on every side."

But if he live according to phase, he uses the *Body of Fate* to clear the intellect of the influence of the *Mask*. He frees himself from emotion; and the *Body of Fate*, 20 derived from Phase 14, pulls back the mind into the supersensual, so changes it that it grows obedient to all that recurs; and the *Mask*, now entirely enforced, is a rhythmical impulse. He gives himself up to the function of the moment, the hope of the moment, and yet is 25 neither immoral nor violent but innocent; he is as it were the breath stirring on the face of the deep; the smile on the face of a but half-awakened child. Nobody of our age has, it may be, met him, certainly no record of such meeting exists, but, were such meeting possible, 30 he would be remembered as a form of joy, for he would

seem more entirely living than all other men, a personi-
fication or summing up of the life of all other men. He
would decide on this or that by no balance of the reason
but by an infallible joy, and if born amid a rigid
5   mechanical order, he would make for himself a place, as
a dog will scratch a hole for itself in loose earth.

Here, as at Phase 16, the ordinary condition is sometimes reversed, and instead of ugliness, otherwise
characteristic of this as of all *primary* phases, there is
10 beauty. The new *antithetical Tincture* (the old *primary*
reborn) is violent. A new birth, when the product of an
extreme contrast in the past life of the individual, is
sometimes so violent that lacking foreign admixture it
forestalls its ultimate physical destiny. It forces upon
15 the *primary* and upon itself a beautiful form. It has
the muscular balance and force of an animal good-
humour with all appropriate comeliness as in the dancing
faun. If this rare accident does not occur, the body is
coarse; not deformed, but coarse from lack of sensitive-
20 ness and is most fitted for rough physical labour.

Seen by those lyrical poets who draw their *Masks*
from early phases, the man of Phase 2 is transfigured.
Weary of an energy that defines and judges, weary of
intellectual self expression, they desire some " conceal-
25 ment," some transcendent intoxication. The bodily
instincts, subjectively perceived, become the cup
wreathed with ivy. Perhaps even a *Body of Fate* from
any early phase may suffice to create this *Image*, but
when it affects Phase 13 and Phase 14 the *Image* will
30 be more sensuous, more like immediate experience.

" The Kings of Inde their jewelled sceptres vail,
And from their treasures scatter pearled hail;
Great Brama from his mystic heaven groans
And all his priesthood moans;
35   Before young Bacchus' eye-wink turning pale."

III

Phase Three

Will—Beginning of Ambition.

Mask (from *P. 17*). *True*—Innocence. *False*—Folly.

Creative Mind (from *P. 27*). *True*—Simplicity. *False* —Abstraction.

Body of Fate (from *P. 13*)—Interest. 5

Out of phase and copying the opposite phase, he gives himself up to a kind of clodhopper folly, that keeps his intellect moving among conventional ideas with a sort of make-believe. Incapable of consecutive thought and of 10 moral purpose, he lives miserably seeking to hold together some consistent plan of life, patching rags upon rags because that is expected of him, or out of egotism. If on the other hand he uses his *Body of Fate* to purify his *Creative Mind* of the *Mask*, if he is content to permit his senses and his subconscious nature to dominate his 15 intellect, he takes delight in all that passes; but because he claims nothing of his own, chooses nothing, thinks that no one thing is better than another, he will not endure a pang because all passes. Almost without intellect, it is a phase of perfect bodily sanity, for, though 20 the body is still in close contact with supersensual rhythm, it is no longer absorbed in that rhythm; eyes and ears are open; one instinct balances another; every season brings its delight.

> " He who bends to himself a joy 25
> Does the winged life destroy,
> But he who kisses the joy as it flies
> Lives in eternity's sunrise."

Seen by lyrical poets, of whom so many have belonged
to the fantastic Phase 17, the man of this phase becomes
an *Image* where simplicity and intensity are united, he
seems to move among yellowing corn or under over-
5 hanging grapes. He gave to Landor his shepherds and
hamadryads, to Morris his " Water of the Wondrous
Isles," to Shelley his wandering lovers and sages, and
to Theocritus all his flocks and pastures; and of what
else did Bembo think when he cried, " Would that I
10 were a shepherd that I might look daily down upon
Urbino." Imagined in some *antithetical* mind, seasonal
change and bodily sanity seem images of lasting passion
and the body's beauty.

IV

PHASE FOUR

Will—Desire for Exterior World.
15 *Mask* (from *P. 18*). *True*—Passion. *False*—Will.
C.M. (from *P. 26*). *True*—First Perception of
Character. *False*—Mutilation.
B.F. (from *P. 12*)—Search.

When out of phase he attempts *antithetical* wisdom
20 (for reflection has begun), separates himself from instinct
(hence " mutilation "), and tries to enforce upon himself
and others all kinds of abstract or conventional ideas
which are for him, being outside his experience, mere
make-believe. Lacking *antithetical* capacity, and all of
25 *primary* that is founded upon observation, he is aimless
and blundering, possesses nothing except the knowledge
that there is something known to others that is not mere
instinct. True to phase, his interest in everything that

happens, in all that excites his instinct (" search "), is
so keen that he has no desire to claim anything for his
own will; nature still dominates his thought as passion;
yet instinct grows reflective. He is full of practical
wisdom, a wisdom of saws and proverbs, or founded upon 5
concrete examples. He can see nothing beyond sense, but
sense expands and contracts to meet his needs, and the
needs of those who trust him. It is as though he woke
suddenly out of sleep and thereupon saw more and
remembered more than others. He has " the wisdom of 10
instinct," a wisdom perpetually excited by all those hopes
and needs which concern his well-being or that of the race
(*Creative Mind* from Phase 12 and so acting from that in
race which corresponds to personality when personality is
unified in thought). The men of the opposite phase, or 15
of the phases nearly opposite, worn out by a wisdom
held with labour and uncertainty, see persons of this
phase as images of peace. Two passages of Browning
come to mind :

> " An old hunter, talking with gods   20
>   Or sailing with troops of friends to Tenedos."

> " A King lived long ago,
>   In the morning of the world,
>   When Earth was nigher Heaven than now :
>   And the King's locks curled,   25
>   Disparting o'er a forehead full
>   As the milk-white space betwixt horn and horn
>   Of some sacrificial bull—
>   Only calm as a babe new-born :
>   For he was got to a sleepy mood,   30
>   So safe from all decrepitude,
>   Age with its bane, so sure gone by,
>   (The gods so loved him while he dreamed)
>   That, having lived thus long, there seemed
>   No need the King should ever die."   35

V

The Opening of the Tinctures

SINCE Phase 26 the *Primary Tincture* has so predominated, man is so sunk in Fate, in life, that there is no
reflection, no experience, because that which reflects,
that which acquires experience has been drowned. Man
5   cannot think of himself as separate from that which he
sees with the bodily eye or in the mind's eye. He
neither loves nor hates though he may be in hatred or in
love. Birdalone in " The Water of the Wondrous Isles "
(a woman of Phase 8 reflected in an *antithetical* mind)
10   falls in love with her friend's lover and he with her.
There is great sorrow but no struggle, her decision to
disappear is sudden as if some power over which she
has no control compelled. Has she not perhaps but
decided as her unknown fathers and mothers compelled,
15   but conformed to the lineaments of her race? Is she not
a child of " Weird," are not all in the most *primary*
phases children of " Weird " exercising an unconscious
discrimination towards all that before Phase 1 defines
their *Fate*, and after Phase 1 their race. Every achieve-
20   ment of their souls, Phase 1 being passed, springs up
out of the body, and their work, now it is passed, is to
substitute for a life, where all is Fate frozen into rule
and custom, a life where all is fused by instinct; with
them to hunger, to taste, to desire, is to grow wise.

25   Between Phase 4 and Phase 5, the *Tinctures* separate,
are said to open, and reflection begins. When closed,
there is an approach to absolute surrender of the *Will*,
first to God, then, as Phase 1 passes away, to Nature, and
the surrender is the most complete form of the freedom
30   of the *Body of Fate* which has been increasing since
Phase 22. When Man identifies himself with his *Fate*,
when he is able to say " Thy Will is our freedom " or

when he is perfectly natural, that is to say perfectly
a portion of his surroundings, he is free even though
all his actions can be foreseen, even though every action
is a logical deduction from that that went before it. He
is all *Fate* but has no *Destiny*.   5

VI

Phase Five

Will—Separation from Innocence.

Mask (from *P. 19*). *True*—Excess. *False*—Limitation.

Creative Mind (from *P. 25*). *True*—Social Intellect.
False—Limitation.   10

Body of Fate (from *P. 11*)—Natural Law.

Out of phase, and seeking *antithetical* emotion, he is
sterile, passing from one insincere attitude to another,
moving through a round of moral images torn from
their context and so without meaning. He is so proud 15
of each separation from experience that he becomes a
sort of angry or smiling Punch with a lath between his
wooden arms striking here and there. His *Body of Fate*
is enforced, for he has reversed the condition of his phase
and finds himself at conflict with a world which offers 20
him nothing but temptation and affront. True to phase,
he is the direct opposite of all this. Abstraction has
indeed begun, but it comes to him as a portion of
experience cut off from everything but itself and therefore fitted to be the object of reflection. He no longer 25
touches, eats, drinks, thinks and feels nature, but sees

it as something from which he is separating himself, something that he may dominate, though only for a moment and by some fragmentary violence of sensation or of thought. Nature is half gone but the laws of nature have appeared and he can change her rhythms and her seasons by his knowledge. He lives in the moment but with an intensity Phases 2, 8 and 4 have never known, the *Will* approaches its climax, he is no longer like a man but half-awakened. He is a corrupter, disturber, wanderer, a founder of sects and peoples, and works with extravagant energy, and his reward is but to live in its glare.

Seen by a poet of the opposite phase, by a man hiding fading emotion under broken emphasis, he is Don Juan or the Giaour.

VII

PHASE SIX

Will—Artificial Individuality.

Mask (from *Phase 20*).   *True*—Justice.   *False*—Tyranny.

Creative Mind (from *Phase 24*).   *True*—Ideality. *False*—Derision.

Body of Fate (from *Phase 10*)—Humanity.

Example : Walt Whitman.

Had Walt Whitman lived out of phase, desire to prove that all his emotions were healthy and intelligible, to set his practical sanity above all not made in his fashion, to cry " thirty years old and in perfect health ! " would have turned him into some kind of jibing demagogue;

and to think of him would be to remember that Thoreau
when he had picked up the jaw-bone of a pig that had
not a tooth missing, recorded that there also was
perfect health. He would, that he might believe in
himself, have compelled others to believe. But using 5
his *Body of Fate* (his interest in crowds, in casual loves
and affections, in all summary human experience) to
clear intellect of *antithetical* emotion (always insincere
from Phase 1 to Phase 8), and haunted and hunted by
the now involuntary *Mask*, he creates an *Image* of vague, 10
half-civilised man, while all his thought and impulse is
a product of democratic bonhomie, of schools, of colleges,
of public discussion. Abstraction has been born but it
is the abstraction of a community, of a tradition, a
synthesis starting, not as with Phases 19, 20 and 21 with 15
logical deduction from an observed fact, but from some
experience or from the whole experience of the individual
or of the community : " I have such and such a feeling.
I have such and such a belief. What follows from
feeling, what from belief? " While Thomas Aquinas, 20
whose historical epoch was nearly of this phase, would
sum in abstract categories all possible experience, not
that he may know but that he may feel, Walt Whitman
makes catalogues of all that has moved him, or amused
his eye, that he may grow more poetical. Experience 25
is all absorbing, subordinating, observed fact, drowning
even truth itself (where truth is conceived of as something apart from impulse and instinct and from the *Will*,
where impulse or instinct begins to be all in all). In a
little while, though not yet, impulse and instinct, 30
sweeping away catalogue and category, will fill the mind
with terror.

VIII

PHASE SEVEN

Will—Assertion of individuality.

Mask (from phase 21). *True*—Altruism. *False*—Efficiency.

Creative Mind (from phase 23). *True*—Heroic senti-
5   ment. *False*—Dogmatic sentimentality.

Body of Fate (from phase 9)—Adventure that excites the individuality.

Examples : George Borrow, Alexandre Dumas, Thomas Carlyle, James Macpherson.

10   At Phases 2, 3 and 4 the man moved within traditional
or seasonable limits, but since Phase 5 limits have grown
indefinite; public codes, all that depend upon habit, are
all but dissolved, even the catalogues and categories of
Phase 6 are no longer sufficient. If out of phase the man
15   desires to be the man of Phase 21; an impossible desire,
for that man is all but the climax of intellectual complexity and all men, from Phase 2 to Phase 7 inclusive,
are intellectually simple. His instincts are all but at their
apex of complexity, and he is bewildered and must soon
20   be helpless. The dissolving character, out of phase,
desires the breaking personality, and though it cannot
possess, or even conceive of personality, seeing that
its thoughts and emotions are common to all, it can
create a grandiloquent phantom and by deceiving others
25   deceive itself; and presently we shall discover Phase 21,
out of phase, bragging of an imaginary naiveté.
     Phase 7 when true to phase surrenders to the *Body
of Fate* which, being derived from the phase where

personality first shows itself, is excited into forms of character so dissolved in *Will*, in instinct, that they are hardly distinguishable from personality. These forms of character, not being self-dependent like personality, are however inseparable from circumstance : a gesture, or a pose born of a situation and forgotten when the situation has passed; a last act of courage, a defiance of the dogs that must soon tear the man into pieces. Such men have a passion for history, for the scene, for the adventure. They delight in actions, which they cannot see apart from setting sun or a storm at sea or some great battle, and that are inspired by emotions that move all hearers because such that all understand.

Alexander Dumas was the phase in its perfection, George Borrow when it halts a little, for Borrow was at moments sufficiently out of phase to know that he was naïve and to brag of imaginary intellectual subjectivity, as when he paraded an unbelievable fit of the horrors, or his mastery of many tongues. Carlyle like Macpherson showed the phase at its worst. He neither could, nor should have cared for anything but the personalities of history, but he used them as so many metaphors in a vast popular rhetoric, for the expression of thoughts that seemed his own and were the work of preachers to angry ignorant congregations. So noisy, so threatening that rhetoric, so great his own energy that two generations passed before men noticed that he had written no sentence not of coarse humour that clings to the memory. Sexual impotence had doubtless weakened the *Body of Fate* and so strengthened the False *Mask*, yet one doubts if any mere plaster of ant's eggs could have helped where there was so great insincerity.

D

IX

Phase Eight

Will—War between race and individuality.

Mask (from Phase 22). *True*—Courage. *False*—Fear.

Creative Mind (from Phase 22). *True*—Versatility. *False*—Impotence.

5   *Body of Fate* (from Phase 8)—The beginning of strength.

Example : The Idiot of Dostoieffsky perhaps.

Out of phase, a condition of terror, when true to phase, of courage unbroken through defeat.

10   From Phase 1 to Phase 7, there has been a gradual weakening in the character of all that is *primary*. Character has taken the disguise of individuality (the *will* analysed in relation to itself), but now, though individuality persists through another phase, personality 15 (the *Will* analysed in relation to the *Mask*) must predominate. So long as the *primary Tincture* predominated, the *antithetical Tincture* accepted its manner of percepttion; and character has been enlarged by the vegetative and sensitive faculties excited by the *Body of Fate*, 20 which are the nearest a *primary* nature can come to *antithetical* emotion. But now the bottle must be burst. The struggle of idealised, or habitual theologised thought with instinct, and that between mind and body, of the waning *primary* with the growing *antithetical*, must be 25 decided, and the vegetative and sensitive faculties must for a while take the sway. Only then can the *Will* be forced to recognise the weakness of the *Creative Mind* when unaided by the *Mask*, and so to permit the involun-

tary *Mask* to change into the voluntary. Every modification or codification of morality has been its attempt, acting through the *Creative Mind,* to set order upon the instinctive and vegetative faculties, and it must now feel that it can create order no longer. It is the very nature of a struggle, where the soul must lose all form received from the objectively accepted conscience of the world, that it denies us an historical example. One thinks of possible examples only to decide that Hartley Coleridge is not amongst them, that the brother of the Brontës may only seem to be because we know so little about him, but that Dostoieffsky's Idiot is almost certainly an example. But Dostoieffsky's Idiot was too matured a type, he had passed too many times through the twenty-eight phases to help our understanding. Here for the most part are those obscure wastrels who seem powerless to free themselves from some sensual temptation—drink, women, drugs—and who cannot in a life of continual crisis create any lasting thing. The being is often born up to four times at this one phase, it is said, before the *antithetical Tincture* attains its mastery. The being clings like a man drowning to every straw, and it is precisely this clinging, this seemingly vain reaching forth for strength, amidst the collapse of all those public thoughts and habits that are the support of *primary* man, that enables it to enter at last upon Phase 9. It has to find its strength by a transformation of that very instinct which has hitherto been its weakness and so to gather up the strewn and broken members. The union of *Creative Mind* and *Mask* in opposition to *Body of Fate* and *Will,* intensifies this struggle by dividing the nature into halves which have no interchange of qualities. The man is inseparable from his fate, he cannot see himself apart, nor can he distinguish between emotion and intellect. He is will-less, dragged hither and thither, and his unemotionalised intellect, gathered up into the mathe-

matical Phase 22, shows him perpetually for object of
desire, an emotion that is like a mechanical energy, a
thought that is like wheel and piston. He is suspended;
he is without bias, and until bias comes, till he has begun
5   groping for strength within his own being, his thought
and his emotion bring him to judgment but they cannot
help. As those at Phase 22 must dissolve the dramatising *Mask* in abstract mind that they may discover the
concrete world, he must dissolve thought into mere im-
10   personal instinct, into mere race that he may discover
the dramatising *Mask* : he chooses himself and not his
Fate. Courage is his true *Mask*, and diversity, that has
no habitual purpose, his true *Creative Mind*, because these
are all that the phase of the greatest possible weakness
15   can take into itself from the phase of the greatest possible
strength. When his fingers close upon a straw, that is
courage, and his versatility is that any wave may float
a straw. At Phase 7, he had tried out of ambition to
change his nature, as though a man should make love
20   who had no heart, but now shock can give him back his
heart. Only a shock resulting from the greatest possible
conflict can make the greatest possible change, that from
primary to *antithetical* or from *antithetical* to *primary*
again. Nor can anything intervene. He must be aware
25   of nothing but the conflict, his despair is necessary, he
is of all men the most tempted—" Eloi, Eloi, why hast
thou forsaken me? "

There are two human types found at each phase and
called *Victim* and *Sage*, the first predominantly
30   emotional, the other predominantly intellectual. Though
not necessary to a first understanding of " The Wheel,"
they must be touched on when describing Phase 22 (a
phase of such great importance at the present moment
of history that it will be described at greater length than
35   the other phases), and for this reason it is necessary to
say that they have an interchange at Phase 8 or at

Phase 22, corresponding to the interchange of the *Tinctures*. Their diagram will be given, while expounding another portion of the system.

X

PHASE NINE

Will—Belief instead of individuality.

Mask (from Phase 23). *True*—Facility. *False*—   5
Obscurity.

Creative Mind (from Phase 21). *True*—Self-Dramatisation. *False*—Anarchy.

Body of Fate (from Phase 7)—Enforced sensuality.

Example : An unnamed artist.   10

Out of phase, blundering and ignorant, the man becomes when in phase powerful and accomplished; all that strength as of metallic rod and wheel discovered within himself. He should seek to liberate the *Mask* by the help of the *Creative Mind* from the *Body of Fate*—that   15
is to say, to carve out and wear the now voluntary *Mask* and so to protect and to deliver the *Image*. In so far as he does so, there is immense confidence in self-expression, a vehement self, working through mathematical calculation, a delight in straight line and right angle;   20
but if he seek to live according to the *primary Tincture*, to use the *Body of Fate* to rid the *Creative Mind* of its *Mask*, to live with objective ambition and curiosity, all is confused, the *Will* asserts itself with a savage, terrified violence. All these phases of incipient personality when   25
out of phase are brutal, but after Phase 12, when true

personality begins, brutality gives place to an evasive capricious coldness—" false, fleeting, perjured Clarence " —a lack of good faith in their *primary* relation, often accompanied in their *antithetical* relation by the most
5 self-torturing scruples. When an *antithetical* man is out of phase, he reproduces the *primary* condition, but with an emotional inversion, love for *Image* or *Mask* becomes dread, or after Phase 15, hatred, and the *Mask* clings to the man or pursues him in the *Image*. It may even be
10 that he is haunted by a delusive hope, cherished in secret, or bragged of aloud, that he may inherit the *Body of Fate* and *Mask* of a phase opposed to his own. He seeks to avoid *antithetical* conflict by accepting what opposes him and his *antithetical* life is invaded. At Phase 9, the
15 *Body of Fate* that could alone purify the mind of a Carlyle, or of a Whitman, is the enemy of a unity which it breaks with sensuality (the rising flood of instinct from Phase 7) and the man if out of phase, instead of mastering this through his dramatisation of himself as a form
20 of passionate self-mastery, and of seeking some like form as *Image*, grows stupid and blundering. Hence one finds at this phase, more often than at any other, men who dread, despise and persecute the women whom they love. Yet behind all that muddy, flooded, brutal self, there
25 is perhaps a vague timid soul knowing itself caught in an antithesis, an alternation it cannot control. It is said of it, " the soul having found its weakness at Phase 8 begins the inward discipline of the soul in the fury of Phase 9." And again, " Phase 9 has the most sincere
30 belief any man has ever had in his own desire."

There is a certain artist who said to a student of these symbols, speaking of a notable man, and his mistress and their children, " She no longer cares for his work, no longer gives him the sympathy he needs, why does he
35 not leave her, what does he owe to her or to her children ? " The student discovered this artist to be a

cubist of powerful imagination and noticed that his head
suggested a sullen obstinacy, but that his manner and his
speech were generally sympathetic and gentle.

XI

Phase Ten

Will—The Image Breaker.

Mask (from Phase 24). *True*—Organisation. *False*—   5
Inertia.

Creative Mind (from Phase 20). *True*—Domination
through emotional construction. *False*—Reformation.

Body of Fate (from Phase 6)—Enforced emotion.

Example : Parnell.   10

If he live like the opposite phase, conceived as *primary*
condition—the phase where ambition dies—he lacks
all emotional power (False *Mask* : " Inertia "), and
gives himself up to rudderless change, reform without
a vision of form. He accepts what form (*Mask* and   15
Image) those about him admire and, on discovering that
it is alien, casts it away with brutal violence, to choose
some other form as alien. He disturbs his own life, and
he disturbs all who come near him more than does
Phase 9, for Phase 9 has no interest in others except in   20
relation to itself. If, on the other hand, he be true to
phase, and use his intellect to liberate from mere race
(*Body of Fate* at Phase 6 where race is codified), and so
create some code of personal conduct, which implies
always " divine right," he becomes proud, masterful and   25
practical. He cannot wholly escape the influence of his
Body of Fate, but he will be subject to its most

personal form; instead of gregarious sympathies, to some
woman's tragic love almost certainly. Though the *Body
of Fate* must seek to destroy his *Mask*, it may now
impose upon him a struggle which leaves victory still
5 possible. As *Body of Fate* phase and *Mask* phase
approach one another they share somewhat of each
other's nature; the effect of mutual hate grows more
diffused, less harsh and obvious. The effect of the *Body
of Fate* of Phase 10 for instance is slightly less harsh
10 and obvious than that of the " enforced sensuality " of
Phase 9. It is now " enforced emotion." Phase 9 was
without restraint, but now restraint has come and with
it pride; there is slightly less need to insist upon the
brutal facts of life that he may escape from their charm;
15 the subjective fury is less uncalculating, and the opposition of *Will* and *Mask* no longer produces a delight in an
impersonal precision and power like that of machinery
(machinery that is emotion and thought) but rather a
kind of burning restraint, a something that suggests a
20 savage statue to which one offers sacrifice. This sacrifice
is code, personality no longer perceived as power only.
He seeks by its help to free the creative power from mass
emotion, but never wholly succeeds, and so the life remains troubled, a conflict between pride and race, and
25 passes from crisis to crisis. At Phase 9 there was little
sexual discrimination, and now there is emotion created
by circumstance rather than by any unique beauty of
body or of character. One remembers Faust, who will
find every wench a Helen, now that he has drunk the
30 witches' dram, and yet loves his Gretchen with all his
being. Perhaps one thinks of that man who gave a
lifetime of love, because a young woman in capricious
idleness had written his name with her parasol upon the
snow. Here is rage, desire to escape but not now by
35 mere destruction of the opposing fate; for a vague
abstract sense of some world, some image, some circum-

stance, harmonious to emotion, has begun, or of something harmonious to emotion that may be set upon the empty pedestal, once visible world, image, or circumstance has been destroyed. With less desire of expression than at Phase 9, and with more desire of action and of command, the man (*Creative Mind* from Phase 20, phase of greatest dramatic power) sees all his life as a stage play where there is only one good acting part; yet no one will accuse him of being a stage player for he will wear always that stony *Mask* (Phase 24 " The end of ambition " *antithetically* perceived). He, too, if he triumph, may end ambition through the command of multitudes, for he is like that god of Norse mythology, who hung from the cliff's side for three days a sacrifice to himself. Perhaps Moses when he descended the mountain-side had a like stony *Mask*, and had cut out of the one rock *Mask* and table.

John Morley says of Parnell, whose life proves him of the Phase, that he had the least discursive mind he had ever known, and that is always characteristic of a phase where all practical curiosity has been lost wherever some personal aim is not involved, while philosophical and artistic curiosity are still undiscovered. He made upon his contemporaries an impression of impassivity, and yet after a speech that seemed brutal and callous, a follower has recorded that his hands were full of blood because he had torn them with his nails. One of his followers was shocked during the impassioned discussion in Committee Room No. 15, that led to his abandonment, by this most reticent man's lack of reticence in allusion to the operations of sex, an indifference as of a mathematician dealing with some arithmetical quantity, and yet Mrs Parnell tells how upon a night of storm on Brighton pier, and at the height of his power, he held her out over the waters and she lay still, stretched upon his two hands, knowing that if she moved, he would drown himself and her.

XII

Phase Eleven

Will—The Image Burner.

Mask (from Phase 25). *True*—Rejection. *False*—Moral Indifference.

Creative Mind (from Phase 19). *True*—Moral reformation. *False*—Self-Assertion.

Body of Fate (from Phase 5)—Enforced belief.

Examples : Spinoza, Savonarola.

While Phase 9 was kept from its subjectivity by personal relations, by sensuality, by various kinds of grossness; and Phase 10 by associations of men for practical purposes, and by the emotions that arise out of such associations, or by some tragic love where there is an element of common interest; Phase 11 is impeded by the excitement of conviction, by the contagion of organised belief, or by its interest in organisation for its own sake. The man of the phase is a half solitary, one who defends a solitude he cannot or will not inhabit, his *Mask* being from a phase of abstract belief, which offers him always some bundle of mathematical formulae, or its like, opposed to his nature. It will presently be seen that the man of Phase 25, where the *Mask* is, creates his system of belief, just as Phase 24 creates his code, to exclude all that is too difficult for dolt or knave; but the man of Phase 11 systematises, runs to some frenzy of conviction, to make intellect, intellect for its own sake, possible, and perhaps, in his rage against rough-and-ready customary thought, to make all but intellect impossible. He will be the antithesis of all this, should he be conquered by his *Body of Fate* (from Phase 5, where the common instinct first unites itself to reflection) being carried off by

some contagion of belief, some general interest, and compelled to substitute for intellectual rage some form of
personal pride and so to become the proud prelate of
tradition.

In Spinoza one finds the phase in its most pure and   5
powerful shape. He saw the divine energy in whatever
was the most individual expression of the soul, and spent
his life in showing that such expression was for the
world's welfare and not, as might seem, a form of
anarchy. His *Mask*, under the influence of his *Body of*   10
Fate, would have forced him to seek happiness in submission to something hard and exterior; but the *Mask*,
set free by a *Creative Mind* that would destroy exterior
popular sanction, makes possible for the first time the
solitary conception of God. One imagines him among   15
the theologians of his time, who sought always some
formula perhaps, some sheep-dog for common minds,
turning himself into pure wolf, and making for the
wilderness. Certainly his pantheism, however pleasing
to his own bare bench of scholars, was little likely to help   20
the oratory of any bench of judges or of bishops.
Through all his cold definitions, on whose mathematical
form he prided himself, one divines some quarrel, not
recorded in his biography, with the thought of his fathers
and his kin, forced upon him almost to the breaking of   25
his heart : no nature without the stroke of fate divides
itself in two.

XIII

The Opening of the Tincture, etc.

JUST before the place in the Great Wheel, where the
word *Heart* is written, the splitting or opening of each
Tincture begins, and increases till Phase 15 and then   30

decreases, until the place where *Head* is written; at which point they close once more. The *antithetical Tincture* is said to open at Phase 11, the *primary* at Phase 12. When the *Tinctures* open, that is to say when observation

5 gives place to experience, when the being attains self knowledge or its possibility, the *Four Faculties* reflect themselves in the experience or knowledge as the *Four Qualities*, the *Will* as *instinct* (or race), the *Mask* as *emotion*, the *Creative Mind* as *reason*, the *Body of Fate*

10 as *desire*.

Before the interchange of the *Tinctures* at Phase 15 the *antithetical* is reflected as *reason* and *desire*, the *primary* as *emotion* and *instinct*, while after Phase 15 this is reversed. *Emotion* and *instinct* when acting as one are

15 *love*, *reason* and *desire hatred*; and in all *phases* before Phase 11 and after Phase 19, except those between Phase 26 and Phase 4, and especially in those phases round Phase 8 and Phase 22 the man knows himself through acted *love* and acted *hate*. Between Phase 26 and Phase

20 4 *love* and *hate* should be themselves unknown being only known as one, as that which is fated.

By *love* is meant love of that particular unity towards which the nature is tending, or of those images and ideas which define it, and by *hate*, hate of all that

25 impedes that unity. In the phases between Phase 12 and Phase 18, the unity sought is Unity of Being, which is not to be confused with. the complete subjectivity of Phase 15, for it implies a harmony of *antithetical* and *primary* life, and Phase 15 has no

30 *primary*. Between Phase 12 and Phase 18 the struggle for this unity becomes conscious and its attainment possible. All the *antithetical* control over *primary* faculties increases; and the being may become almost wholly predestined, as distinguished from the *primary*

35 phases which are fated. It struggles within itself, for it must now harmonise its *instinct* with its *emotion*, its

reason with its *desire*, and not in relation to, or for the sake of, some particular action; but in relation to a conception of itself as Unity. With this change sexual love becomes the most important event of the life, for the opposite sex is nature chosen and fated—*Image* and 5 *Body of Fate.*

At the approach of Unity of Being the greatest beauty of literary style becomes possible, for thought becomes sensuous and musical. All that moves us is related to our possible Unity; we lose interest in the abstract and 10 concrete alike, only when we have said, " My fire," and so distinguished it from " the fire " and " a fire," does the fire seem bright. Every emotion begins to be related, as musical notes are related, to every other. It is as though we touched a musical string that set other strings 15 into sympathetic vibration.

XIV

PHASE TWELVE

Will—The Forerunner.

Mask (from Phase 26). *True*—Self-exaggeration. *False*—Self-abandonment.

Creative Mind (from Phase 18). *True*—Subjective 20 Philosophy. *False*—War between two forms of Expression.

Body of Fate (from Phase 4)—Enforced Intellectual Action.

Example : Nietzsche. 25

The man of this phase is out of phase, is all a reaction, is driven from one self-conscious pose to another, is full of hesitation; or he is true to phase, a cup that remembers but its own fullness. His phase is called the " Fore-

runner " because fragmentary and violent. The phases
of action where the man mainly defines himself by his
practical relations are finished, or finishing, and the
phases where he defines himself mainly through an
image of the mind begun or beginning; phases of hatred
for some external fate are giving way to phases of self-
hatred. It is a phase of immense energy because the
Four Faculties are equisdistant. The *oppositions* (*Will*
and *Mask, Creative Mind* and *Body of Fate*) are balanced
by the *discords* and these, being equidistant between
identity and *opposition,* are at their utmost intensity.
The nature is conscious of the most extreme degree of
deception, and is wrought to a frenzy of desire for truth
of self. If Phase 9 had the greatest possible " belief
in its own desire," there is now the greatest possible
belief in all values created by personality. It is therefore
before all else the phase of the hero, of the man who
overcomes himself, and so no longer needs, like Phase
10, the submission of others, or like Phase 11 conviction
of others to prove his victory. Solitude has been born
at last, though solitude invaded, and hard to defend.
Nor is there need any longer of the bare anatomy of
Phase 11; every thought comes with sound and
metaphor, and the sanity of the being is no longer from
its relation to facts, but from its approximation to its
own unity, and from this on we shall meet with men and
women to whom facts are a dangerous narcotic or
intoxicant. Facts are from the *Body of Fate,* and the
Body of Fate is from the phase where instinct, before
the complications of reflection, reached its most
persuasive strength. The man is pursued by a series
of accidents, which, unless he meet them antithetically,
drive him into all sorts of temporary ambitions, opposed
to his nature, unite him perhaps to some small protesting
sect (the family or neighbourhood of Phase 4 intellectu-
alised); and these ambitions he defends by some kind of

superficial intellectual action, the pamphlet, the violent speech, the sword of the swashbuckler. He spends his life in oscillation between the violent assertion of some commonplace pose, and a dogmatism which means nothing, apart from the circumstance that created it. If, however, he meets these accidents by the awakening of his *antithetical* being there is a noble extravagance, an overflowing fountain of personal life. He turns towards the True *Mask* and having by philosophic intellect (*Creative Mind*) delivered it from all that is topical and temporary, announces a philosophy, which is the logical expression of a mind alone with the object of its desire. The True *Mask*, derived from the terrible Phase 26, called the phase of the Hunchback, is the reverse of all that is emotional, being emotionally cold; not mathematical, for intellectual abstraction ceased at Phase 11, but marble pure. In the presence of the *Mask*, the *Creative Mind* has the isolation of a fountain under moonlight; yet one must always distinguish between the emotional *Will*—now approaching the greatest subtlety of sensitiveness, and more and more conscious of its frailty—and that which it would be, the lonely, imperturbable, proud *Mask*, as between the *Will* and its *discord* in the *Creative Mind* where is no shrinking from life. The man follows an *Image*, created or chosen by the *Creative Mind* from what fate offers; would persecute and dominate it; and this *Image* wavers between the concrete and sensuous *Image*. It has become personal; there is now, though not so decisively as later, but one form of chosen beauty, and the sexual *Image* is drawn as with a diamond, and tinted those pale colours sculptors sometimes put upon a statue. Like all before Phase 15 the man is overwhelmed with the thought of his own weakness and knows of no strength but that of *Image* and *Mask*.

XV

PHASE THIRTEEN

Will—Sensuous Ego.

Mask (from Phase 27). *True*—Self-expression. *False* —Self-absorption.

Creative Mind (from Phase 17). *True*—Subjective
5 Truth. *False*—Morbidity.

Body of Fate (from Phase 3)—Enforced Love.

Examples : Baudelaire, Beardsley, Ernest Dowson.

This is said to be the only phase where entire sensuality
is possible, that is to say sensuality without the inter-
10 mixture of any other element. There is now a possible
complete intellectual unity, Unity of Being apprehended
through the images of the mind; and this is opposed by
the fate (Phase 3 where body becomes deliberate and
whole) which offers an equal roundness and wholeness
15 of sensation. The *Will* is now a mirror of emotional
experience, or sensation, according to whether it is
swayed by *Mask* or *Fate*. Though wax to every
impression of emotion, or of sense, it would yet through
its passion for truth (*Creative Mind*) become its opposite
20 and receive from the *Mask* (Phase 27), which is at the
phase of the Saint, a virginal purity of emotion. If it
live objectively, that is to say surrender itself to
sensation, it becomes morbid, it sees every sensation
separate from every other under the light of its perpetual
25 analysis (*Creative Mind* at a phase of dispersal). Phase
13 is a phase of great importance, because the most
intellectually subjective phase, and because only here
can be achieved in perfection that in the *antithetical* life

which corresponds to sanctity in the *primary* : not self-denial but expression for expression's sake. Its influence indeed upon certain writers has caused them in their literary criticism to exalt intellectual sincerity to the place in literature, which is held by sanctity in theology. At this phase the self discovers, within itself, while struggling with the *Body of Fate*, forms of emotional morbidity, which others recognise as their own; as the saint may take upon himself the physical diseases of others. There is almost always a preoccupation with those metaphors and symbols and mythological images through which we define whatever seems most strange or most morbid. Self-hatred now reaches its height, and through this hatred comes the slow liberation of intellectual love. There are moments of triumph and moments of defeat, each in its extreme form, for the subjective intellect knows nothing of moderation. As the *primary Tincture* has weakened the sense of quantity has weakened, for the *antithetical Tincture* is preoccupied with quality.

From now, if not from Phase 12, and until Phases 17 or 18 have passed, happy love is rare for seeing that the man must find a woman whose *Mask* falls within or but just outside his *Body of Fate* and *Mask*, if he is to find strong sexual attraction, the range of choice grows smaller, and all life grows more tragic. As the woman grows harder to find, so does every beloved object. Lacking suitable objects of desire, the relation between man and *Daimon* becomes more clearly a struggle or even a relation of enmity.

E

XVI

Phase Fourteen

Will—The Obsessed Man.

Mask (from Phase 28). *True*—Serenity. *False*—Self-distrust.

Creative Mind (from Phase 16). *True*—Emotional
5 Will. *False*—Terror.

Body of Fate (from Phase 2)—Enforced Love of the World.

Examples : Keats, Giorgione, Many Beautiful Women.

As we approach Phase 15 personal beauty increases
10 and at Phase 14 and Phase 16 the greatest human beauty
becomes possible. The aim of the being should be to
disengage those objects which are images of desire from
the excitement and disorder of the *Body of Fate*, and
under certain circumstances to impress upon these the
15 full character of the *Mask* which, being from Phase 28,
is a folding up, or fading into themselves. It is this
act of the intellect, begun at conception, which has given
the body its beauty. The *Body of Fate*, derived from
the phase of the utmost possible physical energy, but
20 of an energy without aim, like that of a child, works
against this folding up yet offers little more of objects
than their excitement, their essential honey. The images
of desire, disengaged and subject to the *Mask*, are
separate and still (*Creative Mind* from a phase of violent
25 scattering). The images of Phase 18 and even of Phase
12 have in a lesser degree this character. When we
compare these images with those of any subsequent
phase, each seems studied for its own sake; they float

as in serene air, or lie hidden in some valley, and if they move it is to music that returns always to the same note, or in a dance that so returns into itself that they seem immortal.

When the being is out of phase, when it is allured by *primary* curiosity, it is aware of its *primary* feebleness and its intellect becomes but a passion of apprehension, or a shrinking from solitude; it may even become mad; or it may use its conscious feebleness and its consequent terror as a magnet for the sympathy of others, as a means of domination. At Phase 16 will be discovered a desire to accept every possible responsibility; but now responsibility is renounced and this renunciation becomes an instrument of power, dropped burdens being taken up by others. Here are born those women who are most touching in their beauty. Helen was of the phase; and she comes before the mind's eye elaborating a delicate personal discipline, as though she would make her whole life an image of a unified *antithetical* energy. While seeming an image of softness, and of quiet, she draws perpetually upon glass with a diamond. Yet she will not number among her sins anything that does not break that personal discipline, no matter what it may seem according to others' discipline; but if she fail in her own discipline she will not deceive herself, and for all the languor of her movements, and her indifference to the acts of others, her mind is never at peace. She will wander much alone as though she consciously meditated her masterpiece that shall be at the full moon, yet unseen by human eye, and when she returns to her house she will look upon her household with timid eyes, as though she knew that all powers of self-protection had been taken away, and that of her once violent *primary Tincture* nothing remained but a strange irresponsible innocence. Her early life has perhaps been perilous because of that nobility, that excess of *antithe-*

tical energies, which may have so constrained the fading *primary* that, instead of its becoming the expression of those energies, it is but a vague beating of the wings, or their folding up into a melancholy stillness. The greater
5 the peril the nearer has she approached to the final union of *primary* and *antithetical*, where she will desire nothing; and already perhaps, through weakness of desire, she understands nothing yet seems to understand everything; already serves nothing, while alone seeming
10 of service. Is it not because she desires so little and gives so little that men will die and murder in her service? One thinks of THE ETERNAL IDOL of Rodin : that kneeling man with hands clasped behind his back in humble adoration, kissing a young girl a little below
15 the breast, while she gazes down, without comprehending, under her half-closed eyelids. Perhaps could we see her a little later, with flushed cheeks casting her money upon some gaming-table, we would wonder that action and form could so belie each other, not under-
20 standing that the Fool's *Mask* is her chosen motley, nor her terror before death and stillness. One thinks too of the women of Burne-Jones, but not of Botticelli's women, who have too much curiosity, nor Rossetti's women, who have too much passion; and as we see
25 before the mind's eye those pure faces gathered about the Sleep of Arthur, or crowded upon the Golden Stair, we wonder if they too would not have filled us with surprise, or dismay, because of some craze, some passion for mere excitement, or slavery to a drug.
30 In the poets too, who are of the phase, one finds the impression of the *Body of Fate* as intoxication or narcotic. Wordsworth, shuddering at his solitude, has filled his art in all but a few pages with common opinion, common sentiment; while in the poetry of Keats there
35 is an exaggerated sensuousness, though little sexual passion, that compels us to remember the pepper on the

tongue as though that were his symbol. Thought
is disappearing in image; and in Keats, in some
ways a perfect type, intellectual curiosity is at its
weakest; there is scarcely an image, where his poetry is
at its best, whose subjectivity has not been heightened   5
by its use in many great poets, painters, sculptors,
artificers. The being has almost reached the end of
that elaboration of itself which has for its climax an
absorption in time, where space can be but symbols or
images in the mind. There is little observation even   10
in detail of expression, all is reverie, while in Wordsworth
the soul's deepening solitude has reduced mankind, when
seen objectively, to a few slight figures outlined for a
moment amid mountain and lake. The corresponding
genius in painting is that of Monticelli, after 1870, and   15
perhaps that of Condor, though in Condor there are
elements suggesting the preceding phase.

All born at antithetical phases before Phase 15, are
subject to violence, because of the indeterminate energy
of the *Body of Fate;* this violence seems accidental,   20
unforeseen and cruel—and here are women carried off by
robbers and ravished by clowns.

XVII

PHASE FIFTEEN

Will.	No description ex-
Mask (from Phase 1).	cept that this is a
Creative Mind (from Phase 15).	phase of complete 25
Body of Fate (from Phase 1).	beauty.

Body of Fate and *Mask* are now identical; and *Will*
and *Creative Mind* identical; or rather the *Creative Mind*
is dissolved in the *Will* and the *Body of Fate* in the *Mask.*
Thought and Will are indistinguishable, effort and attain-   30

ment are indistinguishable; and this is the consummation of a slow process; nothing is apparent but dreaming
Will and the *Image* that it dreams. Since Phase 12 all
images, and cadences of the mind, have been satisfying
5   to that mind just in so far as they have expressed this
converging of will and thought, effort and attainment.
The words musical, sensuous, are but descriptions of that
converging process. Thought has been pursued, not as
a means but as an end—the poem, the painting, the
10 reverie has been sufficient of itself. It is not possible,
however, to separate in the understanding this running
into one of *Will* and *Creative Mind* from the running
into one of *Mask* and *Body of Fate*. Without *Mask* and
Body of Fate the *Will* would have nothing to desire, the
15 *Creative Mind* nothing to apprehend. Since Phase 12
the *Creative Mind* has been so interfused by the *antithetical Tincture*, that it has more and more confined its
contemplation of actual things to those that resemble
images of the mind desired by the *Will*. The being has
20 selected, moulded and remoulded, narrowed its circle of
living, been more and more the artist, grown more and
more " distinguished " in all preference. Now contemplation and desire, united into one, inhabit a world where
every beloved image has bodily form, and every bodily
25 form is loved. This love knows nothing of desire, for
desire implies effort, and though there is still separation
from the loved object, love accepts the separation as
necessary to its own existence. *Fate* is known for the
boundary that gives our *Destiny* its form, and—as we
30 can desire nothing outside that form—as an expression
of our freedom. Chance and Choice have become interchangeable without losing their identity. As all effort
has ceased, all thought has become image, because no
thought could exist if it were not carried towards its
35 own extinction, amid fear or in contemplation; and
every image is separate from every other, for if image

were linked to image, the soul would awake from its immovable trance. All that the being has experienced as thought is visible to its eyes as a whole, and in this way it perceives, not as they are to others, but according to its own perception, all orders of existence. Its own body possesses the greatest possible beauty, being indeed that body which the soul will permanently inhabit, when all its phases have been repeated according to the number allotted : that which we call the clarified or Celestial Body. Where the being has lived out of phase, seeking to live through *antithetical phases* as though they had been *primary*, there is now terror of solitude, its forced, painful and slow acceptance and a life haunted by terrible dreams. Even for the most perfect, there is a time of pain, a passage through a vision, where evil reveals itself in its final meaning. In this passage Christ, it is said, mourned over the length of time and the unworthiness of man's lot to man, whereas his forerunner mourned and his successor will mourn over the shortness of time and the unworthiness of man to his lot ; but this cannot yet be understood.

XVIII

PHASE SIXTEEN

Will—The Positive Man.

Mask (from Phase 2). *True*—Illusion. *False*—Delusion.

Creative Mind (from Phase 14). *True*—Vehemence. *False*—Opinionated Will.

Body of Fate (from Phase 28)—Enforced Delusion.

Examples : William Blake, Rabelais, Aretino, Paracelsus, some beautiful women.

Phase 16 is in contrast to Phase 14, in spite of their resemblance of extreme subjectivity, in that it has a *Body of Fate* from the phase of the Fool, a phase of absorption, and its *Mask* from what might have been
5 called the phase of the Child, a phase of aimless energy, of physical life for its own sake; while Phase 14 had its *Body of Fate* from the phase of the Child and its *Mask* from that of the Fool. Fate thrusts an aimless excitement upon Phase 14, while Phase 14 finds within itself
10 an *antithetical* dream; whereas Phase 16 has a dream thrust upon it and finds within itself an aimless excitement. This excitement, and the dream, are both illusions, so that the *Will*, which is itself a violent scattering energy, has to use its intellect (*Creative Mind*) to discrim-
15 inate between illusions. They both illusions, because, so small is the *primary* nature, sense of fact is an impossibility. If it use its intellect, which is the most narrow, the most unflinching, even the most cruel in synthesis, possible to man, to disengage the aimless child (*i.e.*, to
20 find *Mask* and *Image* in the child's toy), it finds the soul's most radiant expression and surrounds itself with some fairyland, some mythology of wisdom or laughter; its own scattering, its mere rushing out into the disordered and unbounded, after the still trance of Phase
25 15, has found its antithesis, and therefore self-knowledge and self-mastery. If, however, it subordinate its intellect to the *Body of Fate* all the cruelty and narrowness of that intellect are displayed in service of preposterous purpose after purpose till there is nothing left but the
30 fixed idea and some hysterical hatred. By these purposes, derived from a phase of absorption, the *Body of Fate* drives the *Will* back upon its subjectivity, deforming the *Mask* until the *Will* can only see the object of its desire in these purposes. It does not hate because it
35 dreads, as do the phases of increasing *antithetical* emotion, but hates that which opposes desire. Capable

of nothing but an incapable idealism (for it has no
thought but in myth, or in defence of myth), it must
because it sees one side is all white, see the other side
all black; what but a dragon could dream of thwarting
a St. George. In men of the phase there will commonly   5
be both natures for to be true to phase is a ceaseless
struggle. At one moment they are full of hate—Blake
writes of " Flemish and Venetian demons " and of some
picture of his own destroyed " by some vile spell of
Stoddart's "—and their hate is always close to madness;   10
and at the next they produce the comedy of Aretino
and of Rabelais or the mythology of Blake, and discover
symbolism to express the overflowing and bursting of the
mind. There is always an element of frenzy, and almost
always a delight in certain glowing or shining images of   15
concentrated force; in the smith's forge; in the heart; in
the human form in its most vigorous development; in
the solar disc; in some symbolical representation of the
sexual organs; for the being must brag of its triumph
over its own incoherence.   20

Since Phase 8 the man has more and more judged what
is right in relation to time, a right action, or a right
motive, has been one that he thought possible or desirable to think or do eternally; his soul would " come into
possession of itself for ever in one single moment "; but   25
now he begins once more to judge an action or motive in
relation to space. A right action or motive must soon
be right for any other man in similar circumstance.
Hitherto an action, or motive, has been right precisely
because it is exactly right for one person only though   30
for that person always. After the change, the belief in
the soul's immortality declines though the decline is
slow, and it may only be recovered when Phase 1 is
passed.

Among those who are of this phase may be great   35
satirists, great caricaturists, but they pity the beautiful,

for that is their *Mask*, and hate the ugly, for that is
their *Body of Fate*, and so are unlike those of the *primary*
phases, Rembrandt for instance, who pity the ugly, and
sentimentalise the beautiful, or call it insipid, and turn
5 away or secretly despise and hate it. Here too are
beautiful women, whose bodies have taken upon themselves the image of the True *Mask*, and in these there is
a radiant intensity, something of " The Burning Babe "
of the Elizabethan lyric. They walk like queens, and
10 seem to carry upon their backs a quiver of arrows, but
they are gentle only to those whom they have chosen or
subdued, or to the dogs that follow at their heels.
Boundless in generosity, and in illusion, they will give
themselves to a beggar because he resembles a religious
15 picture and be faithful all their lives, or if they
take another turn and choose a dozen lovers, die convinced that none but the first or last has ever touched
their lips, for they are of those whose " virginity renews
itself like the moon." Out of phase they turn termagant,
20 if their lover take a wrong step in a quadrille where all
the figures are of their own composition and changed
without notice when the fancy takes them. Indeed,
perhaps if the body have great perfection, there is always
something imperfect in the mind, some rejection of, or
25 inadequacy of *Mask* : Venus out of phase chose lame
Vulcan. Here also are several very ugly persons, their
bodies torn and twisted by the violence of the new
primary, but where the body has this ugliness great
beauty of mind is possible. This is indeed the only
30 *antithetical* phase where ugliness is possible, it being
complementary to Phase 2, the only *primary* phase where
beauty is possible.

From this phase on we meet with those who do
violence, instead of those who suffer it; and prepare for
35 those who love some living person, and not an image of
the mind, but as yet this love is hardly more than the

" fixed idea " of faithfulness. As the new love grows the
sense of beauty will fade.

XIX

PHASE SEVENTEEN

Will—The *Daimonic* Man.

Mask (from Phase 3). *True*—Simplification through
intensity. *False*—Dispersal

Creative Mind (from Phase 13). *True*—Creative
imagination through antithetical emotion. *False*—Enforced self-realization.

Body of Fate (from Phase 27)—Loss.

Examples : Dante, Shelley.

He is called the *Daimonic* man because Unity of Being,
and consequent expression of *Daimonic* thought, is now
more easy than at any other phase. As contrasted with
Phase 13 and Phase 14, where mental images were
separated from one another that they might be subject
to knowledge, all now flow, change, flutter, cry out, or
mix into something else; but without, as at Phase 16,
breaking and bruising one another, for Phase 17, the
central phase of its triad, is without frenzy. The *Will*
is falling asunder, but without explosion and noise. The
separated fragments seek images rather than ideas, and
these the intellect, seated in Phase 13, must synthesise
in vain, drawing with its compass point a line that shall
but represent the outline of a bursting pod. The being
has for its supreme aim, as it had at Phase 16 (and as
all subsequent *antithetical* phases shall have) to hide
from itself and others this separation and disorder, and

it conceals them under the emotional *Image* of Phase 3;
as Phase 16 concealed its greater violence under that of
Phase 2. When true to phase the intellect must turn all
its synthetic power to this task. It finds, not the im-
5   passioned myth that Phase 16 found, but a *Mask* of
simplicity that is also intensity. This *Mask* may represent intellectual, or sexual passion; seem some Ahasuerus
or Athanase; be the gaunt Dante of The Divine Comedy;
its corresponding *Image* may be Shelley's Venus Urania,
10   Dante's Beatrice, or even the Great Yellow Rose of the
Paradiso. The *Will*, when true to phase, assumes, in
assuming the *Mask*, an intensity, which is never dramatic
but always lyrical and personal, and this intensity,
though always a deliberate assumption, is to others but
15   the charm of the being; and yet the *Will* is always aware
of the *Body of Fate*, which perpetually destroys this
intensity, thereby leaving the *Will* to its own " dispersal." At Phase 3, not as *Mask* but as Phase, there
should be perfect physical well-being or balance, though
20   not beauty or emotional intensity, but at Phase 27 are
those who turn away from all that Phase 3 represents and
seek all those things it is blind to. The *Body of Fate*
therefore, derived from a phase of renunciation, is
" loss," and works to make impossible " simplification
25   by intensity." The being, through the intellect, selects
some object of desire for a representation of the *Mask*
as *Image*, some woman perhaps, and the *Body of Fate*
snatches away the object.· Then the intellect (*Creative
Mind*), which in the most *antithetical* phases were better
30   described as imagination, must substitute some new
image of desire; and in the degree of its power and of its
attainment of unity, relate that which is lost, that which
has snatched it away, to the new image of desire, that
which threatens the new image to the being's unity. If its
35   unity be already past, or if unity be still to come,
it may for all that be true to phase. It will then use its

intellect merely to isolate *Mask* and *Image*, as chosen forms or as conceptions of the mind. If it be out of phase it will avoid the subjective conflict, acquiesce, hope that the *Body of Fate* may die away; and then the *Mask* will cling to it and the *Image* lure it. It will feel itself betrayed, and persecuted till, entangled in *primary* conflict, it rages against all that destroys *Mask* and *Image*. It will be subject to nightmare, for its *Creative Mind* (deflected from the *Image* and *Mask* to the *Body of Fate*) gives an isolated mythological or abstract form to all that excites its hatred. It may even dream of escaping from ill-luck by possessing the impersonal *Body of Fate* of its opposite phase and of exchanging passion for desk and ledger. Because of the habit of synthesis, and of the growing complexity of the energy, which gives many interests, and the still faint perception of things in their weight and mass, men of this phase are almost always partisans, propagandists and gregarious; yet because of the *Mask* of simplification, which holds up before them the solitary life of hunters and of fishers and " the groves pale passion loves," they hate parties, crowds, propaganda. Shelley out of phase writes pamphlets, and dreams of converting the world, or of turning man of affairs and upsetting governments, and yet returns again and again to these two images of solitude, a young man whose hair has grown white from the burden of his thoughts, an old man in some shell-strewn cave whom it is possible to call, when speaking to the sultan, " as inaccessible as God or thou." On the other hand, how subject he is to nightmare ! He sees the devil leaning against a tree, is attacked by imaginary assassins and in obedience to what he considers a supernatural voice, creates " The Cenci " that he may give to Beatrice Cenci her incredible father. His political enemies are monstrous, meaningless images. And unlike Byron, who is two phases later, he can never see anything that opposes

him as it really is. Dante, who laments his exile as of
all possible things the worst for such as he, and sighs for
his lost solitude, and yet could never keep from politics,
was such a partisan, says a contemporary, that if a
5 child, or a woman, spoke against his party he would pelt
this child or woman with stones. Yet Dante, having
attained, as poet, to Unity of Being, as poet saw all
things set in order, had an intellect that served the *Mask*
alone, and that compelled even those things that opposed
10 it to serve, was content to see both good and evil.
Shelley, upon the other hand, in whom even as poet unity
was but in part attained, found compensation for his
" loss," for the taking away of his children, for his
quarrel with his first wife, for later sexual disappoint-
15 ment, for his exile, for his obloquy—there were but some
three or four persons, he said, who did not consider him
a monster of iniquity—in his hopes for the future of
mankind. He lacked the Vision of Evil, could not conceive of the world as a continual conflict, so, though
20 great poet he certainly was, he was not of the greatest
kind. Dante suffering injustice and the loss of Beatrice,
found divine justice and the heavenly Beatrice, but the
justice of Prometheus Unbound is a vague propagandist
emotion and the women that await its coming are but
25 clouds. This is in part because the age in which Shelley
lived was in itself so broken that true Unity of Being
was almost impossible, but partly because being out of
phase so far as his practical reason was concerned, he
was subject to an *automatonism* which he mistook for
30 poetical invention, especially in his longer poems. *Anti-*
thetical men (Phase 15 once passed) use this *automaton-*
ism to evade hatred, or rather to hide it from their own
eyes; perhaps all at some time or other, in moments of
fatigue, give themselves up to fantastic, constructed
35 images, or to an almost mechanical laughter.
Landor has been examined in " *Per Amica Silentia*

Lunæ." The most violent of men, he uses his intellect
to disengage a visionary image of perfect sanity (*Mask
at Phase 8*) seen always in the most serene and classic
art imaginable. He had perhaps as much Unity of Being
as his age permitted, and possessed, though not in any full   5
measure, the Vision of Evil.

XX

PHASE EIGHTEEN

Will—The Emotional Man.

Mask (from Phase 4).   *True*—Intensity through
emotion. *False*—Curiosity.

Creative Mind (from Phase 12).   *True*—Emotional   10
Philosophy. *False*—Enforced lure.

Body of Fate (from Phase 26)—Enforced disillusionment.

Examples : Goethe, Matthew Arnold.

The *antithetical tincture* closes during this phase, the   15
being is losing direct knowledge of its old antithetical
life. The conflict between that portion of the life of
feeling, which appertains to his unity, with that portion
he has in common with others, coming to an end, has
begun to destroy that knowledge. " A Lover's Noc-   20
turne " or " An Ode to the West Wind " are probably
no more possible, certainly no more characteristic. He
can hardly, if action and the intellect that concerns
action, are taken from him, recreate his dream life; and
when he says " who am I," he finds it difficult to   25
examine his thoughts in relation to one another, his

emotions in relation to one another, but begins to find it easy to examine them in relation to action. He can examine those actions themselves with a new clearness. Now for the first time since Phase 12, Goethe's saying is

5   almost true : " Man knows himself by action only, by thought never." Meanwhile the *antithetical Tincture* begins to attain, without previous struggle or self-analysis, its active form which is love—love being the union of emotion and instinct—or when out of phase, sentiment-

10   ality. The *Will* seeks by some form of emotional philosophy to free a form of emotional beauty (*Mask*) from a " disillusionment," differing from the " delusions " of Phase 16, which are continuous, in that it permits intermittent awakening. The *Will*, with its closing *anti-*

15   *thetical*, is turning away from the life of images to that of ideas, it is vacillating and curious, and it seeks in this *Mask* from a *phase* where all the functions can be perfect, what becomes, when considered *antithetically*, a wisdom of the emotions. At its next phase it will have fallen

20   asunder; already it can only preserve its unity by a deliberate balancing of experiences (*Creative Mind* at Phase 12, *Body of Fate* at Phase 26), and so it must desire that phase (though that transformed into the emotional life), where wisdom seems a physical accident. Its object

25   of desire is no longer a single image of passion, for it must relate all to social life; the man seeks to become not a sage, but a wise king, no longer Ahasuerus, and seeks a woman who looks the wise mother of children. Perhaps now, and for the first time, the love of a living woman

30   (" disillusionment " once accepted), as apart from beauty or function, is an admitted aim, though not yet wholly achieved. The *Body of Fate* is from the phase where the " wisdom of knowledge " has compelled *Mask* and *Image* to become not objects of desire but objects of knowledge.

35   Goethe did not, as Beddoes said, marry his cook, but he certainly did not marry the woman he had desired, and his

grief at her death showed that, unlike Phase 16 or Phase 17, which forget their broken toys, he could love what disillusionment gave. When he seeks to live objectively, he will substitute curiosity for emotional wisdom, he will invent objects of desire artificially, he will say perhaps, though this was said by a man who was probably still later in phase, " I was never in love with a serpent-charmer before "; the False *Mask* will press upon him, pursue him and, refusing conflict, he will fly from the True *Mask* at each artificial choice. The nightingale will refuse the thorn and so remain among images instead of passing to ideas. He is still disillusioned but he can no longer through philosophy substitute for the desire that life has taken away love for what life has brought. The *Will* is near the place marked *Head* upon the great chart, which enables it to choose its *Mask* even when true to phase almost coldly and always deliberately, whereas the *Creative Mind* is derived from the phase which is called " the wisdom of heart," and is therefore more impassioned and less subtle and delicate than if Phase 16 or Phase 17 were the place of the *Will*, though not yet argumentative or heated. The *Will* at *Head* uses the heart with perfect mastery and, because of the growing *primary*, begins to be aware of an audience, though as yet it will not dramatise the *Mask* deliberately for the sake of effect as will Phase 19.

XX

Phase Nineteen

Will—The Assertive Man.

Mask (from Phase 5). *True*—Conviction. *False*—Domination.

Creative Mind (from Phase 11). *True*—Emotional Intellect. *False*—The Unfaithful.

Body of Fate (from Phase 25)—Enforced failure of Action.

Examples : Gabriele d'Annunzio (perhaps), Oscar Wilde, Byron, a certain actress.

This Phase is the beginning of the artificial, the abstract, the fragmentary, and the dramatic. Unity of Being is no longer possible, for the being is compelled to live in a fragment of itself and to dramatise that fragment. The *primary Tincture* is closing, direct knowledge of self in relation to action is ceasing to be possible. The being only completely knows that portion of itself which judges fact for the sake of actions. When the man lives according to phase, he is now governed by conviction, instead of by a ruling mood, and is effective only in so far as he can find this conviction. His aim is to use an intellect, which turns easily to declamation, emotional emphasis, so that it saves conviction in a life where effort, just in so far as its object is passionately desired, comes to nothing. He desires to be strong and stable, but as Unity of Being and self-knowledge are both gone, and it is too soon to grasp at another unity through *primary* mind, he passes from emphasis to emphasis. The strength from conviction, being derived from a *Mask* of the first quarter, is not founded upon social duty, though that may seem so to others, but is temperamentally formed to fit some crisis of personal life. His thought is immensely effective and dramatic, arising always from some immediate situation, a situation found or created by himself, and may have great permanent value as the expression of an exciting personality. This thought is always an open attack; or a sudden emphasis, an extravagance, or an impassioned declamation of some general idea, which is a more veiled attack. The *Creative Mind* being derived from Phase 11, he is doomed to attempt the destruction of all that breaks or encumbers personality, but this personality is conceived of as a fragmentary, momentary intensity. The mastery of images, threatened or lost at Phase 18, may however be completely recovered, but there is less symbol, more fact. Vitality from dreams has died out, and a vitality from fact has begun which has for its ultimate aim the mastery of the real world. The watercourse after an abrupt fall continues upon a lower level; ice turns to water, or water to vapour : there is a new chemical phase.

When lived out of phase there is a hatred or contempt of others, and instead of seeking conviction for its own sake, the man takes up opinions that he may impose himself upon others. He is tyrannical and capricious, and his intellect is called " The Unfaithful," because, being used for victory alone, it will change its ground in a moment and delight in some new emphasis, not caring whether old or new have consistency. The *Mask* is derived from that phase where perversity begins, where artifice begins, and has its discord from Phase 25, the last phase where the artificial is possible; the *Body of Fate* is therefore enforced failure of action, and many at this phase desire action above all things as a means of expression. Whether the man be in or out of phase, there is the desire to escape from Unity of Being or any approximation towards it, for Unity can be but a simulacrum now. And in so far as the soul keeps its memory of that potential Unity there is conscious *anti-*

5 *thetical* weakness. He must now dramatise the *Mask* through the *Will* and dreads the *Image*, deep within, of the old *antithetical Tincture* at its strongest, and yet this *Image* may seem infinitely desirable if he could but find the desire. When so torn into two, escape when it comes

10 may be so violent that it brings him under the False *Mask* and the False *Creative Mind*. A certain actress is typical, for she surrounds herself with drawings by Burne-Jones in his latest period, and reverse them as they were holy pictures, while her manners are boisterous, dominating

15 and egotistical. They are faces of silent women, and she is never silent for a moment; yet these faces are not, as I once thought, the True *Mask* but a part of that incoherence the True *Mask* must conceal. Were she to surrender to their influence she would become insincere in

20 her art and exploit an emotion that is no longer hers. I find in Wilde, too, something pretty, feminine, and insincere, derived from his admiration for writers of the 17th and earlier phases, and much that is violent, arbitrary and insolent, derived from his desire to escape.

25 The *antithetical Mask* comes to men of Phase 17 and Phase 18 as a form of strength, and when they are tempted to dramatise it, the dramatisation is fitful, and brings no conviction of strength, for they dislike emphasis; but now the weakness of the *antithetical* has

30 begun, for though still the stronger it cannot ignore the growing *primary*. It is no longer an absolute monarch, and it permits power to pass to statesman or demagogue whom however it will constantly change.

Here one finds men and women who love those who

35 rob them or beat them, as though the soul were intoxicated by its discovery of human nature, or found even a

secret delight in the shattering of the image of its desire.
It is as though it cried, " I would be possessed by " or
" I would possess that which is Human. What do I
care if it is good or bad? " There is no " disillusionment," for they have found that which they have sought,   5
but that which they have sought and found is a fragment.

XXI

PHASE TWENTY

Will—The Concrete Man.

Mask (from Phase 6). *True*—Fatalism. *False*—
Superstition.

Creative Mind (from Phase 10). *True*—Dramatisation   10
of Mask. *False*—Self-desecration.

Body of Fate (from Phase 24)—Enforced Success of
Action.

Examples : Shakespeare, Balzac, Napoleon.

Like the phase before it, and those that follow it im-   15
mediately, a phase of the breaking up and subdivision
of the being. The energy is always seeking those facts
which being separable can be seen more clearly, or expressed more clearly, but when there is truth to phase
there is a similitude of the old unity, or rather a new   20
unity, which is not a Unity of Being but a unity of the
creative act. He no longer seeks to unify what is broken
through conviction, by imposing those very convictions
upon himself and others, but by projecting a dramatisation or many dramatisations. He can create, just in that   25
degree in which he can see these dramatisations as

separate from himself, and yet as an epitome of his whole nature. His *Mask* is derived from Phase 6, where man first becomes a generalised form, according to the *primary Tincture*, as in the poetry of Walt Whitman,

5 but this *Mask* he must by dramatisation rescue from a *Body of Fate* derived from Phase 24, where moral domination dies out before that of the exterior world conceived as a whole. The *Body of Fate* is called " enforced success," a success that rolls out and smooths away, that

10 dissolves through creation, that seems to delight in all outward flowing, that drenches all with grease and oil; that turns dramatisation into desecration : " I have made myself a motley to the view." Owing to the need of seeing the dramatic image, or images, as individuals, that

15 is to say as set amongst concrete or fixed surroundings, he seeks some field of action, some mirror not of his own creation. Unlike Phase 19 he fails in situations wholly created by himself, or in works of art where character or story has gained nothing from history. His phase is

20 called " The Concrete Man," because the isolation of parts that began at Phase 19, is overcome at the second phase of the triad; subordination of parts is achieved by the discovery of concrete relations. His abstraction too, affected by these relations, may be no more than an

25 emotional interest in such generalisations as " God," " man," a Napoleon may but point to the starry heavens and say that they prove the existence of God. There is a delight in concrete images that, unlike the impassioned images of Phase 17 and Phase 18, or the declamatory

30 images of Phase 19, reveal through complex suffering the general destiny of man. He must, however, to express this suffering, personify rather than characterise, create not observe that multitude, which is but his *Mask* as in a multiplying mirror, for the *primary* is not yet strong

35 enough to substitute for the lost Unity of Being that of the external world perceived as fact. In a man of action

this multiplicity gives the greatest possible richness or resource where he is not thwarted by his horoscope, great ductability, a gift for adopting any rôle that stirs imagination, a philosophy of impulse and audacity; but in the man of action a part of the nature must be crushed, one main dramatisation or group of images preferred to all others.

Napoleon sees himself as Alexander moving to the conquest of the East, *Mask* and *Image* must take an historical and not a mythological or dream form, a form found but not created; he is crowned in the dress of a Roman Emperor. Shakespeare, the other supreme figure of the phase, was—if we may judge by the few biographical facts, and by such adjectives as " sweet " and " gentle " applied to him by his contemporaries— a man whose actual personality seemed faint and passionless. Unlike Ben Jonson he fought no duels; he kept out of quarrels in a quarrelsome age; not even complaining when somebody pirated his sonnets; he dominated no Mermaid Tavern, but—through *Mask* and *Image*, reflected in a multiplying mirror—he created the most passionate art that exists. He was the greatest of modern poets, partly because entirely true to phase, creating always from *Mask* and *Creative Mind*, never from situation alone, never from *Body of Fate* alone; and if we knew all we would find that success came to him, as to others of this phase, as something hostile and unforeseen; something that sought to impose an intuition of fate (the condition of Phase 6) as from without and therefore as a form of superstition. Both Shakespeare and Balzac used the False *Mask* imaginatively, explored it to impose the True, and what *Lake Harris, the half-charlatan American visionary, said of

* I quote from a book circulated privately among his followers. I saw it years ago but seem to remember it, as now vague, now vulgar, and now magnificent in style.

Shakespeare might be said of both : " Often the hair of his head stood up and all life became the echoing chambers of the tomb."

At Phase 19 we create through the externalised *Mask* an imaginary world, in whose real existence we believe, while remaining separate from it; at Phase 20 we enter that world and become a portion of it; we study it, we amass historical evidence, and, that we may dominate it the more, drive out myth and symbol, and compel it to seem the real world where our lives are lived.

A phase of ambition; in Napoleon the dramatist's own ambition; in Shakespeare that of the persons of his art; and this ambition is not that of the solitary law-giver, that of Phase 10 (where the *Creative Mind* is placed) which rejects, resists and narrows, but a creative energy.

XXII

PHASE TWENTY-ONE

Will. The acquisitive Man.

Mask (from Phase 7). *True*—Self-analysis. *False*—Self-adaption.

Creative Mind (from Phase 9). *True*—Domination of the Intellect. *False*—Distortion.

Body of Fate (from Phase 23)—Triumph of Achievement.

Examples : Lamarck, Mr Bernard Shaw, Mr Wells, Mr George Moore.

The *antithetical Tincture* has a predominance so slight that the *Creative Mind* and *Body of Fate* almost equal it in control of desire. The *Will* can scarcely conceive of a *Mask* separate from or predominant over *Creative Mind* and *Body of Fate*, yet because it can do so there is personality not character. It is better, however, to use a different word, and therefore Phases 21, 22 and 23 are described as, like the phases opposite, phases of individuality where the *Will* is studied less in relation to the *Mask* than in relation to itself. At Phase 23 the new relation to the *Mask*, as something to escape from, will have grown clear.

The *antithetical Tincture* is noble, and, judged by the standards of the *primary*, evil, whereas the *primary* is good and banal; and this phase, the last before the *antithetical* surrenders its control, would be almost wholly good did it not hate its own banality. Personality has almost the rigidity, almost the permanence of character, but it is not character, for it is still always assumed. When we contemplate Napoleon we can see ourselves, perhaps even think of ourselves as Napoleons, but a man of Phase 21 has a personality that seems a creation of his circumstance and his faults, a manner peculiar to himself and impossible to others. We say at once, " How individual he is." In theory whatever one has chosen must be within the choice of others, at some moment or for some purpose, but we find in practice that nobody of this phase has personal imitators, or has given his name to a form of manners. The *Will* has driven intellectual complexity into its final entanglement, an entanglement created by the continual adaption to new circumstances of a logical sequence; and the aim of the individual, when true to phase, is to realise, by his own complete domination over all circumstance, a self-analysing, self-conscious simplicity. Phase 7 shuddered at its own simplicity, whereas he must shudder at his own complexity. Out of phase, instead of seeking this simplicity through his own dominating constructive will, he will parade an imaginary naiveté, even blunder in his work, encourage in himself stupidities of spite or sentiment, or commit calculated indiscretions simulating impulse. He is under the False *Mask* (emotional self-adaption) and the False *Creative Mind* (distortion : the furious Phase 9 acted upon by " enforced sensuality "). He sees the *antithetical* as evil, and desires the evil, for he is subject to a sort of possession by the devil, which is in reality but a theatrical scene. Precisely because his adaptability can be turned in any direction, when lived according to the *primary*, he is driven into all that is freakish or grotesque, mind-created passions, simulated emotions; he adopts all that can suggest the burning heart he longs for in vain; he turns braggart or buffoon. Like somebody in Dostoieffsky's " Idiot," he will invite others to tell their worst deeds that he may himself confess that he stole a half-crown and left a servant-girl to bear the blame. When all turn upon him he will be full of wonder for he knows that the confession is not true, or if true that the deed itself was but a trick, or a pose, and that all the time he is full of a goodness that fills him with shame. Whether he live according to phase and regard life without emotion, or live out of phase, and simulate emotion, his *Body of Fate* drags him away from intellectual unity; but in so far as he lives out of phase he weakens conflict, refuses to resist, floats upon the stream. In phase he strengthens conflict to the utmost by refusing all activity that is not *antithetical* : he becomes intellectually dominating, intellectually unique. He apprehends the simplicity of his opposite phase as some vast systematisation, in which the will imposes itself upon the multiplicity of living images, or events, upon all in Shakespeare, in Napoleon even, that delighted in its independent life; for he is a tyrant and must kill his adversary. If he is a novelist, his characters must go his road, and not theirs, and perpetually demon-

strate his thesis; he will love construction better than
the flow of life, and as a dramatist he will create without
passion, and without liking, character and situation;
and yet he is a master of surprise, for one can never be
sure where even a charge of shot will fall. Style exists 5
now but as a sign of work well done, a certain energy
and precision of movement; in the artistic sense it is
no longer possible, for the tension of the will is too great
to allow of suggestion. Writers of the phase are great
public men and they exist after death as historical monu- 10
ments, for they are without meaning apart from time
and circumstance.

XXIII

Phase Twenty-two

Will—Balance between Ambition and Contemplation.

Mask (from Phase 8). *True*—Self-immolation. *False*
—Self-assurance. 15

Creative Mind (from Phase 8). *True*—Amalgamation.
False—Despair.

Body of Fate (from Phase 22)—The Breaking of
Strength.

Examples : Flaubert, Herbert Spenser, Swedenborg, 20
Dostoieffsky.

The aim of the being, until the point of balance has
been reached, will be that of Phase 21 except that
synthesis will be more complete, and the sense of identity
between the individual and his thought, between his 25
desire and his synthesis will be closer; but the character

of the phase is precisely that here balance is reached and passed, though it is stated that the individual may have to return to this phase more than once, though not more than four times, before it is passed. Once balance has been reached, the aim must be to use the *Body of Fate* to deliver the *Creative Mind* from the *Mask*, and not to use the *Creative Mind* to deliver the *Mask* from the *Body of Fate*. The being does this by so using the intellect upon the facts of the world that the last vestige of personality disappears. The *Will*, engaged in its last struggle with external fact (*Body of Fate*), must submit, until it sees itself as inseparable from nature perceived as fact, and it must see itself as merged into that nature through the *Mask*, either as a conqueror lost in what he conquers, or dying at the moment of conquest, or as renouncing conquest, whether it come by might of logic, or might of drama, or might of hand. The *Will* since Phase 8 has more and more seen itself as a *Mask*, as a form of personal power, but now it must see that power broken. From Phase 12 to Phase 18 it was or should have been a power wielded by the whole nature; but since Phase 19 it has been wielded by a fragment only, as something more and more professional, temperamental or technical. It has become abstract, and the more it has sought the whole of natural fact, the more abstract it has become. One thinks of some spilt liquid which grows thinner the wider it spreads till at last it is but a film. That which at Phase 21 was a longing for self-conscious simplicity, as an escape from logical complication and subdivision, is now (through the *Mask* from Phase 8) a desire for the death of the intellect. At Phase 21 it still sought to change the world, could still be a Shaw, a Wells, but now it will seek to change nothing, it needs nothing but what it may call " reality," " truth," " God's Will " : confused and weary, through trying to grasp too much, the hand must loosen.

Here takes place an interchange between portions of the mind which corresponds, though to represent it in the diagram of the Wheel would complicate the figure, to the interchange between the old and new *primary*, the old and new *antithetical* at Phase 1 and Phase 15. The mind that has shown a predominately emotional character, called that of the *Victim*, through the *antithetical* phases, now shows a predominately intellectual character, called that of the *Sage* (though until Phase 1 has been passed it can but use intellect when true to phase to eliminate intellect); whereas the mind that has been predominately that of the *Sage* puts on *Victimage*.[1] An element in the nature is exhausted at the point of balance, and the opposite element controls the mind. One thinks of the gusts of sentimentality that overtake violent men, the gusts of cruelty that overtake the sentimental. At Phase 8 there is a similar interchange, but it does not display its significance at that blinded and throttled phase. A man of Phase 22 will commonly not only systematise, to the exhaustion of his will, but discover this exhaustion of will in all that he studies. If Lamarck, as is probable, was of Phase 21, Darwin was probably a man of Phase 22, for his theory of development by the survival of fortunate accidental varieties seems to express this exhaustion. The man himself is never weak, never vague or fluctuating in his thought, for if he brings all to silence, it is a silence that results from tension, and till the moment of balance, nothing interests him that is not wrought up to the greatest effort of which it is capable. Flaubert is the supreme literary genius of the phase, and his " Temptation of St. Anthony " and his " Bouvard and Pécuchet " are the sacred books of the phase, one describing its effect upon a mind where all is

(1) These terms will be explained later. They are touched on here to draw attention to a change in Swedenborg, Flaubert and Dostoieffsky at the point of balance.

concrete and sensuous, the other upon the more logical, matter-of-fact, curious, modern mind. In both the mind exhausts all knowledge within its reach and sinks exhausted ·to a conscious futility. But the matter is not
5 more of the phase than is the method. One never doubts for a moment that Flaubert was of the phase; all must be impersonal; he must neither like nor dislike character or event; he is " the mirror dawdling down a road," of Stendhal, with a clear brightness ·that is not Stendhal's;
10 and when we make his mind our own, we seem to have renounced our own ambition under the influence of some strange, far-reaching, impartial gaze.

We feel too that this man who systematised by but linking one emotional association to another has become
15 strangely hard, cold and invulnerable, that this mirror is not brittle but of unbreakable steel. " Systematised " is the only word that comes to mind, but it implies too much deliberation, for association has ranged itself by association as little bits of paper and little chips of wood
20 cling to one another upon the water in a bowl. In Dostoieffsky the " amalgamation " is less intellectual, less orderly, he, one feels, has reached the point of balance through life, and not through the process of his art; and his whole will, and not merely his intellectual will,
25 has been shaken, and his characters, in whom is reflected this broken will, are aware, unlike those of " Bouvard and Pécuchet," and those of the " Temptation " even, of some ungraspable whole ·to which they have given the name of God. For a moment that fragment, that rela-
30 tion, which is our very being, is broken; they are at Udan Adan " wailing upon the edge of nonentity, wailing for Jerusalem, with weak voices almost inarticulate "; and yet full submission has not come. Swedenborg passed through his balance after fifty, and a mind
35 incredibly dry and arid, hard and tangible, like the minerals he assayed for the Swedish government, studies

a new branch of science : the economics and the natural
history of Heaven, and notes that there nothing but
emotion, nothing but the ruling love exists. The desire
to dominate has so completely vanished, " amalgamation " has pushed its way so far into the subconscious,   5
into that which is dark, that we call it a vision. Had he
been out of phase, had he attempted to arrange his life
according to the personal *Mask*, he would have been
pedantic and arrogant, a Bouvard, or a Pécuchet, passing
from absurdity to absurdity, hopeless and insatiable. In   10
the world of action such absurdity may become terrible,
for men will die and murder for an abstract synthesis,
and the more abstract it is the further it carries them
from compunction and compromise; and as obstacles to
that synthesis increase, the violence of their will increases. 15
It is a phase as tragic as its opposite, and more terrible,
for the man of this phase may, before the point of balance has been reached, become a destroyer and
persecutor, a figure of tumult and of violence; or as
is more probable—for the violence of such a man   20
must be checked by moments of resignation or despair,
premonitions of balance—his system will become an instrument of destruction and of persecution in the hands
of others.

The seeking of Unity of Fact by a single faculty,   25
instead of Unity of Being by the use of all, has separated
a man from his genius. This is symbolised in the Wheel
by the gradual separation (as we recede from Phase 15)
of *Will* and *Creative Mind*, *Mask* and *Body of Fate*.
During the supernatural incarnation of Phase 15, we were   30
compelled to assume an absolute identity of the *Will*, or
self, with its creative power, of beauty with body; but
for some time self and creative power, though separating,
have been neighbours and kin. A Landor, or a Morris,
however violent, however much of a child he seem, is   35
always a remarkable man; in Phases 19, 20 and 21 genius

grows professional, something taken up when work is taken up, it begins to be possible to record the stupidities of men of genius in a scrapbook; Bouvard and Pécuchet have that refuge for their old age. Someone has said that
5 Balzac at noonday was a very ignorant man, but at midnight over a cup of coffee knew everything in the world. In the man of action, in a Napoleon, let us say, the stupidities lie hidden, for action is a form of abstraction that crushes everything it cannot express. At Phase
10 22 stupidity is obvious, one finds it in the correspondence of Karl Marx, in his banal abusiveness, while to Goncourt, Flaubert, as man, seemed full of unconsidered thought. Flaubert, says Anatole France, was not intelligent. Dostoieffsky, to those who first acclaimed his
15 genius, seemed when he laid down his pen an hysterical fool. One remembers Herbert Spencer dabbing the grapes upon a lodging-house carpet with an inky cork that he might tint them to his favourite colour, " impure purple." On the other hand, as the *Will* moves further
20 from the *Creative Mind*, it approaches the *Body of Fate*, and with this comes an increasing delight in impersonal energy and in inanimate objects, and as the *Mask* separates from the *Body of Fate* and approaches the *Creative Mind* we delight more and more in all that is
25 artificial, all that is deliberately invented. Symbols may become hateful to us, the ugly and the arbitrary delightful that we may the more quickly kill all memory of Unity of Being. We identify ourselves in our surroundings—in our surroundings perceived as fact—while at the
30 same time the intellect so slips from our grasp as it were, that we contemplate its energies as something we can no longer control, and give to each of those energies an appropriate name as though it were an animate being. Now that *Will* and *Body of Fate* are one, *Creative Mind* and
35 *Mask* one also, we are no longer four but two, and life, the balance reached, becomes an act of contemplation.

There is no longer a desired object, as distinct from
thought itself, no longer a *Will*, as distinct from the process of nature seen as fact; and so thought itself, seeing
that it can neither begin nor end, is stationary. Intellect
knows itself as its own object of desire; and the *Will* 5
knows itself to be the world; there is neither change nor
desire of change. For the moment the desire for a form
has ceased and an absolute realism becomes possible.

XXIV

PHASE TWENTY-THREE

Will—The Receptive Man.

Mask (from Phase 9). *True*—Wisdom. *False*—Self- 10
pity.

Creative Mind (from Phase 7). *True*—Creation
through Pity. *False*—Self-driven desire.

Body of Fate (from Phase 21)—Success.

Examples : Rembrandt, Synge. 15

When out of phase, for reasons that will appear later,
he is tyrannical, gloomy and self-absorbed. In phase his
energy has a character analogous to the longing of
Phase 16 to escape from complete subjectivity : it escapes
in a condition of explosive joy from systematisation and 20
abstraction. The clock has run down and must be wound
up again. The *primary Tincture* is now greater than the
antithetical, and the man must free the intellect from
all motives founded upon personal desire, by the help of
the external world, now for the first time studied and 25
mastered for its own sake. He must kill all thought

G

that would systematise the world, by doing a thing, not
because he wants to, or because he should, but because
he can; that is to say he sees all things from the point
of view of his own technique, touches and tastes and
5   investigates technically. He is, however, because of
the nature of his energy, violent, anarchic, like all who
are of the first phase of a quarter. Because he is without
systematisation he is without a master, and only by his
technical mastery can he escape from the sense of being
10   thwarted and opposed by other men; and his technical
mastery must exist, not for its own sake, though
for its own sake it has been done, but for that which
it reveals, for its laying bare—to hand and eye,
as distinguished from thought and emotion—general
15   humanity. Yet this laying bare is a perpetual surprise,
is an unforeseen reward of skill. And unlike *antithetical*
man he must use his *Body of Fate* (now always his
" success ") to liberate his intellect from personality, and
only when he has done this, only when he escapes the
20   voluntary *Mask*, does he find his true intellect, is he found
by his True *Mask*. The True *Mask* is from the frenzied
Phase 9 where personal life is made visible for the first
time, but from that phase mastered by its *Body of Fate*,
" enforced sensuality," derived from Phase 7 where the
25   instinctive flood is almost above the lips. It is called
" wisdom " and this wisdom (personality reflected in a
primary mirror), is general humanity experienced as a
form of involuntary emotion, and involuntary delight
in the " minute particulars " of life. The man wipes his
30   breath from the window pane, and laughs in his delight
at all the varied scene. His *Creative Mind* being at Phase
7—where instinctive life, all but reaching utmost complexity, suffers an external abstract synthesis—his *Body
of Fate* compelling him to intellectual life being at Phase
35   21; his *Will* phase that of the revolt from every intellectual summary, from all intellectual abstraction, this

delight is not mere delight, he would construct a whole, but that whole must seem all event, all picture. That whole must not be instinctive, bodily, natural, however, though it may seem so, for in reality he cares only for what is human, individual and moral. To others he may seem to care for the immoral and inhuman only, for he will be hostile, or indifferent to moral as to intellectual summaries; if he is Rembrandt he discovers his Christ through anatomical curiosity, or through curiosity as to light and shade, and if he is Synge he takes a malicious pleasure in the contrast between his hero, whom he discovers through his instinct for comedy, and any hero in men's minds. Indeed, whether he be Synge or Rembrandt, he is ready to sacrifice every convention, perhaps all that men have agreed to reverence, for a startling theme, or a model one delights in painting; and yet all the while, because of the nature of his *Mask*, there is another summary working through bone and nerve. He is never the mere technician that he seems, though when you ask his meaning he will have nothing to say, or will say something irrelevant or childish. Artists and writers of Phase 21 and Phase 22 have eliminated all that is personal from their style, seeking cold metal and pure water, but he will delight in colour and idiosyncrasy, though these he must find rather than create. Synge must find rhythm and syntax in the Aran Islands, Rembrandt delight in all accidents of the visible world; yet neither, no matter what his delight in reality, shows it without exaggeration, for both delight in all that is wilful, in all that flouts intellectual coherence, and conceive of the world as if it were an overflowing cauldron. Both will work in toil and in pain, finding what they do not seek, for, after Phase 22, desire creates no longer, will has taken its place; but that which they reveal is joyous. Whereas Shakespeare showed through a style, full of joy, a melancholy vision sought from afar;

a style at play, a mind that served; Synge must fill many notebooks, clap his ear to that hole in the ceiling; and what patience Rembrandt must have spent in the painting of a lace collar though to find his subject he
5 had but to open his eyes. When out of phase, when the man seeks to choose his *Mask*, the man is gloomy with the gloom of others, and tyrannical with the tyranny of others, because he cannot create. Phase 9 was dominated by desire, was described as having the greatest belief
10 in its own desire possible to man, yet from it **Phase 23** receives not desire but pity, and not belief but wisdom. Pity needs wisdom as desire needs belief, for pity is *primary*, whereas desire is *antithetical*. When pity is separated from wisdom we have the False *Mask*, a pity
15 like that of a drunken man, self-pity, whether offered in seeming to another or only to oneself : pity corrupted by desire. Who does not feel the pity in Rembrandt, in Synge, and know that it is inseparable from wisdom. In the works of Synge there is much self-pity, ennobled
20 to a pity for all that lived; and once an actress, playing his Deirdre, put all into a gesture. Concubar, who had murdered Deirdre's husband and her friends, was in altercation with Fergus who had demanded vengeance; " Move a little further off," she cried, " with the
25 babbling of fools "; and a moment later, moving like a somnambulist, she touched Concubar upon the arm, a gesture full of gentleness and compassion, as though she had said, " You also live." In Synge's early unpublished work, written before he found the dialects
30 of Aran and of Wicklow, there is brooding melancholy and morbid self-pity. He had to undergo an æsthetic transformation, analogous to religious conversion, before he became the audacious joyous ironical man we know. The emotional life in so far as it was deliberate had to
35 be transferred from Phase 9 to Phase 23, from a self-regarding melancholy condition of soul to its direct

opposite. This transformation must have seemed to him
a discovery of his true self, of his true moral being;
whereas Shelley's came at the moment when he first
created a passionate image which made him forgetful
of himself. It came perhaps when he had passed from 5
the litigious rhetoric of Queen Mab to the lonely reveries
of Alastor. *Primary* art values above all things sincerity
to the self or *Will* but to the self active, translating and
perceiving.

The quarter of intellect was a quarter of dispersal 10
and generalisation, a play of shuttlecock with the first
quarter of animal burgeoning, but the fourth quarter
is a quarter of withdrawal and concentration, in which
active moral man should receive into himself, and transform into *primary* sympathy the emotional self-realisation 15
of the second quarter. If he does not so receive and
transform he sinks into stupidity and stagnation,
perceives nothing but his own interests, or becomes a
tool in the hands of others; and at Phase 23, because
there must be delight in the unforeseen, he may be brutal 20
and outrageous. He does not, however, hate, like a man
of the third quarter, being but ignorant of or indifferent
to the feelings of others. Rembrandt pitied ugliness,
for what we call ugliness was to him an escape from all
that is summarised and known, but had he painted a 25
beautiful face, as *antithetical* man understands beauty,
it would have remained a convention, he would have
seen it through a mirage of boredom.

When one compares the work of Rembrandt with that
of David, whose phase was Phase 21; or the work of 30
Synge with that of Mr Wells; one sees that in the one the
antithetical Tincture is breaking up and dissolving, while
in the other it is tightening as for a last resistance,
concentrating, levelling, transforming, tabulating. Rembrandt and Synge but look on and clap their hands. 35
There is indeed as much selection among the events

in one case as in the other, but at Phase 23 events seem startling because they elude intellect.

All phases after Phase 15 and before Phase 22 unweave that which is woven by the equivalent phases before
5 Phase 15 and after Phase 8. The man of Phase 23 has in the *Mask*, at Phase 9, a contrary that seems his very self until he use the discord of that contrary, his *Body of Fate* at Phase 21, to drive away the *Mask* and free the intellect and rid pity of desire and turn belief into wisdom. The
10 *Creative Mind*, a discord to the *Will*, is from a phase of instinctive dispersal, and must turn the violent objectivity of the self or *Will* into a delight in all that breathes and moves : " The gay fishes on the wave when the moon sucks up the dew."

XXV

Phase Twenty-four

15 *Will*—The End of Ambition.

Mask (from Phase 10). *True*—Self-reliance. *False*—Isolation.

Creative Mind (from Phase 6). *True*—Construction through humanitarianism. *False*—Authority.

20 *Body of Fate* (from Phase 20)—Objective Action.

Examples : Queen Victoria, Galsworthy, a certain friend.

As the *Mask* now seems the natural self, which he must escape; the man labours to turn all within him
25 that is from Phase 10, into some quality of Phase 24. At

Phase 23, when in what seemed the natural self, the man was full of gloomy self-absorption and its appropriate abstractions, but now the abstractions are those that· feed self-righteousness and scorn of others, the nearest the natural self can come to the self-expressing mastery of Phase 10. Morality, grown passive and pompous,· dwindles to unmeaning forms and formulae. Under the influence·of the *Body of Fate*, the unweaver and *discord* of Phase 10, the man frees the intellect from the *Mask* by unflagging impersonal activity. Instead of burning intellectual abstraction, as did Phase 23, in a technical fire, it grinds moral abstraction in a mill. This mill, created by the freed intellect, is a code of personal conduct, which being formed from social and historical tradition, remains always concrete in the mind. All is sacrificed to this code; moral strength reaches its climax; the rage of Phase 10 to destroy all that trammels the being from without is now all self-surrender. There is great humility—" she died every day she lived "—and pride as great, pride in the code's acceptance, an impersonal pride, as though one were to sign " servant of servants." There is no philosophic capacity, no intellectual curiosity, but there is no dislike for either philosophy or science; they are a part of the world and that world is accepted. There may be great intolerance for all who break or resist the code, and great tolerance for all the evil of the world that is clearly beyond it whether above it or below. The code must rule, and because that code cannot be an intellectual choice, it is always a tradition bound up with family, or office, or trade, always a part of history. It is always seemingly fated, for its sub-conscious purpose is to compel surrender of every personal ambition; and though it is obeyed in pain—can there be mercy in a rigid code?—the man is flooded with the joy of self-surrender; and flooded with mercy—what else can there be in self-surrender?—for those over whom the code can have no rights, children and the nameless multitude. Unmerciful to those who serve and to himself, merciful in contemplating those who are served, he never wearies of forgiveness.

5   Men and women of the phase create an art where individuals only exist to express some historical code, or some historical tradition of action and of feeling, things written in what Raftery called the Book of the People, or settled by social or official station, even as
10 set forth in directory or peerage. The judge upon the bench is but a judge, the prisoner in the dock is but the eternal offender, whom we may study in legend or in Blue Book. They despise the Bohemian above all men till he turn gypsy, tinker, convict, or the like, and
15 so find historical sanction, attain as it were to some inherited code or recognised relation to such code. They submit all their actions to the most unflinching examination, and yet are without psychology, or self-knowledge, or self-created standard of any kind, for they but ask
20 without ceasing, " Have I done my duty as well as so-and-so ? " " Am I as unflinching as my fathers before me ? " and though they can stand utterly alone, indifferent though all the world condemn, it is not that they have found themselves, but that they have been
25 found faithful. The very Bohemians are not wholly individual men in their eyes, and but fulfil the curse, laid upon them before they were born, by God or social necessity.

    Out of phase, seeking emotion instead of impersonal
30 action, there is—desire being impossible—self-pity, and therefore discontent with people and with circumstance, and an overwhelming sense of loneliness, of being abandoned. All criticism is resented, and small personal rights and predilections, especially if supported by habit
35 or position, are asserted with violence; there is great indifference to others' rights and predilections; we have

the bureaucrat or the ecclesiastic of satire, a tyrant who is incapable of insight or of hesitation.

Their intellect being from Phase 6, but their energy, or will, or bias, from Phase 24, they must, if in phase, see their code expressed in multiform human life, the mind of Victoria at its best, as distinguished from that of Walt Whitman. Their emotional life is a reversal of Phase 10, as what was autocratic in Victoria reversed the personal autocracy of Parnell. They fly the *Mask*, that it may become, when enforced, that form of pride and of humility that holds together a professional or social order.

When out of phase they take from Phase 10 isolation, which is good for that phase but destructive to a phase that should live for others and from others; and they take from Phase 6 a bundle of race instincts, and turn them to abstract moral, or social convention, and so contrast with Phase 6, as the mind of Victoria at its worst contrasts with that of Walt Whitman. When in phase they turn these instincts to a concrete code, founded upon dead or living example.

That which characterises all phases of the last quarter, with an increasing intensity, begins now to be plain : persecution of instinct—race is transformed into a moral conception—whereas the intellectual phases, with increasing intensity as they approached Phase 22, persecuted emotion. Morality and intellect persecute instinct and emotion respectively, which seek their protection.

XXVI

PHASE TWENTY-FIVE

Will—The Conditional Man.

Mask (from Phase 11). *True*—Consciousness of Self.
False—Self-consciousness.

Creative Mind (from Phase 5). *True*—Rhetoric. *False*
—Spiritual Arrogance.

Body of Fate (from Phase 19)—Persecution.

Examples : Cardinal Newman, Luther, Calvin, George
Herbert, Mr George Russell (A.E.).

Born as it seems to the arrogance of belief, as Phase
24 was born to moral arrogance, the man of the phase
must reverse himself, must change from Phase 11 to
Phase 25; use the *Body of Fate* to purify the intellect
from the *Mask*, till this intellect accepts some organized
belief : belief rooted in social order : the convictions of
Christendom let us say. He must eliminate all that is
personal from belief; eliminate the necessity for intellect
by the contagion of some common agreement, as did
Phase 23 by its technique, Phase 24 by its code. With a
Will of subsidence, an intellect of loosening and separating, he must, like Phases 23 or 24, find himself in such a
situation that he is compelled to concrete synthesis (*Body
of Fate* at Phase 19 the discord of Phase 11) but this
situation compels the *Will*, if it pursue the False *Mask*,
to the persecution of others, if found by the True *Mask*,
to suffer persecution. Phase 19, phase of the *Body of
Fate*, is a phase of breaking, and when the *Will* is at
Phase 25 of breaking by belief. In this it finds its
inspiration and its joy. It is called the *Conditional Man*,

perhaps because all the man's thought arises out of some particular condition of actual life, or is an attempt to change that condition with a moral object. He is still strong, full of initiative, full of social intellect; absorption has scarce begun; but his object is to limit and bind, 5 to make men better, by making it impossible that they should be otherwise, to so arrange prohibitions and habits that men may be naturally good, as they are naturally black, or white, or yellow. There may be great eloquence, a mastery of all concrete imagery that 10 is not personal expression, because though as yet there is no sinking into the world but much distinctness, clear identity, there is an overflowing social conscience. No man of any other phase can produce the same instant effect upon great crowds; for codes have passed, the 15 universal conscience takes their place. He should not appeal to a personal interest, should make little use of argument which requires a long train of reasons, or many technical terms, for his power rests in certain simplifying convictions which have grown with his character; he 20 needs intellect for their expression, not for proof, and taken away from these convictions is without emotion and momentum. He has but one overwhelming passion, to make all men good, and this good is something at once concrete and impersonal; and though he has hitherto 25 given it the name of some church, or state, he is ready at any moment to give it a new name for, unlike Phase 24, he has no pride to nourish upon the past. Moved by all that is impersonal, he becomes powerful as, in a community tired of elaborate meals, that man might 30 become powerful who had the strongest appetite for bread and water.

When out of phase he may, because Phase 11 is a phase of diffused personality and pantheistic dreaming, grow sentimental and vague, drift into some emotional 35 abstract, his head full of images long separated from life, and ideas long separated from experience, turn tactless and tasteless, affirm his position with the greatest arrogance possible to man. Even when nearly wholly good he can scarce escape from arrogance; what old friend did Cardinal Newman cut because of some shade of theological difference?

Living in the False *Creative Mind* produces, in all *primary* phases, insensitiveness, as living in the False *Mask* produces emotional conventionality and banality, because that False *Creative Mind*, having received no influence from the *Body of Fate*, no mould from individuals and interests, is as it were self-suspended. At Phase 25 this insensitiveness may be that of a judge who orders a man to the torture, that of a statesman who accepts massacre as a historical necessity. One thinks of Luther's apparent indifference to atrocities committed, now by the peasants, now against them, according to the way his incitements veered.

The genius of Synge and Rembrandt has been described as typical of Phase 23. The first phase of a triad is an expression of unrelated power. They surprised the multitude, they did not seek to master it; while those chosen for examples of Phase 24 turn the multitude into a moral norm. At Phase 25 men seek to master the multitude, not through expressing it, nor through surprising it, but by imposing upon it an intellectual norm. Synge, reborn at Phase 25, might interest himself, not in the *primary* vigour and tragedy of his Aran Island countrymen but in their beliefs, and through some eccentricity (not of phase but horoscope) not in those they hold in common with fellow Catholics, as Newman would, but of those they share with Japanese peasants, or in their belief as a part of all folk belief considered as religion and philosophy. He would use this religion and philosophy to kill within himself the last trace of individual abstract speculation, yet this religion and this

philosophy, as present before his mind, would be artificial
and selected, though always concrete. Subsidence upon,
or absorption in, the *spiritual primary* is not yet possible
or even conceivable.

Poets of this phase are always stirred to an imaginative
intensity by some form of propaganda. George Herbert
was doubtless of this phase; and Mr George Russell
(A.E.), though the signs are obscured by the influence
upon his early years of poets and painters of middle
antithetical phases. Neither Mr Russell's visionary
painting, nor his visions of " nature spirits " are, upon
this supposition, true to phase. Every poem, where he is
moved to write by some form of philosophical propaganda,
is precise, delicate and original, while in his visionary
painting one discovers the influence of other men, Gustave
Moreau, for instance. This painting is like many of his
" visions," an attempt to live in the *Mask*, caused by
critical ideas founded upon *antithetical* art. What dialect
was to Synge, his practical work as a co-operative
organiser is to him, and he finds precise ideas and sincere
emotion in the expression of conviction. He has learned
practically, but not theoretically, that he must fly the
Mask. His work should neither be consciously æsthetic
nor consciously speculative but imitative of a central
Being—the *Mask* as his pursuer—consciously apprehended as something distinct, as something never
imminent though eternally united to the soul.

His False *Mask* has shown him what purport to be
" nature spirits " because all phases before Phase 15 are
in nature, as distinguished from God, and at Phase 11
that nature becomes intellectually conscious of its
relations to all created things. When he desires the
Mask, instead of flying that it may follow, it gives,
instead of the intuition of God, a simulated intuition of
nature. That simulated intuition is arrayed in ideal
conventional images of sense, instead of in some form of

abstract opinion, because of the character of his horoscope.

XXVII

Phase Twenty-six

Will—The Multiple Man, also called " The Hunch-back."

5   *Mask* (from Phase 12). *True*—Self-realisation. *False* —Self-abandonment.

Creative Mind (from Phase 4). *True*—Beginning of Supersensual thought. *False*—Fascination of Sin.

Body of Fate (from Phase 18)—The Hunchback is
10   his own *Body of Fate.*

The most difficult of the phases, and the first of those phases for which one can find few or no examples from personal experience. I think that in Asia it might not be difficult to discover examples at least of Phases 26,
15   27 and 28, final phases of a cycle. If such embodiments occur in our present European civilisation they remain obscure, through lacking the instruments for self-expression. One must create the type from its symbols without the help of experience.
20   All the old abstraction, whether of morality or of belief, has now been exhausted, but in the seemingly natural man, in Phase 26 out of phase, there is an attempt to sub-stitute a new abstraction, a simulacrum of self-expression. Desiring emotion the man becomes the most completely
25   solitary of all possible men, for all emotional communion with his kind, that of a common study, that of an interest in work done, that of a code accepted, that of a belief

shared, has passed; and without personality he is forced
to create its artificial semblance. It is perhaps a slander
of history that makes us see Nero so, for he lacked the
physical deformity which is, we are told, first among
this phase's inhibitions of personality. The deformity
may be of any kind, great or little, for it is but symbolised
in the hump that thwarts what seems the ambition of a
Cæsar or of an Achilles. He commits crimes, not because
he wants to, or like Phase 23 out of phase, because he
can, but because he wants to feel certain that he can;
and he is full of malice because, finding no impulse but
in his own ambition, he is made jealous by the impulse
of others. He is all emphasis, and the greater that
emphasis the more does he show himself incapable of
emotion, the more does he display his sterility. If he
live amid a theologically minded people, his greatest
temptation may be to defy God, to become a Judas, who
betrays, not for thirty pieces of silver, but that he may
call himself creator.

In examining how he becomes true to phase, one is
perplexed by the obscure description of the *Body of Fate*,
" the Hunchback is his own *Body of Fate*." This *Body
of Fate* is derived from Phase 18, and (being reflected in
the physical being of Phase 26), can only be such a
separation of function—deformity—as breaks the self-
regarding False *Mask* (Phase 18 being the breaking of
Phase 12). All phases from Phase 26 to Phase 11
inclusive are gregarious; and from Phase 26 to Phase
28 there is, when the phase is truly lived, contact with
supersensual life, or a sinking in of the body upon its
supersensual source, or desire for that contact and
sinking. At Phase 26 has come a subconscious
exhaustion of the moral life, whether in belief or in
conduct, and of the life of imitation, the life of judgment
and approval. The *Will* must find a substitute, and as
always in the first phase of a triad energy is violent and

fragmentary. The moral abstract being no longer possible, the *Will* may seek this substitute through the knowledge of the lives of men and beasts, plucked up, as it were, by the roots, lacking in all mutual relations; there may be hatred of solitude, perpetual forced bonhomie; yet that which it seeks is without social morality, something radical and incredible. When Ezekiel lay upon his " right and left side " and ate dung, to raise " other men to a perception of the infinite," he may so have sought, and so did perhaps the Indian sage or saint who coupled with the roe.

If the man of this phase seeks, not life, but knowledge of each separated life in relation to supersensual unity; and above all of each separated physical life, or action, —that alone is entirely concrete—he will, because he can see lives and actions in relation to their source and not in their relations to one another, see their deformities and incapacities with extraordinary acuteness, and we shall *discover, when we come to consider the nature of *victimage*, that their images beset him in states analogous to hypnogogic vision. His own past actions also he must judge as isolated and each in relation to its source; and this source, experienced not as love but as knowledge, will be present in his mind as a terrible unflinching judgment. Hitherto he could say to *primary* man, " Am I as good as So-and-So? " and when still *antithetical* he could say, " After all I have not failed in my good intentions taken as a whole "; he could pardon himself; but how pardon where every action is judged alone and no good action can turn judgment from the evil action by its side. He stands in the presence of a terrible blinding light, and would, were that possible, be born as worm or mole.

* This topic belongs to the psychology of the system, which I have not yet mastered. I have yet to put together and study many obscure scattered passages in the documents.—W.B.Y., July, 1925.

XXVIII

Phase Twenty-seven

Will—The Saint.

Mask (from Phase 18). *True*—Renunciation. *False*—Emulation.

Creative Mind (from Phase 8). *True*—Spiritual Receptivity. *False*—Pride.

Body of Fate (from Phase 17)—None except Impersonal Action.

Examples : Socrates, Pascal.

In his seemingly natural man, derived from *Mask*, there is an extreme desire for spiritual authority; and thought and action have for their object display of zeal or some claim of authority. Emulation is all the greater because not based on argument but on psychological or physiological difference. At Phase 27, the central phase of the soul, of a triad that is occupied with the relations of the soul, the man asserts when out of phase his claim to faculty or to supersensitive privilege beyond that of other men; he has a secret that makes him better than other men.

True to phase, he substitutes for emulation an emotion of renunciation, and for the old toil of judgment and acknowledgement of sin, a beating upon his breast and an ecstatical crying out that he must do penance, that he is even the worst of men. He does not, like Phase 26, perceive separated lives and actions more clearly than the total life, for the total life has suddenly displayed its source. If he possess intellect he will use it but to serve perception and renunciation. His joy is to be

H

nothing, to do nothing, to think nothing; but to permit the total life, expressed in its humanity, to flow in upon him and to express itself through his acts and thoughts. He is not identical with it, he is not absorbed in it, for if he were he would not know that he is nothing, that he no longer even possesses his own body, that he must renounce even his desire for his own salvation, and that this total life is in love with his nothingness.

Before the self passes from Phase 22 it is said to attain what is called the " Emotion of Sanctity," and this emotion is described as a contact with life beyond death. It comes at the instant when synthesis is abandoned, when fate is accepted. At Phases 23, 24 and 25 we are said to use this emotion, but not to pass from Phase 25 till we have intellectually realised the nature of sanctity itself, and sanctity is described as the renunciation of personal salvation. The " Emotion of Sanctity " is the reverse of that realisation of incipient personality at Phase 8, which the *Will* related to collective action till Phase 11 had passed. After Phase 22 the man becomes aware of something which the intellect cannot grasp and this something is a supersensual environment of the soul. At Phases 23, 24 and 25 he subdues all attempts at its intellectual comprehension, while relating it to his bodily senses and faculties, through technical achievement, through morality, through belief. At Phases 26, 27 and 28 he permits those senses and those faculties to sink in upon their environment. He will, if it be possible, not even touch or taste or see : " Man does not perceive the truth; God perceives the truth in man."

XXIX

PHASE TWENTY-EIGHT

Will—The Fool.

Mask (from Phase 14). *True*—Oblivion. *False*—
Malignity.

Creative Mind (from Phase 2). *True*—Physical
Activity. *False*—Cunning.

Body of Fate (from Phase 16)—The Fool is his own
Body of Fate.

The natural man, the fool desiring his *Mask*, grows
malignant, not as the Hunchback, who is jealous of those
that can still feel, but through terror and out of jealousy
of all that can act with intelligence and effect. It is
his true business to become his own opposite, to pass
from a semblance of Phase 14 to the reality of Phase
28, and this he does under the influence of his own mind
and body—he is his own *Body of Fate*—for having no
active intelligence he owns nothing of the exterior world
but his mind and body. He is but a straw blown by
the wind, with no mind but the wind and no act but a
nameless drifting and turning, and is sometimes called
" The Child of God." At his worst his hands and feet
and eyes, his will and his feelings, obey obscure subconscious fantasies, while at his best he would know all
wisdom if he could know anything. The physical world
suggests to his mind pictures and events that have no
relation to his needs or even to his desires; his thoughts
are an aimless reverie; his acts are aimless like his
thoughts; and it is in this aimlessness that he finds his
joy. His importance will become clear as the system
elaborates itself, yet for the moment no more need be

said but that one finds his many shapes on passing from the village fool to the fool of Shakespeare.

> " Out of the pool,
> Where love the slain with love the slayer lies,
> Bubbles the wan mirth of the mirthless fool.''

Phase One

Will.
Mask (from Phase 15).   } No description except
Creative Mind (from Phase 1). } complete plasticity.
Body of Fate (from Phase 15). }

This is a supernatural incarnation, like Phase 15, because there is complete objectivity, and human life cannot be completely objective. At Phase 15 mind was completely absorbed by Being, but now body is completely absorbed in its supernatural environment. The images of mind are no longer irrelevant even, for there is no longer anything to which they can be relevant, and acts can no longer be immoral or stupid for there is no one there that can be judged. Thought and inclination, fact and object of desire, are indistinguishable (Mask is submerged in Body of Fate, Will in Creative Mind), that is to say there is complete passivity, complete plasticity. Mind has become indifferent to good and evil, to truth and falsehood; body has become undifferentiated, dough-like; the more perfect be the soul, the more indifferent the mind, the more dough-like the body; and mind and body take whatever shape, accept whatever image is imprinted upon them, transact whatever purpose is imposed upon them, and are indeed the instruments of supernatural manifestation, being the final link between the living and more powerful beings. There

may be great joy; but it is the joy of a conscious
plasticity; and it is this plasticity, this liquefaction,
or pounding up, whereby all that has been knowledge
becomes instinct and faculty. All plasticities do not
obey all masters, and when we have considered cycle and   5
horoscope it will be seen how those that are the instruments of subtle supernatural will differ from the instruments of cruder energy; but all, highest and lowest, are
alike in being automatic.

Finished at Thoor, Ballylee, 1922,   10

in a time of Civil War.

BOOK II

WHAT THE CALIPH REFUSED TO LEARN

1. *DESERT GEOMETRY OR THE GIFT OF HARUN AL-RASCHID*

Kusta ben Luka is my name, I write
To Abd Al-Rabban; fellow roysterer once,
Now the good Caliph's learned Treasurer,
And for no ear but his.
         Carry this letter
Through the great gallery of the Treasure House   5
Where banners of the Caliphs hang, night-coloured
But brilliant as the night's embroidery,
And wait war's music; pass the little gallery;
Pass books of learning from Byzantium
Written in gold upon a purple stain,   10
And pause at last, I was about to say,
At the great book of Sappho's song; but no!
For should you leave my letter there, a boy's
Love-lorn, indifferent hands might come upon it
And let it fall unnoticed to the floor.   15
Pause at the Treatise of Parmenides
And hide it there, for Caliphs to world's end
Must keep that perfect, as they keep her song,
So great its fame.
         When fitting time has passed,   20
The parchment will disclose to some learned man
A mystery that else had found no chronicler
But the wild Bedouin. Though I approve
Those wanderers that welcomed in their tents

What great Harun Al-Raschid, occupied
With Persian embassy or Grecian war,
Or those who need his bounty or his law,
Must needs neglect; I cannot hide the truth
5   That wandering in a desert, featureless
As air under a wing, can give bird's wit.
In after time they will speak much of me
And speak but phantasy. Recall the year
When our beloved Caliph put to death
10 His Vizir Jaffer for an unknown reason.
" If but the shirt upon my body knew it
I'd tear it off and throw it in the fire."
That speech was all that the town knew, but he
Seemed for a while to have grown young again;
15 Seemed so on purpose, muttered Jaffer's friends,
That none might know that he was conscience struck—
But that's a traitor's thought. Enough for me
That in the early summer of the year
The mightiest of the princes of the world
20 Came to the least considered of his courtiers;
Sat down upon the fountain's marble edge,
One hand amid the goldfish in the pool :
And thereupon a colloquy took place
That I commend to all the chroniclers
25 To show how violent great hearts can lose
Their bitterness and find the honeycomb.

" I have brought a slender bride into the house;
You know the saying ' Change the bride with Spring,'
And she and I, being sunk in happiness,
30 Cannot endure to think you tread these paths
When evening stirs the jasmine, and yet
Are brideless."

" I am falling into years."

" But such as you and I do not seem old
Like men who live by habit. Every day
I ride with falcon to the water's edge
Or carry the ringed mail upon my back,
Or court a woman; neither enemy,   5
Gamebird, nor woman does the same thing twice;
And so a hunter carries in the eye
A mimicry of youth. Can poet's thought
That springs from body and in body falls
Like this pure jet, now lost amid blue sky,   10
Now bathing lily leaf and fishes' scale,
Be mimicry? "

          " What matter if our souls
Are nearer to the surface of the body
Than souls that start no game and turn no rhyme!   15
The soul's own youth and not the body's youth
Shows through our lineaments. My candle's bright;
My lantern is too loyal not to show
That it was made in your great father's reign."

" And yet the jasmine season warms our blood."   20

" Great prince, forgive the freedom of my speech;
You think that love has seasons, and you think
That if the spring bear off what the spring gave
The heart need suffer no defeat; but I
Who have accepted the Byzantine faith   25
That seems unnatural to Arabian minds,
Think when I choose a bride I choose for ever;
And if her eye should not grow bright for mine,
Or brighten only for some younger eye,
My heart could never turn from daily ruin   30
Nor find a remedy."

          " But what if I
Have lit upon a woman who so shares

Your thirst for those old crabbed mysteries,
So strains to look beyond our life, an eye
That never knew that strain would scarce seem **bright**;
And yet herself can seem youth's very fountain,
5 Being all brimmed with life."

      " Were it but true
I would have found the best that life can give,
Companionship in those mysterious things
That make a man's soul or a,woman's soul
Itself and not some other soul."

      " That love
10 Must needs be in this life and in what follows
Unchanging and at peace, and it is right
Every philosopher should praise that love;
But I being none can praise its opposite.
It makes my passion stronger but to think
15 Like passion stirs the peacock and his mate,
The wild stag and the doe; that mouth to mouth
Is a man's mockery of the changeless soul."

And thereupon his bounty gave what now
Can shake more blossom from autumnal chill
20 Than all my bursting springtime knew. A girl
Perched in some window of her mother's house
Had watched my daily passage to and fro;
Had heard impossible history of my past;
Imagined some impossible history
25 Lived at my side; thought Time's disfiguring **touch**
Gave but more reason for a woman's care.
Yet was it love of me, or was it love
Of the stark mystery that has dazed my sight,
Perplexed her phantasy and planned her care?
30 Or did the torchlight of that mystery
Pick out my features in such light and shade

Two contemplating passions chose one theme
Through sheer bewilderment? She had not paced
The garden paths, nor counted up the rooms,
Before she had spread a book upon her knees
And asked about the pictures or the text;   5
And often those first days I saw her stare
On old dry writing in a learned tongue,
On old dry faggots that could never please
The extravagance of spring; or move a hand
As if that writing or the figured page   10
Were some dear cheek.
        Upon a moonless night
I sat where I could watch her sleeping form,
And wrote by candle-light; but her form moved,
And fearing that my light disturbed her sleep
I rose that I might screen it with a cloth.   15
I heard her voice " Turn that I may expound
What's bowed your shoulder and made pale your cheek ";
And saw her sitting upright on the bed;
Or was it she that spoke or some great Djinn?
I say that a Djinn spoke. A live-long hour   20
She seemed the learned man and I the child;
Truths without father came, truths that no book
Of all the uncounted books that I have read,
Nor thought out of her mind or mine begot,
Self-born, high-born, and solitary truths,   25
Those terrible implacable straight lines
Drawn through the wondering vegetative dream,
Even those truths that when my bones are dust
Must drive the Arabian host.

        The voice grew still,
And she lay down upon her bed and slept,   30
But woke at the first gleam of day, rose up
And swept the house and sang about her work
In childish ignorance of all that passed.

A dozen nights of natural sleep, and then
When the full moon swam to its greatest height
She rose, and with her eyes shut fast in sleep
Walked through the house. Unnoticed and unfelt
5   I wrapped her in a heavy hooded cloak, and she
Half running, dropped at the first ridge of the desert
And there marked out those emblems on the sand
That day by day I study and marvel at,
With her white finger. I led her home asleep
10   And once again she rose and swept the house
In childish ignorance of all that passed.
Even to-day, after some seven years
When maybe thrice in every moon her mouth
Has murmured wisdom of the desert Djinns,
15   She keeps that ignorance, nor has she now
That first unnatural interest in my books.
It seems enough that I am there; and yet,
Old fellow student, whose most patient ear
Heard all the anxiety of my passionate youth,
20   It seems I must buy knowledge with my peace.
What if she lose her ignorance and so
Dream that I love her only for the voice,
That every gift and every word of praise
Is but a payment for that midnight voice
25   That is to age what milk is to a child!
Were she to lose her love, because she had lost
Her confidence in mine, or even lose
Its first simplicity, love, voice, and all,
All my fine feathers would be plucked away
30   And I left shivering. The voice has drawn
A quality of wisdom from her love's
Particular quality. The signs and shapes;
All those abstractions that you fancied were
From the great Treatise of Parmenides;
35   All, all those gyres and cubes and midnight things
Are but a new expression of her body

Drunk with the bitter-sweetness of her youth.
And now my utmost mystery is out :
A woman's beauty is a storm-tossed banner;
Under it wisdom stands, and I alone—
Of all Arabia's lovers I alone—   5
Nor dazzled by the embroidery, nor lost
In the confusion of its night-dark folds,
Can hear the armed man speak.

1923.

2. THE GEOMETRICAL FOUNDATION OF THE WHEEL

I

THE GYRE

FLAUBERT talked much of writing a story called " La Spirale " and died before he began it, but since his death an editor has collected the scheme from various sources. It would have concerned a man whose dreams during sleep grew in magnificence as his life became more and more unlucky. He dreamt of marriage with a princess when all went wrong with his own love adventure. Swedenborg wrote occasionally of gyrations, especially in his " Spiritual Diary," and in " The Principia " where the physical universe is described as built up by the spiral movement of points, and by vortexes which were combinations of these; but very obscurely except where describing the physical universe, perhaps because he was compelled as he thought to keep silent upon all that concerned Fate. I remember that certain Irish countrymen whom I questioned some twenty years ago had seen Spirits departing from them in an ascending gyre; and there is that gyring " tangle of world lines in a fourth dimensional space " of later discoverers, and of course Descartes and his vortex, Boehme and his gyre, and perhaps, were I learned enough to discover

128

it, allusions in many writers back to antiquity. Arrived there I am attracted to a passage in Heraclitus which I can, I think, explain more clearly than his English commentators.

II

EXPANDING AND CONTRASTING GYRES

HAVING the concrete mind of the poet, I am unhappy when I find myself among abstract things, and yet I need them to set my experience in order. I must speak of time and space, though as I accept the argument of Berkeley I think of them as abstract creations of the human mind, limits which it has chosen for itself.

A line is the symbol of time and it expresses a movement—without extension in space—and because emotion has no extension in that space, however much connected with objects that have, a line symbolises the emotional subjective mind, the self in its simplest form. A plane cutting the line at right angles constitutes, in combination with the moving line, a space of three or more dimensions, and is the symbol of all that is objective, and so for certain purposes of nature and, because intellect is the understanding of objects in space, of intellect as opposed to emotion. Line and plane are combined in a gyre, and as one tendency or the other must be always the stronger, the gyre is always expanding or contracting. For simplicity of representation the gyre is drawn as a cone. Sometimes this cone represents the individual soul, and that soul's history—these things are inseparable— sometimes general life. When general life, we give to its narrow end, to its unexpanded gyre, the name of *Anima Hominis*, and to its broad end, or its expanded gyre, *Anima Mundi*; but understanding that neither the soul of man nor the soul of nature can be expressed without

I

conflict or vicissitude we substitute for this cone two
cones, one which is the contact of the mind with *Fate*,
and the other the contact of the mind with *Destiny*.
Destiny being understood to mean all external acts and
5   forms created by the *Will* itself and out of itself, whereas
Fate is all those acts or forms imposed upon the *Will*
from without. It is as though the first act of being, after
creating limit, was to divide itself into male and female,
each dying the other's life living the other's death.

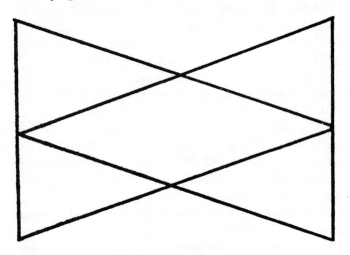

10   These cones are associated with the line and the space
wherein it moves respectively, as though the first gyre
met with another and opposing gyre which has its
greatest expansion, not in space, as we perceive it by
the senses, but in a space perceived by the mind only.
15 We can consider the cones as fixed and use disks or
lines to represent the opposing gyres. It will be seen
presently that these opposing gyres are also beauty and
truth, value and fact, particular and universal, quality
and quantity, the bundle of separated threads as dis-
20 tinguished from those still in the pattern, abstracted
types and forms as distinguished from those that are

still concrete, Man and *Daimon*, the living and the dead, and all other images of our first parents.

When the life of man is growing more predestined, there is something within the depth of his being that resists, that desires the exact contrary; and if his life 5 is growing more fated it desires the exact contrary of that also. As these contraries become sharper in their contrast, as they pull farther apart, consciousness grows more intense, for consciousness is choice. The energy of the one tendency being in exact mathematical pro- 10

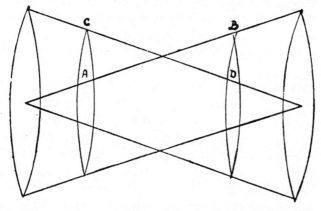

portion to that of the other, the wide gyre marked B for instance in the cone of *Fate* is at exactly the same distance from its widest expanse that the gyre marked C is from its widest expansion. When each gyre has reached the widest expansion, the contradiction in the 15 being will have reached its height. But beside these two expanding gyres there are the two narrowing gyres, marked A D in the figure. As man's intellect, say, expands, the emotional nature contracts in equal degree and vice versa; when, however, a narrowing and a widen- 20 ing gyre reach their limit, the one the utmost contraction the other the utmost expansion, they change places, point to circle, circle to point, for this system conceives the world as catastrophic, and continue as before, one always narrowing, one always expanding, and yet bound for ever to one another. Of this fourfold—two expanding gyres, in nature opposite to one another and two contracting gyres, opposite to one another—we consider the one we identify with the *Will* as deciding the nature of the being. If now we consider these opposing gyres or cones as expressing Man and *Daimon*—those two first portions of being that suffer vicissitude into which *Anima Hominis* and *Anima Mundi* resolve—we can explain much in Parmenides and Empedocles, but especially this in Heraclitus : " I shall retrace my steps over the paths of song that I had travelled before, drawing from my saying a new saying. When Strife was fallen to the lowest depth of the vortex." ("Not as might be supposed," Birkett explains, " the centre but the extreme bound.") " and love has reached the centre of the whirl, in it do all things come together so as to be one only; not all at once, but coming together gradually from different quarters; and as they came together Strife retired to the extreme boundary . . . but in proportion as it kept rushing out, a soft immortal stream of blameless love kept running in." So far all is plain, and it may be this very passage that suggested Flaubert's dreaming man whose life goes wrong as his dream comes right. " For of a truth they (Love and Strife) were afore time and shall be, nor ever can (?) boundless time be emptied of the pair, and they prevail in turn as the circle comes round, and pass away before one another and increase in their appointed time."

And had we more than a few fragments of Empedocles and his school it might not be hard to relate the four gyres of our symbol to heat and cold, light and dark, the pairs of opposites, whether in the moral or physical universe, which permeate his thought. The single cone whose extreme limits are described as *Anima Hominis*,

Anima Mundi, is said in our documents to be formed by
the whirling of a sphere which moves onward leaving an
empty coil behind it; and the double cones by the
separating of two whirling spheres that have been one,
and it may be that we have here what suggested to   5
Parmenides thoughts that seemed to forestall certain of
our latest mathematical speculations. " Where then it
has its furthest boundary it is complete on every side,
equally poised from the centre in every direction like the
mass of a rounded sphere, for it cannot be greater or   10
smaller in one place than another . . . and there is not,
and never shall be any time, other than that which is
present, since Fate has chained it so as to be whole and
immoveable."

III

BLAKE'S USE OF THE GYRES

BLAKE, in the Mental Traveller, describes a struggle, a   15
struggle perpetually repeated between a man and a
woman, and as the one ages, the other grows young. A
child is given to an old woman and

> Her fingers number every nerve
> Just as a miser counts his gold;   20
> She lives upon his shrieks and cries
> And she grows young as he grows old.
> Till he becomes a bleeding youth
> And she becomes a virgin bright;
> Then he rends up his manacles   25
> And bends her down to his delight.

Then he in his turn becomes " an aged shadow " and
is driven from his door, where " From the fire on the
hearth a little female babe doth spring." He must
wander " until he can a maiden win " and then all is   30
repeated for

> " The honey of her infant lips
> The bread and wine of her sweet smile
> The wild game of her roving eye
> Does him to infancy beguile."

> . . . .

> Till he becomes a wayward babe
> And she a weeping woman old "

When Edwin J. Ellis and I had finished our big book on the philosophy of William Blake, I felt that we had no understanding of this poem : we had explained its details, for they occur elsewhere in his verse or his pictures, but not the poem as a whole, not the myth, the perpetual return to the same thing; not that which certainly moved Blake to write it; but when I had understood the double cones, I understood it also. The woman and the man are two competing gyres growing at one another's expense, but with Blake it is not enough to say that one is beauty and one is wisdom, for he conceives this conflict as that in all love—whether between the elements as in Parmenides, " the wanton love " of Aristotle, or between man and woman—which compels each to be slave and tyrant by turn. In our system also it is a cardinal principle that anything separated from its opposite—and victory is separation—" consumes itself away." The existence of the one depends upon the existence of the other.

Blake and his wife signed, in 1789, a document approving the foundation of the Swedenborgian Church, his brother remained a Swedenborgian to the end of his life, his friend Flaxman was a Swedenborgian and a very learned man, and it is possible therefore that he found among fellow-believers a knowledge of gyres and vortexes obtained from Swedenborg himself, though at that time inaccessible in print. Or, upon the other hand, those beings which gave that knowledge as it is in " The Spiritual Diary " may have given it to Blake also.

IV

The Pairs of Opposites and the Dance of the Four Royal Persons

ONE must fix the character of the pairs of opposites, Blake's tyrant and slave, or, to follow Empedocles to the end, " Fire and Water, Earth and the mighty height of Air." Our documents arrange them as in diagram.

The cone of *Fate* and *Mind* is shaded, and all that is external to the *Will* is assumed to be dark, for the light that makes all things visible to the mind comes from the

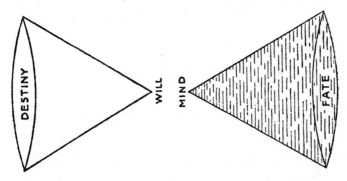

Will itself, our perception of objects, being, as Plotinus insisted, not a passive reception but a state of activity. *Destiny* is here the utmost range possible to the *Will* if left in freedom, and its other name is beauty, whereas *Fate* is the utmost range of the mind when left in its freedom and its other name is truth. But we are no longer dealing with the simple elements but with mixtures, and so we impose these cones, or gyres, upon certain other cones or gyres, which remain fixed and are their containing sphere, and which for simplicity of representation we may place end to end though they are in reality one within the other,—as in the first figure in Sec. II.

By moving the two dotted cones in and out, we can express to the eye the unalterable relation between A

which is the energy, and **B** which is its *Destiny* or beauty,
and that between **C**, which is mind, and **D** which is its
Fate or Truth. As **B B** approaches the wide end of the
right hand cone, **A** approaches the narrow end of its
5   cone, and when this movement is reversed, and **B B**
recedes from the wide end, **A** recedes from the narrow end
of its cone. That is to say when **B** is three quarter
primary and one quarter *antithetical* **A** is three quarter
antithetical and one quarter *primary*, and so on; and

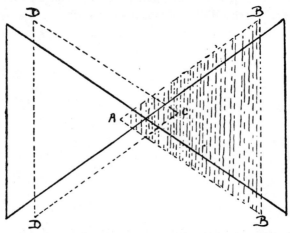

10   the movements of **D D** and **C** coincide exactly with these
movements. That is to say each gyre, for the extremities
of the moving cones are gyres in the fixed cones, preserves
its relation to its own opposite unbroken, though the
nature of each perpetually. changes. In the documents
15   the fixed cones are left out and the relation between the
opposites symbolised by the various relations of the
approaching and separating cones; or the approaching
and separating cones are left out and the opposites
represented by lines cutting the fixed cones.

20   It is, however, cumbersome to use four gyres if two
will serve, as they do if we combine two sets of cones
so that one line includes **B B**, **C C**, and another **D D**,

A A, and so that the same movement causes one line to contract as the other expands.

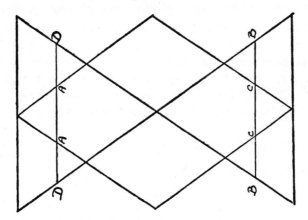

We reach the same end if we consider both sides of the fixed cones as having different meanings, and these fixed cones as placed one within the other. We now obtain our pairs of opposites by considering the four points touched by the two gyres.

5

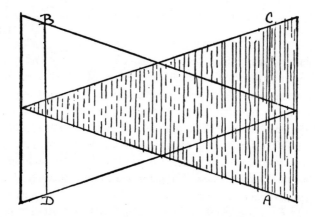

The pairs A B and C D are now so placed that opposites confront one another from opposite sides of the figure, and if we study their movements we have those of the Great Wheel or the Dance of the Four Royal Persons.

Will is *Will,* Mind is *Creative Mind,* Destiny is *Mask,* Fate is *Body of Fate.* They are the *Four Faculties,* and I
5 must leave the definition of their function, given in the section describing the Great Wheel, to explain itself as the system grows familiar, that I may not write at too great length. The figure in the two diagrams just given is that of a person at Phase 12, and as each gyre is now considered

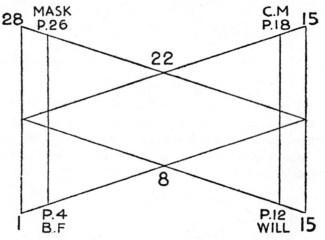

10 as a whirling disc, passing through both inner and outer cones it shows the exact proportion of *antithetical* and *primary* in each of the *Four Faculties.* This proportion is represented in the Great Wheel by the size of the illuminated portion of the Lunar disc at each particular phase.
15 At Phase 12 the Moon is approaching the full in the exact measure as that in which the gyre A C is approaching its greatest expansion. When the greatest expansion of the gyre is reached the phase is Full Moon and so on, and *Will* and *Creative Mind* pass each other at its greatest expan-
20 sion exactly as in the Great Wheel. When we make a symbol combining Sun and Moon, we express the same

thing more completely, for as we have already seen the *primary* may be called Solar, the *antithetical* Lunar. The converse is not always true, for the *Tinctures* belong to a man's life while in the body, and Solar and Lunar may transcend that body. The *Great Wheel* is not, how- 5 ever, an arbitrary symbol for it is a single gyre of a great cone containing, as we shall see presently, twelve cycles of embodiment. Every gyre of every cone is in the same way equal to an entire cone revolving through twenty-eight phases or their equivalent. 10

V

BLAKE AND THE GREAT WHEEL

WE interpret the symbol differently from Blake because his tyrant and slave, slave and tyrant are man and woman out of phase, and their youth occurs at Phases 8 and 22 of our symbol because there is the greatest passion, whereas their old age is at Phase 1 and Phase 15 15 respectively because at those phases the *Primary Tincture* and the *Antithetical Tincture* conquer completely and passion ceases. With us these are the moments of the greatest Beauty and Wisdom respectively because we have mainly studied men true to phase, and 20 when man is true to phase he attains at Phase 1 and Phase 15 relation with his opposite not through conflict but, in so far as one *Faculty* or group of *Faculties* is concerned, through harmony, and is in a Sphere and not a cone. Had I studied men out of phase mainly, I 25 would have had constantly to use Blake's interpretation, as indeed Homer did when he put into the same poem Helen and the Siege of Troy, and as Avicenna did when he wrote " All life proceeds out of corruption." As it is, the system constantly compels us to consider beauty an 30 accompaniment of war, and wisdom of decay.

VI

THE SYMBOLISM OF THE SUN'S PRECESSION AND ANNUAL MOVEMENTS

HITHERTO I have considered the Wheel in relation to the symbolic days of the months, but there are also the twelve symbolic months of the Lunar and Solar year, and

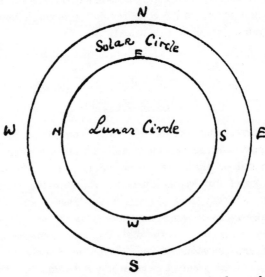

the Solar day. All circles are but a single archetypal
5   circle seen according to different measures of time, and
Solar East, West, the spring and autumn equinoxes,
and sunrise and sunset,. the critical points between
the two Solar extremes, are held to fall upon Phases
15 and 1 respectively of the Lunar circle; and for
10   simplicity we sometimes call Phase 22 Lunar East because
of the Moonrise, Phase 8 Lunar West, Phase 15 Lunar
South, and Phase 1 Lunar North. The fullness of *antithetical* life at Phase 15, and of *primary* life at Phase 1,
fall at moments of extreme strain and shock in all that the
15   Solar circle symbolises. We may represent the two

qualities of life by two circles one within the other which move in opposite directions, the Lunar from West to East according to the Moon's zodiacal movements, the Solar from East to West according to the Sun's daily movement, or as we shall presently see, according to his precessional movement.

The Solar circle represents all that comes from outside the man and is therefore the Bride, the Enemy, the Spiritual Life, the Physical World, though it is only through the *Faculties*, separated form, that he apprehends it. Because there is between the Lunar or natural world and the Solar or spiritual world conflict, the creation of philosophy " from experience " is said " to burn " (? " to consume itself away ") whereas that from revelation gives life. For the same reason spiritual beings are said " to deceive us if they can." The condition of truth is that neither world separate from the other and become " abstract."

VII

The Gyres and Lunar Months of the Great Year

WHEN we come to number gyres and Lunar months in relation to the signs we consider the first gyre as coinciding with the first Lunar phase and as beginning at the centre of a zodiacal sign. We mean by the zodiacal signs not the constellations but mathematical divisions which we shall presently consider.

I. Phase One (Mid Autumn, Lunar North, Cancer, Solar West, Libra).

II. Phases Two, Three and Four.

III. Phases Five, Six and Seven.

IV. Phase Eight (Mid Winter).

V. Phases Nine, Ten and Eleven.

VI. Phases Twelve, Thirteen and Fourteen.

VII. Phase Fifteen (Mid Spring, Solar East, Aries, Lunar South, Capricorn).

VIII. Phases Sixteen, Seventeen and Eighteen (First Lunar Month of Great Year).

IX. Phases Nineteen, Twenty and Twenty-one.

X. Phase Twenty-two (Mid Summer).

XI. Phases Twenty-three, Twenty-four and Twenty-five.

XII. Phases Twenty-six, Twenty-seven and Twenty-eight.

The Solar Months coincide with the signs.

Such a figure as that on page 140 is, however, without movement, for it is without error, it is but the frame, the circle which encloses all, and to show reality we create another figure in the midst consisting of two more circles, the one Solar and the other Lunar, reflections as it were of the Fixed Circles. But for convenience sake I substitute cones for these two inner circles, and when the equinoctial point has just entered Aries—is at Aries 30 that is—superimpose them one upon another and assume that the Solar or Diamond shaped cone has a movement from East to West, and that like an Hour-Glass from West to East.

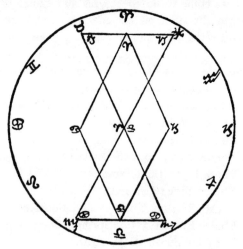

VIII

THE CONES OF THE LUNAR AND SOLAR YEAR

I USE two cones with their narrow ends meeting for *Mask* and *Will*, which I will call the Lunar-cones, and two with their broad ends meeting for the *Creative Mind* and *Body of Fate* which I will call the Solar cones. At the

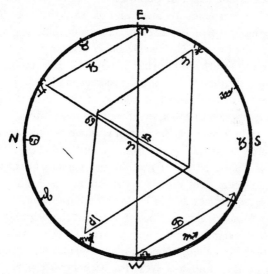

present moment as the equinox is in Pisces, the *Creative* 5
Mind, which is always identified with the East and so
with the equinoctial point, has moved from the historical
starting point in Aries 30 through somewhat more than
one twelfth of the entire circle.

When the Sun at the vernal equinox passed from 10
Taurus into Aries, Eternal Man had his *Will* and *Mask*
at Phase 15 and Phase 1 respectively, and so at Lunar
South and North, and his *Creative Mind* and his *Body
of Fate* at Solar East and West. During the passage
of *Creative Mind* through one sign, starting from solar 15

East, the interior gyre of these Solar and Lunar cones will have made one rotation out of the twelve that complete their circles, and in the Lunar cones that has been a passage from South to North and from North to South again.

It is necessary to notice that as Aries 30, let us say, is the extreme end or East of the Solar cone, and Capricorn 30 the extreme end of the Lunar cone, the 15th Lunar Phase does not begin at Solar East, but that its central moment corresponds to East and so to Aries 30. This means that each of the twelve Lunar divisions begins in the middle of one of the twelve Solar divisions. Starting at East and South we say that the gyre or division corresponding to Phase 15 ends and that corresponding to Phases 16, 17 and 18 begins in the middle of the Solar division that corresponds to Aries, or, if we turn it all into astronomical symbolism, that the first new Moon occurs one half of a Solar month after the Sun has entered Aries. Our figure is based on the Great Year of some twenty-six thousand years, and therefore the Sun enters Aries at the 30th degree and not at 0 as in the annual movement. But the new Moon is always North for it is at the beginning of the twenty-eight phases, and so we get the symbolism of the Cardinal Points once more, for each Solar division begins at East and has West for its central point. The *Will* of Eternal Man during the civilisation that climaxed in Athens and in Rome was passing through a gyre which corresponded to Phase 15 of the Lunar cone and had therefore the greatest possible artistic capacity, and at the foundation of Christianity entered upon the gyre of Phases 16, 17 and 18, while His *Creative Mind* entered upon that of Phases 14, 13 and 12; and at the foundation of the next civilisation His *Will* will have entered the gyre of Phases 19, 20 and 21, while His *Creative Mind* at the moment when the Solar equinox touches the central point of Pisces will have entered that of Phases 11, 10 and 9. As

the Great Year begins at its vernal equinox—Aries 80 not
Aries 0—the next civilisation will correspond to its second
lunar month.   These revolving cones, however, as we
shall see presently, belong to all periods, whether of
history or of individual life, which involve the interaction   5
of *primary* and *antithetical.*

When the Lunar and Solar cones are considered
together, there are two gyres in the Lunar for *Mask* and
Will respectively, and two in the Solar for *Creative Mind*
and *Body of Fate*, and they complete their revolutions   10
once in the course of the Great Year.   The *Creative Mind*
and the *Body of Fate* are only present in the Lunar cones
as an outward limit or obstruction—we shall return to
them presently—as they should act through *Will and
Mask*; and the *Will* and *Mask* are present in the same   15
way in the Solar cones as they should act through *Creative
Mind* and *Body of Fate*.   During the *antithetical* half
of the circle, the mind of the man, as we shall see
presently, is in the Lunar cones, and during the *primary*
half in the Solar.   When they are considered separately,   20
each can move at its own will for it is a complete being,
but we can still keep the same two cones, putting four
gyres into each, and in this case the *Faculties* are not
defined by the points where the gyres touch but by the
gyres themselves, or we may use a double set of cones   25
in each case with two gyres in each.

And now the essential movement is that when *Will*
and *Mask* in the Hour-glass, moving from North to South
respectively, reach " the centre of the whirl " or East
and West respectively, the gyres of *Creative Mind* and   30
Body of Fate start from the extreme ends of the
Diamond, each that is " from the lowest depths of the
vortex."   Sometimes man is said to have only one gyre
in the Solar cones and this is because that of the *Body
of Fate* lies outside his mind, whereas both *Mask* and   35
Will are within the mind of *antithetical* man.   The *Body*

K

of Fate is of course the *Creative Mind* of the *Daimon*, whereas the man's *Creative Mind* is the *Daimon's Body of Fate*, and so outside the being of the *Daimon*. When the Lunar and Solar cones are considered separately, we call the first the cone of the *Faculties* and the second the cone of the *Principles;* and we divide that of the *Faculties* into two cones, the one Solar and the other Lunar; and divide the cone of the *Principles* in the same way. The Four Principles are *Spirit, Celestial Body, Husk* and

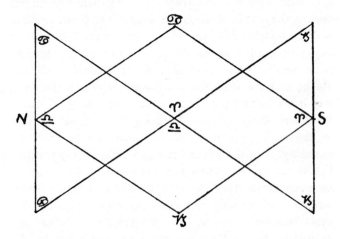

Passionate Body—we shall describe each presently—and they correspond to *Creative Mind, Body of Fate, Will* and *Mask* respectively. In the cone of the *Faculties* we place *Will* and *Mask* in the Lunar cone or the Hour-glass, *Creative Mind* and *Body of Fate* in the Diamond or Solar cone; and in the cone of the *Principles, Husk* and *Passionate Body* in the Hour-glass, *Spirit* and *Celestial Body* in the Diamond. In each set the revolutions of Diamond and Hour-glass round one another create the months, the Solar month being in the cone of the *Principles* which is superimposed.

Upon the diagram of the Great Wheel the words *Head,*

Heart, Loins and *Fall* are written, and they correspond to *Spirit, Passionate Body, Husk* and *Celestial Body* at the opening of the next civilisation, which will be reached when the *Will* of the Great Year is between phase 18 and phase 19. These points have, however, no direct 5 connection with the Great Wheel itself and imply another figure obtained by reducing two pairs of cones to one cone each and crossing them at right angles.

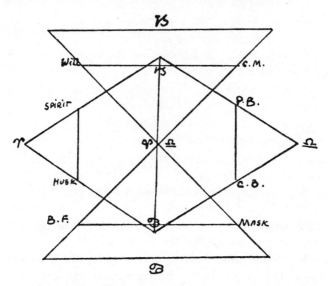

This arrangement is not used by me and is only described here because if superimposed upon the Great 10 Wheel it explains the position upon it by *Head, Heart, Loins and Fall.* They are very confusing unless one remembers that they are made necessary if a single Zodiac with Cancer and Capricorn at North and South respectively is made to represent an entire Wheel. 15

The Diamond in this figure represents a form of existence which lasts through the entire period of twenty-six thousand years, and the Hour-glass—really Hour-glass and Diamond—the Great Wheel or period of

twenty-eight embodiments, say 2200 years, a single
gyre made by the whirling of the two parts of the
Diamond or cone of 26,000 years. The *Faculties* and
Principles marked upon the figure keep their position
5 almost unchanged through the Wheel's domination.

IX

THE MONTHS ALTERNATELY PRIMARY AND ANTITHETICAL

BUT each month in addition to its separate passage
through the phases from 1 to 28 is part of a period of
two months which is itself an entire cone or wheel, and
therefore the months are alternately *antithetical* and
10 *primary*, the lunar months corresponding to 16, 17 and
18, and so to our civilisation, being for instance *primary*.
The *Principles* are properly speaking beyond the
Tinctures, which are physical, but they have a corresponding change, and so it follows that we may say that
15 Christ gave a *primary* revelation at the climax of an
antithetical civilisation and will be followed by His
contrary. Measured by the single month, considered
as the Divine influx of that month alone, He is always
the Eternal Sage—Libra—but measured on the wheel
20 or cone of the double months He is now *Victim* and now
Sage, at East always *Victim*, the sacrificial ram, He who
offers himself in sacrifice to the pitiless *antithetical* mind,
for in this the life of the *Principle* resembles that of the
Faculty and at East strength is renounced. But each
25 quarter of the Great Year is also a cone, and so we say
that the months are in sets of three; and measured by
this measure He is first *Victim* and then *Sage*, and
then once more *Victim*, and so we say that He is
Three Fountains, the first born of Aries and Taurus,
30 the second of Libra and Scorpio, and the third

of Aries and Taurus once more; and the greater circle
is always *primary* in relation to that which turns more
quickly and within.

I see the Lunar and Solar cones first, before they start
their whirling movement, as two worlds lying one within 5
another—nothing exterior, nothing interior, Sun in Moon
and Moon in Sun—a single being like man and woman
in Plato's Myth, and then a separation and a whirling
for countless ages, and I see man and woman as
reflecting the greater movement, each with zodiac, pre- 10
cession, and separate measure of time, and all whirling
perpetually. But this whirling, though it is creative, is
not evil, for evil is from the disturbance of the harmony,
so that those that should come in their season come all
at once or straggle here and there, the gyres thrown 15
together in confusion, and hatred takes possession of all.

X

THE GREAT YEAR IN CLASSICAL ANTIQUITY

BEFORE further explaining these cones which the reader
must have found very troublesome, I would discover if
Antiquity had similar measures. Remembering that
elaborate geometry of the Timaeus and certain numerical 20
calculations in the Republic of which modern scholars
have seventeen incompatible explanations, we may be
certain that a Platonist would have found our measures
naive in their simplicity.

Milton was the first English writer who made philoso- 25
phical use of the obliquity of the ecliptic, but it was
the Sun's annual and not his precessional movement that
enabled Milton in the tenth book of Paradise Lost to
explain the sudden ruin of the climate when Adam was

driven out of Eden. Yet he must have known of the
precession for he had in his library the Byzantine
historian Georgius Syncellus who comments upon it and
upon the Great Year that it defines. It is only now when
5   we realise the antiquity of man that we can know how
vast and how important was the conception of that Year.

    Certain English and German scholars associate the
changes of ancient mythology with the retreat of the Sun
through the Zodiacal Signs, and attribute to his passage
10   at the Vernal Equinox through Gemini such double
Gods and Worthies as Castor and Pollux, Adam
and Eve, Cain and Abel; and all Ox-like Deities
to his passage through Taurus and so on, and discover
in the Zodiac a history of the human soul through life
15   and death, sin and salvation, and consider that Babylonian and other Antiquity meant the Constellations
when it spoke of the Book of Life, the zodiacal constituting the text and those to North and South the
commentary. There are indeed later scholars—I think
20   of M. Cumont especially—who write about this view as
if they were Protestant theologians denouncing the errors
of Rome, and insist that nobody knew anything about
the equinoctial precession until Hipparchus discovered
it a hundred and fifty years before Christ. Dr Alfred
25   Jeremias and Dr Fritz Homell, however, writing,
the one upon the Babylonian Calendar, the other upon the
Babylonian Ages of the world, in " The Encyclopaedia
of Religion and Ethics," proffer recent evidence and
declare that the older view is proved. Dr Homell fixes
30   the date of the first Vernal rising of the various signs
as Cancer 7000 B.C., Gemini 5000 B.C., Taurus 8000 B.C.,
and Aries 1000 B.C. He evidently prefers these round
numbers to the actual periods of a little under 2200
years because we do not know precisely where the
35   ancient mathematical divisions of the Zodiac, if such
there were, began and ended; or even where the ancient

constellations began and ended; and the symbolism expounded in this book is based upon the same dates and
round numbers. He defines a mathematical division or
sign for the opening month of the Great Year which does
not correspond with any possible month of the ordinary   5
year, for the first month of the ordinary year, as we
shall presently see, has its symbolical starting point—its
0 of Aries—at his 15th or central degree, if anything so
vague as his division can have degrees.

Our authorities for the Greek and Roman use of the   10
Great Year which was, Dr Alfred Jeremias and Dr Fritz
Homell think, founded like the Babylonian upon the
precessional movement through the signs, are passages
in the Timaeus—39.D.ff.—in the Republic—545.C.ff.—
in Cicero's Dream of Scipio, and, for its relation to   15
another smaller cycle, in the Fourth Eclogue of Virgil,
and in various commentators upon them. The Babylonian Great Year began when Aries rose at the Vernal
Equinox, and Syncellus says that this was the doctrine of
the " Greeks and Egyptians . . . as stated in the Genica   20
of Hermes, and in the Cyrannid Books," but words put by
Cicero into the mouth of a shade give no especial significance to any particular sign : " By common custom men
measure the year merely by the return of the Sun, or in
other words by the revolutions of one star. But when   25
the whole of the constellations shall return to the positions from which they once set forth, thus after a long
interval re-making that first map of the Heavens, that
may indeed be called the Great Year wherein I scarce
dare say how many are the generations of men. As   30
when in old days, at the coming of Romulus into this
sacred house, the Sun seemed to fail and to be extinguished, so shall the Sun at the same time and position
fail once more and the signs of the Zodiac all return
to their first position and the stars be recalled, and then   35
shall the cycle of the Great Year be full, and of that vast

cycle know that not one twentieth part has passed away." Macrobius translated Cicero's Greek into Latin at the end of the fifth century and said in his commentary that Cicero considered that the Great Year began with an eclipse that coincided with the death of Romulus. " The World Year " or " Revolution of the Universe," as he names it also, " developed only in a profusion of centuries and the idea of it is as follows. All the luminaries and stars that seem fixed in Heaven and whose individual motion human wisdom is unable to perceive or detect are moved for all that. . . . The end of the Great Year is then when all the luminaries and other fixed stars have returned to some one definite position." Thereupon he adds,—and Plato has the same thought which five minutes' arithmetic would have refuted— " The luminaries and the five planets must be in the same position that they were at the beginning of the world year." And this will come about, he thinks, in [1]fifteen thousand years. Twelve thousand, nine hundred and fifty-four, however, is the number Tacitus gives, quoting from a lost work of Cicero's, but to-day we know that the true number is some twenty-six thousand years.

The Fourth Eclogue seems at first sight contradictory for it announces not that the Year has but lately begun but that it is coming to an end. " The latest age of Cumean Song is at hand; the cycles in their vast array begin anew; Virgin Astrea comes, the reign of Saturn comes, and from the heights of Heaven a new generation of mankind descends . . . Apollo now is King and in your consulship, in yours, Pollio, the age of glory shall commence and the mighty months begin to run their course."

Virgil had in his mind not the Great Year as it seems but a period of Ten Ages of upon an average a hundred years apiece, and if we call them a Year, or as I prefer

1. The Greek or Roman Great Year if derived from Hipparchus would surely have been founded upon that 86″ which he thought the least possible annual movement.

half a Year, it can but be because as Macrobius says " a
month is the Moon's Year." This period which was as
Mr Kirby Flower Smith says " divided according to the
ancient solar year " probably began, when a Roman
period, at the Foundation of Rome or at the death of   5
Romulus; and among the Etruscans according to
tradition at 966 B.C., the date of their coming into Italy
perhaps. May I not consider it as stretching from the
beginning of the Great Year according to the dates
selected for that event by Etruscan and Roman   10
respectively, to the moment when the equinox reaches the
centre of Homell's Aries? Macrobius may have named
fifteen thousand years for its length because the time
from the Foundation of Rome to what may have seemed
to him the end of the Tenth Age—4 B.C.[1]—was exactly   15
one-twentieth of the whole, that is to say one half of a
Solar month if he divided the Great Year by ten. Popular
thought may have seen in the Ten Ages the life period
of the Etruscan polity alone, for it is known that the
Etruscans divided a man's life into ten ages and con-   20
sidered that the tenth began with his seventieth year
when, even though he lived to be ninety, soul and body
parted, but I assume that in the Temples, or among those
that spoke through the Sibyl's mouth, the larger measures
of time were known. One might consider that the Great   25
Year and the lesser period had but an accidental
connection were it not that Virgil announced for the
dawn of the Tenth Age an event too great to be expected
once in a thousand years, and certainly expected elsewhere as the supreme event of the world. Plutarch   30
records a trumpet shrilling from the sky to announce the
Ninth Age, Sulla's rise, the long misery of the Roman Civil
War, and Servius, a contemporary of Macrobius, quotes
from the Memoirs of Augustus to prove that the Tenth or

1. Some one gave this date for close of Tenth Age, perhaps some
Etruscan, but I am correcting these pages at Thoor Ballylee and
there is not a reference book in the house.—*July* 1925.

Solar Age and a comet came together in 44 B.C., a little before Virgil wrote his Eclogue; while a scholar of the third century remembers that Etruscan soothsayers foretold that the Tenth Age would bring the Etruscan State
5 to an end. That age brought to the one state death, and to the other re-birth as Empire and three hundred years of peace. So considered Virgil's prophecy ceases to be an act of individual genius and is united to something more profound and mysterious, to an apprehension of a mathe-
10 matical world order. Salomon Reinach upon discovering therein thoughts from some Dionysian mystery of Magna Grecia refused to consider it a poem of compliment upon the expected birth of Cæsar, but I am ready to believe that Virgil to find familiar form for strange and perhaps
15 hitherto unknown emotions summoned up in the same instant the *Spiritual* and the *Physical Primary*. Upon the other hand I see no reason to explain away a prophecy which only differs from many others by its connection with an ancient sideral faith. Kepler
20 foretold the rise of Gustavus Adolphus and even the exact year in which he would die, and Savonarola the Sack of Rome and in what Pope's reign it would be, and many obscure people foresee in the night's dream or the day's premonition events great or trivial.

25 Cicero's belief that the Sun must be eclipsed upon the same place once more, and that of Macrobius that after fifteen thousand years the planets must return to the same position, and that of somebody else that a line drawn from the centre of the earth must thereon pass
30 through them all, suggests that the doctrine of the Great Year was accepted without examination because of its antiquity. Greek and Chaldean astronomers had known for centuries the periods which bring the planets back to the same point, and Macrobius enumerates them—
35 Mars returns in " two of our years," Jupiter in twelve years, and Saturn in thirty, and so on; and that no

one, not even Plato with all his mathematical calculations, calculated the periods back through the World Year implies an acceptance or half acceptance of that Year, not for its astronomical but for its moral value. Our interest in Plato's comment is precisely that he does use it as we use the lunar phases, as if it were the moving hands upon a vast clock, or a picturesque symbolism that helped him to make more vivid, and perhaps date, developments of the human mind that can be proved dialectically. In the Republic he identifies the passage of his typical community through Timocracy, Oligarchy, Democracy, Tyranny, and so back to Aristocracy again, as a passage through Ages of Gold, Silver, etc., that may have seemed to the eyes of the Sibyl and perhaps to the eyes of Virgil identical with some classification of the Ten Ages : he saw what had seemed *Fate* as *Destiny*. In another passage he makes his typical community bring its different periods to an end by carrying some character to excess, and attributes the changes of the year to a like cause.

Macchiavelli may but have spoken as Plato's disciple when he contended that all States must decay, and that all the reformer can do to check decay is bring them back to an earlier condition, his thought being too summary to show him that to push the State backward could but leave it out of phase and so in illusion.

Though I have assumed that the Birth of Christ took place at the symbolic centre of the first Solar month of the Great Year, I do not think it likely that He was born at its exact centre. Indeed the documents from which I have worked say two or three times that the age which preceded the Birth of Christ was longer than that which followed, but as I am unable to find an explanation of this statement—they insist that there is a mathematical explanation—I have ignored it. We have considered that every Divine Birth occurs at a symbolical New Moon, and

as that of Christ occurred at or near the middle of the first
Solar Month we may describe it as marking the First Day
of the Lunar Great Year. A departure from symmetry,
a separation between the Full Moon and the first day of
5   the Solar Month, and of the New Moon from its Fifteenth
Day, would according to our system accompany the
discord of life. What we have called the First Day of
the Lunar Great Year falls at a remarkable place among
the Constellations. The Constellations being of varying
10   lengths and sometimes overlapping have but a vague
connection either with the Twelve Divisions of the Solar
Great Year, or with the Twelve Divisions of the ordinary
year, but they must have dominated the ancient imagination much more than any abstract division of the ecliptic.
15   When I find the position of the vernal equinox at the
birth of Christ upon the only star map within my reach
which has the ancient mythological Zodiacal creatures—
Plate 3 in E. M. Plunkett's " Ancient Calendars "—it
falls exactly upon the line dividing the Horn of the
20   Ram from the Side of the Fish. Probably the Zodiacal
creatures were never drawn precisely alike on any two
maps but the difference was not great, the stars of Ram
and Fish are packed particularly close to one another,
and neither Virgil nor his Sibyl, if they knew anything
25   of the Great Year, could have failed to find the position
of the precessional Sun significant. Three hundred years,
two degrees of the Great Year, would but correspond to
two days of the Sun's annual journey, and his transition
from Pisces to Aries had for generations been associated
30   with the ceremonial death and resurrection of Dionysus.
Near that transition the women wailed him, and night
showed the full moon separating from the constellation
Virgo, with the star in the wheatsheaf, or in the
child, for in the old maps she is represented carrying
35   now one now the other. It may be that instead
of a vague line, the Sibyl knew some star that

fixed the exact moment of transition. I find but four explanations compatible with man's agency, and all four incredible, for Christ being born at or near the moment of transition : that it came of pure chance—that prophecy founded upon observation of the stars created a so general expectation that prophecy brought its own fulfilment—that there has been from time immemorial so exact and unvarying correspondence between the history of mankind and the passage of the constellations men could date at some remote millenium, perhaps when the first month was first described as the month of the Sacrifice of Righteousness, and given the sacrificial Ram. as its symbol, the rise and fall of civilisations as the manager of an office can tell what his clerks will be doing after lunch by a morning consideration of the clock,— that Christianity, like the religion of Serapis at the time of Ptolemy Soter, was deliberately created by unknown men out of what they found.

To show a Redeemer was expected for the middle of a period—in our system the first solar month of an Age, and I suggest in that of Rome—we have not only the Stoical argument that improvement in the arts and sciences was at the expense of the individual soul, and that therefore the moment of maturity was the moment of the soul's need, but the early Christian doctrine that Christ was born in the middle of the sixth period from Adam, and the Persian that Zarathustra was born in the middle of a period of six thousand years " as the heart in the middle of the body." One remembers too, " Times and times and half a time." The Persian and Christian doctrines were identical in essentials, for the Age is a microcosm of the whole. However I but suggest and wait judgment, being no scholar; and it may be, but seek a background for my thought, a painted scene.

The alternation of *antithetical* and *primary* months is certainly Platonic, for his Golden Age men are born old and grow young, whereas in that which follows they are born young and grow old. He, however, made Gold *antithetical*; upon the other hand the Babylonians had the same alternation but began we are told with Silver

5 and the Moon.

XI

THE DEAD AND THE FIXED STARS

BECAUSE the visible world is the sum of the *Bodies of Fate* of all living things, or the sum of the *Creative Minds* of all *Daimons* whether of the living or the dead, what we call *Fate* is, as much as our most voluntary acts, a

10 part of a single logical stream; and the Fixed Stars being the least changing things are the acts of whatever in that stream changes least, and therefore of all souls that have found an almost changeless rest. Berkeley thought if his study table remained when he closed his eyes it

15 could only be because it was the thought of a more powerful spirit which he named God, but the mathematician Poincaré considers time and space the work of our ancestors. With the system in my bones I must declare that those ancestors still live and that time and

20 space would vanish if they closed their eyes.

XII

THE CONES OF INDIVIDUAL LIFE

WHEN we consider the Lunar and Solar cones in relation to individual life, the lower half of one or other, according to whether that life be *primary* or *antithetical*, is the individual phase, and the opposite half the *Mask* or the

25 *Body of Fate* as the case may be, and during the waking

life while in the body, the man may not pass beyond the central point. The opposite state of his being, that which is the activity of his *Daimon*, meets him at the centre, and contact with it is now death and now creation. After death, or in a trance or in ordinary sleep, 5 he enters into that state, as man is always antithetical in relation to his *Daimon* whatever his own phase may be, or whatever that of his *Daimon*, and to die or to sleep is to pass from the Lunar to the Solar cones.

When we translate this into the life of the *Faculties* 10 we mean that in the cones of the *Faculties*, *Will* starting at lunar South, physical maturity, reaches lunar East (Phase 22) at death, and that then life passes into the *Creative Mind* which is in the solar cones—the Diamond— and that, instead of *Will* and *Mask* dominating 15 the being, *Creative Mind* and *Body of Fate* are dominant until the *Will* reaches lunar West (Phase 8) birth. If we translate it into the life of the *Principles*, which are those of spiritual life and, while Natural life continues, of subconscious life, life remains in 20 the *Husk* until East is reached and then passes into *Spirit* which is in the Solar cones at Capricorn. Then the *Spirit* together with the *Celestial Body* which is at Cancer, dominate instead of *Passionate Body* and *Husk*, and continue to do so, moving as we have already 25 described until the *Husk* reaches lunar *West*.

The *Principles* and the *Faculties* change quality and operation according to the side of the cone upon which they travel, for the sides of the Lunar cone where Aries is are associated with *Spirit* or *Creative Mind*, and those 30 where Libra is with *Celestial Body* or *Body of Fate*; whereas in the Solar cones the sides where Capricorn is are associated with *Husk* or *Will*, and those where Cancer is with *Passionate Body* or *Mask*. This change of quality or operation chiefly concerns us in the part of the cones 35 where the mind is, and, as we shall presently see, *Spirit*

during all the first part of the life after death struggles
to separate itself from the *Passionate Body* upon whose
side of the cone it travels, whereas in the second part
of that life it re-unites itself with *Husk*; and during later
5 natural life the *Mask* travels upon the side of its cone
influenced by the *Celestial Body*, whereas in the earlier
part upon that side influenced by the *Husk*.

It is sometimes said that there is only one gyre in the
Diamond, but that means that man can know but one
10 gyre, that of *Spirit* or of *Creative Mind* as the case may
be, and sees the *Celestial Body* or *Body of Fate* as beyond
himself; whereas a man during natural life is in both
Will and *Mask*, and after death—if *Husk* and *Passionate
Body* be sublimated and transformed—he may enter
15 through *Spirit* and *Celestial Body* into the nature of both,
and that is why *antithetical* man after death is in good
and evil, or in light and dark, whereas *primary* man is
in good or evil, light or dark.

XIII

The Four Principles

THE *Husk* is sensuous and instinctive, almost the
20 physical body during life, and after death its record.

The *Passionate Body* is passion, but unlike the *Mask*—
which if permitted to govern the mind is isolating passion,
—is without solitude.

The *Celestial Body* is the portion of Eternal Life
25 which can be separated away.

The *Spirit* is almost abstract mind, for it has neither
substance nor life unless united to the *Passionate Body*
or *Celestial Body*.

Unlike the *Faculties* they do not create separated or
30 abstracted form.

XIV

LIFE AFTER DEATH

AFTER death the consciousness or choice passes into the
Spirit and that should turn wholly to the *Celestial Body*
and submit to it; not to the *Passionate Body* which is now
inseparable from the *Body of Fate* and inaugurates what
is called the *Dreaming Back*. If for the sake of simplicity 5
I count the life before death and the life after as the
two halves of a single Wheel and measure it upon that,
this state probably lasts till that part which corresponds
to Phase 25 is over. It is succeeded by a state called the
Shiftings which lasts until the *Spirit* escapes from the 10
Passionate Body, and the *Celestial Body* from the *Husk*
and they face one another in contemplation and in rest.
Then comes a brief state called *Beatitude* corresponding
perhaps to that moment of contemplation and to Phase 1.
This is followed by the *Going Forth* and the *Foreknowing* 15
during which the *Spirit* is reunited to the *Husk*, and
Celestial Body to *Passionate Body*—now love, not passion
—and after Phase 4 the Soul is dominated by the thought
of the coming life. While the Soul was passing first
through the lower half and then through the upper half of 20
the cone, the cone itself moved so that the Soul is born a
phase further on than that of its previous embodiment.
I have touched upon these things to set them in their
place in the system and touched upon them only, for
I shall describe them in detail later on. 25

XV

THE SUN'S ANNUAL JOURNEY AND THE CHRISTIAN YEAR

WHEN we adopt, as in the Christian Calendar, the Sun's
annual journey as the symbol, we identify the *Celestial
Body* with the Sun, because it moves from Aries to 30

L

Pisces and not in reverse order like the *Spirit* and the
Creative Mind; and we attribute the Birth of Christ to
the winter solstice when the *Husk* is at Phase 8, and His
Conception and also His Crucifixion—He is " slain on the
5   stems of generations "—to the moment when, at the
vernal equinox, the *Husk* is at Phase 15. At least that
is the way we put it in our symmetrical system, but to
the early Christian the problem was more difficult, for
he, or those from whom he learnt, was perplexed by the
10   different beginning and end of the lunar and solar Years.
They tried to settle the matter by a tradition that the
world, and one may conclude the Sun, was created at
the vernal equinox, and the Moon created at the full two
days later, and that as Christ's life must copy the Great
15   Year so begun, His Crucifixion and His Conception took
place two days after the vernal equinox. They did not,
however, celebrate the anniversaries of these events upon
a fixed date but, as if to draw attention to the annual
symbolism and so to the events as always present and
20   recurrent, they selected for their Easter Ceremonies the
first full Moon after the Vernal equinox no matter what
the day of the month, or the Sunday nearest to that moon.
One notices with surprise, however, that though the date
of Conception changed from year to year the Date of
25   Christ's Birth did not. For the first four hundred years
of our era January the 6th was kept Holy as the day of
His Birth. The Christian explanation of the date was an
arbitrary and fantastic calculation, or some childish alle-
gory. Sometimes they calculated the age of the world, and
30   so Christ's relation to the Great Year, by putting together
the lives of Patriarchs, and sometimes pointed out that
January 6th, being twelve days after the winter solstice,
glorified the Twelve Apostles. They had plainly received
the date, as I think Macrobius and Cicero had the doctrine
35   of the Great Year, from the learned men of an older
civilisation, from Greeks and Chaldeans perhaps, perhaps

even from those worshippers of Kore at Alexandria who upon that day carried up from a Temple Crypt a wooden figure marked upon head and hands and knees with a Cross and a Star, crying out " The Virgin has given Birth to the God." If, however, one counts nine lunar months, allowing as the Greeks did twenty-nine and thirty days for each alternately, from the first new Moon after the Annunciation, one finds that the night of the 6th of January is the first upon which the faint Crescent of the Tenth Moon could have shown. The nine and a half months of gestation had passed by, and the Divine Life had been identified with that of the Seasons.

" The White hand of Moses from the bough
  Puts forth, and Jesu from the ground suspires."

The choice of the date, the hesitation which after four centuries chose the winter solstice itself for the birth of Christ, seem much the same choice and hesitation that we ourselves would have gone through, if compelled to decide between Phase 8, where the need for personality first arises, and Phase 9 where personality displays itself. When I was a boy it was customary to consider that the association of events in the Life of Christ with one or other of the four solstices, was the result of competition with Pagan Festivals, but we know now that the association came before competition and that Christianity itself is part of the Sidereal Faith.

Did the great victims of Antiquity, Christ, Cæsar, Socrates—Love, Justice, Truth—die under the first full Moon after the vernal equinox? Christ did, as the date of Easter shows; Cæsar did,—Beware the Ides of March —and the sentence upon Socrates was pronounced when the Sacred Ship sailed for what recent research considers a March Festival at Delos, the renewal of Apollo and the Earth. Did that Festival begin at the new Moon, and the Moon show all but full on the Piræus when the Ship put in to port, and was it full when Socrates drank the Hemlock? When I write these words, and recall the place of the precessional Sun, should there not be a stirring in the roots of my hair? What did ancient Thaumaturgy guard in silence?

According to St. Chrysostom, John the Baptist was conceived at the Autumnal and Christ at the Spring Equinox, which makes them respectively *primary* and *antithetical* when considered in relation to one another, a mid-summer and a mid-winter child. Did Da Vinci, when he painted a St. John that seemed a Dionysus, know that St. John's father begot him when the grape was ripe, and that his mother bore him at the Mediterranean ripening of the corn?

XVI

The Opening and Closing of the Tinctures

THE closing of the Tinctures as described in the section about the Great Wheel is caused by the preoccupation with one another of the *Celestial Body* and the *Spirit*, of the *Creative Mind* and the *Body of Fate*, when the *Will* is between Phase 26 and Phase 4, where Unity with God is possible; whereas their opening between Phases 12 and 18 is caused by the fact that the *Faculties* can be apprehended in their separation within the united being. The fact that one *Tincture* opens or closes before the other is no doubt the effect of the gyres mounting a little higher upon one side of the cone than upon the other.

XVII

The Gyres of the Great Mythologies

A RELIGION or a civilisation belongs also to the lower half of the double cone, and the religion which is the

originating cause of the civilisation is begotten and dies
at the centre. When the lower half of the double cone
is separated off and becomes itself a double cone, what
was the centre is now its North. When it reaches South
of this cone, which I shall now call the History Cone,   5
it finds its doctrinal unity and vigour, its form of Unity
of Being. When later on I study this movement in detail
I will divide this history cone yet once more so that there
is one cone from North to South and yet another from

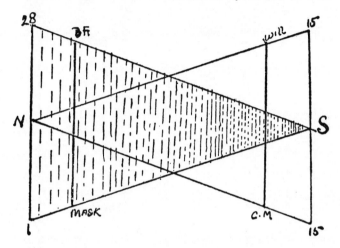

South to North again. Whereas when I examine the life   10
after death and compare it with this life I shall symbolize
each state as one half of a double cone for I have neither
the knowledge nor the talent for an analysis which would
approach the Divine Comedy in complexity.

These are the historical cones in their simplest form,   15
the ordinary double cone of the phases.

Will leaves North at the birth of Christ, and the *Body
of Fate* leaves South, and then when *Will* reaches South
and *Body of Fate* North they change sides and return :
at, say 1200 A.D., they show the position in the figure.   20
But we can also arrange them thus for the same date.

Will starting at A.D.1 travels along the lower side of the shaded cone, reaches 1000 A.D. or South and then moves upon the upper side. The *Creative Mind* starting at 1 A.D. moves along the upper side of the cone till it
5   reaches 1000 A.D. at South and then travels down the lower side. The *Mask* and the *Body of Fate* start also from the North, but whereas the other two *Faculties* had started from the wide ends of the shaded cone, they travel from the narrow end of the unshaded cone. They also

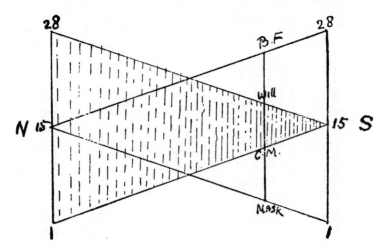

10   travel to South and there change sides and return towards the North. A single line is in this way made to show the position of all the *Four Faculties* as those *Faculties* are placed on the cone of the entire Era of two thousand years, for if this line be itself divided into 28 divisions
15   the 15th in the centre and the 1st at the point nearest the starting point of the *Will* at A.D. 1, it will be found that the points where the sides of cones intersect will show the place of the *Four Faculties* on this greater cone. When the *Will* is so placed that any of
20   the other *Faculties*, if placed upon the line, would lie in the future the corresponding date in a previous Millenium

is taken. When the two thousand years are divided into cones of a millenium each this line has the same office as Head, Heart, Loins and Fall upon the Great Wheel, it shows the relation of the lesser to the greater division.

We show the *antithetical* or *primary* nature of a Faculty at a particular period of time by the converging or diverging nature of the line where it is, without forgetting that each cone has its general *primary* or *antithetical* character. If we consider this figure with a similar figure, which represents the upper half of the cone, there will be two lines parallel, each marking the place of the *Four Faculties* of its half, and we shall get the third diagram in Sec. IV.

Our figure is the ground work of the historical diagram facing page 180 and was probably chosen for it, because it shows at a glance what epochs are affected by what *Faculties*, and there, as it covers two thousand years and shows a movement from North to North (or if you count it upon the whole Wheel from centre to centre) it is divided into two portions of twenty-eight phases. It is upon this figure that the documents I work from place historical events with " approximate accuracy." The movement to South of the entire era is a sinking wave of civilisation, a mounting physical or religious wave; the movement to North the converse. At South of each millennium is a period of artistic creation, that of the first millennium of mainly religious art, that of the other of mainly secular. And as North of the era is solar West, the South solar East, in the first thought is growing more Eastern, and in the second more Western. In the similar period before Christ, that of the Fifth Century B.C., thought was growing Western. Epoch, however, influences epoch as part of the cone of the entire era, by supersensual or ghostly interaction. The diagram facing page 180 is drawn for our epoch and the place of *Will* is affected through its *Creative Mind* by the Age of

Constantine, and when I was at Oxford a few years
ago, a distinguished scholar, now dead, showed me much
elaborate written evidence to prove that an apparition
seen by herself and a friend in the Louvre was the
5 Emperor Constantine.   This influence of age upon age
is said to be through the agency of certain *spirits who
have come to possess what is called a simulacrum, or
permanent illusionary body, created from the representation of themselves most present to the imagination of
10 their time.

But this figure differs in form from that which preceded
it and symbolised the preceding period of two thousand
years, and will differ in form from any figure drawn to
record the influence of a *Second Fountain*. This difference
15 is caused by a movement analogous to the exchange of
the *Tinctures* but instead of the words *primary* and
antithetical we substitute Solar and Lunar.   At each
Fountain the civilisation gyres, those of *Creative Mind*
and *Will* which in this connection we call Lunar, and the
20 gyres of *Mask* and *Body of Fate* which we call Solar,
change cones. Before the birth of Christ, for instance the
Lunar gyres came to the narrow end of their cone, and at
His birth passed into the broad end of the other cone and
so continued to converge. The Solar gyre upon the other
25 hand passed from broad to narrow. The Solar is religious
and physical and the Lunar emotional and intellectual.
This means that as the civil life grew more and more
antithetical in nature the religious grew more and more
primary till the instant of creation was reached.   At

---

* I once heard Sir William Crookes tell how he was informed
through an automatic writer that if he would make a certain
incense " The Magi would be present," and that there followed
words in an unknown tongue which turned out to be ancient
Persian. When read with great difficulty they proved to be a list
of herbs, but no one living seemed to know to what herbs the
names applied. I suspect that the link between periods arising
from their place among the gyres is never broken, no matter how
great the passage of time.

South, however, there is no interchange, but a return,
a change of direction, the gyres which diverged now
converge and vice versa, and this change is called *reflex*
to distinguish it from that of the North which is *active*.

XVIII

The Three Fountains and the Cycles of Embodiment

THE Fountains fall into four sets of three, three in each   5
quarter of Wheel, first of each set beginning at centre
of Phases 1, 8, 15, 22 respectively, second at centre of
next three, third at centre of last three Phases of each
quarter. They may correspond to gold, silver, copper
ages adopted by the Greek poet Aratus instead   10
of Hesiod's four. But what is most clear is that
they are alternately *Victim* and *Sage*, the *Victim* being
called the strong soul because he attains the greatest
strength and renounces it, and the *Sage* the frail soul
because his strength is in that which surrounds him, in   15
his doctrine let us say. Christ, though *Sage*—discovery
of strength, the frail soul—when measured upon the Great
Wheel, when placed as one of the Three Fountains of
His quarter, is *Victim*, Aries, surrenders strength, and
He that is to come will be the frail soul, and as Christ   20
was the *primary* revelation to an *antithetical* age, He
that is to come will be the *antithetical* revelation to a
primary age. The cycles of human rebirth, unlike those
of the Eternal Man, are measured upon the Lunar cone,
and the first is at Lunar North, and these months or   25
cycles had at first their symmetrical relation to the Solar
months of the Great Year, each Lunar cycle starting in
the middle of Solar, but a wheel does not cease to turn
when its first revolution is over, and so it comes about at

last that all the months Solar and Lunar, as it were fell together and were confused one with the other, and yet as if by a kind of crystallisation these months so arranged themselves that all the twelve Lunar months had their
5   beginning in a certain order within each era. So we say that the first cycle sent its first soul into the world at the birth of Christ, and that the twelfth will send its last soul immediately before the birth of the New Fountain. Then there will come the first of a new series,
10 the Thirteenth Cycle, which is a Sphere and not a cone. And yet when I say the first and last souls of a cycle, I do not mean that that cycle comes to an end for it is always beginning and always ending. When we arrange these beginnings within the two thousand years
15 of an era we find that three cycles have their approximate beginning in each five hundred years, and so give that time their character.

There is much else that I must leave to my student, if such there be, to discover as he compares symbol with
20 symbol. His task will be easier than mine, for I had to discover all from unconnected psychological notes and from a few inadequate diagrams. These few pages have taken me many months of exhausting labour, but never once have note and diagram failed to support each other.
25 In judging a man one should not only know his phase but his cycle, for every cycle has a different character, but into these characters I cannot go at present, for I lack information. We retain the same sex for a cycle, and then change it for another cycle, and there are said
30 to be certain cycles between which love is more fortunate than between others, and some where physical beauty is greater and some where mental. The general law is that they follow the same development as the phases.

XIX

Cones of Nations and Movements of Thought

WE have to remember that among the solar and lunar cones that revolve in the circle of the great year are the cones of each separate nation and of every school of thought and action. We give to these cones the name of *Covens*. The *Covens* depend exactly as individuals do upon contact for their intensity, and separated from their opposites " Consume themselves away." Four *Covens*, constituting four *Faculties*, may for instance move round the wheel and pass through their phases as do individual men and women. When a movement of thought, the philosophy of religious spiritualism for instance, becomes vague and sentimental, that may be because contact through the *physical* or *spiritual primary* with some school of psychological investigation at the place, say, of the *Creative Mind* has come to an end. The *Covens* are formed by their *Daimons* out of groups of men and women who become the bodies of the *Daimons* and the *Daimon* of each *Coven* seeks to impress his will upon the three associated *Covens*. When a *Coven* has carried its creative life as far as phase and historical epoch permit, there is a re-birth, or a movement to the next phase.

I myself chose the name *Coven*, that being the name of the groups of Scotch Witches described in the witch trials, for I imagine the Nations and Philosophies as having each, as it were, a witches' cauldron of medicinal or devil's broth in the midst. That which we must deduce from the doctrine is that there can be no philosophy, nation, or movement that is not a being or congeries of beings, and that which we call the proof of some philosophy is but that which enables it to be born. The world is

a drama where person follows person, and though the
dialogue prepares for all the entrances, that preparation
is not the person's proof, nor is Polonius disproved when
Hamlet seems to kill him. Once the philosophy, nation
5 or movement has clearly shown its face, we know that
its chief characteristic has not arisen out of any proof,
or even out of all the past, or out of the present tension
of the drama, or out of any visible cause whatever, but is
unique, life in itself. There can be neither cause nor
10 effect when all things are co-eternal.

XX

THE CONES OF SEXUAL LOVE

I CAN but touch upon the symbolism of sexual love as
it needs more detailed consideration than I can give it
in this book. In all pairs of lovers each is to himself
or herself, *Will*, and the other *Body of Fate*. The cones
15 of their passion are constituted, as the solar and lunar
cones are, out of the first fixed circles, and its progress
should mirror the cones containing the three Fountains
or if we consider the matter differently and take a smaller
Wheel, those from Fountain to Fountain. Love which
20 in this way mirrors the fated and predestined, has three
forms of crisis, each at the end of a constituent
cone, called the first and second *Critical Moments* and
the *Beatific Vision*. Such love has a relation with the
dead similar to that of the Fountains and comes at each
25 crisis under the sway of the thirteenth cone. That
is to say there is harmonization or the substitution of
the sphere for the cone. The *Four Faculties* of passion,
before harmonization, are Desire, which is *Creative Mind*,
Cruelty, which is *Body of Fate*, Service, which is *Will*,

and Domination, which is *Mask*. After harmonization the *Creative Mind* becomes Wisdom, *Body of Fate* Truth, *Will* Love, and *Mask* Beauty. There are also *Initiatory Moments* which create the domination of the symbol, as *Critical Moments* destroy that domination, and these 5 fall where the gyres touch the sides of cones—North and South—and are of an indefinite number. All *antithetical* life, for *primary* life has but a single movement, is seen as if it were a form of sexual life. It becomes vital through conflict and happy through harmonization, 10 and without either is self-consumed. Harmonization is made possible by the recognition of fate—the Lunar cone's recognition of the Solar—but as each is Solar to the other, the destiny of the one is the fate of the other. It is the recognition by Lunar man of the Solar spiritual 15 opposite that is called faith, and it inaugurates religious emotional and philosophical experience.

XXI

COMPLEMENTARY DREAMS

I USE in the section about the state of man after death the term *complementary dream*. When two people meditate upon the one theme, who have established a 20 supersensual link, they will invariably in my experience, no matter how many miles apart, see pass before the mind's eye complementary images, images that complete one another. One for instance may see a boat upon a still sea full of tumultuous people, and the other a boat full of 25 motionless people upon a tumultuous sea. Even when the link is momentary and superficial this takes place, and sometimes includes within its range a considerable number of people. One, for instance, will receive from a dream figure a ripe apple, another an unripe; one a lighted and one an unlighted candle, and so on.

On the same night a mother will dream that her child is dead or dying, the child that her mother is dead, while the father will wake in the night with a sudden inexplicable anxiety for some material treasure. I put an experience of the kind into the poem that begins—

> Was it the double of my dream,
> The woman that by me lay
> Dreamed, or did we halve a dream
> Under the first cold gleam of day.

A whole age may be bound in a single dream, or wheel, so that its creations have all the same character though there is no visible influence.

XXII

THE whole world is regarded as a single being with a relation between East and West like that between *complementary dreams*, Europe being *antithetical* and Asia *primary*. The cardinal points in the Solar and Lunar cones are not merely symbols of the Sun and Moon's path, but are held to refer to the actual geographical points. Probably those in the Solar cones refer to the movement of ideas, and their places of origin, and I shall so consider them, and those in the Lunar cones to the origin of the races themselves in so far as they keep the impression of their first surroundings.

When Joseph Strzygowski says " the inhabitants of the South from the very beginning applied pictorial art to the representation of living creatures " he describes the *antithetical* nature of the South, and he defines the *primary* North when he attributes to it geometrical form and various " non-representational " decorations derived

from handicrafts, and he certainly describes the symbolic
East when he attributes to his eastern nations conceptions
that dazzle and astonish by an impression of power
whether in Priest or King. Perhaps too in his description
of the West as that which absorbs and uses, and is a   5
kind of matrix, he describes our symbolic West also.

XXIII

The Cones—Higher Dimensions

ONE of the notes upon which I have based this book
says that all existence within a cone has a larger number
of dimensions than are known to us, and another identifies
Creative Mind, *Will* and *Mask* with our three dimensions,   10
but *Body of Fate* with the unknown fourth, time exter-
nally perceived. When I saw this I tried to understand a
little of modern research into this matter but found that I
lacked the necessary training. I have therefore ignored
it hitherto in writing this book. The difference between   15
a higher and a lower dimension explains, however, the
continual breaking up of cones and wheels into smaller
cones and wheels without changing the main movement
better than Swedenborg's vortex, his gyre made up of
many gyres. Every dimension is at right angles to all   20
dimensions below it in the scale. If the Great Wheel, say,
be a rotating plane, and the movement of any constituent
cone a rotation at right angles to that plane the second
movement cannot affect the first in any way. In the same
way the rotation of the sphere will be a movement at right   25
angles to a circumference which includes all movements
known to us. We can only imagine a perpetual turning
in and out of that sphere, hence the sentence quoted by
Aherne about the great eggs which turn inside out
without breaking the shell.   30

It seems that ancient men except the Persian and the
Jew who looked to an upward progression, held Nietsche's
doctrine of the eternal return, but if religion and mathematics are right, and time an illusion, it makes no differ-
5 ence except in the moral effect.

XXIV

The Four Principles and Neo-Platonic Philosophy

I HAVE not considered the ultimate origin of things, nor
have my documents thrown a direct light upon it. The
word *Anima Mundi* frequently occurs and is used very
much as in the philosophy of Plotinus. I am inclined
10 to discover in the *Celestial Body*, the *Spirit*, the
Passionate Body, and the *Husk*, emanations from or
reflections from his One, his Intellectual Principle, his
Soul of the World, and his Nature respectively. The
Passionate Body is described as that which links one
15 being to another, and that which rescues the *Celestial
Body* from solitude, and this is part of the office of the
Soul of the World in Plotinus. As actually used in the
documents *Anima Mundi* is the receptacle of emotional
images when purified from whatever unites them to one
20 man rather than to another. The 13th, 14th and 15th
cycles are described as Spheres, and are certainly emanations from the Soul of the World, the Intellectual
Principle and the One respectively, but there is a fundamental difference, though perhaps only of expression,
25 between the system and that of Plotinus. In Plotinus the
One is the Good, whereas in the system Good and Evil
are eliminated before the Soul can be united to Reality,
being that stream of phenomena that drowns us.

BOOK III
DOVE OR SWAN

THE HISTORICAL CONES.

The numbers in brackets refer to phases, and the other numbers to dates A.D. The line cutting the cones a little below 250, 900, 1180 and 1927 shows four historical *Faculties* related to the present moment.

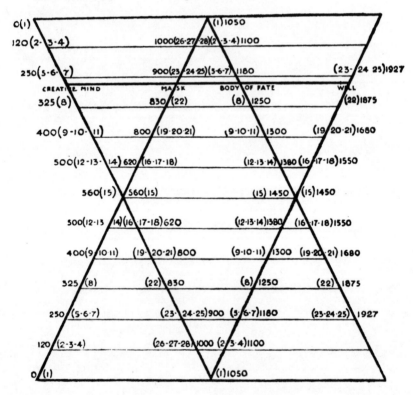

I. LEDA.

A sudden blow : the great wings beating still
Above the staggering girl, her thighs caressed
By the dark webs, her nape caught in his bill,
He holds her helpless breast upon his breast.

How can those terrified vague fingers push   5
The feathered glory from her loosening thighs,
And how can body, laid in that white rush,
But feel the strange heart beating where it lies;
A shudder in the loins engenders there
The broken wall, the burning roof and tower   10
And Agamemnon dead.
                  Being so caught up,
So mastered by the brute blood of the air,
Did she put on his knowledge with his power
Before the indifferent beak could let her drop?   15

2. THE GREAT WHEEL AND HISTORY.

I

ONE must bear in mind that the Christian Era, like the two thousand years, let us say, that went before it, is an entire wheel, and each half of it an entire wheel, that each half when it comes to its 28th Phase reaches
5   the 15th Phase of the entire era. It follows therefore that the 15th Phase of each millenium, to keep the symbolic measure of time, is Phase 8 or Phase 22 of the entire era, that Aphrodite rises from a stormy sea, that Helen could not be Helen but for beleaguered Troy.
10   The era itself is but half of a greater era and its Phase 15 comes also at a period of war or trouble. The greater number is always more *primary* than the lesser and precisely because it contains it. A millenium is the symbolic measure of a being that attains its flexible
15   maturity and then sinks into rigid age.

A civilisation is a struggle to keep self-control, and in this it is like some great tragic person, some Niobe who must display an almost superhuman will or the cry will not touch our sympathy. The loss of control over
20   thought comes towards the end; first a sinking in upon the moral being, then the last surrender, the irrational cry, revelation—the scream of Juno's peacock.

II

2000 B.C. TO 1 A.D.

I IMAGINE the annunciation that founded Greece as made to Leda, remembering that they showed in a Spartan Temple, strung up to the roof as a holy relic, an unhatched egg of hers; and that from one of her eggs came Love and from the other War. But all things are from antithesis, and when in my ignorance I try to imagine what older civilisation she refuted I can but see bird and woman blotting out some corner of the Babylonian mathematical starlight.

Did the older civilisation like the Jewish think a long life a proof of Heavenly favour that the Greek races should affirm so clearly that those whom the Gods love die young, hurling upon some age of crowded comedy their tragic sense? Certainly their tribes, after a first multitudinous revelation—dominated each by its *Daimon* and oracle-driven—broke up a great Empire and established in its stead an intellectual anarchy. At some 1000 years before Christ I imagine their religious system complete and they themselves grown barbaric and Asiatic. Then came Homer, civil life, a desire for civil order dependent doubtless on some oracle, and then (Phase 10 of second Greek millennium) for independent civil life and thought. At, let me say, the sixth century B.C. (Phase 12) personality begins, but there is as yet no intellectual solitude. A man may rule his tribe or town but he cannot separate himself from the general mass. With the first discovery of solitude (Phases 13 and 14) comes, as I think, the visible art that interests us most to-day, for Phidian art, like the art of Raphael, has for the moment exhausted our attention. I recall a Nike at the Ashmolean Museum with a natural unsystematised

beauty like that before Raphael, and above all certain pots with strange half supernatural horses dark on a light ground. Self-realisation attained will bring desire of power—systematisation for its instrument—but as yet
5   clarity, meaning, elegance, all things separated from one another in luminous space, seem to exceed all other virtues. One compares this art with the thought of Greek Philosophers before Anaxagoras, where one discovers the same phases, always more concerned with the
10   truth than with its moral or political effects. One longs for the lost dramatists, the plays that were enacted before Aeschylus and Sophocles arose, both Phidian men.

But one must consider not the movement only from the beginning to the end of the historical cone, but the
15   gyres that touch its sides, the horizontal movement. There is that continual oscillation which I have symbolised elsewhere as a King and Queen, who are Sun and Moon also, and whirl round and round as they mount up through a Round Tower.

20   Side by side with Ionic elegance there comes after the Persian wars a Doric vigour, and the light-limbed dandy of the potters, the Parisian-looking young woman of the sculptors, her hair elaborately curled, give place to the athlete. One suspects a deliberate turning away from all
25   that is Eastern, or a moral propaganda like that which turned the poets out of Plato's Republic, and yet it may be that the preparation for the final systematisation had for its apparent cause the destruction, let us say, of Ionic studios by the Persian invaders, and that all came from
30   the resistance of the *Body of Fate* to the growing solitude of the soul. Then in Phidias Ionic and Doric influence unite—one remembers Titian—and all is transformed by the full moon, and all abounds and flows. With Callimachus pure Ionic revives again, as Furtwingler has
35   proved, and upon the only example of his work known to us, a marble chair, a Persian is represented, and may one

not discover a Persian symbol in that bronze lamp, shaped like a palm, known to us by a description in Pausanias? but he was an archaistic workman, and those who set him to work brought back public life to an older form. One may see in masters and man a   5 momentary dip into ebbing Asia.

Each age unwinds the thread another age had wound, and it amuses one to remember that before Phidias, and his westward moving art, Persia fell, and that when full moon came round again, amid eastward moving thought,   10 and brought Byzantine glory, Rome fell; and that at the outset of our westward moving Renaissance Byzantium fell; all things dying each other's life, living each other's death.

After Phidias the life of Greece, which being *antithe-*   15 *tical* had moved slowly and richly through the *antithetical* phases, comes rapidly to an end. Some Greek or Roman writer whose name I forget will soon speak of the declining comeliness of the people, and in 'the arts all is systematised more and more, and the antagonist recedes.   20 Aristophanes' passion-clouded eye falls before what one must believe, from Roman stage copies, an idler glance. (Phases 19, 20, 21). Aristotle and Plato end creative system—to die into the truth is still to die—and formula begins. Yet even the truth into which Plato dies is a   25 form of death, for when he separates the Eternal Ideas from Nature and shows them self-sustained he prepares the Christian desert and the Stoic suicide.

I identify the conquest of Alexander and the break-up of his kingdom, when Greek civilisation, formalised and   30 codified, loses itself in Asia, with the beginning and end of the 22nd Phase, and his intention recorded by some historian to turn his arms westward shows that he is but a part of the impulse that creates Hellenised Rome and Asia. There are everywhere statues where every muscle   35 has been measured, every position debated, and these statues represent man with nothing more to achieve, physical man finished and complacent, the women slightly tinted, but the men, it may be, who exercise naked in the open air, the colour of mahogany. Every

5 discovery after the epoch of victory and defeat (Phase 22) which substitutes mechanics for power, is an elimination of intellect by delight in technical skill (Phase 23), by a sense of the past (Phase 24) by some dominant belief (Phase 25). After Plato and Aristotle, the mind

10 is as exhausted as were the armies of Alexander at his death, but the Stoics can discover morals and turn philosophy into a rule of life. Among them doubtless—the first beneficiaries of Plato's hatred of imitation—we may discover the first benefactors of our modern individuality,

15 sincerity of the trivial face, the mask torn away. Then in the last three phases of the wheel, a Greece that Rome has conquered, and a Rome conquered by Greece, must adore, desire being dead, physical or spiritual force. This adoration which begins in the second century before

20 Christ creates a world-wide religious movement as the world was then known, which, being swallowed up in what came after, has left no adequate record. One knows not into how great extravagance Asia, accustomed to abase itself, may have carried what soon sent Greeks and

25 Romans to stand naked in a Mithraic pit, moving their bodies as under a shower-bath that those bodies might receive the blood of the bull even to the last drop. The adored image took everywhere the only form possible as the *antithetical* age died into its last violence—a human

30 or animal form. Even before Plato that collective image of man dear to Stoic and Epicurean alike, the moral double of bronze or marble athlete, had been invoked by Anaxagoras when he declared that thought and not the warring opposites created the world. At that sentence

35 the heroic life, passionate fragmentary man, all that had been imagined by great poets and sculptors began to

pass away, and instead of seeking noble antagonists, imagination moved towards divine man and the ridiculous devil. And now sages lure men away from the arms of women because in those arms man becomes a fragment; and all is ready for revelation. When revelation 5 comes athlete and sage are merged; the earliest sculptured image of Christ is copied from that of the Apotheosis of Alexander the Great; the tradition is founded which declares even to our own day that Christ alone is exactly six feet high, perfect physical man. Yet 10 as perfect physical man He must die, for only so can *primary* power reach *antithetical* mankind shut within the circle of its senses, touching outward things alone in that which seems most personal and physical. When I think of the moment before revelation I think of 15 Salome—she too, delicately tinted or maybe mahogany dark—dancing before Herod and receiving the Prophet's head in her indifferent hands, and wonder if what seems to us decadence was not in reality the exultation of the muscular flesh and of civilisation perfectly achieved. 20 Seeking images, I see her anoint her bare limbs according to a medical prescription of that time, with lion's fat, for lack of the sun's ray, that she may gain the favour of a king, and remember that the same impulse will create the Galilean revelation and deify Roman 25 Emperors whose sculptured heads will be surrounded by the solar disk. Upon the throne and upon the cross alike the myth becomes a biography.

III

A.D. 1 TO A.D. 1050

GOD is now conceived of as something outside man and man's handiwork, and it follows that it must be idolatry 30 to worship that which Phidias and Scopas made, and

seeing that He is a Father in Heaven that Heaven will be found presently in the Thebaid, where the world is changed into featureless clay and can be run through the fingers; and these things are testified to from books
5 that are outside human genius, being miraculous, and by a miraculous church, and this church, as the gyre sweeps wider, will make man also featureless as clay or sand. Night will fall upon man's wisdom now that man has been taught that he is nothing. He had
10 discovered, or half-discovered, that the world is round and one of many like it, but now he must believe that the sky is but a tent spread above a level floor, and—that he may be stirred into a frenzy of anxiety and so to moral transformation—blot out the knowledge or half-know-
15 ledge that he has lived many times, and think that all eternity depends upon a moment's decision, and Heaven itself—transformation finished—must appear so vague and motionless that it seems but a concession to human weakness. It is even essential to this faith to declare that
20 God's messengers, those beings who show His will in dreams or announce it in visionary speech were never men. The Greeks thought them often great men of the past but now that concession to mankind is forbidden. All must be narrowed into the sun's image cast out of a
25 burning-glass and man be ignorant of all but the image.

The mind that brought the change, if considered as man only, is a climax of whatever Greek and Roman thought was most a contradiction to its age; but con- sidered as more than man He controlled what Neo-
30 Pythagorean and Stoic could not—irrational force. He could announce the new age, all that had not been thought of or touched or seen, because He could sub- stitute for reason, miracle.

The sacrifice of the 22nd Phase is voluntary and so we
35 say of Him that He was love itself, and yet that part of Him which made Christendom was not love but pity, and

not pity for intellectual despair, though the man in Him, being *antithetical* like His age, knew it in the Garden, but *primary* pity, that for the common lot, man's death seeing that He raised Lazarus, sickness seeing that He healed many, sin seeing that He died.

Love is created and preserved by intellectual analysis, for we love only that which is unique, and it belongs to contemplation not to action, for we would not change that which we love. A lover will admit a greater beauty than that of his mistress but not its like, and surrenders his days to a delighted laborious study of all her ways and looks, and he pities only if something threatens that which has never been before and can never be again. Fragment delights in fragment and seeks possession, not service; whereas the Good Samaritan discovers himself in the likeness of another, covered with sores and abandoned by thieves upon the roadside, and in that other serves himself. The opposites are gone; he does not need his Lazarus; they do not each die the other's life, live the other's death.

It is of course impossible to do more than select a more or less arbitrary general date for the beginning of Roman decay (Phases 2 to 7, A.D. 1 to A.D. 250). Roman sculpture—sculpture made under Roman influence whatever the sculptor's blood—did not for instance reach its full vigour, if we consider what it had of Roman as distinct from Greek, until the Christian Era. It even made a discovery which affected all sculpture to come. The Greeks painted the eyes of marble statues and made out of enamel or glass or precious stones those of their bronze statues, but the Roman was the first to drill a round hole to represent the pupil, and because, as I think, of a preoccupation with the glance characteristic of a civilisation in its final phase. The colours must have already faded from the marbles of the great period, and a shadow and a spot of light, especially where there is

much sunlight, are more vivid than paint, enamel, coloured glass or precious stone. They could now express in stone a perfect composure, the administrative mind, alert attention where all had been rhythm, an exaltation
5   of the body, uncommitted energy. May it not have been precisely a talent for this alert attention that had enabled Rome and not Greece to express those final *primary* phases? One sees on the pediments troops of marble Senators, officials serene and watchful as befits men who
10 know that all the power of the world moves before their eyes, and needs, that it may not dash itself to pieces, their unhurried unanxious never-ceasing care. Those riders upon the Parthenon had all the world's power in their moving bodies, and in a movement that seemed,
15 so were the hearts of man and beast set upon it, that of a dance; but presently all would change and measurement succeed to pleasure, the dancing-master outlive the dance. What need had those young lads for careful eyes? But in Rome of the first and second centuries where the
20 dancing-master himself has died, the delineation of character as shown in face and head, as with us of recent years, is all in all, and sculptors seeking the custom of occupied officials stock in their workshops toga'd marble bodies upon which can be screwed with the least possible
25 delay heads modelled from the sitters with the most scrupulous realism. When I think of Rome I see always those heads with their world-considering eyes, and those bodies as conventional as the metaphors in a leading article, and compare in my imagination vague Grecian
30 eyes gazing at nothing, Byzantine eyes of drilled ivory staring upon a vision, and those eyelids of China and of India, those veiled or half-veiled eyes weary of world and vision alike.

Meanwhile the irrational force that would create con-
35 fusion and uproar as with the cry " The Babe, the Babe, is born "—the women speaking unknown tongues, the

barbers and weavers expounding Divine revelation with all the vulgarity of their servitude, the tables that move or resound with raps—still but creates a negligible sect. All about it is an *antithetical* aristocratic civilisation in its completed form, every detail of life hierarchical, every great man's door crowded at dawn by petitioners, great wealth everywhere in few men's hands, all dependent upon a few, up to the Emperor himself who is a God dependent upon a greater God, and everywhere in court, in the family, an inequality made law, and floating over all the Romanised Gods of Greece in their physical superiority. All is rigid and stationary, men fight for centuries with the same sword and spear, and though in naval warfare there is some change of tactics to avoid those single combats of ship with ship that needed the seamanship of a more skilful age, the speed of a sailing ship remains unchanged from the time of Pericles to that of Constantine. Though sculpture grows more and more realistic and so renews its vigour, this realism is without curiosity. The athlete becomes the boxer that he may show lips and nose beaten out of shape, the individual hairs show at the navel of the bronze centaur, but the theme has not changed. Philosophy alone, where in contact with irrational force—holding to Egyptian thaumaturgy and the Judean miracle but at arms length—can startle and create. Yet Plotinus is as *primary*, as much a contradiction of all that created Roman civilisation as St. Peter, and his thought has its roots almost as deep among the *primary* masses. The founder of his school was Ammonius Sacca, an Alexandrine porter. His thought and that of Origen, which I skimmed in my youth, seem to me to express the abstract synthesis of a quality like that of race, and so to display a character which must always precede Phase 8. Origen, because the Judean miracle has a stronger hold upon the masses than Alexandrian thaumaturgy, triumphs when Constantine

(Phase 8) puts the Cross upon the shields of his soldiers and makes the bit of his war-horse from a nail of the True Cross, an act equivalent to man's cry for strength amid the animal chaos at the close of the first lunar
5   quarter. Seeing that Constantine was not converted till upon his deathbed I see him as half statesman, half thaumaturgist, accepting in blind obedience to a dream the new fashionable talisman, two sticks nailed together. The Christians were but six millions of the sixty or
10 seventy of the Roman Empire but, spending nothing upon pleasure, exceedingly rich like some Nonconformist sect of the eighteenth century; and the world became Christian and " that fabulous formless darkness " as it seemed to a philosopher of the fourth century, blotted
15 out " every beautiful thing," not through the conversion of crowds or general change of opinion, or through any pressure from below, for civilization was *antithetical* still, but by an act of power.

I have not the knowledge (it may be that no man has
20 the knowledge) to trace the rise of the Byzantine state through Phases 9, 10 and 11. My diagram tells me that a hundred and sixty years brought that state to its 15th Phase, but I that know nothing but the arts and of these little, cannot revise the series of dates " approximately
25 correct " but given it may be for suggestion only. With a desire for simplicity of statement I would have preferred to find in the middle, not at the end, of the fifth century Phase 12, for that was, so far as the known evidence carries us, the moment when Byzantium became
30 Byzantine and substituted for formal Roman magnifi- cence, with its glorification of physical power, an archi- tecture that suggests the Sacred City in the Apocalypse of St. John. I think if I could be given a month of Antiquity and leave to spend it where I chose, I would
35 spend it in Byzantium a little before Justinian opened St. Sophia and closed the Academy of Plato. I think I

could find in some little wine shop some philosophical worker in mosaic who could answer all my questions, the supernatural descending nearer to him than to Plotinus even, for the pride of his delicate skill would make what was an instrument of power to Princes and Clerics and a murderous madness in the mob, show as a lovely flexible presence like that of a perfect human body.

I think that in early Byzantium, and maybe never before or since in recorded history, religious, aesthetic and practical life were one, and that architect and artificers—though not, it may be, poets, for language had been the instrument of controversy and must have grown abstract—spoke to the multitude and the few alike. The painter and the mosaic worker, the worker in gold and silver, the illuminator of Sacred Books were almost impersonal, almost perhaps without the consciousness of individual design, absorbed in their subject matter and that the vision of a whole people. They could copy out of old Gospel books those pictures that seemed as sacred as the text, and yet weave all into a vast design, the work of many that seemed the work of one, that made building, picture, pattern, metal work of rail and lamp, seem but a single image; and this vision, this proclamation of their invisible master had the Greek nobility, Satan always the still half divine Serpent, never the horned scarecrow of the didactic Middle Ages.

The ascetic, called in Alexandria " God's Athlete," has taken the place of those Greek athletes whose statues have been melted or broken up or stand deserted in the midst of cornfields, but all about him is an incredible splendour like that which we see pass under our closed eyelids as we lie between sleep and waking, no representation of a living world but the dream of a somnambulist. Even the drilled pupil of the eye, when the drill is in the hand of some Byzantine worker in ivory, undergoes a somnambulistic change for its deep shadow among the

faint lines of the tablet, its mechanical circle, where all else
is rhythmical and flowing, give to Saint or Angel a look
of some great bird staring at miracle. Could any visionary of those days, passing through the Church named
5 with so un-theological a grace " The Holy Wisdom,"
can even a visionary of to-day wandering among the
mosaics of Rome and Sicily, fail to recognise some one
image seen under his closed eyelids? To me it seems
that He, who among the first Christian communities
10 was little but a ghostly exorcist, had in His assent to a
full Divinity made possible this sinking in upon a supernatural splendour, these walls with their little glimmer-
ing cubes of blue and green and gold.

I think that I might discover an oscillation, a revolu-
15 tion of the horizontal gyre like that between Doric and
Ionic art, between the two principal characters of
Byzantine art. Recent criticism distinguishes between
the figures which come from Greece and Rome, their
stern faces suggesting Greek wall-painting at Palmyra,
20 Greco-Egyptian painting upon the cases of mummies,
where characteristic lines are exaggerated as in much
work of our time, and that decoration which seems to
undermine our self-control, and is it seems of Persian
origin, and has for its appropriate symbol a vine whose
25 tendrils climb everywhere and display among their leaves
all those strange images of bird and beast, those forms
that represent no creature eye has ever seen, yet are
begotten one upon the other as if they were themselves
living creatures. May I consider the domination of the
30 first late *antithetical* and that of the second *primary*, and
see in their alternation the work of the horizontal gyre?
Strzygowski thinks that the church decorations where
there are visible representations of holy persons were
especially dear to those who believed in Christ's double
35 nature and that wherever Christ is represented by a bare
Cross and all the rest is bird and beast and tree, we may

discover an Asiatic art dear to those who thought Christ
contained nothing human.

If I were left to myself I would make Phase 15 coincide
with Justinian's reign, that great age of building in
which one may conclude Byzantine art was perfected;   5
but the meaning of the diagram may be that a building
like St. Sophia where all, to judge by the contemporary
description, pictured ecstasy, must unlike the declamatory St. Peter's precede the moment of climax. Of the
moment of climax itself I can say nothing and of what   10
followed from Phase 17 to Phase 21 almost nothing, for
I have no knowledge of the time; and no analogy from
the age after Phidias, or after our own Renaissance can
help. We and the Greeks moved towards intellect but
Byzantium and the western Europe of that day moved   15
from it. If Strzygowski is right we may see in the
destruction of images but a destruction of what was Greek
in decoration accompanied perhaps by a renewed splendour in all that came down from the ancient Persian
Paradise, an episode in some attempt to make theology   20
more ascetic, spiritual and abstract. Destruction was
apparently suggested to the first iconoclastic Emperor
by followers of a Monophysite Bishop, Xenaias, who had
his See in that part of the Empire where Persian influence
had been strongest. The return of the images must, as   25
I see things, have been the failure of synthesis (Phase 22)
and the first sinking in and dying down of Christendom
into the heterogeneous loam. Europe grew animal and
literal; the strength of the victorious party came from
zealots who were as ready as their opponents to destroy   30
an image if permitted to grind it into powder, mix it
with some liquid and swallow it as a medicine. Mankind
for a season would do, not what it would, or should, but
what it could, and accept the past and the current belief
because they prevented thought. In western Europe   35
I think I may see in Johannes Scotus Erigena the last

N

intellectual synthesis before the death of philosophy, but I know little of him except that he is founded upon a Greek book of the sixth century, put into circulation by a last iconoclastic Emperor, though its Angelic Orders 5 might have given, and perhaps did give a theme to the image makers. I notice too that my diagram makes Phase 22 coincide with the break up of Charlemagne's Empire and so clearly likens him to Alexander, but I do not want to concern myself, except where I 10 must, with political events.

Then follows, as always must in the last quarter, heterogeneous art; hesitation amid architectural forms, some book tells me; an interest in Greek and Roman literature; much copying out and gathering together; yet outside 15 a few courts and monasteries I seem to discover an Asiatic and anarchic Europe. The intellectual cone has so narrowed that secular intellect has gone, and the strong man rules with the aid of local custom that needs none, and everywhere the supernatural is sudden, violent, and 20 as dark to the intellect as a stroke or St. Vitus' dance. Men under the Cæsars, my documents tell me, were physically one but intellectually many, but that is now reversed, for there is one common thought or doctrine and town is shut off from town, village from village, 25 clan from clan. The spiritual life is alone overflowing, its cone expanded, and yet this life—secular intellect extinguished—has little effect upon men's conduct, is perhaps a dream which passes beyond the reach of conscious mind but for some rare miracle or vision. I 30 think of it as like that profound reverie of the somnambulist which may be accompanied by a sensuous dream— a romanesque stream perhaps of bird and beast images— and yet neither affect the dream nor be affected by it. It is indeed precisely because this double mind is created 35 at the South that the *antithetical* phases are but, at the best, phases of a momentary illumination like that of a lightning flash. But the South that now concerns us, is not only Phase 15 of its greater era, but the final phase, Phase 28, of its millennium and, in its physical form, human life grown once more automatic. I knew a man once who, seeking for an image of the absolute, saw one persistent image, a slug, as though it were suggested to him that Being which is beyond human comprehension is mirrored in the least organised forms of life. Intellectual creation has ceased but men have come to terms with the supernatural and are agreed that, if you make the usual offerings, it will remember to live and let live; even Saint or Angel does not seem very different from themselves, a man thinks his guardian Angel jealous of his mistress; a King, dragging some Saint's body to a new Church, meets some difficulty upon the road, assumes a miracle, and denounces the Saint as a churl. Three Roman Courtesans who have one after another got their favourite lovers chosen Pope have, it pleases one's mockery to think, confessed their sins, with full belief in the supernatural efficacy of the act, to ears that have heard their cries of love, or received the Body of God from hands that have played with their own bodies. Interest has narrowed to what is near and personal and, seeing that all abstract secular thought has faded, those interests have taken the most physical forms. In monasteries and in hermit cells men freed from the intellect at last can seek their God upon all fours like beasts or children. Ecclesiastical Law, in so far as that law is concerned not with government, Church or State, but with the individual soul, is complete; all that is necessary to salvation is known, but as I conceive the age there is much apathy. Man awaits death and judgment with nothing to occupy the worldly faculties and is helpless before the world's disorder, and this may have dragged up out of the subconscious the conviction that the world was about to end. Hidden, except at rare

moments of excitement or revelation, and even then shown but in symbol, the stream of *recurrence*,* set in motion by the Galilean Symbol, has filled its basin, and seems motionless for an instant before it falls over the
5 rim, and in the midst of the basin I imagine in motionless contemplation, blood that is not His blood upon His Hands and Feet, One that feels but for the common lot, and mourns over the length of years and the inadequacy of man's fate to man. Two thousand years before, His
10 predecessor, careful of heroic men alone, had so stood and mourned over the shortness of time, and man's inadequacy to his fate.

Full moon over, that last Embodiment shall grow more like ourselves, putting off that stern majesty, borrowed
15 it may be from the Phidean Zeus—if we can trust Cefalu and Monreale—and His Mother—putting off her harsh Byzantine image—stand at His side.

IV

A.D. 1050 TO THE PRESENT DAY

WHEN the tide changed and God no longer sufficed, something must have happened in the courts and castles
20 of which history has perhaps no record, for with the first vague dawn of the ultimate *antithetical* revelation man, under the eyes of the Virgin, or upon the breast of his mistress, became but a fragment. Instead of that old alternation, brute or ascetic, came something obscure

---

* The documents distinguish between *recurrence* which is an impulse that begins strongly and dies out by degrees, and *sequence* where every part of the impulse is related to every other. Every phase is a *recurrence*, and *sequence* is related to Unity of Being. If I understand rightly Plato's perfect and imperfect numbers they have much the same meaning. The documents distinguish both *recurrence* and *sequence* from an *allusion*, or unrelated fact. A spirit at Phase 1 sees *allusion* only.

or uncertain that could not find its full explanation for
a thousand years. A certain Byzantine Bishop had said
upon seeing a singer of Antioch, " I looked long upon
her beauty, knowing that I would behold it upon the day
of judgment, and I wept to remember that I had taken   5
less care of my soul than she of her body," but when in
the Arabian Nights Harun Al-Raschid looked at the
singer Heart's Miracle, and on the instant loved her, he
covered her head with a little silk veil to show that her
beauty " had already retreated into the mystery of our   10
faith." The Bishop saw a beauty that would be sanctified
but the Caliph that which was its own sanctity, and it
was this latter sanctity, come back from the first Crusade
or up from Arabian Spain or half Asiatic Provence and
Sicily, that created romance. What forgotten reverie,   15
what initiation it may be, separated wisdom from the
monastery and, creating Merlin, joined it to passion.
When Merlin in Cretien de Troyes loved Ninian he showed
her a cavern adorned with gold mosaics and made by a
prince for his beloved, and told her that those lovers died 20
upon the same day and were laid " in the chamber where
they found delight." He thereupon lifted a slab of red
marble that his art alone could lift and showed them
wrapped in winding sheets of white samite. The tomb
remained open, for Ninian asked that she and Merlin   25
might return to the cavern and spend their night near
those dead lovers, but before night came Merlin grew sad
and fell asleep, and she and her attendants took him " by
head and foot " and laid him " in the tomb and replaced
the stone," for Merlin had taught her the magic words,   30
and " from that hour none beheld Merlin dead or
alive." Throughout the German " Parsifal " there is no
ceremony of the Church, neither Marriage nor Mass nor
Baptism, but instead we discover that strangest creation
of romance or of life, " the love trance." Parsifal in   35
such a trance, seeing nothing before his eyes but the

image of his absent love, overcame knight after knight, and awakening at last looked amazed upon his dinted sword and shield; and it is to his lady and not to God or the Virgin that Parsifal prayed upon the day of battle, and it was his lady's soul, separated from her entranced or sleeping body, that went beside him and gave him victory.

The period from 1005 to 1180 is attributed in the diagram to the first two gyres of our millenium, and what interests me in this period, which corresponds to the Homeric period some two thousand years before, is the creation of the Arthurian Tales and Romanesque architecture. I see in Romanesque the first movement to a secular Europe, but a movement so instinctive that as yet there is no antagonism to the old condition. Every architect, every man who lifts a chisel, may be a cleric of some kind, yet in the overflowing ornament where the human form has all but disappeared and where no bird or beast is copied from nature, where all is more Asiatic than Byzantium itself, one discovers the same impulse that created Merlin and his jugglery. I do not see in Gothic architecture, which is a character of the next gyre, that of Phases 5, 6 and 7, as did the nineteenth century historians ever looking for the image of their own age, the creation of a new communal freedom but a creation of authority, a suppression of that freedom though with its consent, and certainly St. Bernard when he denounced the extravagance of Romanesque saw it in that light. I think of that curious sketchbook of Villars de Honecourt with its insistence upon mathematical form, and I see that form in Mont St. Michel—Church, Abbey, Fort and town, all that dark geometry that makes Byzantium seem a sunlit cloud—and it seems to me that the Church grows secular that it may fight a new-born secular world. Its avowed appeal is to religion alone : nobles and great ladies join the crowds that drag the Cathedral stones, not out of love for beauty but because the stones as they are trundled down the road cure the halt and the blind; yet the stones once set up traffic with the enemy. The mosaic pictures grown transparent fill the windows, and draw all eyes and quarrel one with the other as if they were pretty women, and upon the faces of the statues flits once more the smile that disappeared with archaic Greece. That smile is physical, *primary* joy, the escape from supernatural terror, a moment of irresponsible common life before *antithetical* sadness begins. It is as though the pretty worshippers, while the Dominican was preaching with a new and perhaps incredible sternness, let their imaginations stray and the observant sculptor, or worker in ivory, in modelling his Holy Women has remembered their smiling lips.

Are not the Cathedrals and the Philosophy of St. Thomas the product of the abstraction that comes a little before the Phases 8 and 22, and of the moral synthesis that at the end of the first quarter seeks to control the general anarchy? That anarchy must have been exceedingly great, or man must have found a hitherto unknown sensitiveness, for it was the shock that created modern civilisation. The diagram makes the period from 1250 to 1300 correspond to Phase 8, certainly because in or near that period, chivalry and Christendom having proved insufficient, the King mastered the one, the Church the other, reversing the achievement of Constantine, for it was now the mitre and the crown that protected the Cross. I prefer, however, to find my example of the first victory of personality where I have more knowledge. Dante in the " Convito " mourns for solitude, lost through poverty, and writes the first sentence of modern autobiography, and in the Divine Comedy imposes his own personality upon a system and a phantasmagoria hitherto impersonal; the King everywhere has found his kingdom.

The period from 1300 to 1380 is attributed to the fourth gyre, that of Phases 9, 10 and 11, which finds its character in painting from Giotto to Fra Angelico, in the chronicles of Froissart and in the elaborate canopy upon the stained glass of the windows. Every old tale is alive, Christendom still unbroken; painter and poet alike find new ornament for the tale, they feel the charm of everything but the more poignantly because that charm is archaistic; they smell a pot of dried roses. The practical men, face to face with rebellion and heresy, are violent as they have not been for generations, but the artists separated from life by the tradition of Byzantium can even exaggerate their gentleness, and gentleness and violence alike express the gyre's hesitation. The public certainty that sufficed for Dante and St. Thomas has disappeared, and there is yet no private certainty. Is it that the human mind now longs for solitude, for escape from all that hereditary splendour, and does not know what ails it; or is it that the *Image* itself encouraged by the new technical method, the flexible brush-stroke instead of the unchanging cube of glass, and wearied of its part in a crowded ghostly dance longs for a solitary human body? That body comes in the period from 1380 to 1450 and is discovered by Masaccio, and by Chaucer who is partly of the old gyre, and by Villon who is wholly of the new. Masaccio, a precocious and abundant man, dying like Aubrey Beardsley in his six-and-twentieth year, cannot move us, as he did his immediate successors, for he discovered a naturalism that begins to weary us a little, making the naked young man awaiting baptism shiver with the cold, and St. Peter grow red with exertion as he drags the money out of the miraculous fish's mouth, and Adam and Eve, flying before the sword of the Angel, show faces disfigured by their suffering. It is very likely because I am a poet and not a painter that I feel so much more keenly that suffering of Villon—of the 13th Phase

as man, and of it or near it in epoch—in whom the human
soul for the first time stands alone before a death ever
present to imagination, without help from a Church that
is fading away, or is it that I remember Aubrey
Beardsley, a man of like phase though so different epoch, 5
and so read into Villon's suffering our modern conscience
which gathers intensity as we approach the close of an
era? Intensity that has seemed to me pitiless self-
judgment may have been but heroic gaiety. With the
approach of solitude bringing with it an ever increasing 10
struggle with that which opposes solitude—sensuality,
greed, ambition, physical curiosity in all its species—
philosophy has returned driving dogma out. Even
amongst the most pious the worshipper is preoccupied
with himself, and when I look for the drilled eyeball, 15
which reveals so much, I notice that its edge is no longer
so mechanically perfect, nor, if I can judge by casts
at the Victoria and Albert Museum, is the hollow so deep.
Angel and Florentine noble must look upward with an eye
that seems dim and abashed as though to recognise duties 20
to Heaven, an example to be set before men, and finding
both difficult seem a little giddy. There are no miracles
to stare at, for man descends the hill he once climbed
with so great toil, and all grows but natural again.

As we approach the 15th Phase, as the general move- 25
ment grows more and more westward in character, we
notice the oscillation of the horizontal gyres, as though
what no unity of being, yet possible, can completely fuse
displays itself in triumph.

Donatello, as later Michaelangelo, reflects the hardness 30
and astringency of Myron, and foretells what must follow
the Renaissance; while Jacopo della Guercia, and most
of the painters seem by contrast, as Raphael later on,
Ionic and Asiatic. The period from 1450 to 1550 is
allotted to the gyre of Phase 15, and these dates are no 35
doubt intended to mark somewhat vaguely a period that

begins in one country earlier and in another later. I do
not myself find it possible to make more than the first
half coincide with the central moment, Phase 15 of the
Italian Renaissance—Phase 22 of the cone of the entire
era—the breaking of the Christian synthesis as the corresponding period before Christ, the age of Phidias, was the
breaking of great traditional faith. The first half covers
the principal activity of the Academy of Florence which
formulated the reconciliation of Paganism and Christianity. This reconciliation which to Pope Julius meant that
Greek and Roman Antiquity were as sacred as that of
Judea, and like it " a vestibule of Christianity," became
in the theoretic exploration of Dürer who had visited
Venice within the movement of the gyre, that the human
norm, discovered from the measurement of ancient
statues, was God's first handiwork, that " perfectly proportioned human body " which had seemed to Dante
unity of being symbolised. The ascetic, who had a
thousand years before attained his transfiguration upon
the golden ground of Byzantine mosaic, had not turned
athlete but into that unlabouring form the athlete
dreamed of : the second Adam had become the first.
Because the 15th Phase can never find direct human
expression, being a supernatural incarnation, it impressed
upon work and thought an element of strain and artifice, a
desire to combine elements which may be incompatible,
or which suggest by their combination something supernatural. Had some Florentine Platonist read to Botticelli
Porphyry upon the Cave of the Nymphs? for I seem to
recognise it in that curious cave, with a thatched roof
over the nearer entrance to make it resemble the conventional manger, in his *" Nativity " in the National

---

* There is a Greek inscription at the top of the picture which
says that Botticelli's world is in the " second woe " of the
Apocalypse, and that after certain other Apocalyptic events the
Christ of the picture will appear. He had probably found in
some utterance of Savonarola's promise of an ultimate Marriage

Gallery. Certainly the glimpse of forest trees, dim in the evening light, through the far entrance, and the deliberate strangeness everywhere, gives one an emotion of mystery which is new to painting.

Botticelli, Crivelli, Mantegna, Da Vinci, who fall within 5
the period, make Masaccio and his school seem heavy and common by something we may call intellectual beauty or compare perhaps to that kind of bodily beauty which Castiglione called " the spoil or monument of the victory of the soul." Intellect and emotion, *primary* curiosity 10
and the *antithetical* dream, are for the moment one. Since the rebirth of the secular intellect in the eleventh century, faculty has been separating from faculty, poetry from music, the worshipper from the worshipped, but all have remained within a common fading circle— 15
Christendom—and so within the human soul image has been separated from image but always as an exploration of the soul itself; forms have been displayed in an always clear light, have been perfected by separation from one another till their link with one another and with common 20
associations has been broken; but, Phase 15 past, these forms begin to jostle and fall into confusion, there is as it were a sudden rush and storm. In the mind of the artist a desire for power succeeds to that for knowledge, and this desire is communicated to the forms and to the 25
onlooker. The eighth gyre, which corresponds to Phases 16, 17 and 18 and completes itself say between 1550 and 1650, begins with Raphael, Michaelangelo and Titian,

---

of Heaven and Earth, sacred and profane, and pictures it by the Angels and shepherds embracing, and as I suggest by Cave and Manger. When I saw the Cave of Mithra at Capri I wondered if that were Porphyry's Çave. The two entrances are there, one reached by a stair of a hundred feet or so from the sea and once trodden by devout sailors, and one reached from above by some hundred and fifty steps and used, my guide-book tells me, by Priests. If he knew that cave, which may have had its recognised symbolism, he would have been the more ready to discover symbols in the cave where Odysseus landed in Ithaca.

and the forms, as in Titian, awaken sexual desire—we
had not desired to touch the forms of Botticelli or even
of Da Vinci—or they threaten us like those of Michaelangelo, and the painter himself handles his brush with
5   a conscious facility or exultation. The subject matter
may arise out of some propaganda as when Raphael in
the Camera della Segnatura, and Michaelangelo in the
Sistine Chapel put, by direction of the Pope, Greek
Sages and Doctors of the Church, Roman Sibyls and
10 Hebrew Prophets, opposite one another in apparent
equality. From this on, all is changed and where the
Mother of God sat enthroned, now that the Soul's unity
has been found and lost, Nature seats herself, and the
painter can paint what he desires in the flesh alone, and
15 soon, asking less and less for himself, will make it a
matter of pride to paint what he does not at all desire.
I think Raphael almost of the earlier gyre—perhaps a
transitional figure—but Michaelangelo, Rabelais, Aretino,
Shakespeare, Titian—Titian is so markedly of the 14th
20 Phase as a man that he seems less characteristic—I associate with the mythopæic and ungovernable beginning of the
eighth gyre. I see in Shakespeare a man in whom human
personality, hitherto restrained by its dependence upon
Christendom or by its own need for self-control, burst
25 like a shell. Perhaps secular intellect, setting itself free
after five hundred years of struggle has made him the
greatest of dramatists, and yet because an *antithetical*
art could create a hundred plays which preserved—
whether made by a hundred hands or by one—the unity
30 of a painting or of a Temple pediment, we might, had the
total works of Sophocles survived—they too born of a like
struggle though with a different enemy—not think him
greatest. Do we not feel an unrest like that of travel
itself when we watch those personages, who are so much
35 more living than ourselves, amidst so much that is
irrelevant and heterogeneous, amid so much *primary*

curiosity, and are carried from Rome to Venice, from Egypt to Saxon England, or in the one play from Roman to Christian mythology.

Were he not himself of a later phase, were he of the 16th phase like his age and so drunk with his own wine he had not written plays at all, but as it is he finds his opportunity among a crowd of men and women who are still shaken by thought that passes from man to man in psychological contagion. I see in Milton who is characteristic of the moment when the first violence of the gyre has begun to sink, an attempted return to the synthesis of the Camera Segnatura and the Sistine Chapel. It is this attempt made too late that, amid all the music and magnificence of the still violent gyre, gives him his unreality and his cold rhetoric. The two elements have fallen apart in the hymn " On the Morning of Christ's Nativity," the one is called sacred, the other profane, and his classical mythology has become an artificial ornament, whereas no great Italian artist from 1450 to the sack of Rome saw any difference between them, and when difference came, as it did with Titian, it was God and the Angels that seemed artificial.

The gyre ebbs out in order and reason, the Jacobean poets succeed the Elizabethan, Cowley and Dryden the Jacobean as belief dies out. Elsewhere Christendom keeps a kind of spectral unity for a while, now with one, now with the other element of the synthesis dominant; declamatory statues deface old Churches, innumerable Tritons and Neptunes pour water from their mouths. What had been a beauty like the burning sun fades out in Vandyke's noble ineffectual faces, and the Low Countries, which have reached the new gyre long before the rest of Europe, convert the world to a still limited curiosity, to certain recognised forms of the picturesque constantly repeated, chance travellers at an inn door, men about a fire, men skating, the same pose or grouping, where the subject is different, passing from picture to picture. The world begins to long for the arbitrary and accidental, for the grotesque, the repulsive and the terrible, that it may be cured of desire, and the moment has come for the ninth gyre, Phases 19, 20 and 21, and for the period that begins for the greater part of Europe with 1650 and lasts it may be to 1875.

The beginning of the gyre like that of its forerunner is violent, a breaking of the soul and world into fragments, and has for a chief character the materialistic movement at the end of the seventeenth century, all that comes out of Bacon perhaps, the foundation of our modern inductive reasoning, the declamatory religious sects and controversies that first in England and then in France destroy the sense of form, all that has its very image and idol in Bernini's big Altar in St. Peter's with its figures contorted and convulsed by religion as though by the devil. Men change rapidly from deduction to deduction, opinion to opinion, have but one impression at a time and utter it always, no matter how often they change, with the same emphasis. Then the gyre develops a new coherence in the external scene; and violent men, each master of some generalisation, arise one after another: Napoleon, a man of the 20th Phase in the historical 21st—personality in its hard final generalisation —typical of all. The artistic life, where most characteristic of the general movement, shows the effect of the closing of the *Tinctures*. It is external, sentimental and logical,—the poetry of Pope and Gray, the philosophy of Johnson and of Rousseau—equally simple in emotion or in thought, the old oscillation in a new form. Personality is everywhere spreading out its fingers in vain, or grasping with an always more convulsive grasp a world where the predominance of physical science, of finance and economics in all their forms, of democratic politics, of vast populations, of architecture where styles jostle one another, of newspapers where all is heterogenous, show that mechanical force will in a moment become supreme.

That art discovered by Dante of marshalling into a vast *antithetical* structure *antithetical* material became through Milton Latinised and artificial—the Shades, as Sir Thomas Browne said, " steal or contrive a body "— and now it changes that it may marshal into a still *Antithetical* structure *Primary* material, and the modern novel is created, but even before the gyre is drawn to its end, the happy ending, the admired hero, the preoccupation with desirable things, all that is undisguisedly *Antithetical* disappears.

All the art of the gyre that is not derived from the external scene, is a Renaissance echo growing always more conventional or more shadowy, but since the Renaissance—Phase 22 of the cone of the era—the " Emotion of Sanctity," that first relation to the *Spiritual Primary* has been possible in those things that are most intimate and personal, but not until Phase 22 of the millennium cone will general thought be ready for its expression. A mysterious contact is perceptible first in painting and then in poetry and last in prose. In painting it comes where the influence of the Low Countries and that of Italy mingle, but always rarely and faintly. I do not find it in Watteau but there is a preparation for it, a sense of exhaustion of old interests—" they do not believe even in their own happiness," Verlaine said—and then suddenly it is present in the faces of Gainsborough's women as it has been in no face since the Egyptian sculptor buried in a tomb that image of a princess carved in wood. Reynolds had nothing of it, an ostentatious fashionable man fresh from Rome, he stayed content with fading Renaissance emotion and modern curiosity. In frail women's faces—Lady Bessborough's rises before me—the soul awakes—all its prepossession, the accumu-

lated learning of centuries swept away—and looks out
upon us wise and foolish like the dawn. Then it is
everywhere, it finds the village providence of the
eighteenth century and turns him into Goethe, who
for all that comes to no conclusion, his Faust after his
hundred years but reclaiming land like some Sir Charles
Grandison or Voltaire in his old age. It makes the
heroines of Jane Austen seek, not as their grandfathers
and grandmothers would have done, theological or
political truth, but simply good breeding, as though to
increase it were more than any practical accomplishment.
In poetry alone it finds its full expression for it is
a quality of the emotional nature (*Celestial Body* acting
through *Mask*); and creates all that is most beautiful in
modern English poetry from Blake to Arnold, all that is
not a fading echo, and one discovers it in those symbolist
writers like Verhaeren who substitute an entirely personal
wisdom for the physical beauty or passionate emotion
of the fifteenth and sixteenth centuries. In painting it
shows most often where the aim has been archaistic, as
though it were an accompaniment of what the popular
writers call decadence, as though old emotions had first
to be exhausted. I think of the French portrait painter
Ricard to whom it was more a vision of the mind than
a research, for he would say to his sitter " you are so
fortunate as to resemble your picture," and of Mr Charles
Ricketts, my education in so many things. How often
his imagination moves stiffly as though in fancy dress,
and then there is something,—Sphinx, Danaides—that
makes me remember Callimachus' return to Ionic
elaboration and shudder as though I stared into an
abyss full of eagles. Everywhere this vision or rather
this contact is faint or intermittent and it is always
fragile; Dickens was able with a single book, Pickwick,
to substitute for Jane Austen's privileged and perilous
research the camaraderie of the inn parlour, qualities

that every man might hope to possess, and it did not return till Henry James began to write.

Certain men have sought to express the new emotion through the *Creative Mind*, though fit instruments of expression do not yet exist, and so to establish, in the midst of our ever more abundant *primary* information, *antithetical* wisdom; but such men, Blake, Coventry Patmore at moments, Nietzsche, unlike those who, from Richardson to Tolstoi, from Hobbes to Mill and Spencer, have grown in number and serenity, are full of morbid excitement and few in number. They were begotten in the Sistine Chapel and still dream that all can be transformed if they be but emphatic; yet Nietzsche, when the doctrine of the Eternal Recurrence drifts before his eyes, knows for an instant that nothing can be and is almost of the next gyre.

The period from 1875 to 1927 (Phase 22)—in some countries and in some forms of thought it is from 1815 to 1927—is like that from 1250 to 1300 (Phase 8) a period of abstraction, and like it also in that it is preceded and followed by abstraction. Phase 8 was preceded by the Schoolmen and followed by legalists and inquisitors and Phase 22 was preceded by the great popularisers of physical science and economic science, and will be followed by social movements and applied science. Abstraction which began at Phase 19 will end at Phase 25 for these movements and this science will have for their object or result the elimination of intellect. Our generation has stood at the climax, at what I call in " The Trembling of the Veil " *Hodos Chameliontos*, or has witnessed a first weariness, and when the climax passes will recognise that there common secular thought began to break and disperse. Tolstoi in " War and Peace " had still preference, could argue about this thing or that other, had a belief in Providence and a disbelief in Napoleon, but Flaubert in his

o

St. Anthony had neither belief, nor preference, and so it is that, even before the general surrender of the will, there came synthesis for its own sake, organisation where there is no masterful director, books where the author has disappeared, painting where some accomplished brush paints with an equal pleasure, or with a bored impartiality, the human form or an old bottle, dirty weather and clean sunshine. I too think of famous works where synthesis has been carried to the utmost limit possible, where there are elements of inconsequence or discovery of hitherto ignored ugliness, and I notice that when the limit is approached or past, when the moment of surrender is reached, when the new gyre begins to stir, I am filled with excitement. I think of recent mathematical research, and even my ignorance can compare it with that of Newton—so plainly of the 19th Phase—with its objective world intelligible to intellect; and I recognise that the limit itself has become a new dimension, and that this ever hidden thing which makes us fold our hands has begun to press down upon multitudes. Having bruised their hands upon that limit men, for the first time since the seventeenth century, see the world as an object of contemplation, not as something to be remade, and some few, meeting the limit in their special study, even doubt if there is any common experience, that is to say doubt the possibility of science.

It is said that at Phase 8 there is always civil war, and at Phase 22 always war, and as this war is always a defeat for those who have conquered, we have repeated the wars of Alexander.

I discover already the first phase—Phase 23—of the last quarter in certain friends of mine, and in writers, poets and sculptors admired by these friends, who have a form of strong love and hate hitherto unknown in the arts. It is with them a matter of conscience to live in their own exact instant of time, and they defend their conscience like theologians. They are all absorbed in some technical research to the entire exclusion of the personal dream. It is as though the forms in the stone or in their reverie began to move with an energy which is not that of the human mind. Very often these forms are mechanical, are as it were the mathematical forms that sustain the *physical primary*—I think of the work of Mr Wyndham Lewis, his powerful " cacophony of sardine tins," and of those marble eggs, or objects of burnished steel too drawn up or tapered out to be called eggs, of M. Brancussi, who has gone further than Mr Wyndham Lewis from recognisable subject matter and so from personality ; of sculptors who would certainly be rejected as impure by a true sectary of this moment, the Scandinavian Milles, Meštrović perhaps, masters of a geometrical pattern or rhythm which seems to impose itself wholly from beyond the mind, the artist " standing outside himself." I compare them to sculpture or painting where now the artist now the model imposes his personality. I think especially of the art of the 21st Phase which was at times so anarchic, Rodin creating his powerful art out of the fragments of those Gates of Hell that he had found himself unable to hold together—images out of a personal dream, " the hell of Baudelaire not of Dante," he had said to Symons. I find at this 23rd Phase which is it is said the first where there is hatred of the abstract, where the intellect turns upon itself, Mr Ezra Pound, Mr Eliot, Mr Joyce, Signor Pirandello, who either eliminate from metaphor the poet's phantasy and substitute a strangeness discovered by historical or contemporary research or who break up the logical processes of thought by flooding them with associated ideas or words that seem to drift into the mind by chance ; or who set side by side as in " Henry IV," " The Waste Land," " Ulysses," the *physical primary*—a lunatic among his keepers, a man fishing behind a gas works, the vulgarity of a single

Dublin day prolonged through 700 pages—and the *spiritual primary*, delirium, the Fisher King, Ulysses' wandering. It is as though myth and fact, united until the exhaustion of the Renaissance, have now fallen so

5 far apart that man understands for the first time the rigidity of fact, and calls up, by that very recognition, myth—the *Mask*—which now but gropes its way out of the mind's dark but will shortly pursue and terrify. In practical life one expects the same technical inspira-

10 tion, the doing of this or that not because one would, or should, but because one can, consequent licence, and with those " out of phase " anarchic violence with no sanction in general principles. If there is violent revolution, and it is the last phase where political revolution

15 is possible, the dish will be made from what is found in the pantry and the cook will not open her book. There may be greater ability than hitherto for men will be set free from old restraints, but the old intellectual hierarchy gone they will thwart and jostle one another.

20 One tries to discover the nature of the 24th Phase which will offer peace—perhaps by some generally accepted political or religious action, perhaps by some more profound generalisation—calling up before the mind those who speak its thoughts in the language of our earlier

25 time. Peguy in his Jean of Arc trilogy displays the national and religious tradition of the French poor, as he, a man perhaps of the 24th phase, would have it, and Claudel in his " L'Otage " the religious and secular hierarchies perceived as history. I foresee a time when

30 the majority of men will so accept an historical tradition that they will quarrel, not as to who can impose his personality upon others but as to who can best embody the common aim, when all personality will seem an impurity—" sentimentality," " sullenness," " egotism "

35 —something that revolts not morals alone but good taste. There will be no longer great intellect for a ceaseless

activity will be required of all; and where rights are
swallowed up in duties, and solitude is difficult, creation
except among avowedly archaistic and unpopular groups
will grow impossible. Phase 25 may arise, as the code
wears out from repetition, to give new motives for   5
obedience, or out of some scientific discovery which seems
to contrast, a merely historical acquiescence, with an
enthusiastic acceptance of the general will conceived of
as a present energy—" Sibyll what would you? " " I
would die." Then with the last gyre must come a desire   10
to be ruled or rather, seeing that desire is all but dead,
an adoration of force spiritual or physical, and society
as mechanical force be complete at last.

> Constrained, arraigned, baffled, bent and unbent
>   By those wire-jointed jaws and limbs of wood   15
> Themselves obedient,
>   Knowing not evil or good.

A decadence will descend, by perpetual moral improvement, upon a community which may seem like some
woman of New York or Paris who has renounced her   20
rouge pot to lose her figure and grow coarse of skin and
dull of brain, feeding her calves and babies somewhere
upon the edge of the wilderness. The decadence of the
Greco-Roman world with its violent soldiers and its
mahogany dark young athletes was as great, but that   25
suggested the bubbles of life turned into marbles, whereas
what awaits us, being democratic and *primary*, may
suggest bubbles in a frozen pond—mathematical Babylonian starlight.

When the new era comes bringing its stream of irra-   30
tional force it will, as did Christianity, find its philosophy
already impressed upon the minority who have, true to
phase, turned away at the last gyre from the *Physical
Primary*. And it must awake into life, not Dürer's, nor
Blake's, nor Milton's human form divine—nor yet   35

Nietzsche's superman, nor Patmore's catholic, boasting
" a tongue that's dead "—the brood of the Sistine Chapel
—but organic groups, *covens* of physical or intellectual
kin melted out of the frozen mass. I imagine new
5 races, as it were, seeking domination, a world resembling
but for its immensity that of the Greek tribes—each
with its own Daimon or ancestral hero—the brood of
Leda, War and Love; history grown symbolic, the
biography changed into a myth. Above all I imagine
10 everywhere the opposites, no mere alternation between
nothing and something like the Christian brute and
ascetic, but true opposites, each living the other's death,
dying the other's life.

It is said that the *primary* impulse " creates the
15 event " but that the *antithetical* " follows it " and by
this I understand that the Second Fountain will arise
after a long preparation and as it were out of the very
heart of human knowledge, and seem when it comes no
interruption but a climax. It is possible that the ever
20 increasing separation from the community as a whole
of the cultivated classes, their increasing certainty, and
that falling in two of the human mind which I have
seen in certain works of art is preparation. During the
period said to commence in 1927, with the 11th gyre,
25 must arise a form of philosophy, which will become
religious and ethical in the 12th gyre and be in all things
opposite of that vast plaster Herculean image, final
primary thought. It will be concrete in expression,
establish itself by immediate experience, seek no general
30 agreement, make little of God or any exterior unity, and
it will call that good which a man can contemplate
himself as doing always and no other doing at all. It
will make a cardinal truth of man's immortality that
its virtue may not lack sanction, and of the soul's
35 re-embodiment that it may restore to virtue that long
preparation none can give and hold death an interruption.

The supreme experience, Plotinus' ecstasy, ecstasy of the Saint, will recede, for men—finding it difficult—substituted dogma and idol, abstractions of all sorts, things beyond experience; and men may be long content with those more trivial supernatural benedictions as when Athena took Achilles by his yellow hair. Men will no longer separate the idea of God from that of human genius, human productivity in all its forms.

Unlike Christianity which had for its first Roman teachers cobblers and weavers, this thought must find expression among those that are most subtle, most rich in memory; that Gainsborough face floats up; among the learned—every sort of learning—among the rich— every sort of riches—among men of rank—every sort of rank—and the best of those that express it will be given power, less because of that they promise than of that they seem and are. This much can be thought because it is the reversal of what we know, but those kindreds once formed must obey irrational force and so create hitherto unknown experience, or that which is incredible.

Though it cannot interrupt the intellectual stream— being born from it and moving within it—it may grow a fanaticism and a terror, and at its first outsetting oppress the ignorant—even the innocent—as Christianity oppressed the wise, seeing that the day is far off when the two halves of man can define each its own unity in the other as in a mirror, Sun in Moon, Moon in Sun, and so escape out of the Wheel.

Finished at Capri, February, 1925.

BOOK IV

THE GATES OF PLUTO

1. THE FOOL BY THE ROADSIDE

When my days that have
From cradle run to grave
From grave to cradle run instead;
When thoughts that a fool
Has wound upon a spool
Are but loose thread, are but loose thread;

When cradle and spool are past
And I mere shade at last
Coagulate of stuff
Transparent like the wind,
I think that I may find
A faithful love, a faithful love.

2. THE GREAT WHEEL AND FROM DEATH TO BIRTH

I

STRAY THOUGHTS

CORNELIUS AGRIPPA in " De Occulta Philosophia " quotes from " Orpheus "—" The Gates of Pluto cannot be unlocked, within is a people of dreams," and from that sentence I take the name of this fourth book, in
5 which I must consider the condition from death to birth.

I must speak much of the *Daimon*, and yet we can know nothing of the *Daimon* except by the *Complementary Dream*. She is not phasal and yet we must speak as if she were because she affects human life, now through
10 one *Faculty* and now through another, and if we are to strengthen her influence or to moderate it we must know what these *Faculties* are. She is that being united to man which knows neither good nor evil, and shapes the body in the womb, and impresses upon the mind its form.
15 She is revealed to man in moments of prevision and illumination and in much that we call good and evil fortune, and yet, seeing that she remains always in the Thirteenth Cycle, cannot accompany man in his wanderings, nor can her tutelage of man be eternal,
20 seeing that after many cycles man also inhabits the Thirteenth Cycle and has in a certain way a greater

power than hers. When both are as it were side by side in the same cycle, she like a spirit of the 15th Phase, can communicate with one living man, chosen still doubtless from a cycle beneath her own, whereas the man can communicate with an indefinite number of other men. We can but fall back on image and say that they are united for twelve cycles, and are then set free from one another, she being Full Moon and he Full Sun; though when we consider all with the eyes of living man he is Moon and she the Sun.

Presently I must speak of the *Ghostly Self* by which the creators of this system mean the permanent self, that which in the individual may correspond to the fixed circle of the figure, neither Man nor *Daimon*, before the whirling of the Solar and Lunar cones. It is the source of that which is unique in every man, understanding by unique that which is one and so cannot be analysed into anything else.

I do not think of death as separation from body but from the exclusive association with one body for in no experience possible to the human spirit, as it is known to me, does the human spirit cease to use directly or through the *Record* the senses of living men. Upon the other hand, eye and ear and touch have not always the same range for the living and the dead, nor has the brain of the living, when the dead and the living use it, the same capacity, for the dead are the wisdom of the living. Seeing that the body is a portion of the *Daimon's Body of Fate* it may be said that the *Daimon*, and therefore all associated *Daimons* or Spirits, are nearer to the body than to the intellect. Nor must the dead be thought of as living an abstract life for it is the living who create abstraction which " consumes itself away."

II

The Vision of the Blood Kindred

AT death the man passes into what seems to him afterwards a state of darkness and sleep; there is a sinking
in upon fate analogous to that of the individual cones
at Phase 22. During the darkness he is surrounded by
5 his kindred, present in their simulacrae, or in their Spirits
when they are between lives, the more recent dead the
more visible. Because of their presence it is called the
Vision of the Blood Kindred.

III

The Separation of the Four Principles

THE *Spirit* first floats horizontally within the man's dead
10 body, but then rises until it stands at his head. The
Celestial Body is also horizontal at first but lies in the
opposite position, its feet where the *Spirit's* head is, and
then rising, as does the *Spirit*, stands up at last at the feet
of the man's body. The *Passionate Body* rises straight
15 up from the genitals and stands in the centre. The *Husk*
remains in the body until the time for it to be separated
and lost in *Anima Mundi.* The separation of the
Principles from the body is caused by the *Daimon's*
gathering into the *Passionate Body* memory of the past
20 life—perhaps but a single image or thought—which is
always taken from the unconscious memories of the
living, from the *Record* of all those things which have
been seen but have not been noticed or accepted by the
intellect, and the *Record* is always truthful.

IV

THE AWAKENING OF THE SPIRITS

THE *Spirit* meanwhile has passed from the *Vision of the Blood Kindred* into meditation, but of this meditation we are told little except that it is upon the coming " dissolution of the *Passionate Body* " and that, though in certain cycles it may be prolonged for a very great period, with us it ends with burial. The *Spirit* may appear to the living during this meditation, but if it does so it will show in the likeness of the body as that body was shortly before death. The meditation may be moved and shaped by the Burial Ritual, for the body has become a symbol, and as the *Spirit* has entered upon a condition that is a dream, thoughts inspired among the living by that Ritual can influence its life. Now in its turn the *Spirit* gradually awakens, and it is said that the awaking may begin with the sight of a flower upon the grave where it appears shining amidst the general darkness. In the world where it is now the human soul is seen to give forth light which is transmitted to objects and the thought of some mourner will illuminate the flower. The *Spirit* is somewhere said to appear as a colourless outline until at this awakening it gradually takes upon itself something of the hues of the living man. Its coming to self-knowledge may be long and ·painful. If death has been violent or tragic, *Spirit* and *Passionate Body* may dream that death again and again with intervals of awakening, and in some few cases so dream for a century or more. A gambler killed in a gambling brawl will demand his money, and a man, who has believed that nothing will remain but the decaying body may haunt the house where he has lived as an odour of decay; nor is there any reason why a man may not see reflected

ın a mirror some beloved ghost who, thinking herself
unobserved, will powder her face as in Mr Davies' verse.

> The first night she was in her grave,
> As I looked in the glass
> I saw her sit upright in bed;
> Without a sound it was;
> I saw her hand feel in the cloth
> To fetch a box of powder forth.
>
> She sat and watched me all the while
> For fear I looked her way,
> I saw her powder cheek and chin
> Her fast corrupting clay.
> Then down my lady lay and smiled,
> She thought her beauty saved, poor child.

V

THE RETURN

THE *Spirit* should separate itself from all such dreams
of the *Passionate Body* and seek the *Celestial Body*, and
only when so separate does it cease to dream and know
that it is dead. There are therefore, in what is known as
the *Return*, a *Waking State* and a *Sleeping State* which
alternate, and these states resemble each other in that
in both are sensible images or some impression of sense,
but differ in that during the *Waking State* these images
and impressions of sense are imposed by other beings,
who are bound to the dead man by the events of some
past life, and in that during the *Sleeping State* they are
recovered from the *Record*, by the man's *Spirit* or
Passionate Body, and in that during the *Waking State*

* These states seem analogous to *Sage* (or teacher) and *Victim*
respectively. During the *Waking State* the gyre moves but during
the *Sleeping State* it is stationary.—*Sept. 28.*

alone does he know that he is no longer living. During
this state which is commonly called the *Teaching* he is
brought into the presence, as far as possible, of all sources
of the action he must presently, till he has explored
every consequence, dream through. This passion for   5
the source is brought to him from his own *Celestial
Body* which perpetually, being of the nature of *Fate*,
dreams the events of his life backward through time. If
the thought of the past life permit, he will now perceive
all those persons as they now live or as they have lived,   10
who have influenced him, or whom he has influenced,
and so caused the action, but if he has belonged to some
faith that has not known rebirth he may explore sources
that require symbolical expression.

As he cannot escape the symbols of his life,   15
whatever his belief, he may now see himself surrounded by flames and persecuted by devils. One
remembers the girl in the Japanese play whose
Ghost tells a Priest of a slight sin which seems a
great sin because of its unforeseen and unforeseeable   20
consequences, and that she is persecuted by flames. If
she but touch a pillar, she says, it bursts into flames,
and the Priest who knows that these flames are but
her own conscience made visible, tells her that if she
cease to believe in them they must cease to exist. She   25
thanks him, but the flames return, for she cannot cease
to believe, and the play ends with a dance which is the
expression of her agony.

The *Teaching Spirits*, as the *Waking State* returns and
the first passion declines, may offer him a guidance which   30
seems like that of some familiar institution, hospital, or
school, for they are still the human mind and keep old
habits of thought, but it differs from that of an institution
because these spirits have been a part of his life for
perhaps many centuries. The object of the *Return* is to   35
exhaust pleasure and pain by the display of all the good

P

and evil of his past life, but it is always the old, never new pleasure or pain. He may sometimes visit the living, suggest thoughts or emotions that may amend the consequence of his acts, but cannot, unless through the eyes and ears of some spirit from a later condition, see any that were not a part of his own life. When in the *Meditation* he could but appear to the living in the form he last wore alive, but now he may be seen as of that age at which the event he is about to dream occurred. Most of the spirits at séances are said to belong to this condition.

When the *Spirit* has been for the moment exhausted by the phantasmagoria as it is sometimes called, the *Passionate Body* attracts it to itself, and the *Sleeping State* begins. The *Passionate Body* like the *Celestial Body* never ceases to dream, moving through events, however, not in the order of their occurrence but in that of their intensity, and when the *Spirit* returns to it the *Spirit* is compelled to imitate this dream, having no life except from one or other of the bodies. The man is now in what is called the *Dreaming Back*, and it is now that, according to ancient and modern tradition, the murderer may be seen committing his murder night after night, or perhaps upon the anniversary of its first committal; or it may be that the dream is happy and that the seer but meets the old huntsman hunting once more amid a multitude of his friends and all his hounds, or half tragic and half happy as when the mother, as the folklore of all nations and spiritualistic annals recall, comes to her orphan children. " The Divine returns to the Divinity " through the *Celestial Body*, and to invert *Plotinus* " the Lonely returns to the Lonely " in the dream of the *Passionate Body*, for mother, murderer and huntsman are alone. If the dreamed event was once shared by many, now dead, those many may indeed be present, and yet as each but dreams again without change what happened when they were alive, each dreamer is alone. Should they exchange the thought of the moment, one with another, there would be contrast, conflict, and therefore creation, and the dream would not fade. The dream may be dreamed through by the *Spirit* once, or many times with short or long periods of awakening, but the man must dream the event to its consequence as far as his intensity permit; not that consequence only which occurred while he lived, and was known to him, but those that were unknown, or have occurred after his death. The more complete the exploration, the more fortunate will be his future life, but he is concerned with events only, and with the emotions that accompanied events. Every event so dreamed is the expression of some knot, some concentration of feeling separating off a period of time, or portion of the being, from the being as a whole and the life as a whole, and the dream is as it were a smoothing out or an unwinding. Yet it is said that if his nature had great intensity, and the consequences of the event affected multitudes, he may dream with slowly lessening pain and joy for centuries.

As all the consequences of the event are discovered from the *Record* made by the living—the *Spirit* finding there names, dates, and language to complete the drama, and the *Passionate Body* finding the concrete events— we may say that the dead remain a portion of the living. It is indeed said that where murderer and victim die unknown, and the crime remains unknown, the *Spirit* can find certain facts in its own *Passionate Body*, or from the *Passionate Body* of its victim, but with difficulty, and such a *Dreaming Back* is imperfect. A *Dreaming Back* may be so imperfect or so prolonged that it obsesses the next life and causes rebirth into almost the same circumstances as those already lived through, and generally into the same family. *Teaching Spirits* may assist the dreamer, and many hauntings, many inexplicable sights and sounds, are to cause, among the living, inquiries that passing into the unconscious mind of the enquirer enable the *Passionate Body* or *Spirit* of the dreamer to perfect its knowledge.

5   The *Spirit* can even consult books, records, of all kinds, once they be brought before the eyes or even perhaps to the attention of the living, but it can see nothing there that does not concern the dream. The *Spirit* so dreaming, if it see the living thinks they are a portion
10 of its dream, and is without reflection or the knowledge that it is dead. When the dream ends the *Spirit* withdraws from the *Passionate Body* which continues its purely animal dream. There is, however, the rare event, which may affect either the dreaming back or the waking
15 state, of renewed contact of *Spirit* and *Passionate Body* with the *Husk*. This constitutes the true ghost as distinguished from the dream of the *Spirit* and *Passionate Body*. In this state a spirit may experience for a moment once more pleasure and pain that are not a fading
20 memory. It is said to be dangerous to the living and a hindrance to the dead, and to include incubi and succubi, and perhaps most of those beings the Cambridge Platonist described, when he called the Devil " A Body Politick," and with whom witches made compacts to keep them,
25 by a periodical offering of their blood, from fading out. Seeing that there is no punishment but the prolongation of the *Dreaming back*, and the consequent exclusion of other states, it is among *Spirits* so united to their *Husk* that we discover tempting or evil spirits.

VI

The Return in relation to the Covens

30   THERE are beings which have personality, though their bodies consist of a number of minds held together by

a stream of thought or an event, and these beings, called *Covens*, have their own *Dreaming Back*, *Record Teachings*, and so on, and hold those, who constitute their bodies, even after death and perhaps for many lives. During his individual *Teaching* or *Dreaming Back*, an individual man is among the forms of his *Coven*, the Heaven and Hell of Christianity, the Spheres of Spiritualism, the Faery Hostings of Irish folk-lore, and where there is little change in civilisation and belief these forms may persist for centuries, and it is through these forms that the beings of the 13th Cycle unite the individual destiny to that of a race, or a religion, and make the individual knot coincide with that of the nation and make the untying of one the untying of both.

VII

THE SHIFTINGS

AT the end of the *Return* which corresponds upon the diagram to the gyre associated with phases 23, 24 and 25, the *Spirit* is freed from pleasure and pain and is ready to enter the *Shiftings* where it is freed from Good and Evil, and in this state which is a state of intellect, it lives through a life which is said to be in all things opposite to that lived through in the world, and dreamed through in the *Return*. As the documents are here more than usually obscure and strange and as I am afraid of unconsciously perverting their meaning, I will quote certain passages. If the surroundings of a past life were " good " they are now " evil " and where " evil " " good," and if a man has had good motives " they are now evil, and if evil good . . . . because it is not virtue to be good knowing no evil, nor is it sin to be evil knowing

no good . . . Good is not good if it is not a conquest
of evil, and evil is not evil unless a conquest of good."
And this is amplified later on with the statement that
if one has been in any matter good, knowing evil, or
5 evil, knowing good, one suffers in that matter no transformation. Yet seeing that one is generally good or evil
in ignorance, the state is for most men " the best possible
life in the worst possible surroundings " or the direct
contrary, and this is brought about by no external law
10 but by a craving in the *Principles* to know what life has
hidden, that the *Daimon* who knows intellect but not
good and evil, may be satisfied. Yet there is no suffering
" for in a state of equilibrium there is neither emotion
nor sensation "; and seeing that for all, " in the limits
15 of the good and evil of the previous life, . . . the soul is
brought to a comprehension of good and evil, neither the
utmost evil nor the utmost good can force sensation or
emotion." Evil is that which opposes Unity of Being
and seeing that man seeks his *primary* in woman, and
20 woman her *antithetical* in man, a relationship of sex
displays good and evil in their most subtle and overpower-
ing form. Therefore it is said that in the *Shiftings* men
and women relive their loves, and not as in the *Dreaming
Back* to exhaust pleasure and pain, but that they may
25 separate that which belongs to their true *primary* or true
antithetical from that which seems to, and therefore
exhaust good and evil themselves. The man would
know the woman utterly and so he must relive his love
in all things whereof he was ignorant, turning good
30 fortune into complete tragedy, or tragedy into good
fortune, that he may test his love in every fire; and if
the woman be dead and in like condition she will be
present in reality, but if not, in similitude alone. Yet
whether she be there or not there, the dream will be
35 but the same, for he can see nothing but his dream.
Light loves, loves without mutual recognition, may not

long delay him, for their circumstance and consequence have been exhausted in the *Dreaming Back*, and their effect upon himself has been but little, but strong love given in ignorance may be relived again and again, though not with suffering, for all now is intellect and he is all *Daimon*, and tragic and happy circumstance alike offer an intellectual ecstasy at the revelation of truth, and the most horrible tragedy in the end can but seem a figure in a dance. Yet his dream, like that of the *Dreaming Back*, is not like dreams in sleep, for though it seems to him reality, he sees beside it the love that he actually did live, a reality that seems a dream, for without that he could not bring his soul to quiescence.

In the *Waking State* of *The Shiftings* there is no reliving of the past, and though the soul is taught, there is no teaching, and there is no *Teacher* but the *Celestial Body*, for it is a form of life; the soul is as it were folding up into itself. We can say of it that it is no longer in space, but, in the measure of its truth to phase, in time alone, past and present being within equal reach—for so it is the documents put it—and yet it is more intelligible to say that it has now received from the *Celestial Body* the *Record* of its past existence. It has no memory of its own, apart from this *Record*, having no acquired faculties, and thinks not as man thinks but as *Daimon* thinks. Abstraction has gone, no thread of the cloth can be separated from any other thread, and the whole cloth is unwound. It is now, as the *Shiftings* close, brought by the *Celestial Body* into the presence, not of the source of its good and evil, for it must transcend good and evil, but into that of all typical qualities of its being, and all the associates of its past lives in the order of their phase that it may see their loves and its own as one single wheel; and where the *Celestial Body* is in contact with the beings of the Thirteenth Cycle it may carry to the living messages concerned with

purposes that transcend individual life, or upon the other
hand it may carry from its own *Celestial Body* messages
that concern individual life alone. But when it goes
upon these messages—remembering that it can hear but
5   cannot see, being in time only—it must act through the
intermediary of those in the *Waking State* of the *Return*,
and of Spirits at Phase 1; and should it desire to appear
it must by such intermediary mould into a living image
the most vivid memory of itself found in the unconscious
10   minds of the living, and this image is always that most
generally known, for it is still " suggestible." Sometimes
these messengers make their presence known by some
scent or sound or sight associated with them, and it is
through this scent or sound or sight that they draw upon
15   the physical vitality of a man, or upon the knowledge of
the *Daimon* of this man to whom they are sent, or of that
other who may help the delivery of the message. When
through intermediaries they make use of our eyes, they can
unlike those in the *Return* understand records which have
20   no relation to their own past. They are most commonly
sent to those with whom they have lived in some near
or distant past, and they always " take upon themselves
the exact mental condition of the person they communicate with; if with some person they have injured, they
25   take on the sense of that injury . . . sorrow, suspicion,
self-doubt."

VIII

EXPIATION FOR THOSE IN THE SHIFTINGS AND IN THE RETURN

SEEING that persons are born again and again in association, mother and son at first it may be, then wife and
husband, brother and sister, and that our loves and

friendships are many, each person is a part of a community of spirits and our re-embodiments are governed and caused by passions that we must exhaust in all their forms. As all strong passions are said to contain "cruelty and deceit" and so to require expiation, one deceived as to motive cannot pass out of the *Shiftings* if unable to complete the transposition of life and surroundings, and some other who has sinned in act may be compelled to relive his phase again and again till he has completed the expiation which frees both souls. "An Act" or motive that created action is "expiated in physical life" but an intellectual defect in "spiritual life." So that a man who has been deceived but has not retaliated expiates in the *Shiftings* what, must have found, had he retaliated, an expiation during physical life. Expiation during physical life is caused by the craving to experience that which we have done to another, to reverse in action what the disembodied soul reverses in thought, and we owe it not to that other but to our own *Daimon* which, but for "cruelty or deceit," had found the *Daimon* of that other. The expiation is followed by a prolonged or short mingling of the *Daimons*. Expiation is a harmonisation of being, and we seek out the image, reflected in some living man or woman, of that other being, that we may achieve it in action. It affects that other who must achieve it in thought by *Complementary Dream* for the expiations are simultaneous.

Until an act has been expiated the same circumstance occurs again and again, as though the *Dreaming Back* flowed over into the life that followed. One woman has endured a drunken husband because of a wrong done to a husband in another life, while another expiates, by a life of devotion to an un-loved man, a suicide whereby under some misunderstanding she had deserted a man she loved. During these acts of expiation the life may

be embittered " by an inhibition of the active qualities "
and a suffering which is a " physical emotional and
spiritual, and not moral purgation." And there is always
a sense of being fated. This inhibition, this sense of being
5 fated is not always an unhappiness. A life of voluntary
surrender to another may create an unconscious craving
for its opposite, and this craving may produce a pros-
perous self-appeasing life which is fated and so expiatory.
A Knot is first in the being, and is called a *Knot of*
10 *Destiny*, but in the life that follows, may be in the
events themselves, and uncontrollable by the being, and
is then a *Knot of Fate*. That the expiatory suffering, or
pleasure, may affect a particular disembodied soul, the
Celestial Body of that soul is through its *Spirit* imposed,
15 while in the *Waking State* of the *Shiftings*, as an image
upon some living man or woman, and that man or woman
is then loved, not for his or her own sake but for that of
the dead. Yet this image, not being imposed upon the
desires but upon the unconscious mind, does not create
20 new deception and expiation. There is indeed a condition
of the soul when an image, unexhausted in the *Dreaming
Back*, does impose a physical image upon the desire of
the living, but this is not expiation though it may—if the
same person be dominated by both images—be as it were
25 mixed into expiation. A purgation completed brings
good fortune and happiness, a consciousness of luck.

A race may at times become dominated like an
individual by a subconscious desire for suffering or for
ease, as an expiation for acts done centuries before to
30 some race whose *Coven* has passed into *Daimonic* life.

There are other forms of expiation with which I shall
not concern myself in this book, but there is one on
which I must touch later, for it is that whereby supernatural forms of the more powerful kind are created.

IX

BEATITUDE

AFTER the *Shiftings* the *Spirit* is for a short time " out of space and time," and every other abstraction, and is said not to move in a gyre but in a sphere, being as it were present everywhere at once. *Beatitude* is the result of the expiations of living man and disembodied soul, and the final harmony so established, and it is said that while still living we receive joy from those we have served —choosing tragedy they abandon to us this cast-off joy ?—whereas we receive from those we have wronged, ecstasy, described as the only perfected love and as emotion born when we love that which we hate knowing that it is fated.

In life, seeing that the *Four Faculties* and the *Husk* and *Passionate Body* constrain all, we are in accident and passion; but now *Spirit* and *Celestial Body* constrain all, the one calling up all concrete universal quality and idea, and the other closing it in the unique image. Nor can I consider the *Beatitude* as any state beyond man's comprehension, but as the presence before the soul in some settled order, which has arisen out of the soul's past, of all those events or works of men which have expressed some quality of wisdom or of beauty or of power within the compass of that soul, and as more completely human and actual than any life lived in a particular body. It is the momentary union of the *Spirit* and the *Celestial Body* with the *Ghostly Self* and fades into or is preceded by what is called the *Vision of the Clarified Body*, which is indeed a Vision of our own *Celestial Body* as that body will be when all cycles end.

(Mr Yeats, indulgent to Christian or *primary* prejudice, permits me to say that in the Robartes Papers I find this passage—" The *Celestial Body* is the Divine Cloak lent to all; at the Consummation the Cloak falls for the Christ is revealed." A passage that reminds me of Bardesan's " Hymn of the Soul " where a king's son

5 asleep in Egypt is sent a cloak which is also an image of the body of him to whom it is sent—the *Celestial Body* acting through the *Mask*—and the king's son sets out to his father's kingdom clad in the cloak. I find also that the *Ghostly Self* is so named, not as it might seem

10 because it is shadowy but because the *Beatitude* and the two states that follow correspond to the 13th, 14th and 15th Cycles which correspond in their turn to Holy Ghost, Son and Father.—Owen Aherne.)

X

* The States before Birth, called The Going Forth
and the Foreknowing

WERE the *Spirit* strong enough, or were its human cycles

15 finished, it would remain, as in the *Beatitude*, permanently united to its *Ghostly Self*, or would, after two more states, be reborn into a spiritual cycle where the movement of the gyre is opposite to that in our cycles, and incomprehensible to us, but it will almost certainly pass

20 to human rebirth because of its terror of what seems to be the loss of its own being. Whether it pass to a spiritual or to a human rebirth it must receive in the *Beatitude*—in Cancer—the Cup of Lethe. There all thoughts or images drawn from the *Faculties* during the

25 *Shiftings* or the *Dreaming Back*, or that have remained

---

* The Documents where they describe existence between the *Beatitude* and birth are exceedingly confused and what I have written on the subject is less founded upon what they say than upon my knowledge of the system as a whole.—*Sept. 26.*

in the *Faculties*, must be passed into the *Ghostly Self* and so be forgotten by the *Spirit*. It has now no fixed form, or rather one should say, cannot impose a fixed form upon its intermediaries, or be represented by a fixed correspondence, for it is not in space, nor is it " suggestible " like an inhabitant of the *Shiftings* though like this inhabitant it lives in what is to us darkness. It has, through its intermediaries and our senses and its own darkness, an almost limitless vision of concrete reality, and is in the presence of all those activities whose *Complementary Dream* is in our art, or music or literature, and of those men and women who have finished all their cycles and are called " Those who wait." We may even while we live hear their voices when in a state of trance, but speaking detached and broken sentences, and that which they say is always the greatest wisdom attainable by our soul. It is now, however, that there comes, seeing that it must recover or find its new *Husk*, a craving for deception, for pleasure and for pain, and it passes into the state called the *Foreknowing* and into space among abstracted types and forms; and there, in a reversal of the *Dreaming Back*, it sees events and people that shall influence its coming life upon earth, and as it can see that influence, as can no living man, it is possessed with violent love and hate, a wilful passion comparable to the fated passion of the *Dreaming Back*. Such souls if drunk with prevision may become what are called *Frustrators* and through their power over human emotion, or if helped by more powerful beings over the *Body of Fate* of some living man, prevent, or try to prevent, the beginnings of those things that they fear.

(Robartes told me that while in Arabia his work was constantly interfered with by illness, his own or somebody else's, and that he came to know the presence of *Frustrators* by animal odours like that of the excrement of some beast, or by the smell of a guttering candle. He said that these odours were objective, for anybody who came into the tent smelt them. He blamed the *Frustrators* for the inadequacy and confusion of all his own notes 5 which deal with the life between death and birth, and insisted that the original revelation to Kusta Ben Luka had been, so far as this subject is concerned, left unfinished for the same reason. A curious point of his was that souls immediately before birth frequently 10 thought of themselves as becoming small, and that this called up an imagination of small beasts, birds and flies. He had known, he said, two Arab women who found, one a mouse in her shoe, the other in her bed, the night before their first children were born. He thought that 15 mice, constrained by the imagination of the unborn, were perhaps really there.—Owen Aherne.)

In certain cycles the soul is able within limits to choose into what body it shall be born, but in most it must accept the choice of others. Then comes the sleep in 20 the womb and it must be in this sleep I think that there comes what is called the *Vision of the Friends* to distinguish it from that of the *Blood Kindred*.

In the *Beatitude* and in the states that immediately follow, the man is subject to his *Daimon* only, and there 25 is no alternation of sleep and waking. In the *Beatitude* communication with the living is through that state of soul, where an extreme activity is indistinguishable from an equal passivity.

> " Mind moved but seemed to stop
30 >   As 'twere a spinning top,"

and in the *Going Forth* through those actions and emotions, which are at once conscious and automatic like sudden rage and bodily desire, and nobler emotions cut from the same piece. And yet, through intermediaries, souls in the *Going Forth* can use all forms of communication not peculiar to the *Beatitude*.

The *Going Forth* lasts longer than any state except the *Return*, which may last for generations.

XI

FUNERAL IMAGES, WORKS OF ART, AND THE DEAD

IN the other life, as we have described it, there is no creation of separated form, that being the work of the living, and until the *Beatitude* there is no deliberate selection of form. All antiquity seems to have thought the newly dead " suggestible," compelled even to go where living men commanded. I have a story of a Sligo stable boy who was dismissed by his employer because he had sent her late husband's ghost to haunt a weather-beaten lighthouse, far out in the bay. A dying Mahommedan is sometimes guarded by relatives that he may look upon no ugly woman and so compel the ghostly women he will shortly meet to take her form. A Brahmin once told Florence Farr that he disliked acting because if a man died playing Hamlet he would be Hamlet in the life to come. A Galway woman told a friend of mine she had met this friend's dead husband in an old torn coat, but that if my friend gave a new coat, made to his measure, to some poor man, he would have the use of it. I heard a like story in Munster but there the ghost returned to thank the giver dressed in the new clothes. A king in Heroditus burned the best clothes of the ladies in his neighbourhood that his dead wife might make her choice. A man once told in my hearing a long story of a ghost who appeared at his bedside in a suit of clothes that had, as he proved, by some argument I forget, been copied from a portrait. One thinks of the burial customs of antiquity, all that they hid away in tombs—boats, chairs, oars, and weapons, the realistic statue of the dead man, or the golden mask upon his face—and one may well conclude that all were there to help the *Dreaming Back* of the *Spirit* or its *Waking State* in the *Return*. At some moment of the past it was discovered by some living man, or more likely taught by some dead man, that all being but " suggestion " the clay or wooden image would serve as well as the real boat or the real slave, or even that a painting upon the wall sufficed, for that which made the image serviceable was not its magnitude or its reality but the fervour and precision of the ceremony of dedication, that is to say the might of the " suggestion." The first portraits were statues buried in tombs and buried there, as we believe, to assist the *Spirit* in its *Dreaming Back*, and Strzygowski thinks that the first landscape—a landscape painted or worked in mosaic within the dome of some Mazdian Temple—was " connected with the cult of the dead, the might and majesty of departed spirits." The Christmas before last the spiritualistic paper " Light " described how some woman had been directed by spirits to make a Christmas tree for the pleasure of spirit children. After the toys had served that turn they were to be given to some children's hospital. She and a medium sat beside the tree on Christmas night and she heard the spirit children asking for this or that toy, and older spirits— *Teaching Spirits* doubtless—answering. They seemed to unloose the toy which remained, however, in its place upon the bough.* One recognises in those " synthetic cigars " in " Raymond," a venerable tradition; but may

* The ceremony was repeated last Christmas, and this time the name of the child for whom each toy was intended was by direction of the Spirits written near it. This made the dedication precise with the precision of antiquity.—W. B. Y.

be permitted to consider the scientific language and
explanation as borrowed from the subconsciousness of
the questioner, or from that of some associated person.

XII

* The Spirits at Fifteen and at One

IT is said of the Spirits at Phases 15 and 1 that the first
need help and the second give it. The second give it   5
because they are the instrument of communication
between men and all orders of Spirits, where the
communication shows an automatic element, and they
are also said to give the " Kiss of Life " while the first
give what is called the " Kiss of Death." The Spirits   10
at 15 need help that, before entering upon their embodied
state, they may rid themselves of all traces of the *primary
Tincture*, and this they gain by imposing upon a man or
woman's mind an *antithetical* image which requires
primary expression. It is this expression, which may be   15
an action or a work of art, which sets them free, and the
image imposed is an ideal form, an image of themselves,
a type of emotion which expresses them, and this they
can do but upon one man or woman's mind; their coming
life depending upon their choice of that mind. They   20
suffer from the terror of solitude, and can only free
themselves from terror by becoming entirely *antithetical*
and so self-sufficing, and till that moment comes each
must, if a woman, give some one man her love, and
though he cannot, unless out of phase and obsessed to   25

* Much in this chapter belongs to a part of the system that
requires a more detailed study than I can at present give. I may
be mistaken and only include it because the Documents insist
upon the importance of the form of expiation described. It is
connected with those *critical* and *initiatory moments* touched on
in Book II Sec. XIV.

Q

the creation of a succuba know that his muse exists, he returns this love through the intermediary of an idol. This idol he creates out of an image imposed upon his imagination by the Spirit. This Spirit
5 is said to give the " Kiss of Death " because though she that gives it may persecute other idols, being jealous, the idol has not come out of the man's desire. Its expression is a harmonisation which frees the Spirit from terror and the man from desire, and that which
10 is born from the man, and from an all but completed solitude, is called an *antithetical Arcon*. Such *Arcons* deal with form not wisdom. It is of that Kiss I thought when I made Emer say :

" They find our men asleep, weary with war,
15   Or weary with the chase, and kiss their lips
     And drop their hair upon them; from that hour
     Our men, who yet know nothing of it all,
     Are lonely, and when at fall of night we press
     Their hearts upon our hearts, their hearts are cold."

20   If the Spirit at 15 be a man he must give the " Kiss of Death " to some woman.

There is yet another expiation that follows denial of experience, the wilful refusal of expression. Because of this denial the *Ghostly Self* is famished and so in
25 the succeeding life there comes upon the man a craving to inflict upon himself that which he has inflicted, to make what is called the expiation for the *Ghostly Self*. He will offer his love to some woman who will refuse it, or to some cause that cannot prosper, or he will seek
30 money and find but penury, or knowledge and find but ignorance, he is full of an insatiable desire and yet that desire is unsatisfied because of the curse that is upon him and his secret craving. The *Ghostly Self* is as it were shut up in its own marmorean time-less infinity.
35 That this penury and this fullness may meet in *Comple-*

mentary Dream as in marriage, other spiritual beings
must intervene, using as their instruments still other
spirits, evil perhaps, instruments of the *Ghostly Self*; the
man must receive a violent shock from some crisis created
by supernatural dramatisation. Did Dante acquire in   5
the Thebaid the frenzy that he offered to Beatrice? In
antithetical man this form of Victimage is superimposed upon Victimage for the Dead that the
harmony of human emotions that creates may be
followed or accompanied by acceptance of a super-   10
natural aim. A man feels suddenly for a woman, or
a woman for a man, or—if there has been in both
expiation for the dead and for the *Ghostly Self*,—
each feels for the other an emotion which has become
a supernatural contemplation. I so picture my own   15
Deirdre and Naisi when at the spectacle of triumphant
evil and the approach of death they sit and play at chess,
and I wrote my " Hour Glass " to describe such contemplation, but there the man being *primary* makes no
expiation for the dead. In the one case natural love is   20
brought to the greatest height, and in the other intellectual search, and both reduced to nothing that the soul
may love what it hates, accepting at the same moment
what must happen and its own being, for the *Ghostly
Self* is that which is unique in man and in his fate. This 25
is the moment of the greatest genius possible to that
man or woman, and in it a *primary* or *antithetical Arcon*
of wisdom is begotten by the *Ghostly Self* upon the soul.
The beings who at the bidding of the *Ghostly Self* produce
these dramatisations of evil are the corrective Spirits 30
of Strindberg's Swedenborgian play, called in its English
translation " There are crimes and crimes." These
beings are themselves *Arcons* born through previous
dramatisations. The *Ghostly Self* comes to the man by
symbol and as when that symbol or vesture is not a   35
spirit at 15 it is a spirit from Phase 1, we may speak

of the *primary Arcon* as born from and receiving its body from a spirit at Phase 1. Its soul may be that of any selected spirit. Once born it creates a stream of impersonal expression or search. In every supernatural communication or influence which has a public object there is such an *Arcon* that its supernatural body may give stability and continuity. These beings begotten in tragedy may be brought forth in joy; and all works which are new creation, and so not from desire which can but repeat that which is already known, are brought forth under their influence or under that of beings, born from men and from the spirits at Phase 15. Was it at the Crucifixion or in the Agony in the Garden that the being was begotten whose history imaged itself in that of Christendom?

There are also *Arcons* born from the marriage of a spirit at Phase 1 and a spirit at Phase 15, but these *Arcons* have for their body neither expression nor search but the work of art, the philosophy, or action itself. They are the organic unity of thought.

XIII

COMMUNICATIONS WITH SPIRITS AND THE NATURE OF SLEEP

NO concrete image that comes before the mind in sleep is ever from the memory; for in sleep we enter upon the same life as that we enter between death and birth. Hence we may dream all night of a sweetheart or a friend or a father or a mother and speak to them, and be aware of affection or enmity, and yet if we examine our dream immediately upon waking and before our waking thought has had time to alter the dream, we find that another image has been *substituted, perhaps

---

* I cannot account for the fact that these substituted images often seem not only familiar but that their very form seems to recall the person for whom they are substituted.

very like but more probably quite unlike, perhaps even a table or a chair, and we may discover the nature of our emotion if we study the substitution which is itself a language. The concrete images that have come before us are from one or other of the states before our birth, changed by the mind's automatic phantasy, or from those images of *Anima Mundi* which have some personal link with ourselves, or images from our present life that have evaded the memory and entered the *Record* alone. All these concrete images are associated with the *Passionate Body*; but the abstract intellectual memory of the *Spirit*, that for names and qualities, continues to serve in our sleep, though we cannot connect its contents with recognisable facts. *Spirit* and *Passionate Body* are separating, for it was the waking mind that held them together; and when coherence is attained, as it is at rare moments, it is in some philosophical or symbolical dream where a new centre of coherence is discovered in the *Celestial Body*.

(Robartes told me that at Bagdad he came across an old Judwali doctor who had taken a medical degree in France, and made under his direction certain experiments upon an Arab boy. This boy was a patient of the doctor's for some physical ailment which had no connection with the fact that he talked in his sleep and would answer questions. Sometimes Robartes carried on conversations upon the most profound problems of the soul with an automatic personality which seemed sometimes the boy's own spirit and sometimes an extraneous being. He discovered that the boy's *Passionate Body* continued to dream during these conversations, but he only became aware of this dream when some physical action arising out of it interfered with articulation. Once the sleeper lapped like a cat under the influence of some chance word spoken in his hearing before he fell asleep; upon another occasion he dreamt that his

mouth was full of feathers; and so on. If afterwards
Robartes asked the boy what he had dreamt it was the
dream of the *Passionate Body* and that alone he remembered. Upon one occasion when the boy was lapping
Robartes imitated the barking of a dog as he might for
a child. The boy's terror was great, the beating of his
heart violent and yet Robartes had scarcely made any
attempt at mimicry. Some part of the boy's mind must
have accepted the suggestion deliberately; the dream
must have been a self-created terror. Robartes told me
that the dream of the *Passionate Body* after death was
so created and that the *Spirit* while it shared the dream
could be sufficiently apart from it to see men, scenes,
other spirits, though it could not act or speak outside
the dream.—O. Aherne.)

In our dreams we communicate with the dead in their
Waking State, and these dreams never come to an end
though they are only known to us while we sleep. They
are part of the *Automatic Faculty*, which with that
plastic substance sometimes visible at séances is an
element of personality which corresponds to, without
being identical with, the Spirits at Phase 1. This
Automatic Faculty prolongs, when we walk or breathe,
an act which was in the first instance voluntary, and it
may create, under an impulse from a spirit an automatic
personality which resembles that spirit, more or less
accurately, according to the intensity of the impulse and
the freedom of the *Automatic Faculty* from contrary
impressions.

(During the sleep of the boy I described in a previous
note, Robartes once arranged a code with the automatic
personality. When the boy, who knew nothing of all
this was wide awake, perhaps eating or at some work,
the dream created being would comment upon Robartes'
conversation or action by tapping with the boy's foot
or with his fork or in some similar way. Sometimes he

would speak through the boy's lips and at such moments the boy heard nothing, though the voice was loud and clear, and though he heard everything that Robartes said and every sound in the room and everything that he himself said except those words. Gradually as the automatic personality increased in power it made visible or other signs outside the body of the boy, a sudden light, a sudden heat or cold or some strong fragrance, that of a flower frequently, and this fragrance was generally perceptible to anybody who came into the room. Once Robartes listened to the sleeping boy talking to a number of spirits, and pausing for their answers. The boy spoke to them as though he knew who they were, their capacities, and when they lived. There was something they wanted to tell him that he might know what to do in a certain difficult matter, and that they might be able to impress it on his mind they were evidently insisting that he should go away by himself at a certain hour the next day. He reluctantly consented, being a very sociable person. Next morning he knew nothing of his dream, but when the hour came round said he wanted to be alone and strayed away into the fields. On his return, he said that he had made up his mind what to do in that difficult matter. Robartes' comment was that he had obeyed an order received in sleep without knowing that he did so and received a thought without knowing that it was not his own, and that this showed how strong is the control of the *Daimons* over human life.—Owen Aherne.)

The automatic personality is never perhaps a puppet in the hand of the spirit that created it, but has always not only its own automatic life but that reflected from the man himself. When, however, the creator's control is continuous, the thought and its expression may reveal a mind with powers of co-ordination greater and swifter than those of the embodied mind. One can most easily study these powers in their physical expression, and it has long been known that the hand of the medium can under such influences trace perfect circles or make patterns of sweeping lines with a rapidity and precision no

5 voluntary movement can achieve. A poltergeist has been known to hurl small flat stones through narrow slits in a shutter from a considerable distance, though no living man could have done it from but a few feet off. One notices there and elsewhere that mathematical clarity

10 one would expect from *Daimonic* domination. It is possible even that the first jugglers did not so much imitate the effect of magic as display a sleight of hand, the result of their obsession by an automatic personality.

Primary man in certain periods of thought, Shelley's

15 Ahasuerus, let us say, is able " By dreadful abstinence and conquering penance of the mutinous flesh " to keep his *Automatic Faculty* from desire and fear—hence the symbolic value given to chastity by *primary* philosophers —and so be both vehicle and questioner. His mind has

20 but a single direct movement which may be wholly dominated, whereas an *antithetical* inspiration may demand a separation of vehicle and questioner, a relation like that between Priest and Sybil, Socrates and Diotime, wandering magician and his scryer. This relation, in its

25 highest form, implies a constant interchange of office and such relations may so cross and re-cross that a community may grow clairvoyant. Lover and beloved, friend and friend, son and daughter, or an entire family and *coven*, are brought by the dramatisation of the *Arcons*

30 into such a crisis that the *primary* oppositions and harmonies of the world are exposed in their minds and fates. There must arise in the mind of one, where the bond is between two, a need for some form of truth so intense that the *Automatic Faculty* of the other grows

35 as it were hollow to receive that truth. Should the desire but be to impose a particular form of belief upon others

or upon himself the automatic personalities may exercise their control of thought or of mechanical movement for deception; but if the man desires truth itself that which comes will be the most profound truth possible to his fate. I have, however, but spoken of the communication of truth by intelligible word and there is a continual influence of *Waking Spirits* upon man's destiny by their control of his automatic movements during ordinary life. William Morris sometimes attributes to his heroes lucky eyes and foretells of one that all that he does unwitting shall be well done.

There is, however, communication of waking man and *Sleeping* Spirit, the communication during expiation and during the creation of a work of art, let us say. Self-exhaustion of a man's creative power can make his *Automatic Faculty* plastic to the *Waking* Spirits but it can only be roused into that extremity of creation and so of exhaustion, by conflict. Exhaustion and creation should follow one another like day and night, his creation bringing contact with one form of the *spiritual primary*, his exhaustion with another, and this can only come from a choice forced by conflict with the *physical primary*. When the conflict is sexual and the man and woman each *Victim* for the Dead and for the *Ghostly Self*—each miracle working idol and an object of desire, they give one another a treble love, that for the dead, that for the living, that for the never living. And if those two for whom the victimage had been undertaken be born of the man and of the woman then there is created, both before and after the birth, the position known as that of the *Four Daimons*, and each of the four has been set free from fate.

XIV

The Record and the Memory

I FIND a statement that for the supreme magical work no word or symbol can be used that is still a part of living tradition, whether that tradition is known to the questioner or to the vehicle or not.   Certainly when
5 sleep is interrupted by vision the seer goes back to remote times, and the seer amidst brilliant light discovers myths and symbols that can only be verified by prolonged research.   He has escaped from the individual *Record* to that of the race.   In even a comparatively superficial
10 communication, in so far as the actual mind of the spirit is present, words and symbols are from the individual *Record* and not from the individual memory.   Those things which have no intellectual element, sound of wind and sea for instance, as distinguished, let us say, from
15 speech—constantly pass into the *Record* without passing through the memory, and therefore come most easily to the communicators, hence frequent symbolism even where direct statement is possible.   However all images, languages, forms of every kind used in commun-
20 ications from spirits, have passed through living minds whether in the past or in the present.   All forms are from the *Record*, and almost always from that made by those who are still living, rarely from that made by the spirit itself while living.   Sometimes,
25 however, a spirit may come into contact with his own *Husk*, and through that with his own personal *Record*, or with the *Husk* of another if that other has completely separated himself from it.   It may mistake that *Husk* for its own for it finds it difficult to distinguish
30 between *Husk* and *Husk*.   The recovery, let us say, of a language from such a *Husk* except in the form of whole

sentences imprinted upon the *Record* with their associated
meaning is difficult, and a spirit with knowledge so
acquired may write or speak accurately sentences in
Greek or Latin because the *Husk* when living read or
wrote or spoke such sentences, but will seldom be able   5
to form the simplest Greek or Latin sentence for itself.
It is easier to recover the concrete image than an
abstraction.

XV

THE HERRING FISHERS

MUCH of this book is abstract, because it has not yet
been lived, for no man can dip into life more than a   10
moiety of any system. When a child, I went out with
herring fishers one dark night, and the dropping of their
nets into the luminous sea and the drawing of them up
has remained with me as a dominant image. Have I
found a good net for a herring fisher?   15

XVI

MYTHOLOGY

A BOOK of modern philosophy may prove to our logical
capacity that there is a transcendental portion of our
being that is timeless and spaceless, and therefore
immortal, and yet our imagination remain subjected to
nature as before. The great books—Berkeley's " Prin-   20
ciples of Human Knowledge " let us say—beget new
books, whole generations of books, but life goes on
unchanged. It was not so with ancient philosophy

because the ancient philosopher had something to rein-
force his thought,—the Gods, the Sacred Dead, Egyptian
Theurgy, the Priestess Diotime. He could assume,
perhaps even prove, that every condition of mind dis-
5 covered by analysis, even that which is timeless, spaceless, is present vivid experience to some being, and that
we could in some degree communicate with this being
while still alive, and after our death share in the
experience. We can believe that every school child
10 possesses in some degree all natural faculty displayed by
even the greatest man, for every such child can, if it will,
understand some few lines of Milton or Shakespeare.
That we may believe that all men possess the supernatural faculties I would restore to the philosopher his
15 mythology.

Finished at Syracuse, January, 1925.

8. ALL SOULS' NIGHT

Midnight has come and the great Christ Church bell,
And many a lesser bell, sound through the room;
And it is All Souls' Night
And two long glasses brimmed with muscatel
Bubble upon the table. A ghost may come;   5
For it is a ghost's right,
His element is so fine
Being sharpened by his death,
To drink from the wine-breath
While our gross palates drink from the whole wine.   10

I need some mind that, if the cannon sound
From every quarter of the world, can stay
Wound in mind's pondering,
As mummies in the mummy-cloth are wound;
Because I have a marvellous thing to say,   15
A certain marvellous thing
None but the living mock;
Though not for sober ear;
It may be all that hear
Should laugh and weep an hour upon the clock.   20

X—'s the first I call. He loved strange thought
And knew that sweet extremity of pride
That's called platonic love,
And that to such a pitch of passion wrought
Nothing could bring him, when his lady died,   25
Anodyne for his love.

253

Words were but wasted breath;
One dear hope had he :
The inclemency
Of that or the next winter would be death.

5   Two thoughts were so mixed up I could not tell
Whether of her or God he thought the most,
But think that his mind's eye,
When upward turned, on one sole image fell;
And that a slight companionable ghost
10 Wild with divinity,
Had so lit up the whole
Immense miraculous house,
The Bible promised us,
It seemed a gold-fish swimming in a bowl.

15 On Florence Emery I call the next,
Who finding the first wrinkles on a face
Admired and beautiful,
And knowing that the future would be vexed
With 'minished beauty, multiplied commonplace,
20 Preferred to teach a school
Away from neighbour or friend
Among dark skins, and there
Permit foul years to wear,
Hidden from eyesight, to the unnoticed end.

25 Before that end much had she ravelled out
From a discourse in figurative speech
By some learned Indian
On the soul's journey. How it is whirled about
Wherever the orbit of the moon can reach,
30 Until it plunge into the sun,
And there—free and yet fast,
Being both Chance and Choice—
Forget its broken toys
And sink into its own delight at last.

And I call up MacGregor from the grave,
For in my first hard spring-time we were friends,
Although of late estranged.
I thought him half a lunatic, half knave,
And told him so; but friendship never ends,   5
And what if mind seem changed,
And it seemed changed with the mind,
When thoughts rise up unbid
On generous things that he did
And I grow half contented to be blind.   10

He had much industry at setting out,
Much boisterous courage, before loneliness
Had driven him crazed;
For meditations upon unknown thought
Make human intercourse grow less and less;   15
They are neither paid nor praised.
But he'd object to the host,
The glass because my glass;
A ghost-lover he was
And may have grown more arrogant being a ghost.   20

But names are nothing. What matter who it be,
So that his elements have grown so fine
The fume of muscatel
Can give his sharpened palate ecstasy
No living man can drink from the whole wine.   25
I have mummy truths to tell
Whereat the living mock;
Though not for sober ear
For maybe all that hear
Should weep and laugh an hour upon the clock.   30

Such thought—such thought have I that hold it tight
Till meditation master all its parts,
Nothing can stay my glance

Until that glance run in the world's despite
To where the damned have howled away their hearts,
And where the blessed dance;
Such thought, that in it bound
5   I need no other thing,
Wound in mind's wandering,
As mummies in the mummy-cloth are wound.

Oxford, *Autumn, 1920.*

Notes

The notes herein are keyed to pages and lines: e.g. 5, 15–20 refers to page 5, lines 15 to 20. Titles of section headings (including poems) and the four Books, having no line numbers assigned, are referred to by page numbers and are printed in caps. A list of Abbreviations (pp. 85–6) contains frequently cited terms, societies, and books. Full bibliographical data of all abbreviated book titles will be found in the Bibliography (pp. 87–92), which is confined to works cited in our Editorial Introduction and Notes. Those marked by an asterisk are books Yeats relied upon directly or indirectly in the composition of *VA*. We have been unable to find a system of short titles or abbreviations for many of the rejected manuscripts, typescripts, notebooks, etc.

FRONTISPIECE. The Portrait of Giraldus and the designs of The Great Wheel (facing p. xv) and the unicorn (facing p. 8) were created by Edmund Dulac. He sent Yeats a sketch of Giraldus in an unpublished letter dated 15 Feb 1918, asking if Giraldus Cambrensis were the model. Yeats replied that he was not. Five years later, on 17 Jy 1923, Yeats asked T. Sturge Moore to make 'the big design for the philosophy book', and said that it 'must have a Unicorn in the middle' (*YM 47–8*). But Dulac wrote on 24 Jy that he had 'done a sketch in pencil of the portrait of Gyraldus by an unknown artist of the sixteenth century' (*LWBY* 439), and Yeats wrote apologetically to Moore suggesting that he would ask him 'to do something else for me instead' (*YM* 49). Dulac mailed the sketches on 30 Apr 1925. Yeats was very pleased with this work, writing on 14 Oct that he doubted 'if Laurie would have taken the book but for the amusing deceit that your designs make possible' (*L* 700). Giraldus is mentioned for the first time in the AS on 21 Jan 1919. Near the end of the Script the Control informed Yeats that 'supernormal organ received through a person we will call Gyraldus'. The name is written twice more in response to unrecorded questions. In an early and rejected version of *VA* in the form of a dialogue, Michael Robartes said: 'Giraldus seems to have believed that the ☉ & ☽ actually created antithetical & primary at Gods command for he compares them to the two hands of a cook rolling a piece of dough . . .'.

TITLE PAGE. In GP the title read: '... Giraldus and also Certain Doctrines...'.

ix, *TO VESTIGIA.* For the Dedication generally, see the Editorial Introduction to *VA*. Parallels to 'All Souls' Night' (intended as the Epilogue) are apparent. Yeats preserved a rejected prose version of an Epilogue addressed 'To Vestigia'. Sister of Henri Bergson and widow of MacGregor Mathers, founding Chief of the GD, Moina Mathers was known as Vestigia or Vesty (for Vestigia Nulla Retrorsum, 'No traces behind'), her motto in the GD.

ix, 12–14: *I had not seen you . . . nor what you were doing*. Yeats uses round numbers. Although we cannot date precisely the first draft of the Dedication we can be certain that thirty years had not elapsed since he had last seen Moina in Paris. (He stayed with the Matherses in Apr 1898.) A letter from her dated 5 Jan 1924 suggests that he had talked with her since her return to London (see *LWBY* and Editorial Introduction, p. xliv).

ix, 15: *the Jewish Schemahamphorasch*. Basic study material in the GD, 'The Schemahamphorasch or Divided Name' is explained by MacGregor Mathers in *The Kabbalah Unveiled* (pp. 170–1), a book Yeats knew well: each verse of Exodus 14. 19–21 contains seventy-two Hebrew characters; if the three verses are placed one above another in Hebrew, there will result (reading downward) seventy-two columns of three letters, each expounding the powers of the name Jehovah (IHVH). Also related are the seventy-two leaves in the Cabalistic Tree of Life and the seventy-two rounds in Jacob's ladder. Yeats preserved two manuscript copies of 'The Schemahamphorasch', neither in his hand.

ix, 19: *Florence Farr*. Florence Farr Emery (Sapientia Sapienti Dono Data, 'Wisdom is given to the wise as a gift') was an actress and an important member of the GD, serving for a time as Mathers' 'Representative in the Second Order in London' (*YGD* 21). Yeats noted her death in a letter of Jy 1917 (*L* 628).

x, 3: *a Buddhist monk*. Allan Bennett (Iehi Aour, 'Let there be light'), a member of the GD before he moved to Burma (see *L* 499 and *YGD* 197, n. 82). He was also a good friend of the notorious Aleister Crowley.

x, 5: *A third*. William Thomas Horton (Spes Mea Christus, 'Christ is my hope'), a member of the GD (in 1896) with whom Yeats corresponded sporadically from 1896 to 1919. Yeats wrote the Introduction for Horton's *A Book of Images* (1898) and was influenced by others of Horton's works. Horton's Platonic friend was Amy Audrey Locke, who died in 1916. For what few details are known see *L* 260–3 and *YO* 190–203.

x, 29–30: *our belief that truth cannot be discovered*. In one of his last letters Yeats observed that 'Man can embody truth but he cannot know it' (*L* 922). While the research for *VA* was in progress, Yeats apparently hoped that he could use the experimental method to refute the scientists and discover truth.

x, 33: *a learned brassfounder*. Possibly Thomas Henry Pattinson (*YGD* 197, n. 82).

x–xi, 35f: *"The Summum Bonum"*. The term literally means 'the highest good'. 'The stone of the wise' is the aim of spiritual alchemists. The Adepti of the GD were preoccupied with the quest for the Summum Bonum (see *YGD* 161, n. 57). In the AS for 11 Oct 1918 Yeats asked 'What is the summum bonum?' The Control answered, 'Subjectifying of personal & spiritual objective or oneness with God'. When Yeats then asked what the 'personal objective' is, the Control replied, 'all desire all impulse all individual'.

xi, 4: *in a railway train*. According to Yeats, the Communicators' change from Automatic Writing to Automatic Speaking came on a train in Southern California (*VB* 9). In fact, an account in one notebook of Sleeps suggests that it may have occurred 'on way to San Francisco' from Portland, Oregon, on 24 Mar 1920.

xi, 14–15: *Hodos Chameliontos*. Yeats added this sentence in GP. 'Liber Hodos Chamelionis' or 'Book of the Path of the Chamelion' was the title of a study manual in the GD. Borrowed for the title of Book III of *The Trembling of the Veil* (1922), the phrase became 'Hodos Camelionis'. After being informed by Lous C. Purser that 'the genitive is chameliontos' if used as a Greek word (*LWBY* 436), Yeats changed the spelling. For some details of the use of the manual in the GD, see *YGD* 177, n. 30.

xi, 22: *Dante . . . Baccaccio*. Yeats refers to Ch. 12, 'Qualities and Defects of Dante', in Boccaccio's *Life of Dante* (in *The Earliest Lives of Dante*, pp. 58–9).

xi, 29: *Swedenborg and Blake*. Cf. Yeats's note (wr. 1924) to 'The Friends of the People of Faery': 'A countryman near Coole told me of a spirit so ascending. Swedenborg, in his *Spiritual Diary*, speaks of gyres of spirits, and Blake painted Jacob's Ladder as an ascending gyre' (*M* 123).

xii, 5: *my ignorance of philosophy*. See *VB* 12–20. Yeats frequently expressed regret at his lack of a formal education. But it should be noted that his Instructors warned him not to read philosophy while the AS and Sleeps were in progress. For example, one of the Controls (in an undated Script) said: 'I give you philosophy to give you new images; you ought not to use it as philosophy...'.

xii, 6–8: *As I most . . . in that alone*. See L 781.

xii, 14–15: *thought is nothing without action*. Cf. the remark which Yeats attributes to Goethe: 'Man knows himself by action only, by thought never' (p. 80).

xii, 22: *Beatific Vision*. At one time Yeats intended a more extended treatment of the Beatific Vision, which is discussed several times in the AS and the CF. For example, one card explains: 'Solar Vision followed by Lunar V. brings B.V. Solar—15, Lunar—one, B.V.—apex (center)'. The Solar represents understanding of the Head, the Lunar of the Heart, the Beatific of the Soul. See the brief mention on p. 172 and the discussion of the Beatitude on pp. 235–6.

xii, 27–8: poems like *"The Phases . . . Ego Dominus Tuus"*. In 1922 Yeats commented about 'The Phases of the Moon' and two other poems: 'To some extent I wrote these poems as a text for exposition' (*VP* 821).

xii, 28: *nor spend barren years.* See *VPl* 761 for remarks about *The Player Queen*: 'I wasted the best working months of several years in an attempt to write a poetical play where every character became an example of the finding or not finding of what I have called the Antithetical Self.'

xiii, 3: *Powys Mather's "Arabian Nights".* For Yeats's reading of this edition, see Bushrui, *IER* 291. As with several other foreign-language books, Yeats evidently found the language of a particular edition exciting. See also n. to p. 197, 7–11.

xiii, 6–7: *where Augustus and Tiberius wandered.* Both Augustus and Tiberius built villas on Capri, remains of which are still extant.

xiii, 16–19: *"I have been . . . of the grass".* Since somewhat different versions of the sentence appear in at least two rejected manuscripts, the quotation if not the idea is obviously Yeats's own. A passage from a rejected manuscript in explication of P 25 explains Yeats's meaning: 'I gave up my desire to understand superessential reality, now I must give up my desire to possess it. I must be nothing—an insect in the roots of the grass'. Cf. 'A Dialogue of Self and Soul', especially ll. 57–72. Thatcher (*Nietzsche in England*, 172) suggests that these remarks are reminiscent of the eternal return in *Also Sprach Zarathustra* (see also p. 176).

xv: *BY OWEN AHERNE.* For discussion of the characters Robartes and Aherne see especially the Editorial Introduction herein and Michael J. Sidnell, 'Mr. Yeats, Michael Robartes and Their Circle' (*YO* 225–54). In part at least Aherne was modeled on Lionel Johnson (see *YO* 255–84) and Robartes on MacGregor Mathers (cf. the sketch of him in *A* 182–8).

xv, 18: *the story of Griselda.* By the so-called Griselda Master, who flourished c. 1500 and was influenced by Signorelli; see *The National Gallery Illustrated General Catalogue*, 447, items 912–14. The story is the familiar one from Boccaccio and from 'The Clerk's Tale' in Chaucer's *Canterbury Tales*.

xvi, 16–19: *Mr Yeats had given . . . travesty of real events.* Robartes and Aherne are prominent characters in three early stories: 'Rosa Alchemica' (1896), 'The Tables of the Law' (1896), and 'The Adoration of the Magi' (1897). Only the first story is referred to here.

xvi, 35: *Mr Watkins the book-seller.* John M. Watkins was editor of *Book-Notes* (Mar 1893–Feb 1897), publisher of the writings of the TS, and a bookseller of new and used occult books; his store in Cecil Court was a center for 'tea, talk, and theosophy', as his son Geoffrey N. Watkins comments in 'Yeats and Mr. Watkins' Bookshop' (*YO* 307–10).

xvii, 17–18: *Dr. Dee and his friend Edward Kelly.* In Poland during 1583–5, they were alchemists and spiritualists whose works were studied in the GD.

Yeats was evidently familiar with Dee's published diary (see Taylor, *FPS* 98). *Scrying* is crystal-gazing.

xvii, 26: *'Speculum Angelorum et Hominorum'*. The title of this imaginary volume may be translated as 'Mirror of Angels and Men'. *Hominorum* should be *hominum*, as F. P. Sturm pointed out to Yeats (*FPS* 93–4). In the earliest versions Yeats used *Hominis*.

xvii, 28: *the celebrated Cracow publications*. Apparently Yeats's imagination triumphed over historical reality, since Cracow was a centre of printing in the early sixteenth century rather than the seventeenth. Writing to his illustrator Edmund Dulac about the woodcuts for *VA*, Yeats said that 'your Kracow artist would not have drawn them very carefully. I can give the *speculum* what date you please' (*L* 700). The unimportance of the date is a significant clue; possibly Yeats chose Cracow because Dee and Kelly had been there, because Hannibal Rosselli's six-volume commentary on the *Pymander Hermetis Mercurii Trismegistus* was published there (1585–90), and because the alchemist Michael Sendivogius was connected with the city.

xvii, 32: *curious allegorical pictures*. In the CF, under 'Symbols of Phases', Yeats made a list for all twenty-eight Phases except 12 and 25. Several are suggestive of the three 'curious allegorical pictures': (3) 'Eagle over sea with feet caught in back of sea lion one foot caught by a dolphin. Eagle drags both'; (9) 'leopard, eagle or bird plucking out eyes'; (15) 'man with arrow & stone one in each hand'; (26) 'Hunchback fighting his shadow on ground which bleeds'. In the R-A TS Robartes declared that the *Speculum* 'was indeed full of curious allegorical woodcuts, astronomical diagrams, where drawings of Noah's Ark and the Tables of the Law were mixed up with Zodiacal signs and phases of the moon and geometrical diagrams where cones containing gyres sprang out of each other like strange vegetables'. The unicorn was a basic symbol of the GD. Upon passing the examination for the Degree of 3=8 (Practicus), the aspirant assumed the symbolic title of *monoceros de astris*, which Father John translates as 'the unicorn from the stars' in Yeats's play by that title (*VPl* 659). Yeats informed his sister Lolly in 1920 that 'it is a private symbol belonging to my mystical order. . . . It is the soul' (*L* 662). In the AS for 31 May 1919 the Control informed Yeats that the unicorn was his Daimon. When Yeats asked if he could 'apply symbol of unicorn to new Avatar', the Control said 'No'. On 27 Nov 1920 Yeats noted: 'Unicorn to be kept for Daimon'. For the woman with stone and arrow, cf. *A* 578.

xviii, 5: *an apple, an acorn, a cup*. In the woodcut of The Great Wheel, there are what Yeats calls 'an apple, an acorn, a cup, and what looked like a sceptre or wand' (*VB* 38). In fact, the woodcut depicts only three of these symbolic objects, substituting a flower (possibly a rose) for the acorn. It may be significant that the Guides (in contrast to Controls) who dictated part of the

AS were called by such names as Rose, Flower, Leaf, and Apple (23 May 1920). The four symbols correspond generally to the Tarot suits of cups, wands, swords, and pentacles.

xviii, 8–9: *an unfrocked priest . . . troup of gypsies.* Yeats perhaps echoes Joseph Glanvill's story from *The Vanity of Dogmatizing* (1661) of the wandering gypsy, made famous by Arnold's poem 'The Scholar-Gypsy'. Yeats quotes Glanvill's account in his essay 'Magic' (*EI* 38–40).

xviii, 33: *a tribe of Judwalis.* Called Bacleones in an early manuscript, they were a fictitious group whose name (meaning 'diagrammatists') was probably invented for Yeats by Sir Edward Denison Ross, a great Orientalist. For a good account see Bushrui in *IER* 295–9.

xix, 1–3: *Fanatical in matters . . . I have met.* On 2 June 1900, Yeats wrote to Lady Gregory that George Russell 'and I are the opposite of one another. I think I understand people easily and easily sympathize with all kinds of characters and easily forgive all kinds of defects and vices. I have the defect of this quality. Apart from opinions, which I judge too sternly, I scarcely judge people at all and am altogether too lax in my attitude towards conduct' (*L* 345). See also *A* 432.

xix, 11–12: *"The Way of the Soul between the Sun and the Moon".* This fictitious title combines the titles of two books given to Yeats by friends: W. T. Horton's *The Way of the Soul, a Legend in Line and Verse* (1910) and Cecil French's *Between Sun and Moon: Poems and Wood-Cuts* (1922), which was dedicated to Yeats (see *LWBY* 424). He was perhaps also aware that Tennyson sometimes referred to *In Memoriam* as 'The Way of the Soul'. In one rejected manuscript Robartes says that he 'went to Damascus to speak with a student of "The Way of the Soul"'. Perhaps because the borrowing was too obvious, this title was changed in a rejected typescript to 'The Way of the Souls between the Moon and the Sun'. It was enclosed in parentheses because Yeats intended to replace it with an Arabic translation, probably supplied by Denison Ross: 'I have the name in Arabic', Yeats noted, 'but cannot find it for the moment'. The two Arabs were both quite real, though Kusta Ben Luka was not born (A.D. 820) until after al-Rashid's death (A.D. 809). Yeats might have discovered al-Rashid in *The Arabian Nights* (see p. 197) and in Gibbon's *The Decline and Fall of the Roman Empire*; he might have met Costa ben Luca (spelled variously) in Robert Burton's *Anatomy of Melancholy*.

xx, 1: *djinns.* Bushrui (*IER* 305–6) connects the djinns with Yeats's Daimons, who are much discussed in the AS.

xx, 3: *the little Bloomsbury court.* Yeats maintained a residence at No. 18 Woburn Buildings, London, from Mar 1896 until Dec 1917.

xx, 5: *"No, it will be better".* In the R-A TS, Robartes and Aherne failed to enter because of the probable presence of Ezra Pound, a violent talker who had been rude to Aherne.

xxi, 1: *Thoor Ballylee*. A Norman tower near Gort which Yeats purchased in 1916. The Yeatses spent several months of 1918 (May to Sept) in Ballinamantane, a cottage on Lady Gregory's Coole Park estate, while they supervised the restoration of Ballylee. Moving in for less than a week in Sept, they returned for the entire summer (June to Sept) in 1919 and not again until Apr 1922. 'The Phases of the Moon' (1918) may have been written during the residence at Ballinamantane, though we have discovered no direct references to the poem in the AS of these months.

xxi, 17–20: *St. Clement . . . keeps his mitre*. No orthodox support is to be found for the remarks about either Clement of Alexandria (not a saint, in fact) or Archbishop Passivalli; Yeats's starting point might well have been a biased occultist article. But Clement's disciple Origen did believe in transmigration. The rather obscure Italian Capuchin Luigi Puecher-Passivalli delivered the opening sermon of the Vatican Council of 1869. In the R-A TS, Aherne remarked that a church council found metempsychosis heretical; 'however', he added, 'Leo XII gave me exemption from the Index and I make a distinction between what I investigate as philosopher and what I believe as Christian'. Yeats obviously confused his popes, since Leo XII was pope from 1823–9 and Leo XIII from 1878–1903.

xxii, 2–3: *terror and joy*. These words were particularly associated with *VA*, suggesting the feeling appropriate for a new influx. Several questions in the AS of 2 Aug 1919 are concerned with terror, which is explained as 'the other serenity of isolation' and related to the masculine form of P 15. Earlier (26 Apr) when Yeats asked the Control why the AS was compelled to be 'joyous'—i.e., 'an affirmation of life'—Thomas replied, 'because this script has its origin in human life—all religious systems have their origin in God & descend to man—this ascends'. (See also *E* 425, *L* 901, and *EI* 501, and compare the 'terrible beauty' of 'Easter 1916'.)

xxiii, 13: *The twelve rotations*. This passage is probably meant primarily as mystification suited to the character of Aherne, but see pp. 141–8.

xxiii, 21–2: *great eggs laid by the Phoenix*. The symbol of the egg is explored most fully in Ch. I of Melchiori, *The Whole Mystery of Art*, 164–99. See also p. 175. In an essay published in 1907 Yeats declared: 'We must find some place upon the Tree of Life for the phoenix' nest, for the passion that is exaltation and the negation of the will, for the wings that are always upon fire, set high that the forked branches may keep it safe, yet low enough to be out of the little wind-tossed boughs, the quivering of the twigs' (*EI* 272). The phoenix is a traditional Romantic symbol of rebirth, as in Carlyle's *Sartor Resartus*, Bk III, Ch. V.

3: *THE WHEEL AND THE PHASES OF THE MOON.* Later entitled 'The Phases of the Moon'. See especially the bibliographical data in *VP* and the critical comments in Jeffares' *CCP*. The poem was first printed in *The Wild Swans at Coole* (1919). In *Later Poems* (1922) Yeats attached a note about 'The Phases' and two other *Vision* poems:

> Years ago I wrote three stories in which occurs the names of Michael Robartes and Owen Aherne. I now consider that I used the actual names of two friends, and that one of these friends, Michael Robartes, has but lately returned from Mesopotamia where he has partly found and partly thought out much philosophy. I consider that John Aherne is either the original of Owen Aherne or some near relation of the man that was, and that both he and Robartes, to whose namesake I had attributed a turbulent life and death, have quarrelled with me. They take their place in a phantasmagoria in which I endeavour to explain my philosophy of life and death, and till that philosophy has found some detailed exposition in prose certain passages in the poems named above may seem obscure. To some extent I wrote them as a text for exposition. (Cf. *VP* 821.)

Though 'The Phases' was written in 1918, after Yeats's marriage, it is closely related to his philosophy projected in *PASL* (wr. in 1917, before marriage), part of a logical pattern of development toward *VA*. The first of four complete poems in *VA*, 'The Phases' and 'All Souls' Night' frame the book. Certainly the poem is a 'text for exposition' in that much of it is later developed in greater detail. The setting is Thoor Ballylee.

As to the meaning of the characters in context, the Christian, orthodox Aherne invariably misses the real point, and Robartes and Yeats are much closer; however, Robartes and Aherne are partly two sides of the Yeatsian character, two complementary masks.

After many years of separation, this meeting with Robartes-Aherne signals Yeats's public renewal of interest in occultism. While in private Yeats never forsook his occult interests, his published work had offered less evidence of such concerns for some time; the resurrection of Robartes and Aherne remarkably paralleled the personal and special interest in the occult which dated from Mrs Yeats's mediumistic activity.

Throughout the poem, the magus Robartes has a somewhat abstracted air and never properly responds to Aherne's personal and ideological demands for exclusive attention. The point of view through which the reader's observations are focused is that of Aherne, a fallible and naive narrator, while Robartes cares only for the philosophy which he expounds; hence, those critics are probably correct who suppose the final lines to indicate that the Tower's inhabitant has found his solution to the problem of life in spite of Aherne's malicious glee.

9: *THE DANCE OF THE FOUR ROYAL PERSONS.* Entitled in an early typescript 'Arabian Account of the Origin of the Great Wheel, or as They

Have Named it of the Dance of the Four Royal Persons'. Like most of Yeats's fictions, this one is obviously symbolical. Melchiori points out that, as in the traditional alchemy Yeats learned in the GD, the unification in a dance of the four elements suggests the ultimate aim of life (*The Whole Mystery of Art*, 4). Cf. the Four Quarters of the Great Wheel and other Yeatsian quaternaries (pp. 30–6). In an early version the Caliph was named El Mukledir. Yeats probably identified his own family with 'the King, the Queen, the Prince and the Princess of the Country of Wisdom'. In a record of a Sleep for 24 Mar 1920 George is called the Queen of Cups, Yeats the King of Wands. Numerous times throughout the AS, the Control tells the Yeatses that they are to have two children, a daughter and a son, the third and fourth Daimons. A rejected manuscript makes clear that Yeats had the Tarot deck in mind:

> This story was told to Michael Robartes by a Judwali Doctor at Damascus, & he added a suggestion the four suits of the Tarot, the King, the Queen, Prince & Princess were derived through the Saracens from the dance, and that these cards have in turn given birth to our common court cards.

10, 10: *"some great secret in the marks of their feet"*. This passage is reminiscent of one in *SB* (II, 75–6). An entry dated 4 June 1909 in the Maud Gonne Notebook makes clear that Yeats associated the symbolic dance with the teachings and rituals of the GD:

> Felkin told me that he had seen a Dervish dance a horoscope. He went round & round on the sand bar & then circled to center. He whirled round at the planets making round holes in the sand by doing so. He then danced the connecting lines between planets & fell in trance. This is what I saw in a dream or vision years ago.

Dr Robert W. Felkin was Chief of the Stella Matutina in 1909. For further discussion of the dance see *YGD* 118..See also Kermode, *Romantic Image*, 49–91.

10, 26–7: *He that dies . . . in the story*. This passage is almost identical to line 851 of Yeats's play *The King's Threshold* (*VPl* 309). At one stage Yeats appended the following note to a rejected version of 'The Dance':

> According to the Robartes MSS the Dance of the Four Royal Persons is one of the names for the first figure drawn by the Judwaylis elders for the instruction of youth. It is it seems identical with "The Great Wheel" of Gyraldus.
>
> Owen Aherne

11, 7: *The Judwali doctor of Bagdad*: See n. to pp. 245–6, 20f.

11, 17–18: *"Desert Geometry or The Gift of Harun Al-Raschid"*. In this poem (wr. 1923, pub. Jan 1924) Harun Al-Raschid presents Kusta ben-Luka with a bride who, like Mrs Yeats, unexpectedly begins to provide automatic writing shortly after their marriage. See pp. 121–7.

11, 19–21: *almost similar adventure . . . much later date*. Presumably the later grammarian is a Yeatsian invention, part of an effort to characterize the pedantic and literal Aherne.

12, 5: *Arabic Mansions of the Moon*. Yeats preserved a copy in George's hand of lines 1117–25 and 1129–34 from 'The Franklin's Tale' in W. W. Skeat's edition of Chaucer (IV, 493–4). She drew double lines alongside the second passage, which is concerned with the operation of the twenty-eight mansions of the moon. At the bottom of the page she wrote 'note by Skeat on this passage' and copied , with some changes, his note for line 1130 (V, 392). She also drew double lines alongside three lines citing Johannes Hispalensis' *Epitome Astrologiae*, which explains 'the influence of the moon on these mansions'. According to Jeffares, George typed out the passages from Chaucer, 'whom Yeats had read carefully in 1910' (*WBY* 195). Yeats had, of course, studied lunar-solar symbolism in the TS, the GD, and numerous books, especially Rhys's *Lectures on the Origin and Growth of Religion* (1886).

12, 13: *gold and silver*. These are traditional solar and lunar symbols; their unification would represent perfection, the aim of the alchemist.

13, 5–6: *Murray's dictionary*. One of the names by which the *OED* is known, after its first editor, Sir James Augustus Henry Murray.

14, 2–3: *containing letter S*. Actually, the fascicle *Su–subterraneous* had been issued in Dec 1914 (*OED*, I, xxvi); presumably, Yeats consulted the bound volumes only.

14, 10: *Tinctures*. According to the *OED*, this term's alchemical meaning is 'a supposed spiritual principle or immaterial substance whose character or quality may be infused into material things, which are then said to be tinctured; the quintessence, spirit, or soul of a thing'.

14, 16–17: *strife between the Tinctures*. While retaining its general meanings, *strife* here has especially a Heraclitean sense (see p. 132) suggesting an irreconcilable battle of opposites as the basis of human life.

14: *THE FOUR FACULTIES*. This fourfold division of the personality is at the very heart of Yeats's concept of the self: it is fundamental to Blake's Prophetic Books and the basis of GD rituals and occult doctrines. *Will*, the essential definition of personality, is pure choice and defines the self; what it chooses as ideal personality is *Mask*. *Creative Mind*, something of a misnomer, is less related to Romantic imagination than to philosophical reason, bound by the *Body of Fate* or set of environmental truths which it perceives. Complicating matters, Yeats will later introduce the *Four Principles*, or transcendent aspects of human personality. See n. to p. 30.

14, note: *If Blake had not given "selfhood"*. As this confusing note suggests, Yeats sometimes felt a genuine conflict with the material provided for him by Mrs Yeats; there is tension between what Yeats would have written on his own and what he wrote in an attempt to reconcile his own views with those in the AS. Whereas Yeats's Creative Mind is a rather rational faculty, the roughly synonymous Latin *genius* and the Greek *daimon* suggest a total, transcendental self which altered in perceiving. On 15 Jan 1918 Yeats asked the Control for the 'equivalent in our system to spiritistic guide & Greek daimon' but received an ambiguous reply. Blake's *self* or *selfhood* suggests selfishness, egotism, or egoism: occurring in heaven, the sin of selfhood was the reason for the Fall.

15, 9: *called the Image*. Evidently the Mask is more freely chosen than the Image, which is offered by an external Fate (see p. 63). The term *image* is frequently used in the AS, where it is usually related to symbolic artistic creation.

15, 10: *as intellect was understood*. Yeats is not really concerned with the seventeenth century: he would insist that the intellect is not a *tabula rasa* but shapes, formulates, constitutes, and is equivalent to the imagination of Coleridge's *Biographia Literaria* rather than to the fancy (see *Biographia Literaria*, I, 202).

15, 23–5: *The photograph is fated . . . the Mask is predestined*. The opposition of Fate to Destiny is a recurrent theme of *VA*; whereas the Fated is required by forces external to the self, Destiny is an expression of choice by the self (see pp. 44–5). The distinction is emphasized repeatedly in the AS.

16, 2–6: *An object is sensuous . . . etc.* On two separate occasions Yeats explored these distinctions in the AS. Using the term 'allusion' to refer to concrete images, George recorded that the fire=abstract, a fire=allusion, my fire=sensuous (14 Oct 1919). Two nights later Yeats phrased a rhetorical question which makes an epistomological progression not suggested in *VA*: 'When *the* fire becomes *a* fire & afterwards *my* fire you mean I conclude *my* fire in this life. That it is to say present sensuous memory, one which is in some way impressed, the shape as it were of something in a past life.'

16, 14: *diagram 1*. That is, on p. 13.

16, 15: *Head, Heart, Loins and Fall*. In early drafts Yeats used *Fate* rather than *Fall*. Although the reader may be bothered by the failure of anatomical parallelism in the term *Fall* (as from grace), Yeats had so used the set of four terms as early as 1893, in his and Ellis's *WWB* (I, 262–4; see also I, 347). In the AS for 22 Nov 1917 George drew a diagram with Head, Heart, Fall, and Loins at four quarters and related them to Mars, Saturn, Venus, and the Moon respectively. Yeats asked the Control if he knew Blake's terms 'Head, Heart, Loins'. The answer was 'No but if I can get it from yourselves I may be able to———'. Yeats asked, 'What do you mean by fall'; the Control replied, 'The Beginning of anger and the departure from wisdom', then concluded, 'Head and Heart Anti—Loins & Fall Primary'. Cf. also Yeats's later development in 'The Four Ages of Man', and see his letter of 24 Jy 1934 (*L* 823–5).

16, 19: *will be explained later.* See p. 146, where Yeats relates these points to the transcendental *Principles*.

17, 29: *Commedia del Arte.* In the AS for 17 Jan 1918, when the Control said that 'the Ego chooses the part he plays and writes the words', Yeats responded, 'you have described Commedia Del Arte'. The Control commented: 'That is like the Noh partially, a dramatisation of the soul, it is all great art.'

18, 12–13: *the unity described by Dante in the Convito.* This is one of Yeats's most frequent allusions (see p. 202). Although we cannot identify its precise source, two passages from *Dante's Convito* are illuminating: (1) 'Amongst the works of Divine Wisdom, Man is the most wonderful, considering how in one form the Divine Power joined three natures; and in such a form how subtly harmonized his body must be. It is organized for all his distinct powers; wherefore, because of the great concord there must be, among so many organs, to secure their perfect response to each other, in all the multitude of men but few are perfect' (III, viii, p. 126); (2) 'And when it [the body] is well proportioned and appointed, then it is beautiful throughout and in all its parts; for the due ordering or proportion of our limbs produces a pleasing impression of I know not what of wonderful harmony. . . . And thus to say that the noble nature takes heed for the graces of the body, and makes it fair and harmonious, is tantamount to saying that it prepares it and renders it fit to attain the perfection ordained for it' (IV, xxv, p. 261). In 'William Butler Yeats: A Survey of His Reading' (p. 345) Thomas L. Dume suggests that the particular passage is first borrowed in 'A People's Theatre' (first published 29 Nov–6 Dec 1919) (see *E* 250). In the AS of 13 Oct 1919, before any questions were asked, the Control said 'I want you both to read the whole of Dante's Convito only a little every day—she can read it to you'. The AS contains numerous discussions of Unity of Being, 'a co-equality of Primary & Antithetical' (7 Oct 1921). Earlier Yeats had asked, 'What is unity of being?' The Control replied: 'Complete harmony between physical body, intellect & spiritual desire – *all may be imperfect* but if harmony is perfect it is unity'. It 'cannot exist before 15 or after 19' (3 Sept 1918).

18, 25–6: *The author of "The Imitation of Christ".* Probably Thomas à Kempis, a German monk (cf. *FFT* 6).

18, 28–30: *free Mask is personality . . . enforced mask is character.* Yeats regularly and for some time had made invidious contrasts between personality, which he liked, and character, which he did not; for example, in his preface to *Plays for an Irish Theatre* (1911) he treated character as merely comic (v. tragic) and merely individual (v. universal) (*VPl* 1296–9).

19, 4: *like Landor.* See pp. 78–9.

20: *TRUE AND FALSE MASKS*. In an early notebook Yeats first used the terms 'Good and Bad Masks', then changed them to 'Good and Evil Masks'.

21, 21–2: *sees "a world . . . in a wild flower"*. Slightly misquoted from Blake's 'Auguries of Innocence', ll. 1–2 (Keynes, 431).

22: *TRUE AND FALSE CREATIVE MIND*. Earlier terms for this concept were 'Creative and Evil Genius'.

23: *BODY OF FATE*. This term replaces the earlier 'Passionate Fate'.

24, 7–15: *The Phases . . . are made simple*. In an early notebook Yeats relates water to Heart, air to Head, fire to Loins, and earth to Fall.

25, 1: *the dog bays the Moon*. Cf. *Julius Caesar*, IV.iii.27, in which Brutus says that 'I had rather be a dog, and bay the moon . . .' (*RS* 1125).

25, 2: *the eagle stares on the Sun*. Jeffares (in *CCP* 109–10) connects a similar eagle-image in 'Upon a House Shaken by the Land Agitation' with passages from several of Blake's poems. For the contrast, see Yeats's notes to *Calvary* (1921): 'Certain birds, . . . such lonely birds as the heron, hawk, eagle, and swan, are the natural symbols of subjectivity, especially when floating upon the wind alone or alighting upon some pool or river, while the beasts that run upon the ground, especially those that run in packs, are the natural symbols of objective man' (*VPl* 789).

25, 31–2: *in relation to another part of the System*. See pp. 172–3.

27, 12–14: *St. Peter . . . the crucified Christ*. According to Eusebius, Peter was crucified with head down. Blake suggested that 'The modern Church crucifies Christ with the head downwards'; see 'Blake's Illustrations to Dante', *EI* 138. The Hanged Man of the Tarot Trumps Major (no. xii) is also crucified with head down.

27, 14–15: *"Demon est Deus Inversus"*. That is, 'The devil is the converse of God'. This brief Latin sentence was Yeats's motto in the GD. He probably discovered it in H. P. Blavatsky's *Isis Unveiled* or *The Secret Doctrine*, in which the motto is the heading of a chapter which treats, among other subjects, Solar and Lunar deities. Madame Blavatsky claims that ancient philosophers 'defined evil as the lining of God or Good: *Demon est Deus inversus*, being a very old adage. Indeed, evil is but an antagonizing blind force in nature; it is *reaction, opposition*, and *contrast*,—evil for some, good for others. There is no *malum in se*: only the shadow of light, without which light could have no existence, even in our perceptions.' 'This', she concludes, 'is the "Astral Light", or DEMON EST DEUS INVERSUS' (I, 413, 424). As Yeats suggests in the following sentence, he finds confirmation for his supposedly Heraclitean view that man and god die each other's life, live each other's death, that man and guardian angel may be jealous of one another, and that seasons are antithetical in this world and fairyland. It should be understood that *demon* does not mean *devil*. See n. to p. 220, 6.

27, note: *Light and dark . . . at right angles*. This note, added to the GP, may also be indebted to Madam Blavatsky's *Secret Doctrine* (I, Ch. xi).

29, 6–8: *In the Convito . . . such as he*. In the *Convito*, Dante suggests that a man's physical presence decreases his fame: 'And this is the reason why each prophet is less honoured in his own country; and this is why the good man ought to give his presence to few, and his familiarity to still fewer, in order that his name may be received and not despised' (p. 20). 'When the rivers are poisoned', Yeats wrote to Ethel Mannin, 'take to the mountain well; or go with Dante into exile' (*L* 882).

29, 12: *Guido Cavalcanti*. Yeats probably knew Cavalcanti as poetic technician through Pound. Like Dante, Cavalcanti was active in Florentine politics and was exiled briefly in 1300.

29, 16: *Unity of Being*. See n. to *Convito*, p. 18, 12–13. Yeats related his own situation to Dante's: both belonged at P 17, had achieved Unity of Being, had loved hopelessly, had been 'exiled', and hated abstraction, 'that quality in every phase which impedes unity of being' (AS, 30 Jan 1919).

30: *TABLE OF THE FOUR FACULTIES*. Yeats spent considerable time defining the Faculties and arranging the Table. In one of the notebooks (dated 9 Jy 1923 on the last page) he arranged the first eight Phases in five columns and the remaining twenty in six columns with headings greatly different from the final version: Ego, Good Mask, Evil Mask, Evil Genius, Creative Genius, and Passionate Fate. Ego became Will, Good and Evil Masks were combined, Evil and Creative Geniuses became Creative Mind, and Passionate Fate became Body of Fate. Much of this notebook is concerned with the Four Faculties and such related quaternaries as Four Automatonisms, Four Types of Wisdom, Four Conditions of the Mask, Four Elements, etc.

33: *CHARACTERS OF CERTAIN PHASES*. An early notebook contains another tetradic Character presumably intended for sec. XIII: Four Memories (Mask=Conditional, Ego=Personal, Creative Genius=Spiritual, Passionate Fate=Emotional). Yeats also considered including a tetrad of the Four Daimons (Self=Love, Creative Genius=Wisdom, Mask=Beauty, Passionate Fate=Truth).

34: *GENERAL CHARACTER . . . CERTAIN PHASES*. An early heading was 'Genius of the Divisions of Phases in Wheel & Cone'.

34, note: *the old tenfold year*. See pp. 152–8; this would be the Roman calendar ending with December, the tenth month. Since Yeats's cosmic vision was essentially tetradic, he was disturbed that these two Tables were 'divided into ten divisions' rather than twelve. He rejected a list of 'Automatism of 12 Cycles at Phase 1'.

35, 6: *(10 ,, 25, 26, 27 from 3, 4, 5*. The last set of numbers ought to read 5, 4, 3 in order to be consistent with the rest of this Table; the error (if it is one) is repeated in *VB* 101.

35: At some point, probably after sec. XV, Yeats originally intended to include two septenary Tables: (1) Planes (Physical, Passionate, Spirits of Dead, Celestial Body, Guides etc., Angels, Invisible); (2) Colours (Prayer=Amber, Truth=Blue, Peace=Gray, Heir=Purple, Position= Green, Negation=Red, Space=Yellow).

38, 15–16: *"The uncontrollable mystery upon the bestial floor"*. L. 8 of Yeats's 'The Magi'; in printed texts, 'upon' is 'on'.

39, 14–17: *"But when they . . . on every side"*. Blake's 'The Mental Traveller', ll. 93–6 (Keynes, 427).

39, 27: *the breath stirring on the face of the deep*. See Genesis 1:2.

40, 17–18: *dancing faun*. The old name for the Capitoline Satyr in Rome, a copy of a work by Praxiteles. In Hawthorne's *Marble Faun*, for example, the phrase 'dancing faun' is used in Chapter II in explicit reference to that statue; Yeats would also have been familiar with the phrase from Blake's 'Descriptive Catalogue' (Keynes, 579). The faun was used as an example of physical strength without guiding intelligence.

40, 26–7: *cup wreathed with ivy*. The cup of Bacchus, as in Matthew Arnold's 'Strayed Reveller', ll. 84–5. Keats (ll. 31–5 below) also mentions Dionysus' ivy.

40, 31–5: *"The Kings . . . turning pale"*. Keats's *Endymion*, IV, 263–7.

41, 25–8: *"He who bends . . . in eternity's sunrise"*. See either Blake's 'Eternity', ll. 1–4, or his 'Several Questions Answered', ll. 11–14 (Keynes, 179, 184).

42, 5: *Landor*. 'The Hamadryad' (or tree-nymph) is one of the best-known poems from Landor's *Hellenics* (1847). Yeats was fond of Landor, especially of his *Imaginary Conversations* (1824–9). His name appears frequently in the AS.

42, 6: *Morris*. Yeats knew Morris personally and liked much of his work, especially such medieval romances as *The Well at the World's End* (1896), *The Water of the Wondrous Isles* (1897), and *The Sundering Flood* (1898). See 'The Happiest of the Poets', *EI* 53–64.

42, 7: *Shelley*. Yeats is perhaps thinking of several characters in Shelley's poems, particularly the poet (in *Alastor*) and Ahasuerus the Wandering Jew (in *Hellas*). In a rejected version of the Dedication Yeats quoted two lines (155–6) from *Hellas* about Ahasuerus. One of the Controls in the Sleeps of 1920 is called Alastor.

42, 8; *Theocritus*. His Idylls about the rustic life of his native Sicily are the first examples of pastoral poetry in Greek and have been widely imitated since.

42, 9–11: *did Bembo think . . . "down upon Urbino"*. Bembo and Urbino were symbolic images to Yeats, whose knowledge of both was indebted to L. E. Opdycke's translation of Castiglione's *The Book of the Courtier* (1902), which contains extensive notes. For Bembo, who revised *The Courtier* before publication, see especially Opdycke's Note 42, page 12; secs. 51–72 contain his famous discourse on love. For a description of Urbino, see sec. 2. Yeats repeated Bembo's cry in 'The Bounty of Sweden' (1925; see *A* 545).

43, 4–5: *He is full of . . . saws and proverbs.* Cf. *As You Like It*, II. vii. 156: 'Full of wise saws and modern instances' (*RS* 382).

43, 18: *Two passages of Browning.* The first passage (also quoted in *EI* 409 and *E* 19) is slightly misquoted from Browning's 'Pauline', ll. 323–5. The second is a song from *Pippa Passes*, Part III, ll. 164–77. On 22 Aug 1923 Yeats wrote that George had been guided by a spirit voice to get Browning from the shelf and turn to a particular line in Vol. I, p. 45 (in *The Poetical Works of Robert Browning*, 2 vols. [London: John Murray, 1919]).

44, 8–16: *Birdalone . . . a child of "Weird".* Birdalone falls in love with Sir Arthur (the Black Squire), the lover of her friend Atra. Deciding it best that she depart, Birdalone remarks: 'Now hast thou forgiven me that Weird dragged me in betwixt thy [Atra's] love and thy goodhap; and I have forgiven thee that I am led away by Weird into the waste and the wilderness of love. Farewell.' See *The Collected Works of William Morris*, XX, 256; for other references to Weird (or fate, more usually spelled Wyrd), see pp. 203, 211, 313, 314.

44, 32: *"Thy Will is our freedom".* This line is a variant of Dante's 'In la sua volontade è nostra pace' (*Paradiso*, iii, 85), which Yeats quotes in *EI* 369 and 422. The variant of *freedom* for *peace* is significant.

45, 17: *angry or smiling Punch.* A reference to the Punch-and-Judy show.

46, 14–15: *Don Juan or the Giaour.* In *VB* 113 Yeats inserted 'Byron's' before the titles of the two poems.

46, 26: *"thirty years old and in perfect health".* Slightly misquoted from Whitman's 'Song of Myself' (l. 8).

47, 1–4: *Thoreau . . . perfect health.* See paragraph 11 of 'Higher Laws' in *Walden*, which influenced 'The Lake Isle of Innisfree' (*A* 71–2).

49, 15–19: *George Borrow . . . of many tongues.* Borrow had rather frequent attacks of the horrors: a typescript version of this passage refers to his 'insistence in Lavengro upon his recurring attack of the horrors . . .'. The reference is to Ch. lxxxiv. The protagonist's name suggests 'word-master' because of his linguistic talents. Possibly Yeats was reading or rereading *Lavengro* about this time; in a letter to Olivia Shakespear (dated 28 June 1923) he suggested that incidents in *Lavengro* are 'a little heightened' (*L* 699).

49, 28–9: *Sexual impotence had . . . weakened.* For authority, Yeats might have had in mind either J. A. Froude's posthumous *My Relations with Carlyle* (1903) or Frank Harris's 'Talks with Carlyle' (*English Review*, 1911; repr. in *Contemporary Portraits*, 1915): see G. B. Tennyson, 'The Carlyles', in

DeLaura, *Victorian Prose: A Guide to Research*, 52–3. Yeats's view of Carlyle's work as empty Victorian rhetoric and abstraction is summed up in a letter of 14 Mar 1916, which includes a comparison of Carlyle and Macpherson (*L* 608).

50, 7: *Example*. Yeats had evidently read *The Idiot* by 1922 (*TV* 125); however, as Dume points out (p. 348), Sean O'Casey says that Lady Gregory was shocked in 1924 that Yeats had read nothing by Dostoyevsky, and she supplied him with *The Idiot* and *The Brothers Karamazov* (*Innishfallen, Fare Thee Well*, 255).

50, 25: *vegetative and sensitive faculties*. According to Renaissance and earlier views, man was a microcosm of the world and possessed three souls; he shared the vegetative and sensitive souls with plants and animals but was distinguished from lower orders of creation in the Great Chain of Being by possession of a rational soul, which made him godlike.

52, 26–7: *"Eloi, Eloi, why hast thou forsaken me?"* Except the address to God in Aramaic, these are the translated final words of the crucified Christ. See Matthew 27:46 and Mark 15:34 (also Psalms 22:1). In *VB*, the passage is verbatim on p. 119 but varies in language on p. 239.

52, 29: *Victim and Sage*. Yeats devoted considerable time in the AS to distinguishing between the viewpoint of the Victim, who is antithetical, and the Sage (originally Teacher), who is primary.

53, 10. *Example*. An early draft had no example. See n. to p. 54, ll. 31–2.

54, 2: *"false, fleeting, perjured Clarence"*. From Shakespeare's *Richard III*, I.iv.55 (*RS* 722).

54, 31–2: *a certain artist . . . a notable man*. Wyndham Lewis and Augustus John. (See *Mem* 214–15 and *L* 492–3, 496). In the R-A TS Robartes said: 'I wonder too if I should not place at ten or eleven the genius of Augustus John the images of whose art unlike those of Rembrandt or Valasquez, men of late phases whose intellectual egos have separated themselves from the images of their art, seem accidental and instinctive as though their creator saw from within the race, his soul unfixed and floating.' In a manuscript draft of P 9 Yeats said: 'Last night after I wrote these words I was sitting in the Cafe Royal when I got into conversation with a bullet headed young man who had that short neck which I associate with passion.' He spoke to Yeats, not to 'a student of these symbols', about 'a certain notable man' and his mistress. Yeats observed that the young man was 'a cubist artist of powerful imagination', then added: 'There I thought is my example' – for P 9, that is. According to Robartes, 'in Gyraldus' allegorical woodcut that phase is symbolised by an eagle tearing out a man's eyes' (R-A TS).

56, 2: *woman's tragic love*. Yeats is thinking of Parnell's mistress, Mrs Katharine O'Shea, whose divorce trial led to his downfall. See her account in *Charles Stewart Parnell: His Love Story and Political Life*.

56, 28–31: *One remembers Faust . . . with all his being.* Yeats refers to Goethe's *Faust* rather than Marlowe's, in which Gretchen does not appear. He has in mind especially lines 2603–4, in which Mephistopheles says that, after a diabolic drink, Faust will soon see Helen in any woman.

56, 31–4: *Perhaps one thinks . . . upon the snow.* In Victor Hugo's *The Toilers of the Sea*, Book I, Ch. 1, Déruchette writes the name of Gilliatt in the snow, but with her finger rather than a parasol; perhaps Yeats recalled the incident partly because Walter Pater used it as an illustration in his essay 'Romanticism' (in *Appreciations*). Yeats 'read all Victor Hugo's romances' in his youth (*A* 87).

57, 13: *that god of Norse mythology.* Odin, from the *Hamaval* in the *Elder Edda*. For the same incident, see also *Mem* 146, *VPl* 569, *EI* 321 ('the sacrifice of a man to himself'). Yeats might have known the passage in various contexts; Mrs Yeats read the *Eddas* in 1917 (*L* 635), and Mathers referred to the passage in the GD Flying Roll No. X (cited in King, *Astral Projection*, 121): 'Recall to your mind that passage in one of the Eddas "I hung on the Tree three days and three nights, wounded with a spear, myself a sacrifice offered to my (highest) Self,—Odin unto Odin".' The passage is also cited in Frazer, *The Golden Bough*, V, 290. The GD source recommends itself because it reduces the original nine to three days, but Yeats cites *The Golden Bough* at least twice in the AS.

57, 15–17: *Perhaps Moses . . . Mask and table.* Yeats refers to the descent of Moses from Mount Sinai with the Ten Commandments; see Exodus 34:39.

57, 18: *John Morley says of Parnell.* See Morley's *Recollections*, I, 238: 'In ordinary conversation he was pleasant, without much play of mind; temperament made him the least discursive of the human race'.

57, 25–7: *a follower has . . . with his nails.* See Mrs O'Shea, I, 176–7 and *VP* 835.

57, 32–6: *Mrs Parnell tells . . . himself and her.* Yeats follows Mrs O'Shea's account (II, 153).

58, 7: *Examples.* By 1918 Yeats had classified Spinoza as a mystic but disliked his rationalism (*L* 650). An early manuscript, referring apparently to Spinoza, speaks of those who embrace 'some abstract system of belief, some bundle of almost mathematical principles & convictions'. In the R-A TS, Robartes is more specific: 'at eleven one discovers now a Pantheistic image of man little more precise than my own legs when I study them through the water where I am bathing and now the reason[ed] conviction of Spinoza'. For Yeats's attitude towards Savonarola, see p. 154. and *EI* 227. In a long and rather disorganized AS on 3 Jan 1918, Savonarola appears to be placed in P 20. In the AS for 2 June 1918, Schopenhauer was placed in P 11.

59: *THE OPENING OF THE TINCTURE.* In an early manuscript Yeats first entitled this section 'The Meaning of the word "heart" on the diagram', then 'The Splitting of Antithetical & Primary'.

61, 11–13: *"My fire"* . . . *seem bright*. See n. to p. 16, 2–6.

61: *PHASE TWELVE*. 'Because the hero's crescent is the twelfth' (see p. 5, 1.3), Yeats was preoccupied with this Phase, revising early explanations considerably and shifting several names out of it before he finally settled on Nietzsche alone. In the long list of the AS on 3 Jan 1918 Yeats left P 12 blank. In the AS for 2 June 1918, he listed Nietzsche, Pound, Virgil, Keats, and Tennyson, but crossed out the last two. Still later Robespierre was included. The R-A TS contains a significant passage about Pound which Yeats omitted though he retained Pound's name through an almost finished typescript. Robartes observed: 'I feel more sympathy with twelve where Nietzsche emerges and all men may discover their superman, though the more violent types of the phase among whom I would be sorry to discover your enemy Mr. Pound, not transfigured but transfixed, contemplate the race in some form of his collective opinion till hatred turns the flesh to wood and the nerves to wire.' On 23 May 1918, Yeats asked rhetorically, 'Ezra violence, Nietzsche violence?' but the Control failed to respond. In a fairly late manuscript version Yeats explained that although he had chosen Nietzsche for his 'chief example' he 'would rather have chosen one or two friends of my own whose lives are very open to me'. Pound may have been the only friend Yeats had in mind. A letter to Ethel Mannin explains in part the intellectual hatred Yeats found fascinating in Pound: 'I am a forerunner of that horde that will some day come down the mountains' (L 873). Thatcher observes that Yeats is here echoing Aphorism 900 of Nietzsche's *The Will to Power* (*Nietzsche in England*, 157).

64, 7: *Examples*. In the AS of 2 June 1918 and in the R-A TS, Verlaine and Baudelaire were the two examples for P 13, while Beardsley accompanied Blake 'and perhaps Boehme' at P 16. Dowson was added in a late typescript.

66, 8: *Examples*. The general treatment of Keats had solidified in Yeats's mind well before the assistance of the Instructors: see 'Ego Dominus Tuus' (1915) and M 329. Writing to his father in 1918, Yeats remarked, 'If you accept metempsychosis, Keats was moving to greater subjectivity of being, and to unity of that being, and Shelley to greater objectivity and to consequent break-up of unity of being' (L 653); the placement of Keats on one side of P 15 and of Shelley on the other (p. 75) bears out the tenor of the letter. Keats appears many times in the AS. On 6 and 21 Dec 1917 he was placed in P 12; on 2 June 1918 he was first in P 12, then P 14 with Wordsworth, Iseult Gonne, and Tennyson because all loved the world—i.e., nature. The 'Ode to a Nightingale' is cited several times as an illustration of the daimonic influence on a work of art which already existed in the Anima Mundi. Because thought and images were received by Keats, they 'still remain & can be transmitted to us' even though *'no Keats read by any one during his life time'* (as Yeats summarized the idea in the CF). In the AS on 2 June 1918 Rossetti was first placed in P 14, then moved to P 17. Besides Iseult, Yeats had Helen in mind for P 14. In the R-A TS, Robartes observed 'that Helen would never have set Troy afire if she were not of this phase'.

68, 26: *Sleep of Arthur . . . Golden Stair.* Both are paintings by Sir Edward Burne-Jones: *The Golden Stair* (now in the Tate Gallery) is one of his most famous works; the *Sleep of Arthur* (now in Puerto Rico) is less well known.

68, 32–4: *Wordsworth . . . common sentiment.* The description of his 'soul's deepening solitude' is repeated almost verbatim from the R-A TS, where he was still in P 14. In Jan 1915 Yeats, with Pound as companion, proposed 'to read through the whole seven vols of Wordsworth in Dowden's edition' (*L* 590). Two years later (Feb 1917), in 'Anima Hominis', Yeats described 'Wordsworth withering into eighty years, honoured and empty-witted . . .' (*M* 342).

69, 14–17: *The corresponding genius . . . the preceding phase.* Adolphe Thomas Monticelli was a French painter of the Barbizon group; Charles Conder was a personal acquaintance of Yeats and part of the Decadent movement (see *L* 508–9 and *A* 325, 349). The last paragraph under P 14 was added to a late typescript.

69: *PHASE FIFTEEN.* Because 15 is the Phase of complete beauty, no human life is possible in it. Yeats was, in effect, emphasizing the relationship of physical to spiritual beauty. In the R-A TS Robartes insists that 'all beauty has been, would be or will be physical and that is why those creatures at the Fifteenth phase—though invisible to our eyes—are ponderable and plant their feet upon this earth and why, no longer limited by thought, their eyes have such an eagle gaze'. At this point Yeats made a note (signed John Aherne) which reflects many experiments of the SPR with psychic phenomena: 'It is one of the doctrines of Kusta ben Luka that the retina has an incalculable range and that it is limited by our expectations alone. He explained many miraculous phenomena in this way.' Hearing and touch have 'a like range'.

71, 16–21: *In this passage Christ . . . be understood.* As primary man and Teacher, Christ desired the other world; as antithetical man and Victim, his 'forerunner' (Buddha, in a late typescript) related the physical beauty of this world to the spiritual. 'This cannot yet be understood' until the 'successor' or 'New Messiah' (usually called 'Avatar' in the AS) appears at the end of the present cycle of some 2000 years (see n. to p. 244, 12–15).

71, 28: *Examples.* The AS on 2 June 1918 lists 'Blake, Beardsley, Stephens, Madame Gonne, Cervantes'; the R-A TS names 'Blake and Beardsley and perhaps Boehme'; a later manuscript lists only Blake and Rabelais. What the people Yeats finally chose as examples have in common is somewhat puzzling but may be explained by his thought that the list should include: (1) satirists who hate the ugly and pity the beautiful (like Blake and Rabelais),

(2) 'certain rare sages' (like Paracelsus or the finally rejected Boehme and Cervantes), (3) beautiful women (like Maud Gonne). 'If a man has not loved a woman of the fourteenth or the sixteenth phase', Robartes said, 'he has not known the greatest earthly beauty' (R-A TS).

73, 7–8: *Blake writes of . . . "Venetian demons"*. See Blake's *Descriptive Catalogue*, Number IX: 'These Pictures . . . were the result of temptations and perturbations, labouring to destroy Imaginative power, by means of that infernal machine called Chiaro Oscuro, in the hands of Venetian and Flemish Demons . . .' (Keynes, 582). Blake is, of course, speaking of schools of art.

73, 9–10: *picture of his own . . . "spell of Stoddart's"*. The incident is related in Gilchrist, *Life of William Blake*, 241, and Bentley, *Blake Records*, 180–1.

74, 8: *"The Burning Babe"*. A poem by the Elizabethan Jesuit martyr Robert Southwell.

74, 9–12: *walk like queens . . . at their heels*. The R-A TS reads: 'One marble shape rises before me, a French Diana of the 16th Century; her exquisite head alert she lies half sitting amid the wild deer that in a moment she will destroy, dogs and deer alike gathered about her in fascinated affection: A king's mistress, a quiver of arrows to symbolize that bitter wit that kept ministers in dread, whom the artist solitary it may be as herself saw transfigured as the goddess lingering amid her woodland court after all Olympus elfs had vanished. Was she in truth Diana of Poitiers, was a King of France great enough to love such a beauty and did he turn away at last from that never empty quiver?' In this passage Yeats was thinking of a sculpture of the goddess Diana in the Louvre, formerly attributed to Jean Granjou and frequently seen as a compliment to Diane de Poitiers, mistress of Henry II of France. Among his own books, Yeats could have seen it reproduced in Plate II between pp. 496–7 of vol. 24 of the *EB*. Since Maud Gonne was the most beautiful of all and the only woman named for P 16 in the AS and various early versions of *VA*, Yeats almost certainly intended her as the archetypal queen (Cathleen ni Houlihan?) who bore the quiver of arrows on her back and whose 'virginity renews itself like the moon' (an unidentified quotation which appears twice in *VB*—at pp. 24 and 140).

75, 10: *Examples*. The earliest list includes the following: 'WBY, Shelley, Landor, Dante, Homer, Botticelli, Burne-Jones, Rossetti' (AS, 2 June 1918). Several other times in the AS, the CF, and the Sleeps Yeats placed himself at P 17. For example, in the record of a Sleep dated 6 Jy 1920, he wrote: 'MG [Maud Gonne] 16, myself 17'. An elaborate diagram in the CF has this note: 'individual horoscope WBY may [be] placed to show ascendant at 17'. Although he apparently intended to include himself in *VA*, he does not use his own name in the discussions of P 17 in the R-A TS or other early versions, though he seems to be thinking of himself in numerous passages. The omission of Landor was surely inadvertent (see pp. 78–9), and his name appears under P 17 in *VB* 141.

76, 7: *Ahasuerus*. In Shelley's *Hellas* and *Queen Mab*.

76, 8: *Athanase*. In Shelley's 'Prince Athanase: A Fragment'.

76, 9: *Shelley's Venus Urania*. As Mrs Shelley's note to 'Prince Athanase' asserts, the poem was to have been based on a progression from material to transcendent love; the basic distinction between earthly and heavenly love (Aphrodite Pandemos and Aphrodite Urania) is from Plato's *Symposium* (see *EI* 88–9 and Bornstein, *Yeats and Shelley*, 72–3).

76, 10–11: *Great Yellow Rose of the Paradiso*. See Canto XXX, l. 113. This symbol was standard Rosicrucian background in such works as A. E. Waite's *The Brotherhood of the Rosy Cross*, p. 94.

77, 21: *"The groves pale passion loves"*. Yeats liked the phrase 'pale passion loves' (see *EI* 233 and 376). He may have found 'pale passion' in the 1793 version of Wordsworth's 'Descriptive Sketches', l. 118 (see n. to p. 68, 32–4).

77, 22–3: *Shelley out of phase writes pamphlets*. Including his *Address to the Irish People* (1812), *Declaration of Rights* (1812), *Letter to Lord Ellenborough* (1812), and *Vindication of Natural Diet* (1813).

77, 26–7: *a young man . . . of his thoughts*. See *Alastor*, ll. 248–50, 413, 471, 534–5.

77, 27–9: *an old man . . . "God or thou"*. *Hellas*, ll. 164–5: 'less accessible/Than thou or God!' This section of *Hellas* is quoted at length in *A* 172–3.

77, 30–1: *sees the devil . . . by imaginary assassins*. Yeats is no doubt depending upon Dowden's *Shelley*; see *A* 87. In 1813, Shelley claimed to have been attacked while alone; some have not believed him. In a letter to Hookham, he used the word *assassination* (Dowden, p. 184). According to the wife of one witness, Shelley, who thought he had been fired at through a window, 'bounced out on the grass, and there he saw leaning against a tree the ghost, or, as he said, the devil . . .' (Dowden, p. 188).

77, 33: *"The Cenci"*. Shelley's verse drama about incest and revenge.

78, 1–6: *Dante, who laments . . . woman with stones*. Boccaccio is the contemporary; see *The Earliest Lives of Dante*, 59.

78, 15–17: *there were but . . . monster of iniquity*. In a letter of 6 Apr 1819, Shelley remarked to Thomas Love Peacock: 'I am regarded by all who know or hear of me, except, I think, on the whole five individuals as a rare prodigy of crime & pollution whose look even might infect' (*Letters of Percy Bysshe Shelley*, II, 94).

78, 18: *He lacked the Vision of Evil*. Yeats made the same charge against Emerson and Whitman (*A* 246). According to his Cabalistic learning, Yeats conceived of Evil as an imbalance between opposing forces (see pp. 149 and 176, *M* 357). He wrote at length in the AS (10 June 1918) about the necessity of contraries and the nature of evil: 'In so far as knowledge of evil is attained', the Control said, 'one becomes good but in as far as one is good the visible world becomes evil because it is no virtue to be good knowing no evil—it is no sin to be evil knowing no good.' See n. to p. 229, 24–5.

79, 14: *Examples*. Yeats had a much longer list in the AS of 2 June 1918: Zarathustra, GY [George Yeats], Goethe, Dulac, [George Frederic] Watts, Villon, Plutarch, Montesquieu, Dürer.

79, 20–1: *"A Lover's Nocturne" or "An Ode to the West Wind"*. Yeats must have been quoting from memory the titles of Rossetti's 'Love's Nocturn' (see *EI* 293 and *A* 302) and Shelley's 'Ode to the West Wind'.

80, 5–6: *"Man knows . . . by thought never"*. From Goethe's *Wilhelm Meisters Wanderjahre*: 'Wie kann man sich selbst kennen lernen? Durch Betrachten niemals, wohl aber durch Handeln' (Goethe's *Werke*, VIII, 283).

80, 35: *Goethe did not . . . marry his cook*. According to Beddoes, 'Goethe married his maid servant & drinks brandy' (*Works*, 626). Where Yeats found the passage before 1925 is not known, since the corresponding letter in Gosse's edition of *The Letters . . .* (1894), pp. 119–25, does not contain this passage.

80, 35–6: *he certainly did marry . . . desired*. Charlotte von Stein, whom Goethe loved but who married the Duke of Saxe-Weimar's Master of the Horse.

81, 7–8: *"I was never . . . serpent-charmer before"*. The speaker was Arthur Symons (see *L* 298, *A* 335, *Mem* 97). In a manuscript draft of P 18, Yeats wrote of 'the serpent charmers lover' as 'the one man of this phase I have known intimately'. He 'saw art, life, literature as technical problems, & his life had lacked all momentum but for his bodily lusts'. The manuscript draft of P 18 concludes with the observation that 'in Goethe as in Shelley the influence of Plato or of Christ prevents the phase of either finding perfect antithetical experience'. At the bottom of the page, in parentheses, Yeats added: 'note—Landor hated Plato'.

82, 8: *Examples*. The list in the AS of 2 June 1918 was different: 'Browning, Velasquez, Cromwell'. Yeats's knowledge of Byron was partly based on the Earl of Lovelace's *Astarte* (1905), which Yeats read in 1906 (*L* 468). He might have been aware of the second edition in 1921. In any case, Yeats was aware of Byron's sexual relationship with his half-sister, Augusta Leigh.

84, 11–15: *A certain actress . . . dominating and egotistical*. Yeats refers to Mrs Patrick Campbell. The Control describes her in the AS (21 Nov 1917) as one in whom the antithetical is 'losing' to the primary. Yeats then asked: 'Am I right in supposing that Mrs C's violent egotism is aroused by the interests of her consciousness of Maeterlinck emotion?' The Control answered: 'The egotism in its endeavour to annihilate the Maeterlinck emotion becomes more violent until It has achieved its purpose when it becomes more normal'. Yeats transferred this information to the CF under 'Tinctures'. A rejected section of the manuscript draft refers to Shaw and apparently to Mrs Campbell. Yeats saw her in Maeterlinck's *Bluebird* (*L* 544), and she played Mélisande in *Pelléas and Mélisande* (in 1898 and again in Jy 1904). In *PASL*, Yeats insisted on the distinction between the actress' selfless presence as a Maeterlinck queen and her personal egotism (see *M* 326–7). Yeats referred to her frequently in *L* and probably wrote *The Player Queen* for her. Quiet on stage but boisterous off, she collected Burne-Jones engravings. See *EI* vii (quoting from 'Yeux Glauques' in Ezra Pound's 'Hugh Selwyn Mauberley') and Fitzgerald, *Edward Burne-Jones*, 244.

84, 21–4: *I find in Wilde, too . . . desire to escape*. For Yeats's estimate of Wilde, see *A* 130–9.

85, 14: *Examples*. In the AS of 2 June 1918 Yeats had a different list: Dickens, Shakespeare, Chaucer, Plato, Fielding, Meredith, Anatole France. In the manuscript draft he crossed out Fielding and added 'Balzac, perhaps Ben Jonson'.

86, 12–13: *"I have made . . . to the view"*. Shakespeare, Sonnet 110 (*RS* 1769).

86, 26–7: *a Napoleon may . . . the existence of God*. The incident, which Yeats might have found in the sixth lecture of Carlyle's *On Heroes, Hero-Worship, and the Heroic in History*, has its origin in the *Mémoires* of Napoleon's secretary Bourrienne; see Emil Ludwig, *Napoleon*, p. 120. In the R-A TS, speaking of the fluctuating unity of P 19, Robartes comments that 'Balzac said of Napoleon that he was always the second lieutenant meaning that he was coarse and crude and yet admired him extravagantly as though he recognised a Shakespeare or perhaps a Balzac who had maimed himself'.

87, 8–12: *Napoleon sees himself . . . a Roman Emperor*. In 'Four Years' (1921) Yeats wrote: 'Napoleon was never of his own time, as the naturalistic writers and painters bid all men be, but had some Roman Emperor's image in his head and some condottiere's blood in his heart; and when he crowned that head at Rome with his own hands, he had covered, as may be seen from David's painting, his hesitation with that Emperor's old suit' (see pp. 43–4; 'at Rome' was correctly omitted in *A* 152). Napoleon himself often made the comparision with Alexander.

87, 14–15: *such adjectives as "sweet" and "gentle"*. Both are used by Ben Jonson in his eulogy prefixed to the First Folio of Shakespeare's works.

87, 17: *Unlike Ben Jonson he fought no duels*. Early in his career, Jonson killed one of Henslowe's men in a duel and was briefly imprisoned for his action.

87, 19: *somebody pirated his sonnets*. The standard text of Shakespeare's sonnets, that of the 1609 quarto, is generally presumed to have been pirated.

87, 20: *Mermaid Tavern*. Where Jonson, Shakespeare, and others often gathered.

87–8, 32f: *Lake Harris . . . "of the tomb"*. Slightly misquoted from Thomas Lake Harris's *The Wisdom of the Adepts*, 442. The quotation is echoed in *A* 273. See also *A* 236, *E* 66, and *EI* 410. Yeats became acquainted with Harris's religious writing, much of which (including epic poems) was automatic, through W. T. Horton. After a brief stay in the GD, he had joined The Brotherhood of the New Life, an occult religious order founded by Harris. Horton tried to persuade Yeats to join The Brotherhood in 1896 and loaned him several of Harris's books (only two of the titles can be identified from the correspondence: *God's Breath in Man and in Humane Society* and *The Arcana of Christianity*.

88, 23: *Examples.* The AS of 2 June 1918 had a different list: Milton, Horace, Dr Johnson, Flaubert, Napoleon, Richelieu. In 1934 Yeats called Shaw, Wilde, and Moore 'the most complete individualists in the history of literature, abstract, isolated minds, without a memory or a landscape' (*VP* 834).

90, 15: *Like somebody in Dostoieffsky's "Idiot".* The character is Ferdyshtchenko, and the incident occurs in Chs. 13 and 14, Part I, of *The Idiot*. Yeats refers to the same passage in *A* 433, and there is a curiously similar but entirely personal passage in *Mem* 227. Yeats may not have read the novel by the date of the last-mentioned passage (see n. to p. 50, 7).

91, 20: *Examples.* Besides Swedenborg and Dostoyevsky, the list in the AS of 2 June 1918 included F. W. H. Myers, who is several times mentioned in the Script and elsewhere during the years of Yeats's most extensive spiritualistic experiments. A founder of the SPR and one of its first presidents (in 1900), he was the author of the monumental *Human Personality and Its Survival of Bodily Death* (1903), which Yeats knew well. In the R-A TS Robartes spoke of Flaubert belonging 'to the terrible Twenty-second phase'.

93, note: *These terms will be explained later.* See pp. 169–70.

94, 6–7: *all must be impersonal.* One section of Moore's *Art and Life* (pp. 79–130 and 299–301) deals with Flaubert and 'Impersonal Art'. Moore begins his essay with a quotation from Flaubert's correspondence: 'I believe that great art is scientific and impersonal' (p. 79).

94, 8: *"the mirror dawdling down a road".* The quotation is the epigraph to Ch. xiii, Part I, of Stendhal's *Le Rouge et le noir* (see also II, xiv). Brought to Yeats's attention by his father (see *Passages from the Letters of John Butler Yeats*, 46), it became a favourite literary image which Yeats repeated several times (*A* 358, *OBMV* xxvii, *E* 333 and 373). A late manuscript draft read 'sauntering' rather than 'dawdling'.

94, 30–3: *at Udan Adan . . . "voices almost inarticulate".* The first part of this inexact quotation comes from Blake's *Visions of the Daughters of Albion* (Keynes, 194).

94, 33–4: *Swedenborg passed through.* Cf. *E* 32–3.

96, 4–7: *Someone has said . . . in the world.* Balzac frequently slept during the day and did his work at night while using specially prepared coffee. He discussed his habit in 'Treatise on Modern Stimulants' (see also *E* 271).

96, 11–13: *to Goncourt, Flaubert . . . of unconsidered thought.* Almost certainly Yeats is dependent on Moore's *Art and Life;* if Yeats was thinking of the Goncourt brothers (Edmond and Jules), he might have been recalling remarks by them quoted on p. 133 or 280 (see n. to p. 94, 6–7). However, he might also have been confusing the brothers with Rémy de Gourmont, whose *Problem of Style* Moore quotes on p. 301: 'Far from its being his [Flaubert's] work which is impersonal, the roles are here reversed: it is the man who is vague and a tissue of incoherences; it is the work which lives, breathes, suffers, and smiles nobly . . .'.

96, 13–14: *Flaubert . . . was not intelligent.* Probably Yeats is still dependent on Moore's *Art and Life:* 'Artists cannot be rigidly intellectual, since logic to become practical must yield something to the sensuous illusion in which life is immersed. Anatole France was perhaps feeling after this fact when he made the clumsy assertion that Flaubert was unintelligent' (pp. 134–5).

96, 16: *One remembers Herbert Spencer.* This anecdote was not in the manuscript draft.

97, 15: *Examples.* See Yeats's remarks in 'The Bounty of Sweden': '. . . Synge has described, through an exaggerated symbolism, a reality which he loved precisely because he loved all reality' (*A* 570). The AS of 2 June 1918 also lists Michelangelo, Balzac, and O'Connell as examples.

98, 29: *"minute particulars" of life.* Yeats remembered a favorite line from Blake's *Jerusalem*: 'You shall want all the Minute Particulars of Life' (Keynes, 734). He quoted the last five words in a manuscript draft and rephrased the image in l. 42 ('the minute particulars of mankind') of 'The Double Vision of Michael Robartes', a poem which originated in the AS of 7 Jan 1919. Yeats believed with Blake that 'To Particularize is the Alone Distinction of Merit' (Keynes, 451).

99, 8–9: *Rembrandt . . . anatomical curiosity.* If Yeats was thinking of a literal Christ anatomically imagined, he might have had in mind Rembrandt's *Descent from the Cross* (either the one in Munich or the one in Leningrad); on the other hand, if he intended a view of the world as incarnation, he might have referred to *The Anatomy Lesson of Dr. Nicholas Tulp*. Rembrandt's use of chiaroscuro (as in *The Night Watch*) is justly famous.

99, 10–13: *Synge . . . in men's minds.* Yeats is surely thinking of the contrast between Synge's Christy Mahon in *The Playboy of the Western World* and the traditional hero.

100, 1–2: *Synge . . . hole in the ceiling.* Yeats refers to a statement in Synge's 'Preface' to *The Playboy*: 'I got more aid than any learning could have given me, from a chink in the floor of the old Wicklow house where I was staying, that let me hear what was being said by the servant girls in the kitchen' (*Collected Works*, IV, 53).

100, 3–4: *Rembrandt . . . lace collar.* One of Rembrandt's many talents was his ability to portray minute details of bourgeois clothing.

100, 20–1: *once an actress . . . into a gesture*. Possibly Maire O'Neill, whose 'sincere and restrained' acting in the role of Deirdre was a 'distinct success' to Dublin audiences, through not completely so to Yeats (see *A* 524–5).

100, 24–5: *"Move a little. . . babbling of fools"*. Slightly misquoted from *Deirdre of the Sorrows*: 'Draw a little back with the squabbling of fools when I am broken up with misery' (*Collected Works*, IV, 267).

100, 28–33: *In Synge's early unpublished work . . . man we know*. This observation was longer and more personal in Yeats's manuscript draft of P 23: 'When I went through Synge's work I marked many dialogues & paragraphs & one whole play as not to be published, or used except by the critic or historian. They were Synge before he found his genius, through Aran & dialect.' Yeats took great pride in having urged Synge, in late 1896, to 'Go to the Aran Islands. Live there as if you were one of the people themselves; express a life that has never found expression' (see *Collected Works*, III, 63).

102, 13–14: *"The gay fishes . . . up the dew"*. Not included in the manuscript draft, this is a slightly misquoted line from Blake's *Europe* (Keynes, 243); also quoted in *M* 282.

102, 21: *Examples*. 'A certain friend' was Lady Gregory. In the AS (2 June 1918) Yeats listed Mazarin and Lady Gregory, 'Placens Uxor' (i.e., 'pleasing wife'). In the AS of 2 Jan 1918 Yeats asked, without naming Lady Gregory, 'Where does Placens Uxor come', and was informed, '24'. The Latin phrase comes from one of Horace's Odes (Book II, no. 14, ll. 20–1) concerned with the inevitability of death. In the manuscript draft Yeats listed Queen Victoria and 'a certain personal friend', then crossed out 'personal'. One of the most extensively revised Phases, its original opening may have been an indirect tribute to Lady Gregory: 'The most obviously impressive of all the phases when true to phase.' Lady Gregory is named in *VB* 169.

103, 19: *"she died every day she lived"*. This line from *Macbeth* (IV, iii, 111; *RS* 1333) was used explicitly of Lady Gregory in *Mem* 162 and *A* 457 (see also *M* 116). The manuscript draft reads: 'There is great pride, but an impersonal pride, that of the code itself, & as great humility, a perpetual murmur "the servant of servants". Of such Shakespeare wrote she died every day she lived.'

104, 8–9: *what Raftery called the Book of the People*. Anthony Raftery was a blind Gaelic poet; see Yeats's sketch in *M* 22–30. Yeats found the phrase (also used in l. 44 of 'Coole Park and Ballylee, 1931' and in *E* 215) in Lady Gregory's essay on 'Raftery', in which she speaks of 'The truths of God that he strove in his last years . . . "to have written in the book of the people" ' (*Poets and Dreamers*, 21–2).

104, 13: *Blue Book*. A Blue Book is an official report of Parliament or the Privy Council, so called because of the colour of the covers.

104, 20–1: *"Have I done . . . so-and-so?"* For similar phrasing, see *A* 247 and the characterization of Mary Bell in *VB* 46.

105, 9: *the personal autocracy of Parnell.* According to Mrs O'Shea, Parnell's 'will was autocratic, and once he had made up his mind to any course he would brook no interference, nor suffer anything to stand in his way' (*Charles Stewart Parnell*, II, 243).

106, 7: *Examples.* The AS (2 June 1918) lists 'Luther, Calvin, Ignatius Loyola, George Herbert, G Russell'. The manuscript draft lists only Newman and Luther. It is clear that Yeats looked upon Herbert and AE as well as others named or considered for this Phase as religious reformers. All of them were Teachers and Sages rather than Victims, primary rather than antithetical men. AE is frequently mentioned in the AS. On 20 Jy 1918 the Control observed that 'Russell acts through primary', and Yeats asked if his poetry and Herbert's poetry are 'from Mask'. On 24 Sept 1918, having come to Dublin that day from Ballylee, the Yeatses devoted an entire session to a consideration of the 'reality' of 'Russells story of Irish Avatar'. Yeats asked, 'Where did so many different people get the idea that the child had actually been born?' The Control replied: 'Because the avatar is the fifth generation.' After a long exchange about the child's ancestry, the Control disclosed that 'the avatar is or will be the fifth generation from the mountain (identified by Yeats as Abiegnos, the holy Rosicrucian mountain), and that the fifth generation began after 1895. On 6 Feb 1896 AE had written to Yeats that 'the gods have returned to Erin and have centred themselves in the sacred mountains. . . . I believe profoundly that a new Avatar is about to appear . . .' (*Letters from AE*, 17).

108, 4–5: *what old friend did Cardinal Newman cut.* Yeats may have had any of several people in mind. Possibly he refers to Newman's *A Letter Addressed to the Rev. E. B. Pusey, D.D., on Occasion of His Eirenicon* (1866). Pusey had been one of Newman's fellows in the Oxford Movement before Newman's conversion; though Pusey was attempting to bring the two churches closer together, Newman resented Pusey's presentation of the Catholic doctrine of the Blessed Virgin. Lionel Johnson had supplied some of Yeats's knowledge of Newman; unfortunately, as Yeats discovered, Johnson had imagined some of the meetings which he related as fact (*A* 305–6).

108, 16–18: *Luther's apparent indifference . . . his incitements veered.* Because of repressive measures taken against them during the later fifteenth century, the lower classes in Germany revolted in the Peasants' War of 1524–6; Luther, viewed by many of his time as a revolutionary, opposed the peasants. In the manuscript draft Yeats wrote first, 'One thinks of Luthers rage', then 'One thinks of Luthers incitement of & later repression of the peasantry & of accusations that followed Newman all his life'.

109, 10–16: *Russell's visionary painting . . . Moreau, for instance.* The ideas (including comparison with Moreau), if not the wording, are closely paralleled in *A* 242–3. AE was an amateur painter of considerable talent. Most of his many paintings reflect his visionary apprehension of the unreality of the visible world.

110, 3–4: *"The Hunchback"*. In the AS of 3 Jan 1918 Yeats asked, 'Can there [be] no body of note at 26 & 28', and the Control replied 'yes'. In the manuscript draft for P 26 Yeats wrote: 'I must create from imagination, with some help from legend & from literature.' What literature he used is not clear. Melchiori *The Whole Mystery of Art*, 277–9) is convinced that Yeats's conception of the Hunchback was influenced by Byron's play *The Deformed Transformed*. Other contributing sources were Shakespeare's *Richard III*, Hugo's Quasimodo (see *A* 87), and even 'an old hunchback' painted by his father (*A* 81–2).

111, 8–10: *not because he wants . . . that he can*. Cf. *A* 122 on Florence Farr: 'I formed with her an enduring friendship that was an enduring exasperation—"Why do you play the part with a bent back and a squeak in the voice? How can you be a character actor, you who hate all our life, you who belong to a life that is a vision?" But argument was no use, and some Nurse in Euripides must be played with all an old woman's infirmities and not as I would have it, with all a Sibyl's majesty, because "it is no use doing what nobody wants", or because she would show that she "could do what the others did".'

111, 17: *become a Judas*. Judas is often discussed in the AS. On 26 Jan 1918, the Control observed that 'Judas is creative genius' and placed him in P 8. When Yeats asked how he was 'amalgamation or pity', the Control replied: 'Because he synthesises this pity into a single action—a choice.' That is, he forces Christ to act. Judas's role in *Calvary* (1920) almost certainly grew directly out of this Script, most of which is devoted to the relationship of Christ and Judas.

112, 7–9: *When Ezekiel lay . . . "of the infinite"*. Although the Biblical allusion is to Ezekiel 4: 4 and 13, Yeats refers to Blake's *The Marriage of Heaven and Hell* (Keynes, 154); see *LNI* 205.

112, 18–21: *we shall discover . . . hypnogogic vision*. See p. 243.

112, 25–6: *"Am I as good as So-and-So"*. See p. 104.

112, 32–3: *worm or mole*. In *VB* 179, a paragraph is added here, and the footnote is omitted.

113, 8: *Examples*. In *PP* Yeats crossed out the name of Tagore as third example; in his Introduction (1912) to Tagore's *Gitanjali* (*EI* 387–95), Yeats found several occasions to use the word *saint*. He may have considered it bad taste to canonize the living. In the AS of 3 Jan 1918 both Socrates and Pascal were placed in P 27.

114, 9–26: *Before the self passes . . . through belief*. In the manuscript draft this long passage with some changes was originally placed at the end of the explication of P 25. Yeats explained that the soul 'cannot pass 25, it must reincarnate at 25 till it has turned this emotion—which is a subconscious thought—into "sanctity" itself. That is to say it must give up the endeavour to reach that superessential environment for itself.' Yeats concluded this enigmatic discussion with a poetic passage which he revised and used at the end of the Dedication (see n. to p. xiii, 16–19).

114, 29–30: *"Man does not . . . truth in man"*. Cf. Arthur Symons' essay on 'Maeterlinck as a Mystic': 'Jacob Boehme has said, very subtly, "that man does not perceive the truth but God perceives the truth in man"; that is, that whatever we perceive or do is not perceived or done consciously by us, but unconsciously through us' (*The Symbolist Movement in Literature*, 90).

115, 1: *The Fool*. Sources vary from the Celtic *Amadán-na-Breena* (M 112), to the Tarot Fool known to Yeats through GD documents and works by Mathers, to the fool of the East (A 240), to 'the pure fool of European tradition', like that of *King Lear* (EI 465).

116, 3–5: *"Out of the pool . . . the mirthless fool"*. Misquoted from Sir William Watson's epigram on 'The Play of *King Lear*', which is quoted and identified by Yeats in *LNI* 210.

116, 25: *the more dough-like the body*. Cf. p. 7, 20–1.

119: *BOOK II*. An almost finished typescript is headed Part III; an earlier and clean typescript is headed Book III.

121: *DESERT GEOMETRY OR THE GIFT OF HARUN AL-RASCHID*. Instead of this poem an early typescript contains a section headed 'Where Kusta-ben-Luka got his philosophy'. It is a prose account of some 500 words signed 'Owen Ahearne' containing the narrative details of the poem. This account was published, with some changes and additions, as a note to the poem, then titled 'The Gift of Harun-al-Rashid', in *The Cat and the Moon and Certain Poems* (1924), where Yeats described it as a 'letter of Owen Ahern's, which I am publishing in "A Vision" ' (p. 39). He may have omitted the prose narrative because it is more clearly autobiographical than the poem. For example, a point is made that the 'young bride' had 'fallen in love with the elderly philosopher . . . to the surprise of her friends and relations'. 'They were married but a few days', according to the typescript, when she began to talk in her sleep, and her wisdom was so great that he saw at once that the Caliph had acted under divine guidance, and that she had been brought to him that he who had sought wisdom in libraries might learn all the secrets from an ignorant mouth. . . . She taught him for a number of years, often walking to the border of the desert in her sleep, and there marking upon the sand innumerable intricate symbols' (cf. *VP* 828–30). The fiction is carried still further in the section Yeats intended as Book IV (see pp. 235–6 and 237–8). Unlike Kusta's wife, however, George was no 'ignorant mouth', being well acquainted with occult literature and with experiments in automatic writing.

121, 16: *Treatise of Parmenides*. Yeats may have known Plato's *Parmenides* in the translation of Thomas Taylor, who asserted that Plato intended 'to conceal divine mysteries under the veil of symbols and figures' (*Works of*

Plato, III, 3). More likely, however, Yeats was referring to other books he was reading at this time (see n. on p. 133, 7–14; also *VP* 829).

122, 3: *Or those who need his bounty or his law.* Omitted from *VP* 462.

128, 1–7: *Flaubert talked much . . . own love adventure.* For much of this sub-section, see Jeffares, *The Circus Animals*, 103–14. Summarizing Daphne Fullwood, he suggests that Yeats knew of the Flaubert project only at second hand through Moore's *Art and Life* (see n. on p. 96, 11–13). Yeats preserved several copies of this section, which was much revised in rejected typescripts.

128, 8–15: *Swedenborg wrote . . . that concerned Fate.* Jeffares maintains that 'Yeats did not owe much to Swedenborgian sources' (*The Circus Animals*, 105). But he did know Swedenborg well (see *E* 30–70).

128, 15–18: *I remember that . . . an ascending gyre.* See *M* 123n.

128, 18–19: *that gyring "tangle of world lines in a fourth dimensional space".* In an early version headed 'The Gyres and Higher Dimensions', Yeats wrote: 'I find among my documents the statement that a gyre represents a life lived in a higher dimension . . ., and we may consider the full gyre itself half a rotating four dimensional sphere.' This concept came from a passage in Lyndon Bolton's *An Introduction to the Theory of Relativity* (p. 160), which Yeats misquoted slightly in a rejected typescript: 'The whole of the physical nature is a mathematical diagram, is a mass of these world-lines, existing in a fourth dimensional continuum, like strings in a piece of jelly, and sometimes intersecting one another'.

128, 20: *Descartes and his vortex.* Yeats's knowledge of Descartes' vortexes may have come from J. P. Mahaffy's *Descartes* (see Jeffares, *The Circus Animals*, 106), but Bolton pointed out that 'The immediate predecessor of Newton's theory was the Cartesian theory of Vortices. According to this theory, space is filled with a subtle medium or aether which is in a continual state of whirl, producing vortices which entangle bodies such as the planets and thus cause them to revolve' (p. 168).

128, 20–1: *Boehme and his gyre.* Yeats knew Boehme from William Law's famous edition (1764–81) (see *VB* 23–4). Blake, who read the same edition, said that 'any man of mechanical talents may, from the writings of Paracelsus or Jacob Behmen, produce ten thousand volumes of equal value with Swedenborg's' (Keynes, 158).

129, 2: *passage in Heraclitus.* Yeats's idea of the gyre was probably justified after the fact by the passages cited; the best summary of Yeats's sources may be Melchiori (*The Whole Mystery of Art*, 261–70). Yeats's vortexes were probably based on Blake, theosophy, and especially Rosicrucianism (see Regardie, *The Golden Dawn*, IV, 247 and 251). See also pp. 130, 9 and 132, 12–15.

129, 5–10: *Having the concrete mind . . . for itself.* In the section of the typescript indebted to Bolton (see n. to p. 128, 18–19), Yeats wrote: 'If I did not wish to avoid all argument wherein my concrete mind would do badly what others do well, it would amuse me to follow these arguments of Ouspensky, that birth and death, spring and summer, and all waxing and waning, are but the appearance that immoveable solids take, as we encircle them . . .'.

129, 11–12: *A line is . . . opposed to emotion*. This discussion, which may be indebted to Bolton among others, was part of a section entitled 'Symbols of Time and Space' in the rejected typescript (see n. to p. 128, 18–19). But Yeats found parallels in other sources; see *A* 375 and also Regardie, *The Golden Dawn*, II, 168: 'In this diagram [of the Maltese Cross] are represented the Circle, the Point, the Line, the Cross, the Square and the Cube. For the Circle is the Abyss, the Nothingness, the AIN. The Point is Kether. Now, the Point has no dimension, but in moving, it traces the Line. This gives the first number—Unity—yet therein, lies duality unmanifest, for two Points mark its ends. The movement of the line maketh the Plane or Square thus. . . . The motion of the Point at angles to its first direction and intersecting it maketh the Cross. So therefore, are the Square and the Cross but one Symbol, deriving from the Circle and the Point.'

129, 28–30: *Anima Hominis . . . Anima Mundi*. Meaning 'soul of man' and 'soul of the world', these two phrases are the titles of the two main sections of *PASL*.

130, 9: *each dying the other's life living the other's death*. Apparently, Yeats first recorded this quotation from Heraclitus in 1909 in his Journal (*Mem* 216). Although he might have found it in Thomas Taylor, who quotes it several times, Taylor's translation ('we live their death, and we die their life') is different from the one Yeats used. A more probable source is John Burnet's *Early Greek Philosophy* (1892): 'Mortals are immortals and immortals are mortals, the one living the other's death and dying the other's life' (p. 138). Another citation from Heraclitus (*Mem* 216) is even more obviously indebted to Burnet: 'War is the father of all and the king of all; and some he has made gods and some men, some bound and some free' (p. 136). See also *VB* (67 and 82). Further borrowings from the Pre-Socratic philosophers derive from the first edition of Burnet, which Yeats continued to use rather than editions of 1908 or 1920.

132, 12–16: *Heraclitus: "I shall . . . the extreme bound"*. Here begins a series of quotations from Burnet, whom Yeats confused with F. C. Burkitt, whose *Early Eastern Christianity* (1904) he had read (see *El* 514, *A* 379, and Moore, *The Unicorn* 388 and 401); the quotation is from Empedocles (not Heraclitus), fragments 35–6: 'But now I shall retrace my steps over the paths of song that I have travelled before, drawing from my saying a new saying. When Strife was fallen to the lowest depth of the vortex [note 65: "The 'lowest depth' is not, as might be supposed, the centre; but is the same thing as the 'extreme boundary' (v. 178)"], and Love had reached to the centre of the whirl, in it do all things come together so as to be one only; not all at once, but coming together gradually each from different quarters; and, as they came together, Strife retired to the extreme boundary' (*EGP* 226). Burnet withdrew note 65, interpolated here, from all subsequent editions. Since Yeats quoted the note in both *VA* and *VB*, he obviously continued to rely on the 1892 edition. He corrected *Heraclitus* to *Empedocles* in *VB* 67.

132, 17–23: *"And love has . . . kept running in"*. Empedocles, fragments 35–6 (*EGP* 211–12).

132, 25–30: *"For of a truth . . . their appointed time"*. Cf. Burnet's translation of Empedocles: 'For, of a truth, they [i.e. Love and Strife] were aforetime and shall be: nor ever, methinks, will boundless time be emptied of that pair. And they prevail in turn as the circle comes round, and pass away before one another, and increase in their appointed turn' (*EGP* 223).

133, 7–14: *"Where then it . . . whole and immoveable"*. See Parmenides in Burnet: 'Where, then, it has its farthest boundary, it is complete on every side, equally poised from the centre in every direction, like the mass of a rounded sphere; for it cannot be greater or smaller in one place than in another. [Here, Yeats goes back to the preceding paragraph in Burnet.] And there is not, and never shall be, any time other than that which is present, since fate has chained it so as to be whole and immovable' (*EGP* 187). A passage in a rejected typescript refers to these lines: 'A book of mathematics tells me that I am to understand an obscure passage in Parmenides as the description of a higher dimensional solid under the symbol of a stick thrust into running water. The stick thrust into the surface of the water creates a series of whorls and eddies very comparable to our gyres, whereas in the mathematics of today "The physical history of every object is its world-line".' See Bolton, p. 160.

133: *BLAKE'S USE OF THE GYRES*. In a fairly late typescript, sec. III and sec. IV (p. 135), both without headings, were interchanged. For the quotations from 'The Mental Traveller' see Keynes, 425–6. The poem is most important to the understanding of *VA*. Much of the AS of 9 Apr 1919 draws a parallel between Blake's poem and the System. The relationship of the poem to Yeats's cyclical theories is also suggested in the record of a 'meditation' of 3 Oct 1920: 'But she [George] had got the words continually repeated "He grows old as she grows young" from Blake's Mental Traveller. . . . He [the Control] said that the C[elestial] B[ody] grew young reaching its climax of youth at the man's death while the P[assionate] B[ody] grew old, reaching its greatest age at Death. After death the PB grew young & the CB old; until birth came round again birth being the CB's time of greatest age, while in it (birth) and youth of PB climaxed.'

134, 7–8: *our big book on the philosophy of William Blake*. Yeats refers to *WWB*. Commentary on 'The Mental Traveller' appears in II, 34–6.

134, 19: *as in Parmenides*. Almost certainly, Yeats has again confused the

Pre-Socratic philosophers; whereas Parmenides has little to say of love in any connection, Empedocles has a great deal (see p. 132, 17–30, and *EGP* 245–71).

134, 23–4: *"consumes itself away"*. Cf. p. 141, 14, and p. 221, 33. As the concordances to Yeats's poems and plays make clear, *consume* was one of his favourite words. It appears several times in the AS and in poems written during this time and later. A sentence in a rejected typescript clarifies Yeats's meaning: 'Thought dies when tension dies fading out through a process of abstraction—"All things separate from their opposites consume themselves away" '.

134, 26: *Blake and his wife signed*. See Bentley, *Blake Records*, 35.

134, 27–8: *his brother remained a Swedenborgian*. The brother was James Blake. See Bentley, *Blake Records*, 2.

134, 29: *his friend Flaxman was a Swedenborgian*. See Bentley, *Blake Records*, 440–1, n6.

135, 2–4: *to follow Empedocles . . . "height of Air"*. See Burnet: 'Fire and Water and Earth and the mighty height of Air' (*EGP* 222).

135, 8–9: *as Plotinus insisted*. Yeats refers to *Enneads*, IV. vi, 1–2. Yeats's favourite philosopher, Plotinus was available, first through the translations of Thomas Taylor, then through the stylistically admirable translation of his friend Stephen MacKenna. But Yeats sometimes disapproved of Plotinus's abstract thought (see 'The Tower', l. 146, and n. in *VP* 826).

139, 7: *as we shall see presently*. In GP Yeats underlined these words and placed a big X in the margin. Why is not clear.

139, 28–9: *as Avicenna did . . . "out of corruption"*. Avicenna is the common English name for an Arab philosopher and physician influenced by Aristotle and the Neoplatonists. Yeats is probably indebted to Flaubert's *The Temptation of St. Anthony* (tr. by D. F. Hannigan, 1895): . . . existence proceeds from corruption' (p. 162). See also *M* 276.

140: *THE SYMBOLISM OF THE SUN'S PRECESSION AND ANNUAL MOVEMENTS*. In one of the typescripts this section was headed 'The Equinoctial Points'.

140, 4–5: *All circles are but a single archetypal circle*. Among the miscellaneous papers there is a sheet with a diagram of circles containing many numbers and several circles, one within the other. According to a note in George's hand, the fifth is the circle of the 'Perfect Man'. Besides the 28 Phases, this circle incorporates three sets of numbers representing divisions of the single circle: '10 soul, 12 mind, 22 ascent'. These numbers may signify the 10 limbs on the Tree of Life and 10 degrees in the GD, the 12 signs of the Zodiac, and the 22 petals in the Rosicrucian rose. There are, of course, many ramifications for all three.

141, 14: *"to consume itself away"*. See n. to p. 134, 23–4 and p. 221, 33.

141, 16: *"to deceive us if they can"*. Yeats observed more than once in the AS that the spirits would deceive. In fact, he called one whole class of spirits 'Frustrators'. According to Everard Feilding in a letter of 1 Apr 1933, Yeats had argued (in a lost letter) that 'in the unconscious there is a will to cheat *and to be found cheating*' (*LWBY* 553).

141, 22–4: *We mean by the zodiacal signs . . . consider*. With one difference ('describe' rather than 'consider') this sentence was inserted in GP.

141–2, 25f: *I . . . XII*. 'Mid Autumn', 'Mid Winter', 'Mid Spring', 'Mid Summer', and 'First Lunar Month of Great Year' were inserted in PP.

142, 12–13: *to show reality*. In GP this phrase read: 'to get mankind'. For an amplification of Yeats's meaning, see n. to p. 140, 4–5.

144, 6: *Aries 30*. Each of the twelve signs of the Zodiac is divided into one-twelfth of the complete circle, or thirty degrees. Aries 30 is therefore the end of Aries and the beginning of the following sign, Taurus.

145, 29–33: *"the centre of the whirl" . . . "from the lowest depths of the Vortex"*. See n. to p. 132, 12–16.

149, 7–8: *like man and woman in Plato's myth*. In Plato's *Symposium*, secs. 189f., Aristophanes explains that originally there were three sexes: male, female, and androgynous; Yeats, in an urge for unity, has simplified the myth by stressing this third group. He may have been indebted to Coleridge. In the R–S TS Aherne remarks: 'I remember the passage in the Table Talk, he said that all great minds are androgynous.' See also 'Among School Children', l. 15.

149: *THE GREAT YEAR IN CLASSICAL ANTIQUITY*. From various sources (Duhem, *Le Système du monde*, I, 65–85, 275–96; Petrie, *The Revolutions of Civilization*, 9–10; etc.), Yeats had learned that, according to such ancient philosophers as Plato, man developed through a series of cultural stages analogically similar to the year; each stage developed biologically, like Frazer's year-gods in *The Golden Bough* or like an individual, and each ultimately fell before a new victor. Astrologically (or astronomically), the length of each stage was marked by the return of the equinoctial sun 'to its original place in the constellations' (*E* 395). Before modern astronomy, the length of time required for the precession of the equinoxes was in doubt, as indicated by Yeats's references below to disputed passages in Plato.

149, 19–20: *that elaborate geometry of the Timaeus*. See *Timaeus*, secs. 35f.

149, 21: *calculations in the Republic*. See *Republic*, VIII, secs. 546f. The number of explanations was changed from 17 to 14 in *VB* 248.

149, 25–9: *Milton was the first . . . of the climate*. In *Paradise Lost*, X, 668–78, following the Fall, seasonal change is brought about either by the tilting of the earth's axis from the ecliptic or by a change in the course of the sun.

150, 1–4: *Yet he must . . . that it defines*. According to Saurat, 'In the time of Milton all that was known of this book [the Book of Enoch] was a rather long fragment preserved by the Byzantine historian Georgius Syncellus in his *Chronographia*. This book was published by Goar in Paris in 1657. Professor Hanford, in his article on the "Chronology of Milton's Private Studies", gives a list of the Byzantine historians that were in Milton's library in 1658, and Syncellus is in the list under his other name of Georgius Monachus' (*Milton: Man and Thinker*, 254).

150, 7–15: *Certain English and . . . sin and salvation*. Here begins a series of passages based upon *Encyclopaedia of Religion and Ethics*, which Yeats purchased with money from the Nobel Prize in 1923. This passage is based upon Alfred Jeremias, 'Ages of the World (Babylonian)', I, 185–6.

150, 15–19: *consider that Babylonian . . . South the commentary*. Cf. Jeremias: 'In the Babylonian concept of the universe, which regards everything earthly as a copy of a heavenly prototype, the zodiac . . . is the broad "Way" on the heavens, c. 20 degrees, upon which the sun, the moon, Venus and the four other moving stars (planets) known to antiquity, trace out their course; while the other stars, the fixed stars, seem to stand still on the ball of the revolving heavens. The moving stars were regarded as interpreters of the divine will. The heaven of fixed stars was related to them like a commentary written on the margin of a book of revelation' (*ERE*, I, 184).

150, 19–20: *I think of M. Cumont especially*. See Franz Cumont, *Astrology and Religion Among the Greeks and Romans*: 'the Orientals never had a suspicion of this famous precession before the genius of Hipparchus discovered it' (p. 5). In *VB* 252 Yeats conceded that written evidence justified Hipparchus' position as discoverer of precession.

150, 29–32: *Dr Homell fixes . . . Aries 1000 B.C.* See Hommel, 'Calendar (Babylonian)', *ERE*, III, 77.

151, 17–19: *The Babylonian Great . . . the Vernal Equinox*. See Jeremias in *ERE*, I, 186.

151, 19–21: *Syncellus says that . . . "the Cyrannid Books"*. Yeats gives the source in *VB* 254n: Emmeline M. Plunket, *Ancient Calendars and Constellations*, 17.

151–2, 21f: *words put by Cicero . . . part has passed away*. See the *Somnium Scipionis*, VII, 3–4. Dume points out (p. 171) that the same passage is quoted in Pierre Duhem, *Le Système du monde*, I, 283. However, although Yeats undoubtedly read sections of this work (see *VB* 67) by the time of composition of *VA*, he could not have derived all of this passage from Duhem's French, and his source must have been something other.

152, 2: *Macrobius translated Cicero's Greek into Latin*. This is incorrect, as F. P. Sturm pointed out to Yeats (Taylor, *FPS* 93). While Cicero wrote some Greek, the work in question—the *Somnium Scipionis*, the conclusion of Cicero's *De Re Publica*—was in Latin, and Macrobius wrote a commentary on it in the fifth century.

152, 3–6: *in his commentary . . . "The World Year"*. From Macrobius's commentary, II, xi, 8–11 and 13.

152, 19–21: *Twelve thousand . . . work of Cicero's*. This passage is borrowed directly from Duhem (I, 283), who identifies Cicero's lost work as the *Hortensius* and Tacitus's work as *De Claris Oratoribus Dialogus*, Ch. VI.

152, 25–31: *"The latest age . . . run their course"*. From the Fourth Eclogue of Virgil, often called the 'Messianic Eclogue' because of Christian interpretations of its prophetic content. See also *M* 310, *E* 150, and ll. 9–12 of the first of Yeats's 'Two Songs from a Play'.

153, 2–4: *This period which . . . "ancient solar year"*. See Kirby Flower Smith, 'Ages of the World (Greek and Roman)', *ERE*, I, 200.

153, 6–8: *among the Etruscans . . . into Italy perhaps*. See G. Herbig, 'Etruscan Religion', *ERE*, V, 538; the date should be 967, not 966.

153, 12–17: *Macrobius may have . . . Great Year by ten*. This appears to be pure speculation on Yeats's part.

153, 17–23: *Popular thought may . . . soul and body parted*. Cf. Herbig, *ERE*, V, 538: 'The *libri fatales* assigned to human life a duration of twelve hebdomads; but, when life had extended to ten hebdomads, or seventy years, man could no longer delay the incidence of fate by propitiatory rites. From that stage onwards he must ask nothing more from the gods; and even if he should survive for other two hebdomads, yet his soul is really sundered from his body. . . . The doctrine of the periods of human life was adapted also to the life of the Etruscan city-state . . .'. Religious rites could maintain the city 'until the tenth *saeculum*, and . . . thereafter fate took its inexorable course'.

153–4, 30f: *Plutarch records . . . to an end*. Yeats had evidently been reading Mayor, *et al.*, *Virgil's Messianic Eclogue: Its Meaning, Occasion, & Sources*, 121–2: 'Servius . . . quotes the Memoirs of Augustus to the effect that the soothsayer Vulcatius had interpreted the appearance of the comet at the funeral games held in honour of Caesar, as denoting the end of the ninth age and the beginning of the tenth. Plutarch (*Vita Sullae*, 7), speaking of the signs which foreboded the rise of Sulla, mentions in particular the piercing and terror-striking sound of a trumpet which came from a clear sky, and was understood to announce the end of the eighth stage of the great year. Censorinus (*De Die Natali*, 17) adds that the Etruscan soothsayers believed that, when the tenth stage was completed, there would be an end of the Etruscan name. Servius, in his note on this line, says that, according to the Sibyl, the last age is the tenth, the age of the Sun or Apollo. In the existing Sibylline books . . . the tenth age is also mentioned as the concluding age of the world's history.' The details from Plutarch's life of Sulla may owe something to the translation of the passage in Petrie's *The Revolutions of Civilization* (pp. 9–10), to which a similar passage in *VB* 253 is indebted.

154, 10–13: *Salomon Reinach . . . birth of Caesar*. While the original is an article by Reinach in *Revue de l'histoire des Réligions* for Nov 1900, Yeats depended upon a summary by W. Warde Fowler in 'The Child of the Poem', in Mayor, *et al.*, *Virgil's Messianic Eclogue*, especially pp. 59–64.

154, 13–14: *but I am ready to believe that Virgil*. In GP this passage read: 'but I, like the Christians of fifteen centuries, find nothing incompatible in believing that Virgil', etc.

154, 19–21: *Kepler foretold . . . he would die*. Yeats's reference should have been, not to Johann Kepler, but to Tycho Brahe, whose predictions upon the observation of a new star in Cassiopeia in 1572 were generally applied to Gustavus Adolphus (including the date 1632, the year in which Gustavus defeated Wallenstein but was himself killed).

154, 21–2: *and Savonarola . . . it would be*. Yeats confused Savonarola's regular condemnations of, and dire prophecies for, Rome with the prophecies for Florence reported from him during the final days of his life. See, e.g., Villari, *Life and Times of Girolamo Savonarola*, 752: 'It is said that he also added these words: "Bear well in mind that these things will come to pass when there shall be a Pope named Clement".'

154, 25–6: *Cicero's belief that . . . place once more*. See p. 151, 22f.

154, 26–28: *that of Macrobius . . . same position*. See p. 152, 4f.

154, 28–30: *that of somebody . . . through them all*. See Duhem, who quotes from a fragment of Berosius preserved in Seneca's *Natural Questions*, III, xxviii and xxix, which he thinks was based upon the now-lost *Meteorology* of Posidonius: 'Le globe . . . prendra feu quand tous les astres, qui ont maintenant des cours si divers, se réuniront dans le Cancer et se placeront de telle sorte les uns sous les autres qu'une ligne droite pourrait traverser tous leurs centres' (I, 70). See also II, 214.

154, 34: *Macrobius enumerates them*. In his *Commentary*, II, xi, 7.

155, 10–16: *In the Republic . . . the Ten Ages*. Here Yeats inexactly summarizes from Plato's *Republic*, VIII, secs. 544–7.

155, 16–20: *In another passage . . . a like cause*. *Republic*, VIII, sec. 564.

155, 21–6: *Machiavelli may . . . in illusion*. The ultimate source of this passage is Machiavelli's *Discourses*, I, 2, 3–13 and III, 1, 1–5; see also Butterfield, *The Statecraft of Machiavelli*, 30–3, 48–9. While Machiavelli was usually more optimistic than a cyclical view of history allows, there are passages in his works to support Yeats's statements.

155–6, 35f: *We have considered . . . the Lunar Great Year*. The coming of an Avatar or New Messiah is mentioned frequently in the AS. On 27 Jan 1918 (and several other times) the Control informed Yeats that this cycle began '2026 years ago'; on 17 Apr and 26 May 1918 the date of the Divine Birth of the 'new Christ' is set at 2100.

156, 15–20: *When I find . . . of the Fish*. On the chart facing p. 40 in Plunket's *Ancient Calendars*. The line to which Yeats refers is labeled 'Initial Point Gregorian Zodiac Fixed by Hipparchus at Equinox 150 B.C.'.

157, 16–18: *religion of Serapis . . . they found*. Cf. J. G. Milne, 'Graeco-Egyptian Religion', *ERE*, VI, 376: 'As a matter of fact, Serapis came into theological existence at Alexandria in an altogether unusual manner: he was virtually the result of the investigations of a body of philosophers and priests, who collected from all sources and fused together whatever ideas or attributes would be of service for their new conception. . .'. The group of scholars and priests was later referred to as 'Ptolemy's committee'.

157, 22–3: *Stoical argument that . . . the individual soul.* See Kirby Flower Smith, 'Ages of the World (Greek and Roman)', *ERE*, I, 196. After discussing the Stoic view expressed by Aratus that ideal happiness lies only in the past, Smith summarized the underlying principle: 'We mean the conclusion stated above, that advance in the arts of civilization is at the expense of the character, health, and happiness of the individual.'

157, 25–7: *early Christian . . . period from Adam.* Possibly from St Augustine, *The City of God*, XXII, xxx, but if so only by confusion; see Gaston Bonet-Maury, 'Ages of the World (Christian)', *ERE*, I, 190.

157, 27–29: *the Persian . . . "of the body".* See Nathan Söderblom, 'Ages of the World (Zorastrian)', *ERE*, I, 206: 'The period of mankind being fixed at 6000 years, Zarathrushtra [sic], who was born thirty years before the end of the former 3000 years, and whose first intercourse with the celestial beings begins the second trimillenium, makes his appearance in the middle of human history'. Söderblom then quotes from an appropriate Zoroastrian text, the *Sad Dar*; in this passage, the Creator is speaking to Zarathustra: 'I have created thee at the present time, in the middle period; for it is three thousand years from the days of Gayomard till now, and from now till the resurrection are the three thousand years that remain. . . . For whatever is in the middle is more precious and better and more valuable . . . as the heart is in the middle of the whole body . . . and as the land of Iran is more valuable than other lands, for the reason that it is in the middle.'

157, 29–30: *One remembers too . . . "and half a time".* Revelation 12:14: 'And to the woman were given two wings of a great eagle, that she might fly into the wilderness, into her place, where she is nourished for a time, and times, and half a time, from the face of the serpent.' See also Daniel 12: 7.

157, 32–4: *However I but suggest . . . for my thought.* This sentence was inserted in GP.

157–8, 36f: *Golden Age . . . and grow old.* From Smith, 'Ages of the World (Greek and Roman)', *ERE*, I, 197–8.

158, 3–5: *upon the other . . . and the Moon.* From Jeremias, 'Ages of the World (Babylonian)', *ERE*, I, 187.

158, 13–16: *Berkeley thought . . . named God.* See Bishop George Berkeley, *A Treatise Concerning the Principles of Human Knowledge*, I, 3 and I, 6; more generally, see Torchiana, *W. B. Yeats and Georgian Ireland*, Ch. Six ('God-Appointed Berkeley').

158, 16–18: *mathematician Poincaré . . . our ancestors.* Yeats's knowledge of

Jules Henri Poincaré probably derived from Henry Adams, as a passage in *E* 434 indicates: 'The mathematician Poincaré, according to Henry Adams, described space as the creation of our ancestors, meaning, I conclude, that mind split itself into mind and space.' Perhaps Yeats had in mind Ch. 31 of *The Education of Henry Adams*, 454–5; see also *EI* 503. Yeats became interested in Adams because of his historical theories, especially in *The Degradation of the Democratic Dogma* (see *L* 666).

161: *LIFE AFTER DEATH*. In one typescript this is the title of a considerably longer section which includes discussion of the Four Principles of sec. XIII.

162, 4–5: *"slain on the stems of generations"*. From Blake's 'Descriptive Catalogue', No. V (Keynes, 578). Blake's word was 'generation' rather than 'generations'.

162, 11–14: *They tried . . . two days later*. See Lake, 'Christmas', *ERE*, III, 606. The unknown writer of *De Pascha Computus* 'first establishes the fact that the first day of creation was at the vernal equinox, when everything breaks into life, and the day and night are equal, for God divided them equally (Ch. 3). Moreover, the moon (created two days later) was created full.'

162, 16–22: *They did not . . . to that moon*. See James G. Carleton, 'Calendar (Christian)', *ERE*, III, 89: 'As Christians made their Paschal anniversaries coincide in season with the Passover, so, for a long period, they were satisfied to accept the Jewish computation of the time of that festival, which should fall on the first full moon after the vernal equinox.' For 'the Sunday nearest', see *ERE*, III, 88, where the wording is not so close to Yeats's.

162, 25–7: *For the first . . . of His Birth*. Probably from Lake, 'Christmas', *ERE*, III, 601–5.

162, 29–31: *Sometimes they calculated . . . lives of Patriarchs*. Yeats is probably thinking of the complicated argument of *De Pascha Computus*, summarized by Lake in 'Christmas', *ERE*, III, 606.

162, 31–3: *sometimes pointed out . . . the Twelve Apostles*. See Lake, 'Christmas', *ERE*, III, 607: for Ephraim Syrus, 'not the equinox, but the solstice, is the important point, and he regards Jan. 6 as representing 12 days after the winter solstice, Dec. 25; and these days refer on the one hand to the twelve Apostles, and on the other to the twelve months'.

163, 1–5: *worshippers of Kore . . . "to the God"*. See Lake, 'Epiphany', *ERE*, V, 332. Explaining pagan backgrounds for the Christian choice of 6 Jan as Epiphany, he writes of 'a story in Epiphanius . . . as to the feast which used to be held in Alexandria in the Koreion, or Temple of Kore, on Jan. 6. He says that on the eve of that day it was the custom to spend the night in singing and attending to the images of the gods. At dawn a descent was made to a crypt, and a wooden image was brought up, which had the sign of a cross, and a star of gold, marked on hands, knees, and head. This was carried round in procession, then taken back to the crypt; and it was said that this was done because "the Maiden" had given birth to "the Aeon".'

163, 5–7: *If, however, one . . . for each alternately*. See H. J. Rose, 'Calendar (Greek)', *ERE*, III, 107: 'The Greek year of 12 lunar months contained, as has been said, 354 days, the months having alternately 30 days . . . and 29 days . . .'.

163, 13–14: *"The White hand . . . the ground suspires"*. Somewhat misquoted from FitzGerald's 'Rubáiyát of Omar Khayyám', ll. 15–16.

163, 21–6: *When I was . . . the Sidereal Faith*. When Yeats was young, it was customary to interpret deities as solar, as did Sir John Rhys in his *Celtic Heathendom* (cf. *VP* 807–11). *Sidereal*, on the other hand, means *astral*.

163, 30: *Beware the Ides of March*. Shakespeare, *Julius Caesar*, I. ii. 18 (*RS* 1106).

163, 31–3: *sentence upon Socrates . . . Festival at Delos*. See John Burnet, 'Socrates', *ERE*, XI, 665: 'As, however, Socrates was condemned at the beginning of the Delian festival, which appears to have fallen in March . . .'. Plato's *Phaedo*, sec. 59, explains that Socrates' execution was displayed because his sentencing came during a religious festival celebrating Theseus's salvation of Athens from the burden of sacrifice to the Minotaur.

164, 6–8: *According to St. Chrysostom . . . Spring Equinox*. Loosely based on Lake, 'Christmas', *ERE*, III, 607. See also *Mem* 101, *A* 386, *JS* 90–1, and *VPl* 962.

164, 10–14: *Did Da Vinci . . . of the corn?* See *VB* 212 for more explicit references. Indebted to Coventry Patmore's essay 'The Precursor', according to F. A. C. Wilson, 'Yeats saw St. John as the precursor and necessary antithesis of Christ, natural love where Christ was supernatural, "a midsummer child" where Christ was "a midwinter" ' (*W. B. Yeats and Tradition*, 67–8). To Yeats, that is, Dionysus and St John the Baptist were antitheses to Christ. See also Yeats's general dependence on Lake, 'Christmas', *ERE*, III, 607.

166: A footnote deleted in GP was intended for this page: 'In one or two diagrams, not given here, the phases of the Millenium are divided into ten divisions or cones, and this may come from comparison with the Ten Epochs of Sybilline prophecy. See also tables on page —.'

167, 1–4: *When the two thousand . . . to the greater division*. This sentence was inserted in GP.

168, 1: *when I was at Oxford*. The Yeatses maintained a residence at Oxford from Jan to Mar 1918, and again from Oct 1919 to Mar 1922. There Yeats gained much information for *VA* from research and from living scholars, and there he wrote 'All Souls' Night'.

168, 2–5: *a distinguished scholar . . . the Emperor Constantine*. The distinguished scholar was Charlotte Anne Elizabeth Moberly, Principal of St Hugh's Hall, Oxford. With Eleanor Frances Jourdain, she wrote *An Adventure*, published pseudonymously in 1911 by 'Elizabeth Morison and Frances Lamont', describing their visionary apprehension of Marie Antoinette and the gardens of Versailles as they were laid out in her time. See *VB* 227 n2.

VPl 970, *EI* 406 and 414, *VBWI* 348–9, and *Proceedings of SPR*, 25 (1911), 353–60. *An Adventure* and its authors are mentioned several times in the AS. On 30 Jan 1918, a month after moving to Oxford, Yeats is aware of a great psychic 'disturbance which might have resulted in stopping this work'. He concludes that the first of three stages of the work is finished, and he asks the Control, 'Do you wish us to find certain mystic associates here in Oxford?' The reply is, 'Yes but only the order and philosophic'. Yeats then suggests that they may have been brought to Oxford for this purpose and wishes to be directed to people who might help with 'psychic things'. Several questions later, he asks, 'Do you wish us to seek out the authors of "The Adventure"?' 'Yes', the Control responds, 'she expects you both.' Yeats obviously thought Miss Moberly was 'one of the people in Oxford with whom you wish us to work'. *An Adventure* is discussed again on 31 Jan, 5 Mar, and 17 Mar; and Yeats wrote to Miss Moberly to ask her opinion concerning the appearance of the spirit of her dead father, Bishop George Moberly, to Elizabeth Radcliffe in 1912 (see *YO* 145). Despite her own 'psychical experience', Miss Moberly's reply was very cautious: 'For the sake of science', she wrote on 20 Mar 1918, 'I would willingly listen to any so called "communication" from my father, but I should try not to surrender my best judgment for any marvel. . .'. She thanked Yeats for 'expressing your great anxiety to unravel all the truth', but offered no assistance (*LWBY* 347–8).

168, note: *I once heard Sir William Crookes*. A distinguished scientist and President of the SPR (1896–99), Crookes remained active in the Society until his death in 1919. Since Yeats was an Associate Member from 1913 to 1928, he must have known Crookes personally, and he surely read Crookes' articles as well as his *Researches in the Phenomena of Spiritualism* (1874) (cited by an incorrect title in *VPl* 935).

169, 9–11: *They may correspond . . . of Hesiod's four*. Probably this passage is based on Smith, 'Ages of the World (Greek and Roman)', *ERE*, I, 196: 'The five ages of Hesiod are reduced [by Aratus] to three—An Age of Gold, of Silver, and of Bronze.' However, Smith found five ages in Hesiod (v. Yeats's four) and spoke of a bronze (rather than copper) age in Aratus; either Yeats was understandably confused or he had additional sources.

170, 28: *We retain the same sex for a cycle*. There is considerable discussion in the AS about the alternation of sexes as the soul goes through the cycles.

171, 4–5: *name of Covens*. Yeats associated the lore of witchcraft with psychic phenomena, and had read several books on the subject. See, for example, two essays and notes in *VBWI* 302–65. He had used the term *coven* in *PASL* (*M* 356). For further details see Editorial Introduction, p. xxii.

171, 23: *I myself chose the name Coven*. On the night of 26 Nov 1920 Yeats 'asked leave to alter terminology, "Coven" for "Group" "Unicorn" for "Group Mind"'. Much of his information about Scotch Witches may have

---

come from a book he liked very much: Robert Kirk's *The Secret Commonwealth of Elves, Fauns, & Fairies* (1691), edited with 'comment by Andrew Lang' in 1893 (see *VBWI* 337–44 and *YO* 87). In Kirk also he would have read that Daimons 'are said to be of a midle Nature betuixt Man and Angel' (p. 5). In *VB* 209 Yeats connects the Daimons with angels. His conception of 'reality as a congeries of beings' is mentioned briefly in 'pages from a Diary in 1930' (*E* 305, 309–10), and summarized succinctly in 'Seven Propositions' (Ellmann, *The Identity of Yeats*, 236–7). See also Moore, *The Unicorn*, 378–9, and Taylor, *FPS* 100–1; and cf. n. to pp. 228–9, 31f.

172: *THE CONES OF SEXUAL LOVE.* This section is particularly confusing: Yeats seems to have wanted to introduce certain terms to make the System complete, but without explaining them adequately (cf. *L* 715). For example, he does not indicate any relationship between the *Beatific Vision* and the *Beatitude*, which he describes later (pp. 235–6). He used the term *Beatific Vision* in his original note to 'The Second Coming' (*VP* 824), but dropped it from *VB*.

173, 3–5: *Initiatory Moments . . . Critical Moments.* These terms are discussed extensively in the AS, the CF, and the Sleeps. Most likely Yeats decided not to explain them in detail because they refer to crises and resolutions in his personal relationships with women (chiefly but not only George, Olivia Shakespear, and Iseult and Maud Gonne). Much of the discussion in the AS suggests several fairly specific dates which the well-informed student of Yeats can relate to known biographical events. See Editorial Introduction, pp. xxiii–xxiv.

173: *COMPLEMENTARY DREAMS.* The origin of the complementary dream is not the memory, as Yeats was informed by the Control on 8 Jan 1919: 'In nervous states you are more closely linked psychically; the nightmare of one runs along this link, creates a shock to the other, & the wire acts on the dreamer. That form gave the dream.' A further explanation, during the same session, casts some light on the creative process in Yeats: 'I gave you dream each', the Control said, 'now I give you two more in one—at castle.' The eight lines following record the basic imagery of 'Towards Break of Day' (originally called 'A Double Dream'), the first stanza of which is quoted on p. 174. On the day before (7 Jan) Yeats had received the imagery, in a diagram and broken sentences, for a more famous poem based on a complementary dream—'The Double Vision of Michael Robartes'. Compare Yeats's early experiments with Tatwa cards to evoke 'complementary dreams, or reveries' (*A* 259).

174, 8–11: *Was it the . . . gleam of day.* From Yeats's 'Towards Break of Day', ll. 1–4. Cf. n. to p. 173: *COMPLEMENTARY DREAMS.*

174–5, 26f: *When Joseph Strzygowski . . . symbolic West also.* Josef Strzygowski was an eminent Austrian art critic whose *Origin of Christian Church Art* (trans. in 1923) Yeats read and began to cite in works published in 1924 (*VPl*

805, *A* 580). From *Orient oder Rom* onwards, Strzygowski attempted to show the influence of non-Roman (especially Persian) art upon early Christian and Byzantine work. The book is difficult, and in *VB* 257–8 Yeats was both more specific in his references to Strzygowski's theories and also less confident about their correspondences to his own. The first quotation is apparently not from *Origin*, but cf. p. 104: 'The origin of Southern art, with its representational ideal, is on the contrary to be sought in the subject; from the beginning it pursued the imitation of nature.' For the North, see *Origin*, p. 103: 'Non-representational art was born out of handicraft; it was from handicraft that art sprang into being in the North and among the nomadic shepherd peoples.' For the East, see p. 41: In the East 'the people were at once to be instructed in the faith and dazzled by magnificent display'; see also pp. 47, 161–2, and 223. For the West, see p. 249: 'Throughout the centuries before the rise of Gothic art it was the function of Western Europe to act as a kind of mirror for all movements coming from the East . . .'.

175, 19–20.: *Swedenborg's vortex . . . of many gyres*. See n. to p. 128, 8–15.

175, 28–30: *hence the sentence . . . breaking the shell*. In a rejected typescript this idea, somewhat expanded, followed immediately after the four lines from 'Towards Break of Day': 'These dreams and meditations are now complementary as when two people dream or meditate, the one of Helen's birth from an egg, and the other the birth from an egg of Castor and Pollux, the creation of beauty and the creation of war, and so, necessary parts of the same story . . .' (See n. to p. xxiii, 21–2).

176, 1–3: *It seems that . . . the eternal return*. See Söderblom, 'Ages of the World (Zoroastrian)', *ERE*, I, 209–10: 'The Persian periods do not imply an eternal repetition, as in the developments of Aryan speculation and religion in India and Greece, and sometimes in modern thought (e.g. Nietzsche . . .). [The Persian concept of history as progressive rather than cyclical] has arisen only twice in the history of human thought—in the only two ancient prophetic religions, one Aryan, one Semitic—in Zarathustrianism and in Mosaism.' Nietzsche's doctrine is expressed in *Also Sprach Zarathustra*, Ch. 46.

176: *THE FOUR PRINCIPLES AND NEO-PLATONIC PHILOSOPHY*. For Plotinus, see above, n. to p. 135, 8–9. There is a revised but still hesitant version of this passage in *VB* 193–5. This comparison is rather strained, though details cannot be pointed out: Nature is not a major term in Plotinus, as Yeats seems to indicate, for Plotinus is trinitarian in a pagan sense; *Soul of the World* is not MacKenna's wording (cf. 'All-Soul') but probably derives from Yeats's reading of the Cambridge Platonists. If Yeats had in mind specific passages from Plotinus's *Enneads*, he does not make them clear.

177: *BOOK III: DOVE OR SWAN*. In all early versions the title of this Book was simply 'History'.

179: *LEDA*. Written 18 Sept 1923, the poem was first published in the *Dial* (June 1924), where Yeats explained that he wrote it 'because the editor of a political review asked me for a poem'. When his friend the editor (AE) told Yeats that his 'conservative friends would misunderstand the poem' (*VP* 828), it was withdrawn. Beginning from a request for an appropriately current political work, Yeats ended with an overtly anachronistic one; his cyclical theory, however, parallels Greek and modern influxes as 'contemporary' (in Flinders Petrie's sense: see *The Revolutions of Civilization* [p. 81], a work cited by Yeats in *E* 312–16). The poem thus summarizes symbolically the Greek origins of Western civilization and also predicts a renascence. In GP the first half line reads 'The great bird drops'.

180, 1–5: *One must bear . . . the entire era.* Throughout Book III, history may be seen as consisting of thousand-year periods which are alternately religious and secular, but it may also be seen as combining such periods into longer ones which begin with a religious dispensation either primary or antithetical and then lead into a secular civilization of the same type; the primary religious dispensation beginning with Christ thus gives way to a primary secular civilization beginning at 1000 A.D., and an antithetical religious dispensation is due about the year 2000, the rough beast of 'The Second Coming' (see *VB* 262–3).

180, 16: *A civilisation . . . self-control.* Cf. *E* 150: 'A civilisation is very like a man or a woman. . . .' Such remarks clearly relate Yeats to a Romantic quest to trace any culture to a hero or founder in a kind of humanistic organicism. The AS contains much discussion of the coming of an antithetical Avatar or New Messiah, at about 2100.

180, 17: *some Niobe.* In Greek mythology, Niobe (usually) had seven sons and seven daughters; for bragging of the numerical superiority of her offspring to those of Leto, her children were killed by Leto's—Apollo and Artemis; Niobe was transformed into a weeping stone.

180, 22: *the scream of Juno's peacock.* This passage should be compared to 'Meditations in Time of Civil War', sec. III ('My Table'), ll. 31–2 ('it seemed / Juno's peacock screamed'), and Yeats used the peacock in at least seven other poems and two plays. The peacock or Argos Panoptes (not to be confused with Argos the child of Zeus and Niobe) was originally a man; set by Hera to watch the cow Io (whom Zeus desired in one form or another), he was killed by Hermes (sent by Zeus), and his eyes were put by Hera into the peacock's tail. But the peacock's cry seems to have been an ornithological observation rather than a classical allusion.

181: *2000 B.C. TO 1 A.D.* In early versions this section was divided into two parts: (1) 2000 B.C. to 500 B.C.; (2) 500 B.C. to 1 A.D. (which had two subheadings: (1) 'The Climax of Aesthetic Power' and (2) 'The Rise of Secular Power').

181, 1–5: *I imagine . . . the other War.* See Jeffares, *CCP*, on 'Leda and the Swan' and Melchiori, *The Whole Mystery of Art, passim,* for numerous sources of Yeats's interest. Yeats probably learned of the worship of Leda's eggs from two books he knew well: Pausanias, *The Description of Greece* (Bk. III, Ch. xvi), and Jacob Bryant, *A New System; or An Analysis of Ancient*

Mythology (3rd ed., II, 64–85). In 1901 Yeats wrote a long note about the influence of Bryant on Blake in Lady Gregory's copy of the first edition.

181, 8–9: *Babylonian mathematical starlight.* In *VB* 268 n1 Yeats clarifies his opening by a reference to astrology. He would have read of Babylonian astrology in *ERE* (see above, p. 151), in Burnet's *EGP*, 21–2, and in Cumont's *Astrology and Religion Among the Greeks and Romans*, 18 (see n. to p. 150, 19–20): the alliance of learning and belief was unusually strong in 'Babylon, where we see a practical polytheism of a rather gross character combined with the application of the exact sciences, and the gods of heaven subjected to the laws of mathematics'; in Ch. 2, 'Babylon and Greece' (pp. 22–41), Cumont suggests that astrology entered Greek and Roman thought from Babylon.

181, 10–14: *Did the older . . . their tragic sense?* As to the Jewish feeling about long life, presumably Yeats was thinking of such Biblical passages as Exodus 20:12, I Kings 3: 11–14, or Psalms 91: 16. The Greek sentiment is widely diffused; cf. Plautus, *Bacchides*, IV. 7.18: 'He whom the gods favour dies in youth'. Yeats liked to think that the Irish belonged to the Greek tradition: 'Not only Achilles but our own Cuchulain also, as competent men have thought, coming from that tribal fermentation' (rejected typescript).

181, 14–17: *Certainly their tribes . . . an intellectual anarchy.* Presumably the 'great Empire' of Minoan culture on Crete (*c.* 3000–1200 B.C.) was broken up by the invading Greek tribes (2000–1000 B.C.), who brought with them an Indo-European language. It is difficult to adjust Yeats's System to history: while the former would place the Ledean annunciation at 2000 B.C. (two millenia before Christ, who was two millenia before the rough beast of 'The Second Coming'), the latter would set the fall of Troy—and, by implication, Leda—at 1250 (1184 B.C. was the traditional date). In any case, Yeats wished to stress the polytheistic, individualistic nature of Greek religion in contrast to the subsequent Christian revelation but like the current one (for which see his note to 'The Second Coming', *VP* 823–5). One of the notebooks with extensive records of Sleeps contains considerable discussion of cycles and Masters in relation to history: 'The First Master is monotheistic, the Second philosophic . . . the Third Master is polytheistic. "All races are unified through polytheism" . . . because of its diversity it produces character' (probably 6 Jan 1921). Christ, the First Master, came at P 1, and P 15 was of great importance to his age. The Second Master (a 'multitudinous Avatar') will appear at 2100, and Yeats was preparing the way for his coming: 'As 2nd Master is at 2, 3, 4 the phases 16, 17, 18 have been of great importance historically & persons belonging to those phases are greatly important as preparation for 2nd Master' (9 Feb 1921).

182, 1: *beauty like that before Raphael.* Yeats changed 'of Botticelli' to 'before Raphael' in PP. The early Yeats was much influenced, primarily through his father, by the Pre-Raphaelites.

182, 16–19: *which I have symbolised . . . through a Round Tower.* 'Under the Round Tower' is a direct outgrowth of an AS (20 Mar 1918) at Glendalough, the site of a ruined monastic centre which contains one of Ireland's famous round towers. The Control informed Yeats that 'the medium must meditate on the image of shuttle spiral & funnel'. He asked if the tower was a symbol of the Passionate Body and was informed that it was a symbol of the 'abundant flowing life'. 'Did you bring us here because of round tower', he responded, and received an ambiguous reply: 'Is put in *your mind* for a purpose.' Allegorically, Yeats and his new bride are the 'King and Queen, who are Sun and Moon also'.

182, 25–6: *a moral propaganda . . . of Plato's Republic*. See Books II and III of the *Republic*, especially III, sec. 398, where Plato explains that it may be necessary for the guardians of the republic to cast out poets who tell immoral tales.

182, 31–3: *Then in Phidias . . . abounds and flows*. That is, like the life which the round tower symbolizes. There are similar remarks on Phidias and Callimachus in *EI* 225: see also *A* 475, where Yeats had apparently read of Phidias in Plutarch's life of Nikias. At this point in one typescript Yeats wrote: 'But Greece has an intellect so keen, and a population so small, and is so essentially of the Phases near to the Full Moon that it runs rapidly through the more *primary* phases of its stream and what takes centuries in a nation fundamentally *primary* takes but a few generations.'

182, 33–5: *With Callimachus . . . Furtwingler* [sic] *has proved*. See Furtwängler, *Masterpieces of Greek Sculpture*, 450–1: 'In any case, the artist [Callimachus] belonged to the same Ionicizing school, which tended to a wide divergence from the Pheidian style. . . .' Furtwängler devoted considerable space to Callimachus.

182, 35–6: *only example . . . Persian is represented*. Furtwängler describes the 'armchair found in front of the Pronaos of the Parthenon' (p. 441); he does not, however, mention that the chair was of marble, nor does he refer to the Persian. If Yeats implies that the chair was an extant example of Callimachus' work, then he reverses his view in 'Lapis Lazuli', l. 29, perhaps having accepted the more usual scholarly view that the chair should not be attributed to Callimachus.

183, 1–3: *Persian symbol . . . description in Pausanias?* For a description of the lamp, see Thomas Taylor's *Description of Greece*, I, 70, and n. in III, 215–19. The lamp is mentioned in 'Lapis Lazuli', ll. 33–4. If Yeats read Pausanias, he was surely impressed by the fact that the lamp had been made for a statue of Minerva in 'a place which is now called the *tower*'. Also see Furtwängler, p. 437.

183, 3: *he was an archaistic workman*. Furtwängler uses the term *archaistic* several times in references to Callimachus (pp. 438–9).

183, 4–5: *those who set . . . an older form*. Yeats probably refers to Nikias, whom Furtwängler describes as 'the head of the conservative party, and personally a man of strictly orthodox belief and timid piety' (p. 432). Furtwängler conjectures that Nikias favoured the building of the Erechtheion (as representing the 'old religion') rather than the Parthenon; supposedly it was Nikias who commissioned a Palladion by Callimachus (p. 438).

183, 17–19: *Some Greek . . . of the people.* Possibly Yeats is thinking of a passage from Longinus quoted by Gibbon in *The Decline and Fall of the Roman Empire* (I, 58) and by H. G. Wells in *The Outline of History* (II, 495)—Yeats owned a copy; however, Longinus is rather late (*c.* A.D. 213–73). See also J. P. Mahaffy, *Social Life in Greece from Homer to Menander* (pp. 433–4), citing Cicero's *De Natura Deorum* i, 28 and the 21st oration of Dion Chrysostom.

183, 24: *to die into . . . still to die.* Cf. Yeats's poem 'The Coming of Wisdom with Time', l. 4: 'Now I may wither into the truth'.

183, 25–8: *Yet even . . . Stoic suicide.* Yeats sees in Plato a kind of asceticism or other-worldliness preparing for the Stoic justification of suicide and for the monasticism of the Thebaid (see n. to p. 186, 2). This sentence was inserted in GP.

184, 18: *must adore . . . physical or spiritual force.* Yeats uses the term *adore* in a specifically religious sense; he had learned of emperor-worship in such works as *The Age of Justinian and Theodora* by W. G. Holmes, who used the phrase 'adoration of the Emperor' (I, 95).

184, 25–7: *Mithraic pit . . . last drop.* Yeats might have read of the taurobolium in Frazer, *The Golden Bough*, V, 274–5, or in Grant Showerman, 'Taurobolium', *EB*, XXVI, 455. He might also have read of it in *The Oriental Religions in Roman Paganism*, by Franz Cumont, who, like Yeats, twice used the metaphor of the shower-bath (pp. 71–2 and 208). See also Wells, *The Outline of History*, II, 543.

184, 30–4: *Even before Plato . . . created the world.* In a rejected typescript, Yeats had written: 'Yet even before Plato that collective image of man created by Stoic and Epicurean alike, the moral equivalent of the Hellenic statues, soon to become their antithesis, has been evoked by Anaxagoras when he declares that thought and not the warring of opposites created the world.' In contrasting Anaxagoras with such earlier philosophers of opposites as Heraclitus, Yeats may have been thinking of passages from the former in Burnet, *EGP* 259–60; more likely, however, he has in mind a passage quoted by Burnet (p. 267) from Plato's *Phaedo* (sec. 97) in which Socrates remarks, 'I once heard a man reading a book, as he said, of Anaxagoras, and saying it was Mind that ordered the world and was the cause of all things.'

185, 6–8: *earliest sculptured image . . . Alexander the Great.* Yeats's idea is very close to that in a book he admired, Mrs Arthur Strong's *Apotheosis and After Life*: she speaks of the 'apocalyptic-messianic character that centred about Alexander looked upon as the "Prince of Peace" who was to return and unite all mankind under his rule in a brotherhood of love', and she stresses the influence of 'his portraiture, idealised into a type', upon 'the plastic conception of the Christian God' (pp. 280–1). Unlike Yeats, however, she does not speak of 'the first' sculptured image.

185, 9–10: *Christ alone is . . . perfect physical man.* A favorite bit of Yeats's folklore: for an almost identical passage written in 1902, see *M* 43.

185, 21–4: *I see her anoint . . . favour of a king.* See *E* 291: 'Where did I pick up that story of the Byzantine bishop and the singer of Antioch, where learn that to anoint your body with the fat of a lion ensured the favour of a king?'

185, 24–7: *the same impulse . . . the solar disk.* Yeats's primary authority was probably Mrs Strong's *Apotheosis*, which is particularly concerned with the deification of the Roman emperors and the way in which this process prepared for artistic portrayals of Christ. She speaks of a lead medallion with images of 'Diocletian and his colleague, who, with their solar nimbi, resemble two enthroned apostles' (pp. 96–7, see also p. 103). Cf. Cumont, *Astrology and Religion Among the Greeks and Romans*, 53–6.

185, 26–7: *Upon the throne . . . becomes a biography.* This closing sentence of sec. II replaces a more extended manuscript passage about 'myth or talismanic image': 'I am not concerned with historical uncertainty as to what Christ really thought or said or did, for only that which has created Christendom is Christianity, & remains that miraculous or creative force.' Cf. also *A* 468: 'In Christianity what was philosophy in Eastern Asia became life, biography and drama.'

185: *A.D. 1 TO A.D. 1050.* A complete cycle in itself, 1050 years is also half the larger cycle which will end in 2100 with the coming of the New Messiah. One manuscript and a typescript divided the period into smaller units and related them to Phases. The first section was headed 'Phase 1. A.D. 1 to A.D. 100'.

186, 2: *the Thebiad* [sic]. A section of desert near Thebes in Egypt is particularly associated with early Christian monasticism such as that of St Anthony. Among Yeats's sources of knowledge were Hannay's *The Spirit and Origin of Christian Monasticism* and *The Wisdom of the Desert*, Flaubert's *The Temptation of St. Anthony*, and Gibbon, Ch. XXXVII. Yeats put his knowledge to use in the poem 'Demon and Beast', especially ll. 43–50; see also *E* 301 and *A* 307 and 314.

186, 9: *man has been taught that he is nothing.* Yeats may have been influenced by Dalton, *Byzantine Art and Archaeology*: 'The Emperor Marcus Aurelius expressed one truth when he said that everything which is beautiful is beautiful in itself and terminates in itself. But to the artists of the Middle Ages, whether in East or West, this was false doctrine. To them the individual was nothing, the immanent idea or *eidos* was both a type and an ensample' (p. 37). See also Jeffares, *CCP* 252.

186, 9–11: *He had discovered . . . many like it.* Yeats was aware of Greek discoveries from his reading of Duhem and Burnet. See Burnet's account of

Diogenes of Apollonia: 'The earth itself is round, that is to say, it is a disc; for the language of the doxographers does not point to the spherical form' (p. 365). The theory of the plurality of worlds is also given in accounts of Anaximander (p. 64), Anaximenes (p. 82), Anaxagoras (p. 295), and Leukippos (p. 358). Furthermore, as Yeats read in Duhem, Aristarchus of Samothrace was one among several early figures of astronomy to endorse the heliocentric theory (I, 418–23).

186, 13–19: *he may be stirred . . . to human weakness.* Cf. *EI* 436: 'Our moral indignation, our uniform law, perhaps even our public spirit, may come from the Christian conviction that the soul has but one life to find or lose salvation in: the Asiatic courtesy from the conviction that there are many lives.'

186, 19–23: *It is even . . . mankind is forbidden.* Yeats is here contrasting the Greek daimon with the Christian angel (which, etymologically, means *messenger*). The source for his view of the Greek daimon is not to be limited but includes especially Plutarch's *Moralia*. This contrast serves as one example of the numerous sets of parallels and contrasts which Yeats attempts to establish between various cultures (see p. 195 for a further reference to angels).

186–7, 35f: *He was love itself . . . that He died.* The contrast between love (an antithetical emotion) and pity (a primary emotion) is frequently made in the AS. The distinction is most forceful in a discussion of Judas and Christ (26 Jan 1918) which is important to an understanding of Yeats's *Calvary*: Christ's pity is 'an objective realisation of a collective despair'; Judas, 'the creative genius only', 'does not pity' (cf. *VPl* 789–91). See also *VB* 41, *L* 876, and n. to p. 111, 17.

187, 23: *Roman decay . . . to A.D. 250.* This date is close to the one (248 A.D.) which Gibbon cites as the turning-point for the worse in Roman history (Ch. VII). At this place an early manuscript is headed: 'Phases 2 to 7. A.D. 100 to A.D. 300'.

187, 24–7: *Roman Sculpture . . . the Christian era.* See Mrs Strong, *Roman Sculpture*, p. 10, where she declares that Roman art 'only becomes of paramount importance in the historic chain in the second century after Christ'. A long entry in one of the notebooks containing records of Sleeps cites Mrs Strong's *Roman Sculpture*. Speaking of P 27 ('always the union with external strength'), Yeats observed: 'I do not feel that very old people were creative—I have seen something like them though [with] less kindness in roman faces in the procession, perhaps of the altar of peace in Mrs Strongs book—but their culture is subjective. Will the second master (from 16, 17 or 18) find among such his disciples, & use their objective method as Christ when he personified himself in Judas used the subjective classical method.'

187, 27–34: *It even made . . . its final phase.* This passage, through the end of the paragraph, forms another of Yeats's cultural motifs or contrasts, centering upon the artistic depiction of eyes, parallel to the one on spirits (p. 186). Cf. Yeats's 'The Statues', l. 20.

188, 13: *riders upon the Parthenon*. At least as early as 1906, Yeats spoke of 'the young horsemen on the Parthenon' (*El* 292). And he had surely read Pater's observation in the essay on 'Winckelmann' in *The Renaissance*: 'If a single product only of Hellenic art were to be saved in the wreck of all beside, one might choose perhaps from the "beautiful multitude" of the Panathenaic frieze, that line of youths on horseback, with their level glances, their proud, patient lips, their chastened reins, their whole bodies in exquisite service' (p. 181).

188, 22–6: *sculptors seeking . . . most scrupulous realism*. Cf. Elie Fauré, *Ancient Art*, the first volume of his *History of Art* (Yeats owned a copy): 'Sarcophagi and statues were made in advance: the orator dressed in his toga, the general in his cuirass, the tribune, the quaestor, the consul, the senator, or the imperator, could be supplied at any time. The body was interchangeable. The head was screwed on to the shoulders' (pp. 284–5).

188, 26–33: *When I think . . . and vision alike*. This passage carries forward the motif of eyes (see p. 187, 27–34); cf. 'Lapis Lazuli', l. 56.

188, 34: *Meanwhile the irrational force*. At this point the manuscript has a division: 'Phases 8 & 9. A D 300 to 450'. A revised typescript is changed to 'Phase 8. A D 325 to 395'.

188, 35–6: *"The Babe, the Babe, is born"*. From Blake's 'The Mental Traveller', l. 95 (Keynes, 427).

189, 2–3: *the tables that move or resound with raps*. Yeats was primarily interested in the study of the mental rather than the physical phenomena of spiritualism, but he attended many seances in which the medium communicated by means of raps on the table, and he had read such books as Lodge's *Raymond*, which discuss the phenomenon (see n. to p. 240, 32–3).

189, 4–12: *All about it . . . their physical superiority*. Cf. Holmes, *The Age of Justinian and Theodora*, describing the Roman Empire under Anastasius: 'In earlier times a Roman proconsul in his spacious province was almost an independent potentate during his term of office, the head alike of the civil and military power. But in the new dispensation no man was intrusted with such plenary authority, and each contracted province was ruled by a purely civil administrator, whilst the local army obeyed a different master. For fuller security, each of these in turn was dependent on a higher civil or military officer, to whom was delegated the collective control of a number of his subordinates. Again a shift of authority was made, and the reins of government were delivered into fewer hands, until, at the head of the system, the source of all power, stood the Emperor himself' (I, 332). That the Romans adapted their own deities to fit and coalesce with those of Greece (the great cultural influence) is a commonplace.

189, 12–18: *All is rigid . . . . that of Constantine.* See Gibbon: 'Since the time of the Peloponnesian and Punic wars, the sphere of action had not been· enlarged; and the science of naval architecture appears to have declined. . . . The principles of maritime tactics had not undergone any change since the time of Thucydides; a squadron of galleys still advanced in a crescent. . . . Steel and iron were still the common instruments of destruction and safety; and the helmets, cuirasses, and shields of the tenth century did not, either in form or substance, essentially differ from those which had covered the companions of Alexander or Achilles' (VI, 92–4).

189, 20–3: *The athlete . . . has not changed.* Here Yeats carries forward the theme of the athlete. Cf. p. 184, 30–4.

189, 30: *Ammonius Sacca.* Ammonius, Alexandrian philosopher and teacher of Plotinus, is usually considered the founder of Neoplatonism; his second name literally indicates that he had been a sack-carrier.

189, 31: *Origen.* One of the most learned of the early church fathers, Origen studied under Clement of Alexandria and knew thoroughly the pagan Platonic philosophy, probably a point of attraction to Yeats. In 1928 he wrote that Origen was the only 'Father of the Church . . . I have read or rather dipped into' (*L* 734).

190, 1: *puts the Cross . . . of his soldiers.* Constantine I defeated Maximian, one of his many contenders for the throne, at the battle of the Milvian Bridge near Rome (A.D. 312); shortly before this battle, Constantine supposedly had his vision of the flaming cross in the sky ('*In hoc signo*', etc.). Beginning with an empire divided between East and West, he eventually became sole emperor and placed his capital at Constantinople, establishing Christianity as the state religion in 324. For use of the cross, see Gibbon, II, 299.

190, 2–3: *makes the bit . . . the True Cross.* St. Gregory of Tours asserted that two of the nails with which Christ was crucified were used to make a bit for the bridle of Constantine's horse, while a third adorned his statue.

190, 5–6: *Seeing that Constantine . . . upon his deathbed.* While Constantine had turned the Empire towards Christianity earlier, he did not receive full conversion until his death (see Gibbon, II, 289).

190, 6–7: *half statesman, half thaumaturgist.* Like Gibbon (II, 305–6), Yeats stressed that the conversion was partly genuine and partly political: 'In an age of religious fervour, the most artful statesmen are observed to feel some part of the enthusiasm which they inspire.'

190, 13: *"that fabulous formless darkness"*: Ellmann (*The Identity of Yeats*, 262) and Jeffares suggest that this phrase came from Proclus, 'whom Yeats read in Thomas Taylor's translation' of *The Six Books of Proclus . . . on the Theology of Plato* (1816) (*CCP* 291). According to E. R. Dodds, however, the Greek conception of the Church as 'a fabulous and formless darkness mastering the loveliness of the world' came from Eunapius's *Vita Maximi* (see *Select Passages Illustrating Neoplatonism*, 8). Yeats repeated the phrase in *E* 377 and alluded to it in the opening song from *The Resurrection* (*VPl* 902), also published as one of 'Two Songs from a Play' (*VP* 437). Yeats follows the wording in Dodds.

190, 19–21: *I have not . . . Phases 9, 10 and 11*. At this point the manuscript contains a heading for Phases 10 through 16, A.D. 450 to 600, changed in a revised typescript to Phases 9 to 21, A.D. 395 to 830. Despite Yeats's avowal in the manuscript that he was 'too ignorant to do more than comment here & there', he had studied Byzantine history in W. G. Holmes, O. M. Dalton, Mrs Arthur Strong, Gibbon, the *Encyclopaedia Britannica*, and the *Cambridge Mediaeval History* (see Jeffares, *CCP* 252). Several strongly anti-Christian passages of the manuscript and revised typescript were softened or omitted from *VA*.

190, 24–5: *"approximately correct" . . . for suggestion only*. This passage is both a testimony to Yeats's genuine belief in his Instructors and also an indication of his occasional embarrassment at the data supplied by them.

190, 35–6: *before Justinian opened . . . Academy of Plato*. Justinian opened St Sophia at Christmas 537 and closed the Academy of Plato at Athens in 529.

191, 7: *flexible presence . . . perfect human body*. Like Byzantium generally, this sentence suggests Unity of Being. Cf. pp. 18, 28, 71.

191, 13: *spoke to the multitude and the few alike*. Perhaps Yeats had in mind a famous passage from Gregory Nyssen's 'Oratio de deitate Filii et Spiritus Sancti': 'This city [Constantinople] . . . is full of mechanics and slaves, who are all of them profound theologians, and preach in the shops and in the streets. If you desire a man to change a piece of silver, he informs you wherein the Son differs from the Father; if you ask the price of a loaf, you are told, by way of reply, that the Son is inferior to the Father; and if you inquire whether the bath is ready, the answer is, that the Son was made out of nothing.' Yeats would have found this passage quoted in Gibbon (III, 142–3), in Holmes (I, 280n), and possibly in Hegel's *The Philosophy of History* (III, iii, 3, p. 339).

191, 27–30: *The ascetic . . . midst of cornfields*. As Yeats could have learned explicitly from articles on asceticism in *EB* or *ERE*, the word *ascetic* implies practice and was once referred to the discipline of the Greek athlete. An exact reference to the ascetic as 'God's athlete' in Alexandria has not been found, but cf. a book Yeats read, Hannay's *Spirit and Origin of Christian Monasticism*: [in Eusebius] 'there is mention of Apphianus, an "athlete of piety". . . , that is to say, an ascetic. This metaphorical use of the word athlete to denote an ascetic striver after perfection probably had its origin in St. Paul's writings. It is common in the accounts of the fourth-century Egyptian hermits' (p. 81). See also Hannay, *The Wisdom of the Desert*, 21 and 143. The conjunction of athlete and ascetic is another of Yeats's attempts to relate different cultures (cf. n. to p. 186, 19–23).

192, 5: *"The Holy Wisdom"*. A literal translation of the name of the cathedral in Constantinople, Hagia Sophia. Yeats liked the phrase (see *EI* 431).

192, 7: *Rome and Sicily*. Rephrased in *VB* 280 to 'Ravenne or in Sicily'.

192, 12–13: *these walls with . . . green and gold*. The reference is to mosaics, in which Yeats delighted (see 'Sailing to Byzantium', stanza III).

192, 17–29: *Recent criticism distinguishes . . . themselves living creatures*. Yeats is probably thinking rather generally of Strzygowski's *Origin of Christian Church Art* and of the summary of Strzygowski's position (among others) in Dalton's *Byzantine Art and Archaeology*, pp. 14–15, Chs. 12–13, and pp. 700–3. Loosely, the contrast is between representational (Western) art on the one hand and non-representational or merely decorative (Eastern) on the other.

192–3, 32f: *Strzygowski thinks . . . contained nothing human*. See Ch. VI, especially p. 149, of Strzygowski's *Origin of Christian Church Art*. The question is Christological, dealing with the nature(s) of Christ and also with artistic representations (leading into the Byzantine problem of Iconoclasm, mentioned below). Yeats projected the differing views of Christ's nature in *The Resurrection*, which he began to write in 1925.

193, 12–14: *and no analogy . . . can help*. Yeats reminds the reader that in his System the Age of Phidias, the Age of Justinian, and the Renaissance are parallel as fifteenth Phases of millennial eras; however, because alternate eras are parallel, those after Phidias and after the Renaissance—though parallel to one another—are both antithetical and therefore not parallel to the era after Justinian (a primary cycle).

193, 16–21: *If Strzygowski is . . . spiritual and abstract*. Yeats evidently has in mind no particular passage of Strzygowski, but see Ch. VI, 'Non-Representational Church Art, and the Subsequent Anti-Representational Movement'. Generally, Yeats again contrasts the Greek, Western, and Representational against the Persian, Eastern, and Non-Representational.

193, 21–5: *Destruction . . . had been strongest*. Prohibition of image worship was first required by Leo III in 726. Monophysitism holds that Christ has but a single nature, the view of the Coptic but not of the Roman Catholic Church. Yeats's source for the rather obscure Bishop Xenaias is unknown (though he is mentioned in Ch. 47 of Gibbon). At this point the manuscript contains the heading 'Phases 16 to 25. A D 600 to 900', changed in the revised typescript to 'Phase 22. A D 630 to 900'.

193–4, 35f: *In Western Europe . . . the image makers*. Born and educated in Ireland, Erigena had a special appeal for Yeats. In the manuscript Yeats wrote: 'Am I right . . . in considering Johannes Scotus Erigena not as the first schoolman but the last Christianized Greek philosopher, & so a necessary part of the final abstraction & synthesis before submission to fate. My friend Larminie, an Irish poet & folklorist translated him & has left the manuscript in a Dublin library where now one friend & now another turns its pages &

perhaps tells me what he finds.' Erigena, who went to the court of Charlemagne about 847, translated from Greek into Latin the works of Dionysius the Areopagite and wrote, Yeats said, 'an exposition of the orders of the angels according to the vision of Dionysius' (i.e., *The Celestial Hierarchy*). Michael III (839–67) was the 'last iconoclastic Emperor', but the one most responsible for spreading the Neoplatonic doctrines of Dionysius was Michael II (Duhem, III, 44–7).

194, 6–10: *I notice too . . . with political events*. That is, in the years of 830 to 900. Cf. p. 183, 29–32.

194, 11: *Then follows . . . in the last quarter*. At this point the manuscript contains the heading 'Phases 26, 27, 28. A D 900 to A D 1000'; 'or 1100' was crossed out.

194, 32: *a romanesque stream . . . and beast images*. Possibly this passage is influenced by Strzygowski's assessment of Northern and Eastern influence on Romanesque. He traces East Iranian motifs on one church—'the vine-scroll with enclosed animals'—and asserts that comparison 'reveals that fusion of Iranian and Greek art which succeeded the displacement of the latter in late Roman times, and led gradually to the development of Byzantine art on the Mediterranean, of "Romanesque" in the West, and to the complete triumph of Iranian art in the world of Islam' (pp. 112–14).

195, 17–22: *Three Roman Courtesans . . . their own bodies*. See Gibbon: 'The influence of two sister prostitutes, Marozia and Theodora, was founded on their wealth and beauty, their political and amorous intrigues: the most strenuous of their lovers were rewarded with the Roman mitre, and their reign may have suggested to the darker ages the fable of a female pope. The bastard son, the grandson, and the great-grandson of Marozia, a rare genealogy, were seated in the chair of St. Peter; and it was at the age of nineteen years that the second of these became the head of the Latin Church.' Bury adds only that 'John XI was the legitimate, not the bastard, son of Marozia; and it is not true that her great-grandson was Pope' (V, 297–8 and n. 140a).

196, 9–12: *Two thousand years before . . . to his fate*. Christ's predecessor, 2000 years before, had been antithetical. Because his concern had been for the individual and for the beauty of sensuous experience, he had 'mourned over the shortness of time'. So too will the New Messiah, Christ's successor.

196, 13–17: *Full moon over . . . at His side*. Yeats suggests, somewhat anachronistically, that the Norman cathedrals at Cefalù (begun 1131) and Monreale in Sicily (founded 1174) in their Byzantine majesty reflect the old, trans-human religion; though borrowed from a very Humanistic outlook, the Greek image now reborn as Humanism gradually transcends religious monotheism once more. See E 317 and Dalton, *Byzantine Art and Archaeology*, 410–12.

196: *A.D. 1050 TO THE PRESENT DAY*. The typescript heading is 'Phases 1–8. A D 100 to 1220'. Yeats changed 1000 to 1050 in GP.

196, note: The AS and Sleeps contain numerous references to and definitions of sequence and recurrence.

197, 2–6: *A certain Byzantine . . . "of her body"*. Henn's claim (*The Lonely Tower*, 148–9) that Yeats derived this story from Helen Waddell's *The Desert Fathers* (1936) is obviously wrong. But he is correct that Yeats's source is 'The Life of St Pelagia the Harlot'. The tale is widespread, found in such collections as *The Legenda Aurea*; Yeats demonstrated familiarity with a similar tale in *The Celtic Twilight* (M 49). See also E 291.

197, 7–11: *Arabian Nights . . . "of our Faith"*. From 'The Tale of the Girl Heart's-Miracle, Lieutenant of the Birds' in *The Book of the Thousand Nights and One Night*, IV, 440: 'The Khalîfah rose from his throne and, going down to the girl, very gently returned the little silk veil to her face, as a sign that she belonged to his harîm, and that the fairness of her had already retreated into the mystery of our Faith'. See n. to p. xiii, 3.

197, 18–32: *When Merlin . . . "dead or alive"*. Yeats's source was William Wells Newell's *King Arthur and the Round Table*: '. . . Merlin told the story, how a prince of that land had loved a damsel, and . . . had wrought a chamber in the rock . . . where with great joy their lives had been spent; and how both had died on the same day, and had been laid in the chamber, where they had received their delight.' Merlin showed Niniene a cavern 'adorned with mosaic of gold'. Merlin alone could raise the rock; under it were the lovers, 'wrapped in winding sheets of white samite'. Niniene said Merlin was truly enchanted: 'Thus speaking, she bade her attendants take him by the hand and feet, lay him in the tomb, and replace the stone. This with pains they accomplished; and the damsel by her spells, sealed the slab, so that it might never be removed; from that hour, none beheld Merlin, dead or alive' (II, 137–9). See also EI 484–5.

197, 32–4: *Throughout the German . . . Mass nor Baptism*. See Wolfram von Eschenbach, *Parzival: A Knightly Epic*: 'It is very curious that, constantly as Baptism is insisted upon as essential to salvation, the equal necessity for the Second Great Sacrament of the Faith is passed over. It is perfectly true that Wolfram's knights attend Mass, and that Mass is apparently celebrated with regularity, but here their obligation seems to end; never once do we hear of one of his knights communicating, even Gamuret, when dying, though he receives absolution, does not receive the viaticum . . .' (II, 196–7). Yeats knew this book well.

197–8, 35f: *Parsifal in such a trance . . . sword and shield*. For the now-familiar Wagnerian *liebestod* see Eschenbach, especially Vol. I, in which Kunnewaare's squire comes on Parzival and sees 'A helmet all battle-dinted, and a shield which yet traces bore / Of many a bitter conflict that was foughten for lady fair' (I, 161, ll. 70–1). The theme receives extended treatment in Vol. I, 160–70.

198, 21–5: *I do not see . . . communal freedom*. The *locus classicus* of Gothic freedom is 'The Nature of Gothic' in John Ruskin's *The Stones of Venice*, but Blake in many places and Morris in *Gothic Architecture* similarly suggest that Gothic architecture allowed the workmen to cooperate yet express their individual views freely; Yeats's own description of Byzantium (p. 191) expresses a similar viewpoint. At about this place in the manuscript Yeats made the next division: 'A D 1220 to 1300'.

198, 27–9: *St. Bernard . . . in that light*. In Ch. 12 of *Apologia ad Gulielmum sancti Theodorici abbatem*, St Bernard of Clairvaux expresses his opposition to the aesthetic tendencies of the Clunaic monks and town bishops; he describes Romanesque sculpture, which he considers unworthy of monks.

198, 29–30: *I think of . . . mathematical form*. Villard de Honnecourt was a thirteenth-century French architect whose book of drawings (Paris, 1858) contains sketches of machines, architecture, monuments, human figures, and animals; sometimes geometrical figures are superimposed on humans, animals, etc.

198, 31: *Mont St. Michel*. Yeats visited Maud Gonne in Normandy in May 1910, and they saw Mont-Saint-Michel together; see *Mem* 249 and *EI* 340. He had also read Henry Adams' *Mont-Saint-Michel and Chartres* (1904): 'I have read all Adams and find an exact agreement even to dates with my own "law of history"' (*L* 666).

199, 11: *Dominican*. The Dominican order was founded by St Dominic in 1216.

199, 16–17: *the Cathedrals and the Philosophy of St. Thomas*. A stray observation at the end of a notebook devoted chiefly to Sleeps makes clear that Yeats's source was Adams: '1150 to 1250 given by Henry Adams as time when man most felt his unity in a unified world. He seeks its expression "in Amiens Cathedral & the Works of Thomas Aquinas"' (see *The Education of Henry Adams*, 435).

199, 27–8: *the achievement of Constantine*. This passage is also indebted to Adams. In the notebook cited above Yeats wrote: '325 A D (8) to 400. Constantine (Constantinople founder 324 (Gibbon) Henry Adams takes 310 as significant date "cross took the place of the legions" coming of unification by Church).' Cf. Adams: '. . . the nearest approach to the revolution of 1900 was that of 310, when Constantine set up the Cross' (*The Education*, 383).

200, 1: *The Period from 1300 to 1380*. In the manuscript this division was headed 'A D 1300 to 1450'.

200, 26–7: *Masaccio . . . like Aubrey Beardsley*. Masaccio (whose real name was Tommaso Guidi) is usually said to have lived from 1401 to 1428, one more year than Yeats allows him; Yeats's friend Beardsley lived from 1872 to 1898.

In the manuscript Yeats reminded himself with a note to 'Bring in Masaccio, Donatello, Villon, Chaucer. Compare them together & contrast with Giotto & Dante & his school which like the art of the Cathedrals still celebrates Christendom mainly. We lost ourselves in Christendom when we share their thoughts, but from Masaccio on it is Christendom & ourselves—then Christendom goes'. Another of the notes in the notebook of Sleeps cited above is pertinent: '1250 to 1300. Apparently struggle to establish Kingly Power. Note C[haucer's] allusions to King Arthur.' According to an entry for 20 Dec 1920, Yeats had confirmation of his theory about this period from one of his Controls: 'was looking through some books of history to find why 1250 is the start of 50 years attributed to phase 8 & wondered if St. Clovis consolidation of his power was typical of his period when George heard a voice say "Percys Reliques Vol III poem 5". This proved to be a ballad about Arthurs struggle with his barons & so confirmed the opinion.' (The poem cited is 'The Legend of King Arthur'.) This notebook contains several entries about and diagrams of the cones. On 9 Dec 1920, 'George began cones' and that night '"Carmichael" [the Control] gave confirmation of classification of division of historical cones being divided among phases as covens are divided'.

200, 30–4: *naked young man . . . by their suffering*. Yeats alludes to three of Masaccio's paintings, all in the Brancacci Chapel in Florence: *The Baptism of the Neophytes*, *The Rendering of the Tribute Money*, and *The Expulsion of Adam and Eve*.

200–1, 36f: *suffering of Villon . . . the close of an era?* For significant comments by Yeats on François Villon, see *L* 583 and *A* 273 and 310. After a life of crime and several narrow escapes from death sentences, Villon disappeared, leaving his partly serious, partly humorous *Testament*, or will.

201, 23: *man descends the hill*. Immediately preceding these words, in a much-revised typescript, Yeats finally crossed out a sentence which related the gyres to Irish art: 'The work of the iconoclasts and of those unknown artists who covered the books of Durrow and of Kells with whirling gyres and forms that represent no living thing is reversed.'

201, 30–1: *Donatello . . . astringency of Myron*. For Myron, Yeats may be thinking of comments in Furtwängler's *Masterpieces of Greek Sculpture*, 181; later he observes that 'the ancient orators name him among the last masters of the severe style' (p. 182).

202, 1–10: *I do not myself . . . Paganism and Christianity*. Attempting to compare two periods of two thousand years each, Yeats finds that at the 22nd Phase of the earlier—500 B.C.—and of the later—1500 A.D.—there were 'renaissances' in which man turned from religious to secular values; a second comparison is the movement, in the earlier cycle, to Plato, and, in the later, to the Platonic Academy of Cosimo de' Medici headed by Marsilio Ficino. On p. 181, Yeats even views Greek art on the basis of a Pre-

Raphaelite model, equating Phidias and Raphael and finding earlier art preferable.

202, 10–12: *This reconciliation . . . "a vestibule of Christianity"*. Having learned from Blake that 'All Religions Are One' (Keynes, 98) and from Thomas Taylor that the Greeks had taught the Christians, Yeats sought 'the reconciliation of Paganism and Christianity'. His thinking was no doubt indebted to numerous sources. See in particular F. X. Kraus in 'Medicean Rome'; after describing the work of Julius II, Kraus adds: 'Not only Judaism, but also Graeco-Roman paganism, is an antechamber to Christianity . . .' (*Cambridge Modern History*, II, 6). Yeats follows Kraus in attributing 'this fusion . . . of Christian emotionalism and Pagan intellect' to the Florentine Academy: 'Ficino, before old age brings caution, speaks of Christianity as a development of Greek Philosophy' (rejected typescript).

202, 16–18: *"perfectly proportioned human body" . . . unity of being symbolised*. See note to p. 18, 12–13.

202, 18–22: *The ascetic, who . . . become the first*. See n. to p. 191, 27–30, as well as 'Long-legged Fly', ll. 21–2. For purposes of comparison and contrast, Yeats suggests that the Renaissance (part of a distinctively Christian two-thousand-year cycle) has as its emblem of Unity of Being not the athlete of the preceding pagan cycle but rather the Edenic Adam, prelapsarian and without the disabilities entailed by the Fall. In artistic terms, the distinctive image of the epoch is Adam as defined by Michelangelo on the roof of the Sistine Chapel: see also 'Under Ben Bulben', ll. 45–52.

202, 28–9: *Had some Florentine . . . Cave of the Nymphs?* Yeats knew Porphyry's *De Antro Nympharum* in Thomas Taylor's translation, *On the Cave of Nymphs* (reprinted by the TS in 1895) as early as 1901, when Part II of 'The Philosophy of Shelley's Poetry' was written (*EI* 82). In both manuscript and typescript of *VA* Yeats attributed the book to Proclus.

202–3, 32f: *his "Nativity" in the National Gallery*. The *Mystic Nativity* of Sandro Botticelli is described in *The National Gallery Illustrated General Catalogue*, which translates the inscription given in Yeats's note as follows: 'I Sandro painted this picture at the end of the year 1500 (?) in the troubles of Italy in the half time according to the 11th chapter of S. John in the second woe of the Apocalypse in the loosing of the devil for three and a half years then he will be chained in the 12th chapter and we shall see clearly (?) [damage] as in this picture' (p. 62; insertions are from the *Catalogue*). The Yeatses visited Capri in 1925, where he finished this section and the Dedication (see pp. xiii and 215).

203, 5: *Botticelli, Crivelli, Mantegna*. At this point both manuscript and typescript contain a heading: 'A D 1450 to 1500'.

203, 8–10: *kind of bodily . . . "of the soul"*. Also cited in *Mem* 157. The quotation came from *The Book of the Courtier*: 'Therefore Beautie is the true monument and spoile of the victory of the soule, when she with heavenly influence beareth rule over martiall and grosse nature, and with her light overcometh the darkenesse of the bodie' (p. 311 in Hoby's translation).

203, 21–3: *Phase 15 past . . . rush and storm*. Because 'the Fifteenth Phase of the Moon is supernatural', it is passed over with no comment about its significance in history. At about this point in the manuscript Yeats indicated the next division, then marked through the following: '1500 to —— Phases 16, 17, & 18'. The terminal date was to have been 1640.

204, 1: *the forms . . . awaken sexual desire*. See 'Under Ben Bulben', ll. 45–52: passages such as this are reminiscent of the theory of eugenics Yeats developed in *On the Boiler* (1939).

204, 6–8: *Raphael . . . Sistine Chapel*. Pope Julius II directed the work of Michelangelo in the Sistine Chapel and that of Raphael in the Camera della Segnatura, also in the Vatican.

205, 15–19: *The two elements . . . an artificial ornament*. Milton's 'On the Morning of Christ's Nativity' (1629) stresses the silencing of the pagan oracles at the coming of Christ; though Milton was vastly learned in classical mythology, he ultimately condemned it (see e.g., *Paradise Lost*, VII, 1–39).

206, 8: *The beginning of the gyre*. In a rejected section of the manuscript the next division (for Phases 19, 20, and 21) came at this point: '1640 to 1880'. The revised version begins: 'I find among my "documents" the statement that the nineteenth lunar phase "did all the harm".'

207, 6–7: *the Shades . . . "contrive a body"*. In *Religio Medici*, Browne declares his firm belief in the reality of witches: 'I could believe that Spirits use with man the act of carnality, and that in both sexes; I conceive they may assume, steal, or contrive a body, wherein there may be action enough to content decrepit lust, or passion to satisfie more active veneries . . .' (I, xxx). Yeats alludes to the same passage in *E* 69; also see *M* 267.

207, 18: *"Emotion of Sanctity"*. Yeats is apparently quoting his Instructors. Compare, for example, a sentence from the CF: 'The highest form of soul is sanctity of intellect.' The manuscript draft casts some light on Yeats's meaning: 'Before the self passes from 22 it is said to attain what is called "the emotion of sanctity" & this emotion is described as contact with the life beyond death.' He defined sanctity as the 'renunciation of personal salvation'.

207, 27–8: *"they do not . . . own happiness"*. Yeats is paraphrasing the third line of the second stanza of Verlaine's 'Claire de la lune': 'Ils n'ont pas l'air de croire à leur bonheur. . .'. This poem and its collection, *Fêtes galantes*, are indebted to the painting of Jean Antoine Watteau: see Verlaine's *Oeuvres completes*, I, 26–7, and Antoine Adam, *The Art of Paul Verlaine*, 79–81. Yeats had met Verlaine: see *A* 341–2, *EI* 270–2, and *UP*, I, 397–9.

207, 32–4: *Reynolds had nothing . . . and modern curiosity*. By tradition, Yeats would have been prepared to dislike the work of Sir Joshua Reynolds, whose stay in Rome (1749–52) emphasized study of Raphael and Michelangelo; like his idol Blake, who made extensive adverse marginal comments upon the *Discourses* of Reynolds, Yeats would have reacted strongly against Reynolds' aesthetic and epistemological theories.

207, 35–6: *Lady Besborough's rises before me.* Probably Yeats is thinking of Reynolds' portrait of Henrietta Frances, Viscountess Duncannon and Countess of Bessborough, which is reproduced in a book Yeats read and liked: Granville Leveson Gower, *Private Correspondence, 1781–1821*, I, facing p. 88 (see *L* 678–9).

208, 3: *the village providence.* Cf. *E* 277: 'To Balzac indeed it [the solution of the social question] was but personal charity, the village providence of the eighteenth century . . .'. See also *L* 233n and *UP*, I, 334–5; Yeats apparently refers to the eighteenth-century idea of benevolence.

208, 4–7: *Goethe . . . in his old age.* Cf. *Mem* 158: 'Faust in the end was only able to reclaim land like some officer of the Agricultural Board.' Yeats claims that the Faust of Part II (written in Goethe's elder years) expresses nothing more than a good-hearted eighteenth-century desire as did the hero of Samuel Richardson's novel *Sir Charles Grandison* (1753). Similarly, in his later years, Voltaire defended the cause of religious freedom.

208, 23–4: *The French portrait painter Ricard.* Louis Gustave Ricard was best known for his still life and portraits in the classical manner. See *UP* II, 385n.

208, 26–32: *Charles Ricketts . . . full of eagles.* Ricketts founded the Vale Press and, with Charles Shannon, edited *The Dial* (1897–9). Some measure of his effect on Yeats may be gained from numerous letters of Yeats's and from *Self-Portrait Taken from the Letters and Journals of Charles Ricketts, R.A.* Ricketts illustrated the first edition of Oscar Wilde's poem 'The Sphinx' (1894). Yeats included 'the Charles Ricketts of *The Danaides*, and of the earlier illustrations of *The Sphinx*', among 'the great myth-makers and mask-makers' (*A* 550). Ricketts made three wood engravings for Sturge Moore's *Danaë: A Poem* (London: Hacon and Ricketts, 1903).

208–9, 34f: *Dickens was able . . . began to write.* See Yeats's essay on 'The Modern Novel' (*Irish Times*, 9 Nov 1923), quoted in Torchiana's *W. B. Yeats and Georgian Ireland*:

> Sometime in the middle of the eighteenth century there came into the faces of women, as painted by the great painters, an exquisite subtlety which they called a mark of high breeding. They got it in Gainsborough and one or two painters before him, and they got it in the first volume of "Sir Charles Grandison." Then he found the same thing in the novels of Jane Austen. These novels were simply a description, an elaboration, of the pursuit of good breeding—that was to say, a quality which only a few happily nurtured people ever found. Then he did not find that pursuit again until they got to the writings of Henry James.

He discovered, about five years ago, the particular devil that spoiled that celebrated quality in literature. "Pickwick" was the devil. In "Pickwick" the qualities celebrated were qualities any man could possess: good humour, a certain amount of openness of heart, kindness—qualities which everyman might hope to possess; they were democratic qualities. It gave them the kind of sculpture they saw in Dublin, like Tom Moore and the statue in Leinster Lawn. That smile of vacuous benevolence came out of "Pickwick." (p. 212)

See also the passage in *Lady Gregory's Journals* (p. 262) cited by Torchiana. In the AS for 24 Jan 1918, the Control suggests that Dickens's art, like that of Keats, Wordsworth, and Tennyson, is 'incomplete' because of 'love of world'—that is, 'material good'.

209, 11–12: *They were begotten in the Sistine Chapel.* See pp. 204–5.

209, 13–16: *yet Nietzsche . . . the next gyre.* See n. to p. 176, 1–3. In 1902, Yeats wrote excitedly to Lady Gregory about his discovery of 'that strong enchanter': 'I have read him so much that I have made my eyes bad again. . . . Nietzsche completes Blake and has the same roots' (*L* 379).

209, 17: *The period from 1875 to 1927*. First headed 'Phases 22 to 28' in the manuscript, then 'Phase 22' in a much-revised typescript, this section gave Yeats considerable trouble. 'Phases 8 and 22 are themselves phases of abstraction', he wrote, 'and are preceded and followed by abstraction; phase 8 was preceded by the Schoolmen, followed and accompanied by legalists and inquisitors, and phase 22 was preceded by the popularisation of physical, social and economic science and has been accompanied and will be followed by economic and social movements, movements of applied science in some sense or other of an abstract and probably violent kind.'

209, 30: *Hodos Chameliontos*. See n. to p. xi, 14–15. A rejected sentence states explicitly what Yeats intended to suggest: 'The 22 phase . . . is that of our own epoch—Hodos Chameliontos—as I called it in "The Trembling of the Veil"—and when it has passed away it will be recognized as that wherein broke all that concerns the common thought.'

210, 14–15: *I think of recent mathematical research*. Perhaps Yeats is thinking of *The Education of Henry Adams*, Ch. 31, in which the work of various modern scientists and mathematicians ('since Bacon and Newton') suggested to Adams that 'Chaos was the law of nature; Order was the dream of man' (p. 451); the older, unified scientific view had passed into a scientific relativism in which—as Poincaré had said—Euclidean geometry is not necessarily more true but only more convenient than non-Euclidean types (p. 455). From this point to the end of the paragraph Yeats made numerous revisions in the typescript. One surprising rejection is the following sentence: 'Then, as in the novels, the painting, the philosophy, nature suddenly appears in all her violence and terror returns, so to the individual comes the sense of fate which Dostoievsky calls "Gods Love" a knowledge that the world cannot be changed, a doubt of general progress.'

210, 17–18: *I recognise . . . a new dimension.* Possibly Yeats was thinking of a passage in Bolton's *Introduction to the Theory of Relativity* in which he dealt with "The Limited Universe": 'The curvature of space, or of the aether, leads to the conclusion that any region, if sufficiently extended, may eventually bend round into itself, and thus that the universe of experience may be limited' (pp. 170–1). The new dimension would be time.

210, 26: *possibility of science.* At this point, 'Dove or Swan' breaks off in *VB*, perhaps because the prophetic commentary of the remainder was too personal and conjectural.

210, 27–30: *It is said . . . wars of Alexander.* At the current P 22 some parallel to Alexander the Great must be expected, but Yeats offers no hint of the identity of the parallel. At P 22 always occurs a defeat for such previous conquerors as Alexander: some unidentified hero should now be conquered. A revision in the typescript reads: 'We have in our great war repeated the wars of Alexander.'

210, 31: *I discover already the first phase.* Both manuscript and revised typescript contain a heading here: 'Phases 23–24–25'. At this point Yeats omitted approximately 700 words and drastically revised the remainder of Book III, perhaps because the prophetic tone was too personal or too harsh. A few lines will illustrate:

> Hitherto I have described the past or but the near future, but now I must plunge beyond the reach of the senses. . . . Though I think that I too can describe the mind of the future, I must, if I am not to make the description so abstract that it is unintelligible, imagine circumstance which will be at least as unlike the actual future as the water clock [of Alexandria] is unlike my watch. Then too I am *Antithetical* in nature, and find it impossible to see the joy that belongs to *Primary* Phases. . . . Men will come to eat and house and travel in much the same way and in one another's company, . . . as difference of wealth lessens, all grows uniform and rigid, leisure for that aimless brooding which is the manure at the tree's root will cease, and . . . men's minds grow barren through hatred. . . . I find in my documents a statement that population will decline through pestilence and famine and accidents of nature, and I interpret these words as said of what a follower of Heraclitus said of Epochs, and I understand that to mean that man's desire for truth and for the good, as we call his desire to be fated, has now been fulfilled according to the measure of his capacity, and that change must come from without . . . , and it will be in all things the opposite of that which founded Christianity. . . . I see it rise among all those who have resisted or suffered defeat in the defence of some rank, physiological or intellectual, which has sought its own expression, and as

satisfying all who thirst for whatever if hierarchical or distinguished. . . .
Young and confident they must be, because what we symbolise as the
Tower inherits all that once belonged to the Catacombs, and violent
because those spiritual energies that have come down from the Sermon
on the Mount, through the impersonality of our empirical sciences are
now exhausted.

211, 8–9: *"cacophony of sardine tins"*. Yeats recalls a comment quoted in
Richard Aldington's review of Lewis's *"Timon of Athens"*. *A Portfolio of Drawings*: 'One youthful person assured me that Mr. Lewis' work was a "cacophony of sardine-tins" ' (*The Egoist*, I, No. 1 [Jan 1914], 11). See also *L* 608.

211, 9–11: *those marble eggs . . . of M. Brancussi*. See Ezra Pound, 'Brancusi'
(1921), *Literary Essays of Ezra Pound*: '. . . Brancusi has set out on the mad-
deningly more difficult exploration toward getting all the forms into one
form. . . . Plate No. 5 shows what looks like an egg. . . . I don't know by what
metaphorical periphrase I am to convey the relation of these ovoids to
Brancusi's other sculputure. As an interim label, one might consider them
as master-keys to the world of form—not "his" world of form, but as much
as he has found of "the" world of form' (pp. 442–3).

211, 15: *Meštrović*. The Yugoslav sculptor Ivan Meštrović was condemned
by Wyndham Lewis in *Blast*, No. 2; see William C. Wees, *Vorticism and the
English Avant-Garde*, 203. In 1928, when Yeats reported to the Irish Senate
on the work of his Committee to choose coins for the Free State, he spoke of
Mestrovic, who received an invitation too late to compete: 'Carl Milles and
Ivan Mestrovic, sculptor and medallist, have expressed in their work a
violent rhythmical energy unknown to past ages, and seem to many the
foremost sculptors of our day' (*SS* 163).

211, 21–5: *Rodin creating . . . said to Symons*. From about 1880 until 1910,
Auguste Rodin was at work on the bronze doors entitled *Porte de l'enfer*. For
Rodin's remark to Symons, see *Studies in Seven Arts*: 'Every figure that
Rodin has created is in the act of striving towards something: a passion, an
idea, a state of being, quiescence itself. His "Gates of Hell" are a headlong
flight and falling, in which all the agonies of a place of torment, which is
Baudelaire's rather than Dante's, swarm in actual movement' (p. 15).

211–12, 35f: *a lunatic among . . . Ulysses' wandering*. The lunatic suffering from
delirium is the protagonist of Pirandello's *Henry IV* (1922); the man fishing
behind the gas works is a symbolic figure in Eliot's *The Waste Land* (1922)
(see ll. 187–90); the single Dublin day of Ulysses's wandering is that of
Leopold Bloom in Joyce's *Ulysses* (1922).

212, 25–7: *Peguy . . . would have it*. Charles Péguy, a French patriot, publisher, poet, and devoted Roman Catholic, was the author of the play *Le
Mystère de la charité de Jeanne d'Arc* (1910), which was read to Yeats by Iseult
Gonne (see *E* 264 and *M* 368). But Yeats admitted that he found Péguy
unappealing unless he imagined himself a peasant (*YM* 26).

212, 28: *Claudel in his "L'Otage"*. Paul Claudel was a French Roman Catholic poet, essayist, and dramatist, whom Yeats had studied with the aid of Iseult Gonne in 1917 (*M* 368). Also in 1917, he had seen Claudel's modern miracle play *L'Annonce faite à Marie* in English translation (*L* 626). Though Yeats declared that Péguy's 'Christianity is of course for us impossible' (*YM* 26), he found valuable examples for the young in 'these men in whom an intellectual patriotism is not distinct from religion' (*E* 265), and used his connections to find productions for the dramatic works of Claudel and Péguy.

213, 9–10: *"Sibyll . . . I would die"*. This is a translation of the passage from Ch. 48 of the *Satyricon* of Petronius Arbiter used as epigraph to Eliot's *The Waste Land*.

213, 14–17: *Constrained . . . evil or good*. From 'The Double Vision of Michael Robartes', ll. 9–12. GP also included ll. 13–16. The poem grew out of a session of AS on 7 Jan 1919. Directed by the Control, George drew a full-page symbolic sketch of the rock of Cashel and the ruined church in County Tipperary. When Yeats asked 'Why have you made this drawing?', the Control informed him that he should study the 'historical & spiritual past' and suggested Cashel by means of broken phrases about the church, the castle on the hill, and Cormac, who is also referred to in the Script of 8 Jan.

213, 28–9: *mathematical Babylonian starlight*. See n. to p. 181, 8–9.

213, 35: *Milton's human form divine*. See Blake's 'The Divine Image' and 'A Divine Image' (Keynes, 117 and 221; see also pp. 521, 651, and 755). Dürer and Milton were not included in the typescript, which read: '"The human form Divine" as Blake understood those words . . .'.

214, 1: *Nietzsche's superman*. See p. 5, 1–3 and n. to p. 61, P 12. Nietzsche had a place in the System from an early date. In the AS of 1 Jan 1918, Yeats was informed by the Control that Nietzsche and his most famous superman, Zarathustra, should be placed in Phases 12 and 18. Informed also that the man at P 12 has the 'wisdom of intellect' rather than instinct, Yeats asked, 'Why wisdom of head at 12?' He learned that 'it is generally a propaganda, a will to change forms of existing thought; a metaphysician is a nihilist not a creator'.

214, 2: *"a tongue that's dead"*. Yeats recalls incorrectly a phrase from the last line of Coventry Patmore's 'Dead Language'. Yeats had read Patmore as early as 1909 (*LNI* 72, *E* 199, *Mem* 190, *L* 526).

214, 8: *Leda, War and Love*. The typescript closed Book III with a sentence about Leda intended to remind the reader of the poem, which served as epigraph: 'I remember that from the eggs of Leda, which symbolise perhaps the birth of the Greek civilisation, were born not only Helen, but Castor and Pollux.' Cf. n. to p. 175, 28–30, and *VB* 268.

214, 9: *biography changed into a myth*. Cf. p. 185, 28: at the coming of Christ 'the myth becomes a biography'.

214, 9–13: *Above all I imagine . . . dying the other's life*. This sentence was substituted for a much stronger one in GP: 'Victory bringing control of the world's surface must come to those who have made life a preparation for war and so established life in the terror and sweetness of solitude that every act of war is an act of creation and the solitude of each the tribal solitude.' Cf. p. 130, 9.

215, 1: *Plotinus' ecstasy*. Yeats was recalling a well-known statement by Porphyry that Plotinus had four times achieved 'conjunction' with deity and that he had composed his books from the contemplation and intuition of divinity (see, for example, Thomas Taylor's *Philosophical and Mathematical Commentaries*. . . II, 235). In a rejected Epilogue 'To Vestigia' Yeats suggested that he and his fellow students in the GD 'came to think that nothing mattered but to return to the one', an experience 'so rare' that 'it came . . . to Plotinus but once'.

215, 5–6: *as when Athena took Achilles*. Cf. 'The Phases of the Moon' (p. 5, 1) and *The Resurrection* (VPl 917). Yeats made the same reference in the rejected Epilogue: '& think it is best to be like Plotinus, it may be better to see ghosts than to chop logic. What else did Achilles when Athena came behind & took him by the yellow hair.' See also *Iliad*, I, 197.

215, 6–8: *Men will no longer . . . in all its forms*. This sentence was inserted in GP.

215: *Finished at Capri, February, 1925*. Because of high blood pressure, Yeats went on tour in late 1924: to Sicily in Nov, to Capri in Feb 1925, and then to Rome (Jeffares, *WBY* 237); he cannot have spent much time in Capri: 'a week of beautiful weather in Capri following two months of clear skies in Sicily' (Hone, 367).

217: *THE GATES OF PLUTO*. 'The most unfinished of my five books' as Yeats recalled (VB 23), it is nevertheless the most exciting because it attempts to explain 'the way of the soul' with which *VA* is primarily concerned. In a clearly unsatisfactory manuscript fragment (dated 'about 1929' by Curtis Bradford) of 'The Soul in Judgment' (*VB*, Book III), Yeats wrote the following 'footnote':

> "A Vision" contains a long section called the "Gates of Pluto" that now fills me with shame. It contains a series of unrelated statements & inaccurate deductions from the symbols & were little but hurried notes recorded for my own future guidance. I have not the knowledge at present to do more than substitute for that section the few following paragraphs.

Twelve pages later Yeats concluded in the same vein with a much-revised section which may be reconstructed as follows:

I have written fragmentary paragraphs wishing to postpone almost all that concerns the state of dead till greater knowledge comes or greater strength for a meditation that is followed by sleepless nights, and because the resolution to discuss [certain facts of my life] in their detail events [in my own life] that I had sooner consider my secret is still lacking [I told enough, for any] a mind that will follow the patterns in meditation can find [all] what I know & more perhaps, & will at any rate forgive me [that] if I [take up return] go back to what I suppose is my true business [of verse writing] before I am too old to [turn a rhyme round a verse] shape [?] a rhyme. [Words in brackets were crossed through by Yeats.]

219: *THE FOOL BY THE ROADSIDE*: ll. 18–29 of 'The Hero, the Girl, and the Fool'. This poem was first printed as 'Cuchulain the Girl and the Fool' in *Seven Poems and a Fragment* (1922), where the Fool's remarks were preceded by seventeen lines of discussion between Hero and Girl (possibly Yeats and Iseult Gonne; see *CCP* 307). Omission of this introductory section emphasizes the wise Fool's vision of unified truth beyond the grave.

219, 1: *When my days that have*. Cf. *VP* 449: 'When all works that have'.

220: *THE GREAT WHEEL*. In an early typescript this section was entitled 'Death, the Soul, and the Life after Death'.

220, 1–3: *Cornelius Agrippa . . . "people of dreams"*. Yeats liked to quote from the work of the Renaissance Cabalist Heinrich Cornelius Agrippa von Nettesheim, whose *Three Books of Occult Philosophy or Magic* he must have read in the 1651 translation because it is the only one which includes Book III (Dume 119–20). In 'Swedenborg, Mediums and the Desolate Places' Yeats quoted the sentence from Orpheus in a longer passage (from Ch. xli) suggesting that after death spirits must atone for their unexpiated sins imaginatively, in dreams (See *VBWI* 332 or *E* 63, also *VB* 23).

220, 6: *The Daimon. Daimon* is one of Yeats's more confusing terms, partly because he changed its meaning over a period of time. Before *PASL* (1918), he used the etymologically identical term demon in the common sense of a malevolent spirit (e.g. *M* 284–6). By the time he came to write *PASL*, he had a better though confused idea of the Daimon, apparently derived from Heraclitus (*M* 336; cf. Burnet, *EGP* 270) and more especially from Plutarch's essay 'On the Genius of Socrates' (*E* 59, *M* 335). Yet the term's ambiguity had certainly been known to him earlier than *PASL*; among his sources were the GD (see n. to p. 27, 14–15, for his GD motto *Demon Est Deus Inversus*); probably Plato's *Phaedo* and *Ion* (*Mem* 84 and cf. *UP*, I, 399); Blake (Keynes, 98); Henry More (*M* 351), Philoponus (*E* 62); Cornelius Agrippa (*M* 354). As Moore observes, Yeats here distinguishes Daimon from permanent self or Ghostly Self (*The Unicorn* 287–8, 368). Apparently Yeats wished to distinguish between (1) a permanent self, called either Ghostly Self (p. 221) or permanent Daimon (*M* 335, n1), a portion of the self which would—as all occultists and romantics believed—be above time and change; and (2) the spirit of an illustrious dead man who would form a temporary union with that incarnate spirit most nearly his opposite. See also Wilson, *W. B. Yeats and Tradition*, 244–5.

220, 7–8: *Complementary Dream*. This significant phrase replaced 'correspondence and symbol' in PP. For further information, see the n. to p. 173, sec. XXI.

220, 18: *Thirteenth Cycle*. On 13 Aug 1920, in a long Sleep, the Control discussed the significance of this cycle or cone (sometimes confused) to men and Daimons: 'All Daimons are in 13th Cone, but there are also perfected men there from whom they differ in form & colour. He [Dionertes] would not however at the time go into these forms & colours, as he did not want to get into symbolism.' The symbolism of colours had been explained to Yeats on 28 May: 'Purple signifies for the living the Anima Mundi, & for the Spirits, the 13th cycle which is their Anima Mundi. Our Anima Mundi seems to include the thought & emotion of the world, everything that is *not Fate*. We inquire in purple about interdependence of Spirits & Guides—Spirits & Angels—.' The symbolism of blue, yellow, and rose is also explained.

221, 2–3: *she . . . can communicate with one living man*. On 13 Aug 1920 the Control explained: 'The Daimons were more powerful than the men, but had only one man each (human being) in their charge though they might interest many in carrying out that charge, while the perfected men were in relation each with many men.'

221, 8–10: *though when we consider . . . and she the Sun*. These lines were inserted in GP.

221, 11: *Ghostly Self*. Yeats explained in the CF: 'G.S. does not incarnate but has a correspondential relation with spirit which does.' From the Ghostly Self 'issues either the illumination or the slow spiritual vision. . . . The knowledge is always there.'

221, 33: *"consumes itself away"*. See n. to p. 134, 23–4 and to p. 141, 14.

222: *THE VISION OF THE BLOOD KINDRED*. In a note to 'The Second Coming' (wr. Jan 1919) Yeats said that according to the Judwalis subjective man 'has a moment of revelation immediately after death, a revelation which they describe as his being carried into the presence of all his dead kindred' (*VP* 824). Beginning with this section, the remainder of *VA* is greatly indebted to experimental techniques and publications of the SPR and its members, many of whom were acquaintances of Yeats. Of these, perhaps the most important was Frederic W. H. Myers, a founding member of the SPR, whose monumental *Human Personality and Its Survival of Bodily Death*, 2 vols (1903), Yeats surely read with interest—in particular 'Introduction' (Ch. I), 'Phantasms of the Dead' (Ch. VII), 'Trance, Possession, and Ecstasy' (Ch. IX), and 'Epilogue' (Ch. X).

222: *THE SEPARATION OF THE FOUR PRINCIPLES*. This entire section is essentially a rephrasing of the record of a Sleep for 31 May 1920 'dictated by Dionertes'. Informing Yeats that he is dead and surrounded by 'all those of blood relationship in past lives', Dionertes speaks of the significance of ritual and the flowers on his grave, which enable him 'to enter into the thoughts of the living to discover my own identity'. He then describes with illustrations, 'the separation':

> When I recognize myself, I leave the grave, rising up from my body but horizontally for that is the position of complete subjectivity—When I have regained all knowledge of self necessary I shall separate into the four particles thus

The illustration which follows is well described by Yeats in *VA*. The horizontal form of the 'husk' with 'head' and 'feet' marked is at the bottom. Floating horizontally above it, the 'PB rises from generation'. At the head of the husk the 'celestial body rises from feet', and at the feet of the husk the 'spirit rises from head'. Above the Passionate Body is a sketch of a star to suggest 'light so brilliant that the eye looking upon it sees radiating lines issuing from it'. Calling this explanation 'all the dull preliminary', Dionertes promised to 'go on tomorrow'. In the description of the horizontally floating spirit Yeats may be recalling one of Blake's striking illustrations to Robert Blair's *The Grave* entitled *The Soul hovering over the Body reluctantly parting with Life*. Note that 'Principles' are called 'Particles' at this date (also on 19 June).

222, 22: *Record*. See n. to p. 250, sec. XIV.

223, 9–19: *The meditation may be moved . . . illuminate the flower*. In the record of a sleep for 31 May 1920 the Control explained the significance of both ritual and flower:

> The ritual is a discipline of thought, and intensifies thought. The flowers set on my grave are the only light I see. It is through these flowers that I am first able to enter into the thoughts of the living to discover my own identity. Until I have found that I may not leave my body.

224, 2–14: *Mr. Davies' verse*. The quotation is from W. H. Davies' 'Body and Spirit' (ll. 13–24). Yeats printed seven of Davies' poems in *OBMV*, perhaps after consultation with Dorothy Wellesley (*L* 859).

224: *THE RETURN*. The record of a Sleep dated 18 Oct 1921 explains this and related terms succinctly: 'In the teachings the spirit is prepared for the other world; in the Return he studies his past life in relation to that world; in the Shiftings he gets rid of all memory of that life though not necessarily of still earlier lives.' Yeats had explored the subject in the AS on 10 June 1918, asking the Control if he should 'tell us about the return before you speak of the shiftings'. He learned that 'the return is simply a reliving of life in the moral sphere', 'a replica of old life' rather than 'a new free will'. But Yeats remained uncertain: in the record of a Sleep for 20 Apr 1921, he asked himself, 'Is state called "return" an error. I divine only

1. Dreaming back = return of gyre from center or movement of ego from 15 to 22
2. Shifting = gyre in $\diamondsuit$ or movement of ego from 22 to 8
3. State before birth = movement of gyre to center or movement of ego from 8 to 15'.

224: *note.* A late notebook (the first date is 4 Jy 1923) contains considerable discussion of *Waking State* and *Sleeping State*. It also contains a list of the characteristics of 'Teacher & Victim' in two parallel columns—Thin Man—Fat Man, Frail soul—Strong soul, vision is emotional—vision is intellectual, etc. This note was inserted in GP on 28 Sept 1925.

225, 17–28: *One remembers . . . her agony.* Yeats is summarizing the Noh play *Motomezuka*, which he must have read in M. C. Stopes, *Plays of Old Japan: The No* (1912). Yeats also summarized the work in *VPl* 777 and *E* 65–6. An entry in a late notebook refers to this play (see n. to p. 226, 13).

226, 13: *phantasmagoria.* Seldom used in *VA*, this word appealed to Yeats and became more important in later writing. He made some effort to define the term in a notebook entry for 27 Nov [1923]:

Phantasmogaria is result of Principles foreseeing their future in Shiftings. Phantasmogaria antithesis of [dreaming back] dreamed even as Shiftings is of the life. We are not solitary in phantasmogaria—see Japanese story of two lovers—but only meet those who are in [dreaming back] dreamed event. [Words in brackets crossed through by Yeats.]

226, 28–30: *as when the mother . . . comes to her orphan children.* This visitation of the spirit of a dead mother belongs to a category described by Myers as 'visions of consolation' (II, 374). His appendix to Ch. VII, consisting chiefly of extracts from the *Proceedings of the SPR*, records many visions in several categories.

226, 30–2: *"The Divine . . . the Lonely".* While Yeats obviously depended upon the famous close of Plotinus's *Enneads*, VI, ix, 11, his translation here most closely corresponds to two lines of 'The Dark Angel' by his friend Lionel Johnson: 'Lonely, unto the Lone, I go; / Divine, to the Divinity' (see *YGD* 183, n22). In 1909 when Yeats used the famous image as an epigraph to his brief introduction to the Cuala Press edition of Synge's *Poems and Translations*, he either forgot that Plotinus was the source or did not know: '"The Lonely returns to the Lonely; the Divine to the Divinity." *Proclus*' (*EI* 306). The typescript also mistakenly cites Proclus.

227, 15: *some knot.* In the early AS Yeats used the word 'knot' as a synonym for 'complex'. Thinking primarily of Iseult Gonne's mental unrest, he asked the Control to 'give Freudian analysis' in defining a complex, and was informed that 'A complex is any knot of hidden thought lying in the subconscious that originates in some passion or violent emotion.' Continuing to question, Yeats was told that 'knots are action impressed forcibly on man from outside . . . , the effect of Karma as implied in each incarnation' (AS, 22 Nov 1917). That is, he recorded in the CF, '"Knots" are part of astral body, that is of P.A.M. [Personal Anima Mundi]. Every knot creates an abnormality.' In the record of a Sleep dated 3 Nov [1923] Yeats wrote: 'In dreaming back, after period of dreaming back, comes waking state & in this those who have been part of events that brought about "knot" now dreamed back display in a kind of "marionette show" the covens of that knot & event.'

228, 5–8: *The Spirit can even consult books . . . the dream.* The theory that a spirit may direct a living person to books and records is a commonplace in the history of spiritualistic experiment. Yeats and Lady Gregory sought to find a codicil to Hugh Lane's will by this method; during the Sleeps of 1920 and later Yeats was directed by the Control to several literary works which had some bearing on the subject being explored: Morris's *The Sundering Flood* (on 6 Oct), Blake's 'The Mental Traveller' (on 26 Nov), Percy's *Reliques* (on 20 Dec), and Browning's *Poems* (on 22 Aug 1923).

228, 18–19: *a spirit may experience . . . pleasure and pain.* During the Sleep of 30 Aug 1920 after 'speaking for some time', the Control was interrupted first by a bird's cry and then by the clock striking 12; he informed Yeats that 'sounds like that are sometimes a great pleasure to us'.

228, 22–3: *the Cambridge Platonist . . . "A Body Politick".* Yeats is quoting from Joseph Glanvill's *Saducismus Triumphatus* (1681): 'But I attempt something more particularly, in order to which I must premise, that the *Devil* is a name for a *Body Politick*, in which there are very different *Orders* and *Degrees of Spirits*' (p. 89). Yeats quotes the same phrase in 'Witches and Wizards and Irish Folk-lore' (*VBWI* 304) and cited Glanvill's book in the notes (p. 339).

228–9, 31f: *a number of minds held together by a stream of thought.* This concept, related to Yeats's theory of the Anima Mundi, runs throughout the *VA* documents. A series of Sleeps (19–29 Nov 1920) was devoted primarily to what the Control called the 'Group Mind', which he explained on 19 Nov:

> Trains of thought are however continuous taken from one mind to be finished by another according to a different process. A & perhaps many others start some train of thought, the "Group Mind" takes this thought & chooses the daimon of B who is given the train of thought to finish. Only thus does an Era come to an end. The group mind is conscious but has no subconsciousness.

The following night the Control explained further that

> the group minds are created by a small number of living personalities
> who may, or may not, know each other. . . . Each group mind has a
> correspondence with one of the eight triads [of related Phases]. . . . In
> addition to these group minds there are family minds, rare minds, etc.

On 26 Nov Yeats inquired 'if the interaction of groups & group minds' might
not be described as a 'psychic reacter'; he also asked and received permission 'to alter terminology. "Coven" for Group, "Unicorn" for Group
Mind'. See also n. to p. 171, 23.

229, 7–8: *the Spheres of Spiritualism*. Theosophists, for example, taught that
after death man had to pass through a series of purgatorial planes or
spheres. Yeats was influenced by but did not accept the concept of the seven
planes described in many books he knew. The most important were those of
Madame Blavatsky and A. P. Sinnett, whose *Growth of the Soul* (1896), in a
chapter on 'The Seven Principles', is most detailed: 'Each plane of Nature,
as we ascend through the refinements of the Cosmos, is constituted of
different orders of matter, each order being subject to modifications on its
own plane' (p. 156). One of Yeats's notebooks lists an order of the Seven
Planes to fit the System: see n. to p. 35 on Planes and Colours.

229, 8: *the Faery Hostings of Irish folk-lore*. Yeats had studied Irish folklore
during much of his mature creative life, as his two essays in *VBWI* suggest.
On at least three separate occasions in the AS he sought to relate this
knowledge to theories incorporated into the system of *VA*. On 6 Jan 1918, he
asked 'To what extent is soul at 15 analogous to man or woman of faery?'
The Control replied: 'The people of faery, the souls at one & fifteen and all
other legendary states are but parts of one truth. The truth is in all but in
some more concealed by fable & dreams than in others.' On 12 February
Yeats was informed that 'The faeries in Ireland' are 'p[assionate] b[ody]
images, pictures, sometimes a spirit from 15'. On 11 Apr, he asked if the
faeries are 'the old inhabitants in a distinct race', and was told, 'Yes, on side
of movement up or down' (of the spiral of history, presumably).

229: *THE SHIFTINGS*. On 12 June 1918 Yeats asked the Control, 'Why do
you use the word shiftings in the plural?' He replied, 'Because it may be one
spiral movement or two'. Yeats then asked several questions about the
spiral, the cone, and the movement of the shiftings in the funnel, etc. See
also n. to p. 224, sec. V.

229, 24–5: *I will quote certain passages*. Yeats is quoting almost exactly but
combining two or three answers in the AS for 10 June 1918. Long and
important (52 questions by Yeats), this Script is concerned with The Return,
Shiftings, Teachings, and Dreaming Back. The first of a series of questions
dealing with the nature of good and evil will suggest what Yeats was concerned with: 'In so far as one knew good one becomes good, in so far as one

knew evil one sees, feels, & tastes & smells evil?' The Control answered 'No, No. In so far as knowledge of evil is attained one becomes good but in as far as one is good the visible world becomes evil because it is no virtue to be good knowing no evil & it is no sin to be evil knowing no good.' Three questions later Yeats poses a very perceptive paradox for which the Control has no satisfactory answer: 'If the result has been to become good why is return in the visible world made evil?' See n. to p. 78, 18.

230, 12: *Yet there is no suffering*. In the AS for 12 June 1918, Yeats asked, 'Is there no place of punishment?' and was informed: 'No, . . . the punishment is during the funnell dreaming back.' That is, all souls *'are equal'*.

230, 18: *Evil is that which opposes Unity of Being*. Evil is manifested in abstraction (see p. 231, 26). 'Abstraction', Yeats wrote in one notebook, 'is that quality in every phase which impedes unity of being (& ? of world)'. Abstraction is worst at Phases 5, 6, 7, 22, 24, and 25.

231, 16–17: *no Teacher but the Celestial Body*. The following discussion of the Celestial Body is related to questions by Yeats and the opening statement of the Control in AS for 12 June 1918: 'The celestial body is that portion of the divine influx which is separable and divisible.' Yeats asked, 'Separable from the soul & divisible in itself?' and learned that it is 'Separable & divisible from the entire into the particular & then incarnate'.

232, 11–13: *Sometimes these messengers make their presence known by some scent or sound or sight*. In the notebooks of the Sleeps for 1920 and 1921 there are numerous accounts of such spiritual manifestations. On 5 Sept 1921 Yeats recorded the explanation of a favourite Control:

> We spoke with Dionertes of the different fragrances which come in the house from time to time. He said "one has to distinguish between the fragrances which emphasize the thought & are from the record & those which are created by various spirits as their sign or in the process of materialising". He himself has no special fragrance associated with him as he is in the Shiftings & therefore is a kind of telephone between us & a central group of spirits. He can however create fragrances for special purposes.

After some further discussion of fragrances which various orders of spirits might use, Dionertes 'told us that all future communicators . . . would have an individual scent, but that he would not tell us what these scents would be or with whom connected'. Yeats added a note 'about apparitions seen by Interpreter during William Michael's illness 2 days after birth. . . . The Interpreter gave them forms from her subconscious.' Yeats had been warned of his son's illness by 'the burnt feather smell in the passage' (12 Sept). By means of smells and sounds he and George also received warnings of the machinations of various Frustrators. One who betrayed himself (on 7 October) by the smell of burnt candle grease was 'antithetical to the system'. 'A bringer of unbalance in a high imaginative sense' (he belonged to P 28), he had sought to disrupt through 'an attack upon the instruments of communication'. By means of bells or faint whistles, the Controls sometimes indicated people 'they did not like' (F. P. Sturm) or did like (W. F. Stead); and they informed Yeats about methods of protection (especially the burning of incense) against evil spirits and influences. Months later (in May 1922) he learned that scents were sometimes associated with symbols (violets for the tower) and myths (incense for the voyage).

233, 4: *As all strong passions are said.* One typescript reads: 'In all great passions there is said in our documents to be "cruelty and deceit" which require expiation.'

233, 31–2: *One woman has endured.* Preceding this sentence, one typescript reads: 'The documents give examples.'

234, 2–3: *"physical emotional and spiritual, and not moral purgation".* This is quoted from the answer to the first question for the AS of 27 Jy 1919: 'When you say "victim for" do you mean "sufferer instead of"?' Yeats asked; the Control replied: 'No—I mean a definite physical emotional & spiritual—*not moral*—purgation—process undergone by living person for another *not* in place of that other.'

234, 25–6: *A purgation completed brings good fortune.* Yeats's conclusion from a question and answer in AS for 27 Jy 1919: 'What effect on ghostly self is the purgation?' 'Brings nearer to body'.

235: *BEATITUDE.* This and its companion term, Beatific Vision, are vague and ambiguous, in part because Yeats felt incapable of satisfactory explanation (see pp. xii, 20–3). There are no entries for Beatitude in the CF and only two for Beatific Vision. In both of these he struggled rather unsuccessfully for clarity through codification: 'Solar Vision followed by Lunar V. bring B.V.' He spoke of achieving Beatific Vision in three stages as they are perceived on the cones: Solar—15, Lunar—1, B.V.—Apex (Center); Solar understanding of Head, Lunar of Heart, Beatific of Soul; Solar is knowledge of third, Lunar is vision of third, B.V. is experience of third; Solar is Chance, Lunar is Choice, B.V. is ('neither Choice nor Chance'). 'B.V. come[s] from being free of Hatred'; and Hatred, which 'is always subjective self deception', may be purged 'by revelation of motives . . . your own' (Yeats's ellipsis).

235, 1–2: *for a short time "out of space and time".* At this point in the typescript Yeats wrote: 'I quote the documents without claiming to understand except vaguely that it [the Spirit] is free from limitation to any one place or to that which decides life, cause, operation and effect past present and future. . .'.

235, 27–9: *which is indeed a Vision . . . all cycles end.* This clause was added in GP; 'when all cycles end' first read 'at the consummation of time', then 'end of all our cycles'.

235–6, 30f: *Mr. Yeats . . . Owen Aherne*. This parenthetical paragraph was inserted in a much-revised page of the typescript.

236, 1–3: *"The Celestial Body . . . is revealed"*. This quotation is a condensation of four questions and answers in the AS of 1 Feb 1918. Yeats: 'Why is the spirit body the immortal body?' Control: 'Because the celestial body is the cloak of Christ.' Yeats: 'Is the spirit in a sense the body of Christ, it being the immortal body?' Control: 'It is difficult to say yes because a million years hence may have been mere [?] mists but if you believe the symbolism & not the historical Christ it is so'. Yeats: 'PB dark, CB light, spirit flash between?' Control: 'Yes the CB is the divine cloak lent to all egos, at the consummation the cloak falls away for the Christ is revealed.' Yeats: 'The spirit then is the true ego?' Control: 'Yes but it is throughout incarnation subsidiary to CB, it cannot act alone, that is most unfortunate.' Yeats is thinking of Christ as the archetypal Avatar or New Messiah who appears at the beginning of every 2000-year cycle. 'In dreaming back of CB' events recur 'correspondentially', not exactly, 'as in life'.

236, 4: *Bardesan's "Hymn of the Soul"*. Bardesanes was a Syrian Gnostic; in 1926, Yeats wrote to Sturm: 'I wonder if you know the works of Bardeasan [sic]. He described—they say—a monthly re-creation of all things by a configuration of the ☉ & ☽. And that excites me especially as he had my doctrine of Mask & Celestial Body—see his Hymn of the Soul—' (Taylor, *FPS* 90). See also *VPl* 807. Yeats's source was F. C. Burkitt's *Early Eastern Christianity* (1904); see *A* 379.

236, 23: *in Cancer—the Cup of Lethe*. Cf. Yeat's note to 'Among School Children' (*VP* 828).

236, note. Inserted in GP on 26 Sept 1925.

237–8, 33f: *Robartes told me . . . Owen Aherne*. This parenthetical paragraph was inserted after the typescript, which contains part of the material in a different form. The most important addition is the term *Frustrators*. Although Frustrators (usually Leo Africanus) occasionally interfered with the AS, they do not become important until the period of the Sleeps, especially in 1921. The accounts of five Sleeps 7, 14, 16, 18, 19 Oct) are devoted primarily to a discussion between the Control (Dionertes) and Yeats (but recorded by George) of the nature and danger of two kinds of Frustrators. The first 'are connected with . . . the covens'; they 'are from those phases' opposite to 14, 15, and 16—that is, 28, 1, and 2. The second is a 'personal frustrator' and 'may come from any phase because it may act upon any emotion'. Since 'the personal frustrators never make their presence known by evil odours', it is clear that Yeats is primarily concerned with the other kind—'the Frustrators of System'. When Yeats pressed the Control 'as to their nature he said that to go into that was to explore the nature of evil which he could not do till conditions were better'. Yeats was told that 'old age & sickness & death are not the result of frustration', that 'the Frustrators are the antithesis to all that lives', and that prayer 'would help against frustration'. They led Yeats to numerous incorrect conclusions (often marked 'wrong') in the AS, and they deceived him into failing to record Sleeps for an extended period (15 Jan—2 May 1922). Fortunately, as Yeats recorded several times, they announced their presence by foul odours (see n. to p. 232, 11–13 and *VB* 16). But Yeats was familiar with the phenomenon of odours as concomitants of seances long before the experiences recorded in the AS and Sleeps, as a note in *VBWI* makes clear: 'The sudden filling of the air by a sweet odour is a common event of the Séance room. It is mentioned several times in the "Diary" of Stainton Moses' (p. 365).

Yeats was also familiar with such spiritualistic folklore as that in the account of the two Arab women. According to the typescript, he was well acquainted with the 'two girls', 'one of a family where is second sight, and the other second sighted herself'. 'May I not discover in these mice the shape-changers approaching birth and mastered by the thought of feebleness and littleness', he asked, then added: 'Legend is full of such apparitions before a child is born.'

238, 20–2: *and it must be . . . the Blood Kindred.* This sentence replaced the following in GP: 'which is to birth what the *Vision of the Blood Kindred* is to death, and a foreknowledge of the future life, and a knowledge that such a life is the desire of the soul'.

238, 29–30: *"Mind moved but . . . a spinning top".* Slightly misquoted ('but' for 'yet') from Yeats's 'The Double Vision of Michael Robartes' ll. 43–4. See n. to 'COMPLEMENTARY DREAMS', p. 173.

239, 3–4: *The Going Forth . . . generations.* Yeats is recalling the end of Blake's *Jerusalem*, especially these lines:

> Human Forms identified, living, going forth & returning wearied
> Into the Planetary lives of Years, Months, Days & Hours.
>
> (Keynes, 747)

'Going and returning are the typical eternal motions', Yeats explained; 'they characterize the visionary forms of eternal life' (*WWB*, I, 401).

239: *FUNERAL IMAGES, WORKS OF ART, AND THE DEAD.* This section is not in the typescript, but Yeats preserved a manuscript draft which includes some material not in the final version.

239, 16–19: *A Brahmin once . . . life to come.* Also related in *M* 355.

239, 25–7: *A king in Heroditus* [sic]*. . . make her choice.* The king in Herodotus's *History* was Periander of Corinth (Book V, Ch. 92). In the manuscript Yeats said, 'I cannot find the exact reference'. See *E* 69n and *M* 98.

239–40, 27f: *A man once told in my hearing.* Originally Yeats wrote 'A man once told a society I belong to. . .', referring most likely to the SPR, to which he belonged at this time.

240, 18–22: *and Strzygowski thinks . . . "of departed spirits".* Strzygowski writes that the concept of Hvarenah 'is connected with the cult of the dead, representing the might and majesty of departed spirits. Hvarenah is the power that makes running water gush from springs, plants sprout from the soil, winds blow the clouds, and men come to birth. It governs the courses of sun, moon, and stars' (p. 118). Strzygowski says nothing of the first landscape.

240, 25: *Christmas tree for . . . spirit children.* Yeats recalls two articles by R. H. Saunders: ' Story of a Christmas Tree; Children of Both Worlds', *Light*, XLIII, no. 2191 (6 Jan 1923), 7, and 'A Christmas Tree in the Spheres', *Light*, XLIV, no. 2243 (5 Jan 1924), 5. See also n. at end of p. 240.

240, 32–3: *One recognizes in . . . a venerable tradition.* Sir Oliver Lodge's *Raymond, or Life and Death with Examples of the Evidence for Survival of Memory and Affection After Death* (1916) is named after the author's son, killed in battle on 14 Sept 1915. Much of the book is a record of Lodge's communication with his dead son; Part III, entitled 'Life and Death', is Lodge's argument for 'belief in continued existence', communication of mind with mind, and related subjects. The discussion of the 'synthetic cigars' appears in the record of a sitting with a famous medium, Mrs Gladys O. Leonard, on 3 Dec 1915. Feda, her Control, was explaining life in the spirit world to Sir Oliver: 'A chap came over the other day who *would* have a cigar. "That's finished them," he thought. He means he thought they would never be able to provide that. But there are laboratories over here, and they manufacture all sorts of things in them. . . . It's not the same as on the earth plane, but they were able to manufacture what looked like a cigar.' Someone who smoked four of the synthetic cigars disliked them, 'and now he doesn't look at one'. Sir Oliver noted that 'some of this Feda talk is at least humorous' (p. 197). In the manuscript Yeats first wrote that the cigars had 'caused much amusement to readers of "Raymond"'.

240, 33: *a venerable tradition.* At this point the manuscript contains a sentence which refers to the kind of folk traditions recorded in *VBWI*: 'They [synthetic cigars] remind me of a Connemara grave yard where it is or was till lately the custom to lay full pipes upon the graves.'

241, 9–10: *"Kiss of Life" . . . "Kiss of Death".* Years later, in 1934, Yeats wrote about his poem 'He and She': 'When George spoke of Michael's preoccupation with Life as Anne's with death she may have subconsciously remembered that her spirits once spoke of the centric movement of phase 1 as the kiss of Life and the centric movement of phase 15 (full moon) as the kiss of Death' (*L* 829).

241, Note: *I may be mistaken . . . expiation described.* This sentence was added in GP.

242, 11: *Arcon.* Possibly Yeats was thinking of one definition of *Archon* given by the *OED*: 'A power subordinate to the Deity, held by Gnostics to have made the world'. On 27 Nov 1920 Yeats asked the Control 'if I might modify terminology & he accepted the following—Instead of Avatars, Arcons'. 'Such *Arcons* deal with form not wisdom' was added in GP.

242, 13–19: *made Emer say . . . "hearts are cold"*. With two minor alterations Yeats quotes from *The Only Jealousy of Emer* (ll. 213–17) as it appeared in *Plays and Controversies* (1923). Throughout most of the time during which the AS and Sleeps were being recorded, Yeats was preoccupied with *The Only Jealousy*, in which he, George, Maud, and Iseult were projected in the four main characters. In the AS of 20 Nov 1917 he was informed by the Control that 'there is a symbolism of the growth of the soul' in the Cuchulain plays. On 21 Dec in a long Script he learned that his 'own sin exactly correspond[s] to those of C[uchulain]' and that George (Emer), Iseult (Eithne), and Maud (Woman of the Sidhe) represent race, passion, and love in that order. On 7 Jan 1918 Yeats asked, 'Who will C love?' The Control replied, 'I cannot tell you till you know yourself and you do know I think but perhaps unconsciously.' When he asked if it were Emer, the Control did not reply. He had been told (on 6 Jan) that *The Only Jealousy* belonged to P 12, the heroic phase. The lines from the play were inserted after the typescript.

242, 22–34: *There is yet another expiation . . . time-less infinity*. This ambiguous passage appears to refer indirectly to Maud Gonne's refusal to marry Yeats. Although veiled, the corresponding passage in the typescript is clearer:

> There is the means of equilibrium, but not as yet equilibrium, marriage. The first denial of experience was the work of the spirit at Fifteen that imposed an image or fixed idea, and if this is to be marriage other spiritual beings must intervene, instruments of the *Ghostly Self*, for unlike the equilibrium which follows expiation for the dead man cannot will it.

A related sentence, crossed out in GP, is also illuminating: 'Upon the other hand a man out of phase may receive through some Spirit at Phase 1, not the "Kiss of Life" but a fixed idea, a perversion as it were of the "Kiss of Death," a cold obsession.' In both these passages concerning rejection of experience (i.e., exchanging the 'Kiss of Life' for a 'fixed idea'), Yeats almost certainly refers to Maud. In the AS of 6 Sept 1919 the Control described her as a 'tall woman' of 'fixed ideas', and Yeats noted in the CF that 'Killing PB makes spirit stronger (Hence M G's fixed idea)'. Directly related, of course, is the fact that Maud is represented as the Woman of the Sidhe who is strongly criticized in the speech by Emer (George) from *The Only Jealousy* (ll. 14–19; see n. to p. 242, 13–19). Also apropos is the substitution of the sentence ending 'time-less infinity' for a more obvious one in GP: 'The *Ghostly Self* upon the other hand, having desired experience in vain, ceases to expend itself, becomes as it were full and stationary.' Cf. also 'A Prayer for My Daughter', ll. 57–64. Maud had become the archetype of the 'fixed idea' and the 'cold obsession'.

242, 35: *this penury and this fullness.* Probably an allusion to Plato's myth in *Symposium*, secs. 202–5, and to Plotinus's commentary in *Enneads*, III, v, 7–9. Love's parents are Plenty and Poverty (variously translated); love is thus explained as the desire of deprived mortals for the transcendent.

243, 5–6: *Did Dante acquire in the Thebaid.* See n. to p. 186, 2.

243, 15–18: *my own Deirdre and Naisi . . . my "Hour Glass".* The final versions of *The Hour-Glass* were written while the AS was being recorded, and the title itself assumes an added dimension from the fact that the hour-glass is a geometric figure of symbolic significance often discussed in the Script. On 21 Dec 1921 Yeats alluded to the source of the play (Lady Wilde's short story called 'The Priest's Soul') in a note: 'Priest play reaction from Hawks.Well'. The priest is a primary man, Cuchulain is antithetical. On the same day, in a rejected question, Yeats asked the Control to give him 'a modern illustration of "priest play"'.

243, 32: *"There are crimes and crimes".* This play by August Strindberg was first produced in 1899; it was presented at the Abbey Theatre on 6 Mar 1913.

244, 12–15: *Was it at the Crucifixion . . . of Christendom.* As the great initiate, the First Master, or the Avatar, Christ is discussed many times in the AS, CF, and Sleeps. In a long and significant AS on 1 Jan 1918, the Control informed Yeats that 'time is God, space is Christ, eternity Holy Ghost'. Although the incarnate Christ is primary, the excarnate Christ is antithetical in the form of the Holy Ghost. The placement of Christ in various Phases is often confusing. As incarnate Messiah he is in P 15, as excarnate P 1: '1st Masters are objective because of the supernatural nature of 15 & 1 which have a subjective life separate from the objective world' (undated note, after Jan 1921). A few days later, in a dictated statement about the three Masters, Yeats said: 'As 1st Master was at 1, 15 was of great importance in his age' (9 Feb). In the CF he noted that 'Christ = 22 in certain relations' (see n. to p. 71, 16–21). That is, his combination of primary and antithetical characteristics varies at different points on the wheel: 'Christ at N objective in an objective cycle, . . . at W subjective in an objective cycle, . . . at S subjective in a subjective cycle, . . . at E objective in a subjective cycle.' On this date, 12 Dec 1920, the Control informed Yeats that 'he would not use that word [Christ] again'. Because Christ's life was archetypal, representing an entire cycle of history, Yeats asked the Control if he could 'place events of Christ's history on diagram of lunar phases'. The answer was 'yes—one nativity, first appearance as spiritual being in temple at 4, temptation on mountain 8, sermon on mount 11, crucifixion at one, vigil in garden 24, last supper 18, I cant remember 22 *later*, miracles all at 15' (2 Jan 1918). With one variation (last supper also at 15) this was recorded in a notebook containing numerous other lists, and is several times referred to elsewhere.

244–5, 21f: *No concrete image . . . the Celestial Body.* Phrasing and content of this passage are very close to those of the note published in 1921 to 'An

Image from a Past Life' (*VP* 821–3). Despite the deliberately misleading dates in this note (12 and 15 May 1917), it is based directly upon many experiences and much discussion recorded in the AS.

245, 19: *Celestial Body.* At this point in GP Yeats crossed out an extension of his sentence: 'or as it is sometimes called in the Rhythmical Body' (a term he apparently decided not to use).

245–6, 20f: *Robartes told me . . . outside the dream.* This parenthetical insert attributed to Owen Aherne has a complicated history. At one stage a much-expanded version (four typed pages) entitled 'Michael Robartes and the Judwali Doctor' was planned for the first section of Book IV. In fact, the Yeatses had themselves conducted the experiments described. As the doctor in the typescript said, 'I was always told Kusta-ben-Luka or his wife [i.e., Yeats and George] would come if we could find the right sleeper'. The doctor observed also that 'the sleeper, if it was the sleeper, had strange gifts of abstraction and arrangement, as though the mind had been purged of some gross element'. 'It was these conversations with a sleeping man', according to Aherne, 'that enabled Robartes to adapt the thought of Kusta-ben-Luka to modern necessities, and to find a European expression for the Arabian Law of history.' With slight variations George had actually experienced the sensations of the lapping cat, the mouth full of feathers, and others described in several Sleeps of 1920. On 30 Sept Yeats recorded (in George's handwriting) that the Control (Dionertes) 'was interrupted by George making a lapping sound. He said "She dreamed herself a cat, & that she is lapping up something from the floor". I said "What is to be done". He said "Pretend you are a dog". I could think of nothing better than to say "Bow wow" as one does to a child. To my surprise the Interpreter sprang away from me in great terror & lay panting for a long time after.' George had very similar experiences on several occasions; at another time she had hooted like an owl (Aherne recounted this in the typescript). The episode of the feathers was recorded on 26 Aug 1920. Conditions for the 'Sleep' had not been good because of George's 'turbulent dreams':

> The most persistent of these was that her mouth was full of feathers. I had to draw out the feathers; *one*, from the back of her throat. He [the Control] said that the cause of this was that some weeks ago I had spoken [he had] of M.G. [Maud Gonne] as a goose shedding feathers; & that every time now I mentioned 16 [Maud's Phase] that dream recurred.

On another occasion (10 September) George 'dreamt that her mouth was full of moss & kept trying to blow the moss out'.

246–7, 30f: *During the sleep . . . over human life.* This parenthetical paragraph is an extension of the one on pp. 245–6. A few lines near the end of the typescript are an excellent general description of the Yeatses' method:

He brought his suggestions to the sleeper that they might be rejected, accepted, or modified. When the voice itself took the initiative the method of exposition was always that adopted according to legend by Kusta-ben-Luka's wife. A series of statements would be made that could not be reconciled with the system as a whole until that particular subject was exhausted.

248, 1–5: *it has long been known . . . can achieve*. See Yeats's 'Preliminary Examination of the Script of E[lizabeth] R[adcliffe]' (1913): 'I had already made the experiment of getting Miss R to draw an object with her eyes open and then a complex mathematical form with her eyes closed. She drew badly with her eyes open but the complicated mental image was well drawn, the bounding line returning into itself exactly.' When Yeats tried to draw a similar but simpler form with closed eyes, he 'got the proportions wrong' and 'did not join the line' (see Harper, *YO* 156).

248, 15–16: *"By dreadful abstinence . . . the mutinous flesh"*. From Shelley's *Hellas*, ll. 155–6, this is one of Yeats's favorite passages. It is also quoted in *A* 172 and in a rejected version of the Dedication of *VA*.

248, 23–4: *Priest and Sybil, Socrates and Diotima, wandering magician and his scryer*. There were numerous Greek and Roman sibyls, perhaps the most famous being the Cumaean Sibyl who acted as Aeneas' guide to the Underworld (*Aeneid*, Book VI). Diotima was the prophetess of Mantineia from whom Socrates supposedly learned the nature of love (Plato's *Symposium*, secs. 201–12). John Dee and Edward Kelly were probably the magician and scryer in Yeats's mind (see n. to p. xvii, 17–18).

249, 9–11: *William Morris sometimes . . . be well done*. See *EI* 55 and 423, *L* 846 and *OBMV* xxxii. Yeats is perhaps thinking of Ralph's lucky eyes in *The Well at the World's End*: 'thou seemest to me to have a lucky look in thy eyes' (*Collected Works*, XVIII, 29; cf. also XVIII, 306, and XIX, 14). For the second part of his comment Yeats may be recalling the father's remarks to the passive Ralph, 'O son . . . whatsoever thou dost, that thou dost full well' (XIX, 215). Possibly Yeats supplied 'unwitting' in unconscious imitation of Morris's frequent alliteration. In a long and important meditation of 3 October 1920, Yeats discussed at some length the symbolic significance of another of Morris's quest romances, *The Sundering Flood*. Cf. n. to p. 42, 6.

249, 31: *Four Daimons*. In one sense, at least, they are the Daimons of Yeats, George, Anne, and Michael (see n. to 'CHARACTERS OF CERTAIN PHASES', p. 33), representing wisdom, love, beauty, and truth in that order. During one of the Sleeps (13 Aug 1920) the Control 'explained the correspondence between the 4 Daimons & the Four Faculties' and informed Yeats that 'the coming epoch will have a 3rd Daimon character though 4th Daimon will be working in it'.

250: *THE RECORD AND THE MEMORY*. Discovered as a term late in the psychical research for *VA*, 'Record' seems virtually to replace 'Anima

Mundi', the focal concept and term of the first recorded questions in the AS (8 Nov 1917). The 'personal Record' should be compared to the 'Personal Anima Mundi', which is much discussed in the AS. The most important of the notebooks containing accounts of Sleeps (28 May 1920 to 9 Feb 1921) is marked *Records* on the cover. On 17 Aug 1920, in a discussion of daimonic experience and knowledge, Yeats 'reminded Dionertes that images in the spiritual memory are never from one's own memory but from some other's, a stranger or an intimate'. One note on 'Record' in the CF suggests that Yeats discovered the term during the period of the Sleeps: 'Scents, touch, fragrances, sounds which do not awaken intellect are drawn from record. What awakens thought—human voice say—passes into memory as distinct from record.'

250, 21: *in the past or in the present.* At this point in GP Yeats cut the following sentence: 'nor is there any form characteristic of a life we can only know by symbol and correspondence.'

251, 2–6: *a spirit with knowledge . . . sentence for itself.* The SPR experimented extensively with clairvoyants and mediums who spoke and wrote, usually in broken sentences, languages about which they presumably had no knowledge. For Yeats's account of such experiments see the essay on Miss Radcliffe's Script (Harper, *YO* 130–71).

251, 15: *a herring fisher.* Cf. *Mem* 104.

251: *MYTHOLOGY.* Inserted in GP on a typed sheet, this section was not part of the book when it was 'Finished at Syracuse, January, 1925'.

251–2, 20f: *The great books.* The idea incorporated in the next few lines is much expanded in Yeats's Introduction to Hone and Rossi's *Bishop Berkeley* (1931), particularly in a well-known passage in sec. XI:

> 'God', 'Heaven', 'Immortality', those words and their associated myths define that contemplation [of a pure activity]. . . . Giambattista Vico has said that we should reject all philosophy that does not begin in myth, and it is impossible to pronounce those three words without becoming as simple as a camel-driver or a pilgrim. (*EI* 409)

252, 3: *Diotime.* See n. to p. 248, 23–4.

253–6: *ALL SOULS' NIGHT.* Written in Nov 1920 and published in Mar 1921 (in *The New Republic* and *The London Mercury*), the poem was substituted for a prose Epilogue addressed 'To Vestigia', which may have been rejected because Yeats decided to dedicate the book to her rather than Horton, to the living rather than the dead (see p. x, 23–6). Horton (first identified as H, then as X, in l. 21) remained anonymous until the publication of *The Collected Poems* (1933). Horton, Florence Farr Emery, and MacGregor Mathers, the three dead friends whose ghosts are summoned, had been 'old fellow students' in the GD. Thinking of them as well as Moina Mathers, Allan

Bennett, and others, Yeats said (in a rejected version of the Dedication): 'I write my poetry too more often than not for people who are dead, or estranged.'

He was, of course, aware that All Souls' Night was 'the night before the Irish *Samhain*', which 'was the proper time for prophecy and the unveiling of mysteries' (Rhys, *Lectures*, 514). He had most likely read a chapter devoted primarily to the Feast of All Souls in Frazer's *The Golden Bough* (VI, 51–83; see also X, 224, and *E* 84). It may be significant that Yeats had only recently returned to Oxford from Dublin, after a serious 'operation of my throat & consequent slow recovery' (Sleeps, 19 Nov 1920).

Abbreviations

A   *Autobiographies*. London: Macmillan, 1955.

AS   Automatic Script (see Intro., p. xii).

CCP   Jeffares, *A Commentary on the Collected Poems* (see Bib.).

CF   Card File (see Intro., p. xii).

E   *Explorations*. London: Macmillan, 1962.

EB   *The Encyclopaedia Britannica*, 11th ed. (see Bib.).

EGP   Burnet, *Early Greek Philosophy* (see Bib.).

EI   *Essays and Introductions*. New York: Macmillan, 1961.

ERE   *Encyclopaedia of Religion and Ethics* (see Bib.).

FFT   *Fairy and Folk Tales of Ireland*. Gerrards Cross: Colin Smythe, 1973.

FPS   *Frank Pearce Sturm: His Life, Letters, and Collected Work*. Ed. Richard Taylor. Urbana: Univ. of Illinois, 1969.

FY   *Four Years*. Dundrum: Cuala Press, 1921.

GD   The Hermetic Order of the Golden Dawn.

GP   Yeats's galley proofs for *VA* (now in the possession of Senator Michael B. Yeats).

IER   Jeffares and Cross, *In Excited Reverie* (see Bib.).

JS   *John Sherman & Dhoya*. Ed. Richard J. Finneran. Detroit: Wayne State Univ., 1969.

Keynes   *The Complete Writings of William Blake* (see Bib.).

L   *The Letters of W. B. Yeats*. Ed. Allan Wade. London: Rupert Hart-Davis, 1954.

LNI   *Letters to the New Island*. Ed. Horace Reynolds. 1934; rpt. London: Oxford Univ., 1970.

LWBY   *Letters to W. B. Yeats*. Ed. Richard J. Finneran, George Mills Harper, and William M. Murphy. 2 vols. London: Macmillan, 1977.

M   *Mythologies*. New York: Macmillan, 1959.

Mem   *Memoirs*. Ed. Denis Donoghue. London: Macmillan, 1972.

OBMV   *The Oxford Book of Modern Verse*. Oxford: Clarendon, 1936.

OED   *The Oxford English Dictionary* (see Bib.).

P   Phase, as the term is used by Yeats in *VA*.

PASL *Per Amica Silentia Lunae*. London: Macmillan, 1918.

PP Yeats's page proofs for *VA* (now in the possession of Senator Michael B. Yeats).

R-A TS The Robartes-Aherne typescript (see Intro., p. xxviii).

RS *The Riverside Shakespeare* (see Bib.).

SB *The Speckled Bird*. Ed. William H. O'Donnell. 2 vols. Dublin: Cuala Press, 1973–4.

SPR The Society for Psychical Research.

SS *The Senate Speeches of W. B. Yeats*. Ed. Donald R. Pearce. London: Faber and Faber, 1961.

TS The Theosophical Society.

TV *The Trembling of the Veil*. London: T. Werner Laurie, 1922.

UP *Uncollected Prose by W. B. Yeats*. Ed. John P. Frayne and Colton Johnson (vol. 2 only). 2 vols. New York: Columbia Univ., 1970, 1976.

VA *A Vision: An Explanation of Life Founded upon the Writings of Giraldus and upon Certain Doctrines Attributed to Kusta Ben Luka*. London: T. Werner Laurie, 1925.

VB *A Vision*. London: Macmillan, 1962.

VBWI *Visions and Beliefs in the West of Ireland, Collected and Arranged by Lady Gregory: With Two Essays and Notes by W. B. Yeats*. rpt. New York: Oxford Univ., 1970.

VP *The Variorum Edition of the Poems of W. B. Yeats*. Ed. Peter Allt and Russell K. Alspach. New York: Macmillan, 1957.

VPl *The Variorum Edition of the Plays of W. B. Yeats*. Ed. Russell K. Alspach. London: Macmillan, 1966.

WBY Jeffares, *W. B. Yeats: Man and Poet* (see Bib.).

WWB *The Works of William Blake*. Ed. Edwin John Ellis and William Butler Yeats. 3 vols. London: Bernard Quaritch, 1893.

YGD Harper, *Yeats's Golden Dawn* (see Bib.).

YM *W. B. Yeats and T. Sturge Moore: Their Correspondence, 1901– 1937*. Ed. Ursula Bridge. London: Routledge and Kegan Paul, 1953.

YO Harper, *Yeats and the Occult* (see Bib.).

Bibliography

Books marked with an asterisk are those Yeats relied upon directly or indirectly in the composition of VA.

Adam, Antoine. *The Art of Paul Verlaine*. Tr. Carl Morse. New York: New York Univ., 1963.

*Adams, Henry. *The Education of Henry Adams: An Autobiography*. Boston: Houghton Mifflin, 1918.

Beddoes, Thomas Lovell. *The Letters of Thomas Lovell Beddoes*. Ed. Edmund Gosse. 1894: rpt. New York: Benjamin Blom, 1971.

———. *The Works of Thomas Lovell Beddoes*. Ed. H. W. Donner. London: Oxford Univ., 1935.

Bentley, G. E. *Blake Records*. Oxford: Clarendon, 1969.

Blake, William. *The Complete Writings of William Blake*. Ed. Geoffrey Keynes. London: Oxford Univ., 1966.

*Blavatsky, H. P. *The Secret Doctrine*. 2 vols. 1888; rpt. Pasadena, Cal.: Theosophical Univ. Press, 1963.

*Bolton, Lyndon. *An Introduction to the Theory of Relativity*. New York: Dutton, 1921.

The Book of the Thousand Nights and One Night. Rendered into English from the Literal & Complete French Translation of Dr. J. C. Mardrus by Powys Mathers. 4 vols. 2nd ed. London: George Routledge, 1937.

Bornstein, George. *Yeats and Shelley*. Chicago: Univ. of Chicago, 1970.

*Bryant, Jacob. *A New System; or An Analysis of Ancient Mythology*. 3 vols. London, 1774–6.

*Burkitt, Francis Crawford. *Early Eastern Christianity*. London: John Murray, 1904.

*Burnet, John. *Early Greek Philosophy*. London: Adam and Charles Black, 1892.

Butterfield, H. *The Statecraft of Machiavelli*. London: G. Bell, 1940.

The Cambridge Modern History. Ed. A. W. Ward, G. W. Prothero, and Stanley Leathes. 13 vols. Cambridge: Cambridge Univ., 1902–11.

*Castiglione, Baldassare. *The Courtier*. Tr. L. E. Opdycke. London: Duckworth, 1902.

——. ——. Tr. Sir Thomas Hoby. London: J. M. Dent, 1956.

*Chaucer, Geoffrey. *The Complete Works*. Ed. W. W. Skeat. 6 vols. Oxford: Clarendon, 1894.

Coleridge, Samuel Taylor. *Biographia Literaria*. Ed. John Shawcross. 2 vols. Oxford: Oxford Univ., 1907.

*Cumont, Franz. *Astrology and Religion Among the Greeks and Romans*. Tr. J. B. Baker. New York and London: G. P. Putnam's Sons, 1912.

——. *The Oriental Religions in Roman Paganism*. Tr. Grant Showerman. Chicago: Open Court, 1911.

*Dalton, O. M. *Byzantine Art and Archaeology*. Oxford: Clarendon, 1911.

*Dante. *Il Convito: The Banquet of Dante Alighieri*. Tr. Elizabeth Price Sayer. London: George Routledge and Sons, 1887.

DeLaura, David J., ed. *Victorian Prose: A Guide to Research*. New York: Modern Language Association of America, 1973.

*Davies, John Llewelyn, and David James Vaughan, eds. *The Republic of Plato*, new edition. London: Macmillan, 1885.

*Dodds, E. R., ed. *Select Passages Illustrating Neoplatonism*. London: Society for Promoting Christian Knowledge, 1923.

Dostoevsky, Fyodor. *The Idiot*. Tr. Constance Garnett. New York: Macmillan, 1948.

*Dowden, Edward. *The Life of Percy Bysshe Shelley*. 1886; rpt. New York: Barnes and Noble, 1966.

*Duhem, Pierre. *Le Systeme du monde: Histoire des doctrines cosmologiques de Platon à Copernic*. 10 vols. Paris: Librairie Scientifique A. Hermann et Fils, 1913–59.

Dume, Thomas Leslie. 'William Butler Yeats: A Survey of His Reading.' Diss. Temple Univ., 1950.

The Earliest Lives of Dante. Tr. James Robinson Smith. New York: Frederick Ungar, 1963.

Ellmann, Richard. *The Identity of Yeats*. New York: Oxford Univ., 1954.

Encyclopaedia Britannica. 11th ed. 1910–11.

Encyclopaedia of Religion and Ethics. Ed. James Hastings. 13 vols. Edinburgh: T. & T. Clark, 1908–26.

*Eschenbach, Wolfram von. *Parzival: A Knightly Epic*. Tr. Jessie Weston. 2 vols. 1894; rpt. New York: G. E. Stechert, 1912.

*Fauré, Elie. *History of Art*. Tr. Walter Pach. 5 vols. 1921–30; rpt. Garden City, N. Y.: Garden City Publishing Co., 1937.

Bibliography

Fitzgerald, Penelope. *Edward Burne-Jones: A Biography*. London: Michael Joseph, 1975.

*Flaubert, Gustave. *The Temptation of St. Antony*. Tr. D. F. Hannigan. London: H. S. Nichols, 1895.

*Frazer, Sir James George. *The Golden Bough*. 12 vols. 3rd ed. 1907–15; rpt. New York: Macmillan, 1951.

*Furtwängler, Adolf. *Masterpieces of Greek Sculpture: A Series of Essays on the History of Art*. Tr. Eugénie Sellers. New York: Scribner's, 1895.

*Gibbon, Edward. *The History of the Decline and Fall of the Roman Empire*. Ed. J. B. Bury. 7 vols. London: Methuen, 1909–14.

Gilchrist, Alexander. *Life of William Blake*. Ed. Ruthven Todd. London: J. M. Dent, 1942.

*Glanvill, Joseph. *Saducismus Triumphatus: Or, Full and Plain Evidence Concerning Witches and Apparitions*. Intro. Coleman O. Parsons. 1681; rpt. Gainesville, Fla.: Scholars' Facsimiles and Reprints, 1966.

Goethe, Johann Wolfgang von. *Goethes Werke*. Ed. Enrich Trunz et al. 14 vols. Hamburg: Christian Wegner Verlag, 1964–7.

*Gower, Granville Leveson. *Private Correspondence, 1781–1821*. Ed. Castalia, Countess Granville. 2 vols. London: John Murray, 1916.

Gregory, Lady Isabella Augusta. *Lady Gregory's Journals*. Ed. Lennox Robinson. New York: Macmillan, 1947.

*———. *Poets and Dreamers*. London: John Murray, 1903.

*Hannay, James O. *The Spirit and Origin of Christian Monasticism*. London: Methuen, 1903.

*———. *The Wisdom of the Desert*. London: Methuen, 1904.

Harper, George Mills. *Yeats's Golden Dawn*. London: Macmillan, 1974.

———, ed. *Yeats and the Occult*. Yeats Studies Series. Toronto: Macmillan, 1975.

*Harris, Thomas Lake. *The Wisdom of the Adepts: Esoteric Science in Human History*. 1884; rpt. New York: A. M. S. Press, 1975.

Hegel, G. W. F. *The Philosophy of History*. Tr. J. Sibree. 1858; rpt. New York: Dover, 1956.

Henn, T. R. *The Lonely Tower: Studies in the Poetry of W. B. Yeats*. 2nd ed. London: Methuen, 1950.

*Holmes, W. G. *The Age of Justinian and Theodora*. 2 vols. London: G. Bell, 1912.

Hone, Joseph. *W. B. Yeats, 1865–1939*. 2nd ed. London: Macmillan, 1962.

Jeffares, A. Norman, ed. *The Circus Animals: Essays on W. B. Yeats*. London: Macmillan, 1970.

——. *A Commentary on the Collected Poems of W. B. Yeats*. London: Macmillan, 1968.

——. *W. B. Yeats: Man and Poet*. New Haven: Yale Univ., 1949.

——, and K. G. W. Cross, eds. *In Excited Reverie: A Centenary Tribute, W. B. Yeats, 1865–1939*. London: Macmillan, 1965.

Kermode, Frank. *Romantic Image*. London: Routledge and Kegan Paul, 1957.

King, Francis, ed. *Astral Projection: Ritual Magic and Alchemy by S. L. MacGregor Mathers and Others, Being Hitherto Unpublished Golden Dawn Material*. New York: Samuel Weiser, 1971.

*Kirk, Robert. *The Secret Commonwealth of Elves, Fauns & Fairies*. Ed. Andrew Lang. London: David Nutt, 1893.

*Lodge, Oliver. *Raymond, Or Life and Death*. 6th ed. London: Methuen, 1916.

Mahaffy, J. P. *Social Life in Greece from Homer to Menander*. 7th ed. London: Macmillan, 1907.

*Mathers, S. L. MacGregor. *The Kabbalah Unveiled*. London: George Redway, 1887.

*Mayor, Joseph B., W. Warde Fowler, and R. S. Conway. *Virgil's Messianic Eclogue: Its Meaning, Occasion, & Sources*. London: John Murray, 1907.

Melchiori, Giorgio. *The Whole Mystery of Art: Pattern into Poetry in the Work of W. B. Yeats*. London: Routledge and Kegan Paul, 1960.

*[Moberly, C. A. E., and E. F. Jourdain.] *An Adventure*. London: Macmillan, 1911.

*Moore, T. Sturge. *Art and Life*. London: Methuen, 1910.

Moore, Virginia. *The Unicorn: William Butler Yeats' Search for Reality*. New York: Macmillan, 1954.

*Morley, John, Viscount. *Recollections*. 2 vols. New York: Macmillan, 1917.

*Morris, William. *The Collected Works*. 24 vols. 1910–15; rpt. New York: Russell and Russell, 1966.

Myers, Frederic W. H. *Human Personality and Its Survival of Bodily Death*. 2 vols. 1903; rpt. New York: Longmans, Green, 1954.

National Gallery Illustrated General Catalogue. London: National Gallery Publications Department, 1973.

*Newell, William Wells. *King Arthur and the Table Round*. 2 vols. London: A. P. Watt, 1897.

O'Casey, Sean. *Mirror in My House: The Autobiographies of Sean O'Casey*. 2 vols. New York: Macmillan, 1956.

*O'Shea, Katherine. *Charles Stewart Parnell: His Love Story and Political Life*. 2 vols. London: Cassell, 1914.

The Oxford English Dictionary. Ed. James A. H. Murray et al. Corrected reissue. 13 vols. Oxford: Clarendon, 1933.

Pater, Walter. *The Renaissance*. New York: Modern Library, n. d.

*Petrie, W. M. Flinders. *The Revolutions of Civilization*. 1911; rpt. New York: Peter Smith, 1941.

*Plotinus. *The Enneads*. Tr. Stephen MacKenna. 2nd ed. London: Faber and Faber, 1956.

*Plunket, Emmeline Mary. *Ancient Calendars and Constellations*. London: John Murray, 1903.

Pound, Ezra. *Literary Essays*. Ed. T. S. Eliot. Norfolk, Conn.: New Directions, 1954.

Regardie, Israel. *The Golden Dawn: An Account of the Teachings, Rites and Ceremonies of the Order of the Golden Dawn*. 4 vols. 3rd ed. River Falls, Wis.: Hazel Hills Corp., 1970.

*Rhys, John. *Lectures on the Origin and Growth of Religion as Illustrated by Celtic Heathendom*. 2nd ed. London: William and Norgate, 1892.

Russell, George. *Letters from AE*. Ed. Alan Denson. London: Abelard-Schuman, 1961.

Salvadori, Corinna. *Yeats and Castiglione: Poet and Courtier*. Dublin: Allen Figgis, 1965.

*Saunders, R. H. 'A Christmas Tree in the Spheres'. *Light*, 44, No. 2243 (5 Jan 1924), 5.

*———. 'A Story of a Christmas Tree: Children of Both Worlds'. *Light*, 43, No. 2191 (6 Jan 1923), 7.

*Saurat, Denis. *Milton: Man and Thinker*. London: Jonathan Cape, [1924].

Shakespeare, William. *The Riverside Shakespeare*. Ed. G. Blakemore Evans et al. Boston: Houghton Mifflin, 1974.

Shelley, Percy Bysshe. *The Letters of Percy Bysshe Shelley*. Ed. Frederick L. Jones. 2 vols. Oxford: Clarendon, 1964.

Sinnett, A. P. *The Growth of the Soul*. London: The Theosophical Publishing Society, 1896.

*Strong, Mrs. Arthur. *Apotheosis and After Life: Three Lectures on Certain Phases of Art and Religion in the Roman Empire*. London: Constable, 1915.

———. *Roman Sculpture from Augustus to Constantine*. London: Duckworth, 1907.

*Strzygowski, Josef. *Origin of Christian Church Art*. Tr. O. M. Dalton and H. J. Braunholtz. Oxford: Clarendon, 1923.

*Symons, Arthur. *Studies in Seven Arts*. London: Constable, 1906.

*———. *The Symbolist Movement in Literature*. 1899; rpt. New York: Dutton, 1958.

Synge, J. M. *Collected Works*. 4 vols. London: Oxford Univ., 1962–8.

Taylor, Thomas, tr. *The Description of Greece, by Pausanias*. London, 1794.

———. *The Philosophical and Mathematical Commentaries of Proclus*. 2 vols. London, 1788–9.

———. *The Works of Plato*. 5 vols. London, 1804.

Thatcher, Davis S. *Nietzsche in England, 1890–1914: The Growth of a Reputation*. Toronto: Univ. of Toronto, 1970.

Torchiana, Donald T. *W. B. Yeats & Georgian Ireland*. Evanston: Northwestern Univ., 1966.

Verlaine, Paul. *Oeuvres complètes*. Ed. Jacques Borel et al. Paris: Club des Libraires de France, 1959.

Villari, Pasquale. *Life and Times of Girolamo Savonarola*. London: T. Fisher Unwin, 1899.

Waite, Arthur Edward. *The Brotherhood of the Rosy Cross*. London: W. Rider, 1924.

Wees, William C. *Vorticism and the English Avant-Garde*. Toronto: Univ. of Toronto, 1972.

Wells, H. G. *Outline of History*. 3 vols. 1940–1 ed. New York: Triangle Books, 1940.

Wilson, F. A. C. *W. B. Yeats and Tradition*. New York: Macmillan, 1958.

Yeats, John Butler. *Passages from the Letters of John Butler Yeats*. Ed. Ezra Pound. Dublin: Cuala Press, 1917.

Index to *A Vision*

Index to Editorial Introduction and Notes